GERLL ZINE DISTRO
THE AMOUNT of time you devote to reading benefits you in two ways: it provides pleasure, and it increases your information and knowledge.
SPRING '95
Giant Robot
MAKING FIREWORKS! TOURING CHINA! WRESTLING IN JAPAN! PRODUCING JOHN WOO'S GANGSTER FLICKS! BEING ULTRAMAN!
A Magazine for You
No. 4. $4
TEMP SLAVE
WORK! WORK!
IT'S OK.. THIS JOB'S ONLY TEMPORARY!
ISSUE 7
AD OF THE MONTH
Part-time
SAUSAGE PLANT
Looking for exp. person to tie, hang, cut & pack sausages. M-Thurs., 8am-2pm. Call Continental Sausage.
MORE PAGES! SAME LOW PRICE!
$2
COMETBUS
#35½
TEN YEARS OF
SKRUB FLIERS
25¢
GIRL FRENZY
3
The double life of Moranique: Art Movies panned
Carol Swain interviewed · Comix Galore
Manifest Manifestoes: SCUM & More!
Princess
sexy
inside
and lots more that will amaze you!
Holy titclamps
issue no. 15
File Under "Queer"
$3
girl
Veronica
germs
No. 3
BIKINI KILL
A COLOR AND ACTIVITY BOOK
THE SUMMER FROM HELL/CANADA ISSUE
BAMBOO GIRL
#2
Things to gawk at:
KAPANG!!
$2
TEENAGE GANG DEBS
TEEN FAG
MAGAZINE
DAMAGE CONTROL SPECIAL:
NAMBLA
PRO-LIFE QUEERS
BAD BAD HOMOS
ACTION GIRL GUIDE
number one
one dollar
kitty club
Making a Run for the Border? Not on These Guys...
POCHO MAGAZINE
¡NAFTA!
THE ANTI-IMMIGRATION ISSUE!
STUMBLE
#7
Blah, Blah, Blah, Blah, Blah,Blah, Blah,
Blah, Blah, Blah, Blah,Blah, Blah,
THE ADVENTURES OF BIGGIRL
BG
SOMETIMES SEEING IS NOT BELIEVING
¿WHO'S BEEN NUTRI-LIZING YOUR MIND?
BOILER ANGEL
#ATE
MCD 1991
50¢
afraid of the truth
the never ending search for something new
issue # 5
idiot nation
fanzine 6
$5½
THE DEATH OF AMERICA
RIOT grrrl
threadbare
CU01276517

PUBLISHER/EDITOR:	V. Vale
PRODUCTION MANAGER:	Marian Wallace
LAYOUT:	Thaddeus Croyle, C. Francesca Tussing, Stacy Wakefield
GRAPHIC DESIGN:	Matthew Petty
DESIGN CONSULTANTS:	Curium Design
TEXT INTERNS:	Andrea Fortus, Jennifer Ryan, Yimi Tong
STAFF INTERNS:	Rachel Aronowitz, Jeannie Bail, Calico Brown, Mia Ellis, Rachel Forsman, Jennifer Lasky, Gloria Orbegozo, Rykarda Parasol, Cate Sullivan
PHOTOGRAPHY:	Olivier Robert, Robert Waldman
PRODUCTION CONSULTANTS:	Andrea Reider, Valentine Marquesa Wallace
COMPUTER CONSULTANTS:	Mason Jones, Ron Klatchko
SENIOR EDITOR (NYC):	Chris Trela
RESEARCH:	Nico Ordway
PUBLICITY:	Barbara MacDonald
THANKS FOR SUPPORT:	Steve Bade, Mindy Bagdon, Johnny Bartlett, Liz Borowski, Diane Cantwell, Comic Relief (Chuck Sperry, Kristine Anstine), Claire Dannenbaum, John Finkbeiner, Charles Gatewood, Caroline Hèbert, Marguerite & Stephen Holloway, Carrell McCarthy, Joaquin Miller, Scott Owen, Teresa Piccolotti, Tiffanie Ragasa, Catherine Reuther, Mary Ricci, Seth Robson, Rock Ross, Ken Sitz, Ricky Trance, Justin Welsh
FINANCIAL ADVISORS:	Carol & Dennis Hamby
LAWYER:	David S. Kahn, Esq.

©1996 V. Vale
ISBN: 0-9650469-0-7
Library of Congress Catalog Number: 96-90163

BOOKSTORE DISTRIBUTION: SUBCO, PO Box 160 or 265 South 5th, Monroe OR 97456.
TEL: 800-274-7826 FAX: 503-847-6018
NON-BOOKSTORE DISTRIBUTION: LAST GASP, 777 Florida St, San Francisco CA 94110.
TEL: 415-824-6636. FAX: 415-824-1836.
U.K. DISTRIBUTION: AIRLIFT, #8 The Arena, Mollison Ave, Enfield, Middlesex U.K. EN3 7NJ.
TEL: 181-804-0400. FAX: 181-804-0044.

For a catalog send SASE or 2 IRCs to:
V/SEARCH
20 Romolo #B
San Francisco CA 94133
TEL: (415) 362-1465
FAX: (415) 362-0742

Printed in Hong Kong by Colorcraft, Ltd.

10 9 8 7 6 5 4 3 2 1

Front cover: Photo of Lynn Peril by Olivier Robert; Photoshop by Su Obraz & Matt Petty
Back cover: Photo by Anne Greenwood and Scott Gregory. Photoshop by Matt Petty and Sean T.

Table of Contents

- 4 ♦ Introduction
- 6 ♦ Thrift SCORE
- 22 ♦ Beer Frame
- 34 ♦ Crap Hound
- 50 ♦ Housewife Turned Assassin
- 68 ♦ Meat Hook
- 74 ♦ X-Ray
- 88 ♦ Mystery Date
- 106 ♦ AK Distribution
- 114 ♦ Outpunk
- 130 ♦ Fat Girl
- 150 ♦ Bunnyhop
- 155 ♦ History of ZINES
- 160 ♦ Quotations
- 170 ♦ ZINE Directory
- 174 ♦ Catalog
- 182 ♦ Index

From The Editor

WHAT IS A ZINE?

♦ **Alt.Culture:** "An independent, not-for-profit, self-publication . . . The name 'zine' comes from an abbreviation of the punk-era 'fanzine' (itself a corruption of 'magazine,' which itself dates from postwar Hollywood)."

♦ **Factsheet Five:** "A small handmade amateur publication done purely out of passion, rarely making a profit or breaking even. Sounds like 'zeen.'"

♦ **Weird Flower #6:** "What separates a zine from a magazine is not only budget, but the quirkiness, the individuality, the spirit and yes, even the unavailability that made finding a good read make your day. Maybe this is an overly romantic view, but zines were/should be . . . honest, raw and exciting."

♦ **New Musical Express:** "Why write a fanzine? Boredom, anger, yearning, excitement, hope, egotism, to sell 'em, to corrupt other less fortunate mortals to *your* brilliant taste, to care, create, caress, carp, to find your own alternatives, to communicate, to wander freely off at multi-tangents, stumble blissfully over historical mistakes and express yourselves . . . unfettered by commercial constraints, necessities, good taste, deadlines, libel suits, love of position, power, money . . . When people mock and ask me why I love fanzines so much, I just laugh knowingly and say, 'Have you considered the alternatives?'"

♦ **S.F. Examiner:** "The name 'zine,' short for 'fanzine,' a science-fiction fan magazine, may be new, but small, self-published pamphlets and newsletters date all the way back to Ben Franklin's *Poor Richard's Almanac*, which was launched in 1757. Dadaist manifestoes of the early 1900s continued the trend and started a design style adopted by many of today's zine editors. Science-fiction zines proliferated in the 1920s and '30s, followed by punk rock zines in the 1970s. Today's zines cover political rantings, sex and sexual politics, hobbies, music, movies and just about every other topic that's conceivable—and many that aren't."

♦ **Junk Mail Backlash:** "There's no money to be made and no fame to be had. There's no wages, bosses, advertisers or deadlines, so there's nothing to temper the style or encourage any filler. *It's the only truly free press that there is.*"

♦ **Homegrown:** "The simplest zine is one sheet of legal-sized paper copied on both sides and folded three times, trimmed and stapled to make a 16-page 'mini' zine. This can be produced in one night, and part of its appeal is the diminutive size. Zines have negated the necessity for hours of careful, anal-retentive editing and adherence to perfectionistic production standards. In zines, *message* again assumes ascendancy over *form.*"

♦ **Arthur Cravan:** "Every child begins life as an artist, and every great artist is a born *provocateur.*"

♦ **Mimi Parent:** "Knock hard—life is deaf."

Empowered by the "DO IT YOURSELF" (DIY) philosophy of the punk rock revolt of the '70s, thousands of dissatisfied, savvy malcontents are expressing their authentic thoughts and feelings via the cheapest print medium available: xeroxed zines. There are other affordable means of independent communication, including stickers, flyers, posters, newsletters, home-made cassettes, 7″ vinyl singles, and pixelvision filmmaking using discontinued Fisher-Price cameras whose "film" is a cheap standard cassette tape. However, the zine remains the fastest, most conveniently reproducible and effective means of getting a substantial message across.

Why zines? They are a grassroots reaction to a *crisis* in the media landscape. What was formerly *communication* has become a fully implemented *control process.* Corporate-produced advertising, television programming and PR campaigns dictate the 21st century, "anything goes" consumer lifestyle. TV networks, newspapers and magazines have been taken over by a handful of business culture financiers who co-opt and exploit any emerging "youth revolt" as soon as it begins to manifest. The oft-lamented homogenizing effect of worldwide mass media is now a *reality.*

Investigative journalism in mainstream media is a thing of the past, and even when corruption in politics or business is exposed, the revelations are immediately forgotten—there is no *follow-up.* Gone are the budgets for in-depth reporting which brought us Watergate and the Civil Rights movement; instead, the emphasis is on simulated depictions of "real life" crime—the weirder, the better. "Truth" has been replaced by ever-escalating thresholds of fleshly titillation and violence, while the *real* crime is, naturally, underreported: domestic violence against women. It's not considered newsworthy; it's too commonplace.

Zines are often produced by illicit means, but many also challenge copyright laws and outdated legalistic notions involving intellectual property ownership. As a rule, they appropriate newspaper articles, magazine headlines and photos—all without permission. Sometimes with this contextual change the inherent absurdity of an article or photo speaks for itself; on other occasions the "found" materials require modification. For example, "Snoopy" and "Family Circus" cartoon strips, with hilarious, sexually-explicit text replacing the original dialogue, have been circulating uncredited in an underground zine format for years. Every "official" comic begs for such *improvement.*

Techniques of collage and detournement occur quite naturally to anyone armed with scissors, glue stick, a pen and a sense of humor. With few resources, one can puncture a million-dollar ad campaign: lampoon a political candidate or mock a $10,000 Calvin Klein billboard with a 10-cent sticker. Many zines, in fact, contain stickers to encourage activism. And with today's widespread access to a home computer and *Photoshop* software, no image is safe from a seamless act of sacrilege. ("Want a photo of the Pope consorting with a sheep? *Easy!*")

Innovative appropriation can have its price, though—particularly if the creators are courageous enough to make themselves identifiable. Zines such as *BUNNYHOP* and *Hey There, Barbie Girl!* have been subjected to censorship-by-threat-of-lawsuit and suffered destruction, while the creators of intentionally over-the-top, provocative zines like *Boiled Angel* and *Pure* have been prosecuted and convicted in criminal courts. Those who despise liberating thought continue to use vague "obscenity" definitions in their pinch-nosed crusades against artistic freedom of expression—particularly during election years.

Possessed of a certain cachet these days is the medium of the "e-zine" (a zine published solely on the Internet). But censorship on the net is already a reality; the FBI has used the Internet to entrap persons suspected of being "kiddy porn" voyeurs. Who would voluntarily consent to submitting their communiqué to a pay-as-you-go, centrally controlled surveillance system? To date e-zines also seem to be quite superficial: too "cleanly" presented, and lacking in randomness and collage elements—*the cut-up factor*—which makes paper zines puzzling, sometimes messy, yet endearing and multi-dimensional.

Proponents of the e-zine extol its instant availability, easy updating, alleged ecological advantage and its cheapness as it takes advantage of cutting-edge technology: "The Net is free!" (That is, until you get your monthly phone and credit card bill.) The Internet has been hailed as the communications innovation of the glorious future; the business section of every daily paper has a "news" story promoting it. While arguably every person's web site is a zine, and there are plenty of optimistic projections about how e-zines will replace paper zines, nevertheless, access to computers and scanners is still for the privileged few, and part of the appeal of a zine is its power to grant a voice to the most underprivileged in society, including citizens of high school age who have few resources. Desktop publishing programs demand a certain sophistication, whereas a paper zine can be created overnight with virtually no "art training" or computer expertise. Also, e-zines lack the human touch—many paper zines are personally hand-colored and accompanied by handwritten letters bearing drawings. Browsing e-zines on the World Wide Web could *potentially* net rewarding information, but as of this writing the most uncompromising and subversive zines are only available on paper.

Zines are difficult to locate; there is no central source or network (although *Factsheet Five* makes a marathon attempt). Zines demand the personal communication inherent in a *relationship*—and personal communication always requires energy, sensitivity, thought, foresight and *time*. Having discredited TV, magazines, newspapers and most radio, zine creators have discovered a vast resource of *time* that can be used to some very satisfying and creatively prankish ends. And when one is forced to work at a job, the challenge remains as to how to maximize one's personal benefit from the situation, since these days *all* jobs are temp jobs. Some zine creators have even stooped to sabotage *(boss: "What the HELL could have happened to that computer file?!"),* and this provides material for a future zine. Many a zine has been produced at a job, or helped to counteract job alienation.

Zines provide pure inspiration and encouragement to create one's own radical culture and ideas. Among some high school and punk rock circles, the creation of a zine has become a modern-day *rite of passage*, and the proliferation of zines by high-schoolers (one of the least privileged classes) is heartening. The tragedy of the zine movement is the lack of accessibility to back issues. Some of the greatest zines ever produced are virtually impossible to obtain today—e.g., *SCAM* by the uncompromising punk provocateur, Iggy (who steadfastly refused mass media attention); hundreds of zines associated with feminist Riot Grrrl activism; or the earliest issues of *Dishwasher* by Dishwasher Pete—notable for having pranked David Letterman by sending an imposter in his place to appear on the latter's overrated TV spectacle.

It is a general principle that *consorting with mass media has a damaging effect upon any attempts at social revolution.* The sole person to exploit mass media on his *own terms* has been the Unabomber—and his attempts at revolution are questionable, to say the least. Whenever major media report about anything cutting-edge or ground-breaking, they misrepresent it. This technique of reportage was partially described over a century ago: "Damned by faint praise." It is no coincidence that when features on "the zine revolution" appear in the press, the political potential of zines is downplayed in favor of the novelty/cuteness angle. With few exceptions, the zines which receive the most publicity are ones serving the status quo value system. Allegedly "cutting-edge" zines that promote "ironic" sexism, homophobia and racism (supposedly to "push the reader's buttons and make people think") simply reflect conservative mainstream values, where shock for shock's sake has become a commonplace marketing technique.

If communication can be viewed as food, then everything the mass media serves has been depleted of nourishment by corporate self-serving agendas. Amidst this landscape of lies, the zine movement has arisen everywhere like hydra of discontent. Finally original, fresh and *truthful* communication between individuals is proliferating on a massive scale. This is a movement without leaders or spokespersons, and there are no rigidifying standards dictating what may or may not be presented.

As a response to media being irrelevant and generally misleading, idiosyncratic personal publishing has proliferated *en masse*. This has been facilitated by the technology of the stand-alone photocopier, which grants access to cheap or free printing. Since photocopying became widely available in the '70s, over 50,000 zines have emerged and spread in America alone—mostly through the mail, with little publicity. Flaunting off-beat interests, extreme personal revelations and social activism, zines directly counter the *pseudo-communication* and glossy lies of the mainstream media monopoly. For many, zines have provided a purpose to a life which formerly appeared hopeless or nihilistic; as one zine creator put it, "Zining is *life,* and I know I would die without it." (Johanna Novales, *YAWP!)*

A Situationist slogan once declared, "In a society that abolishes adventure, the only adventure is in abolishing that society." The best zines participate in that adventure.

—V. Vale, San Francisco, 1996

Thrift SCORE

AL HOFF publishes *Thrift SCORE*, the zine about thriftin' (subscription $4, sample copy $1 plus two stamps from PO Box 90282, Pittsburgh PA 15224). Articles such as "Can '70s Clothing Hurt You?," "How to tell Alpaca from Acrylon" and "75 Things I Hate About Shopping in Thrift Stores" enlighten and inspire fellow thrifters. A San Francisco native with a degree in film, Al Hoff now lives in Pittsburgh in a large old tiki-and-treasure-laden house with her husband Pat Clark.

♦ *VALE: Why did you publish* **Thrift SCORE***?*
♦ AL HOFF: First of all, I always "thrifted," but it increasingly became more of an *obsession*—I went from once a month to every weekend. There's so much great stuff to be retrieved out of thrift stores, yet no one discusses this as a concept or a lifestyle. Thrifting involves many different groups of people: poor people, art people, students. I had friends who thrifted a lot; one day we were talking and realized that no one had ever written about thrifting: "Hey, someone should write a book!"

A few months later I had a "temp" job and during work I started making notes on what might be interesting topics to cover. I also raised "issue" questions like "Why is something valuable when it's at the mall, but not at the Salvation Army?"

♦ *V: Also, certain objects then undergo a transition from the thrift store to the antique store—*
♦ AH: Right—why is something "junk" in one place and "collectible" in another? Thrift stores provide the necessities of life for poor people: is it ethical for more affluent, privileged art student types to be snatching things away from them? If I buy 25 lunch boxes, am I part of this problem?

In the fall of '93, my husband remarked, "There's a million people who would read a zine about thrifting." I said, "No way—*everybody* does a zine! Also, I don't know how to get it out there. I just don't want to do it." I was completely resistant to the idea. Then I got a free on-line account. On New Year's Eve I had nothing to do (that's pathetic!), so I started cruising these teenage groups and asked them, "Would anyone be interested in reading a zine about thrift shopping?" I just threw this out there in cyberspace. Half a dozen kids wrote back: "Ohmigod, I would just *die* if somebody did a zine about thrifting!" This was like throwing a ball out into the universe and having it bounce back.

My motivation isn't to propagate some underground cause; my reason for publishing is to talk about buying too much completely cool stuff that you don't really need.

I printed 100 copies of my first issue. Within eight months it had become a "hot" zine; I found myself getting lots of attention. In retrospect, I had missed an obvious point: most people who do zines also thrift, so I immediately got a lot of attention from other zines. This was great; people were very positive. If you print something about your musical taste or political opinions, people are more divided. Thrift shopping has more of a general appeal; it doesn't matter what bands you listen to, you still go to thrift stores.

♦ **V: *You had almost overnight fame—***
♦ AH: A lot of it was luck: producing something at the right time and place. The zine community is so huge and vibrant, with the *alt.zines* group on the Internet and *Factsheet Five* as a key publication. All of the mass media want to tap into this "zine thing." When I started publishing, I hadn't read a zine for years except *Murder Can Be Fun,* and I only got that because the publisher sent it to me for free. I was completely out of the zine loop; I didn't have a clue.

There are an infinite number of zines and it's impossible to track them all. A lot of people aren't interested in funneling their zine through *Factsheet Five* or any central point, and that's sad. There are a handful of zines that get a lot of exposure and distribution, and getting a good plug in one of them can be just as helpful as a good review in *Factsheet Five.* A few zines are well-known outside the zine community, such as *Ben Is Dead* and *Bunnyhop,* which you see at Barnes & Noble. These have glossy covers and look more like magazines. There's a lot of discussion as to whether these qualify as zines; you could write a whole book on the politics of zines. I don't actually know any zine creators in my town, but for two years I've been following all these discussions on the Internet—all these rants about what constitutes a true zine, what is punk, and who is "selling out."

♦ **V: *What are some of the issues involved in "selling out"?***
♦ AH: People complain if you make money, that's considered bad; if you solicit ads and make a profit, that's considered bad. If you sell something you've written to a publication that's considered too mainstream; that's bad. And parleying your zine into a television appearance or a book deal means you haven't remained "true" to the Alternative/Underground/Free Press ideal.

However, these are not issues for me. Personally, I've never worried about whether I'm on the "cutting edge." My motivation is not to propagate some underground cause; my reason for publishing is to talk about buying too much completely cool stuff that you don't really need. Tonight I was watching a TV interview with a man who got a heart transplant and behind him was a knick-knack shelf with the most amazing 12″ statue of Elvis Presley—I couldn't stop staring at it.

♦ **V: *That'll be in a thrift store someday—***
♦ AH: Maybe sooner than you think!

Al Hoff at "Ohio's best thrift store." Photo: Pat Clark

♦ **V:** *When did the term "thrifting" begin? Many years ago, people used the term "sale-ing" (as in going to garage sales)—*
♦ **AH:** I just heard *that* term last year for the first time. I can't trace the etymology, but I started using "thrifting" as a verb at least 10 years ago. The '80s was all about turning nouns into verbs; it's no longer "to

> **No one makes a profit, and sometimes the more zines you sell, the more money you lose! . . . All my time and thought and insight are completely free! Like everybody else, I do this for pleasure.**

have an impact on," it's "impacting." I guess "thrifting" is an abbreviation of "thrift shopping" (which is a mouthful) or "going to the thrift store to shop."

I didn't get a computer until the fall of '93, and four months later I put out a zine—that computer made it possible. That's why we have so many zines now; the technology is at people's fingertips and it's so easy. It takes a lot more effort to do a zine on a typewriter or to write one by hand. I still do a lot of cutting and pasting because I don't have very sophisticated software, but I'm at that terrible point where I can no longer be creative by hand—now all my writing is done on the computer. And the more you do it, the faster you get!

I don't have a scanner, even though they're a few hundred dollars now. I'm still pretty primitive; I cut out pictures and glue them down onto sheets of paper. Some zine people get horrified: "You *glue* the photos down?" [laughs] I'll get a scanner someday. But if I won the lottery, I'd buy one of those really fancy xerox machines with collating, stapling—the whole thing. The downside of zines is that copying is becoming less cheap, plus the cost of paper is going up. No one makes a profit, and sometimes the more zines you sell, the more money you lose! Personally, I hate to charge more than a dollar—it's a nice, fair number. I sell five sheets of paper (folded in half and stapled) for a dollar. Some people charge two dollars for that much paper, but I think that's kind of a rip-off.

♦ **V:** *What about your time?*
♦ **AH:** All my time and thought and insight are completely free! Like everybody else, I do this for pleasure. There's so much fun to be gotten from feedback; it's affirming to write something and have people respond: "What you wrote was great!" That's worth more than money.

A big motivating factor is: I love getting mail. When you do a zine (unless you're someone like Jim Goad) the mail you get is all positive. People don't take the time to write unless they have something nice to say. Every day someone sends me something nice and congratulatory.

♦ **V:** *How do you pay the rent?*
♦ **AH:** I'm *married.* [laughs] I used to work; I had a long series of stupid temp jobs and then I had a "real" job for five years. It was a temp job that turned into a real position with a growth software company—I started at the bottom and could have gone to the top. I was overpaid and slated to become a "big success" at this job—but I *hated* it! Finally I quit. When we moved to Pittsburgh, which is a cheap place to live, my husband got a good job and I said, "Remember those two years when you were unemployed and I worked? Now it's my turn not to work." In theory, there was going to be an equal exchange of labor time, but I think I passed my deadline on that!

My husband is completely supportive of what I do. For years I was miserable doing "the wrong thing" and I sort of stumbled on doing "the right thing." Now I'm extremely lucky. I have such respect for people who have a full-time job and put out a decent zine; I frankly don't know how they do it. I have *mucho* free time and still can't get *Thrift SCORE* out on time! It's so much work: answering mail, writing articles, going to the Post Office—whatever.

It hasn't been bad, though—the zine pretty much supports itself. If you send me a dollar, that pays for my actual printing and mailing costs. And if someone orders five at once, I make a really slim profit because then it costs less to mail. Stores who sell it

Cover of Thrift SCORE #1

Spring 1994 — **Issue One**
Thrift SCORE
a 'zine about thriftin'
It's a PURSE!   It's a PHONE!
It's a PURSE that IS a PHONE!
- WEIRDEST Things Ever Thrifted
- Stuff You See in Every Thrift
- 70's Clothing - Can It Hurt You?

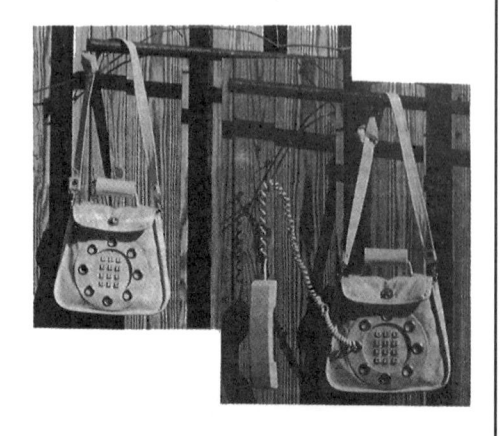

PLUS: Retro-Tennis Shoes (uh oh!), the Wide World of Thrifts, Useful Info, Useless Info, Cool Pix and More More More.

$1

on consignment get a discount, so I don't really see any profit from them, but then again I'm not really in it for profit. But it's not running me into the ground.

I may not have a job now, but I do a lot of housewifely things to compensate. I iron my husband's shirts and make dinner. Actually, I'm not a very good housewife. I grew up in the '70s in San Francisco and was completely indoctrinated with feminist ideals of what women should do. They shouldn't be housewives, they shouldn't stay home and make dinner—my mother's idea was: "If I *don't* teach you these things, you won't be trapped into doing them!" In Pittsburgh, if you tell people you're a housewife and stay home, they say, "That's great!" But in San Francisco people give you a boatload of grief: "Why don't you have your own career? This seems *wrong.*"

I moved to Pittsburgh because I knew it would be easier and cheaper to live, and because it had the best thrift stores I'd ever seen. I refused to move to any suburb—I just can't live there. I moved to a relatively stable city where I could surround myself with *things.*

♦ **V:** *What kinds of things?*
♦ **AH:** I'm looking at three armchairs, a Barcalounger, a velvet couch, the top halves of four mannikins, some of those horrible dashboard dolls whose heads bob up and down on springs, a piggy bank that looks like Bert from *Sesame Street,* a metal picnic basket, and a rotary phone from the '70s that looks like a white donut—it cost three dollars in Akron, Ohio. I have a table from an old diner, lots of shoes and plastic dinnerware. Our new house has a metal sink, and when we moved here I immediately broke a china plate in it. I thought, "I'm going to get some cool plastic dinnerware from the '50s—Melmac." It was incredibly popular and was made in all these weird shapes and colors. I thought it would be hard to find; people told me it was highly collectible: "In New York it's going for $35 a plate!" But in a month's time I found over a hundred pieces; it comes in these enormous grab-bags for two dollars a bag.

♦ **V:** *Is it really lightweight?*
♦ **AH:** No, it's fairly heavy—that's what distinguishes it. It has almost the same heft as china, and it's very hard. I recently did a test: I threw a Melmac bowl and a ceramic bowl from a third floor window. As you might imagine, the ceramic bowl shattered beyond repair while the Melmac bowl was completely unharmed!

♦ **V:** *What colors does it come in? White?*
♦ **AH:** It doesn't usually come in white, because white plastic looks cheap. Because it was so easy to make in any color, the manufacturers went nuts with colors. Yellow, green, blue, and pink pastels are very common. I have a few black pieces, which are a bit unusual. It was literally made in a rainbow of colors. I wrote a history of Melmac by researching '50s magazine articles in the library and no sooner had I finished than I discovered a book published by one of those "collectibles" presses. It said, "Melmac is hot! It's a '50s collectible that no one has discovered." It had price lists in the back and a bowl was supposedly worth $15. In all fairness, the author had done a lot of research. A lot of what he had written was almost identical to what I had written—he had consulted the same sources.

♦ **V:** *How do you do your research?*
♦ **AH:** I do most of it at the library. If there's a new book on a subject, I go to Barnes & Noble and just sit there all day, read it, and take notes. Since I stopped working, I won't allow myself to buy any new books. It's ridiculous—I can't spend seven dollars on a new book, but I can go out this weekend and spend $20 on used books because they have cool covers (even though I'll never read them). There's no logic to this at all—well, in theory the used books are a better deal, even if I never read them—they're 25 cents apiece. New books are very expensive; even a supermarket novel is seven dollars. I never buy those new, but once in awhile I do read them; anything that makes the best-seller list goes to a thrift store—guaranteed! You'll see *Jurassic Park* in every thrift store you visit.

I keep lists of books; if I see a book that looks interesting, I'll make a note of it in a little notebook. Occasionally, the most unlikely book (a very specialized book that maybe sold five copies when new) shows up at a thrift store and when you find it, that's a great score! Not only have you beaten the system (you didn't pay $30 for it), but you got it by mining this tiny vein—there's maybe three copies out there in thrift stores, and you got one of them.

> **I need a cutlery tray right now. And rather than spend three dollars for a new one at the hardware store, I will wait (and I can wait as much as two years) until I find the one I want at a thrift store for 50 cents.**

♦ **V:** *Don't you also collect '50s etiquette guides and cookbooks?*
♦ **AH:** Lynn Peril won't like this, but I buy them to cut 'em up for clip art—they have great photos and illustrations. I do *not* feel good about this; I try to pick books that are in bad shape or are less than a dollar—forlorn copies where some kid has ripped out a page or scribbled in it.

I have a huge collection of pulp paperbacks; those are still easy to find. I buy them for no other reason than the great covers—a lot of times the pages are disintegrating. We just bought a house and I'm going to figure out some way to display them so you can see a whole wall of these covers. It's a shame when they sit in bookcases—all you can see is the spines. I have many, many decorating plans, but none of them ever come to fruition.

♦ **V: Why not?**

♦ AH: Because I just keep *buying* stuff—I don't put the time into doing anything except buying! I have mountains of fabric that I'm going to "do something with" someday; I have lots of extra furniture. Whenever I buy a new chair, I have to throw an old one away!

♦ **V: Maybe you're responding to some previous imperative of want in your childhood—**

♦ AH: I was thinking about that today: "Why do I have this need to have so much stuff?" But as a child I wasn't deprived of anything. I think I just have a *love of objects*. I take tremendous comfort in being surrounded by objects. My living room looks like the set of *Sanford and Son,* with all this stuff piled up on other stuff. Remember how he would shuffle around looking for something: "I know it's here *somewhere*." That's my house.

There are things that I truly need, like I need a cutlery tray right now. And rather than spend three dollars for a new one at the hardware store, I will wait (and I can wait as much as two years) until I find the one I want at a thrift store for 50 cents. And that's a true need—something functional. I also have any number of collections that have to be supported. If I see something I already have one or two of, then I have to get it. I always have to start new collections because the old stuff disappears.

♦ **V: What do you mean?**

♦ AH: I'll start collecting something and then never see it again. China's like that—I'll be collecting one pattern and then *bam*—it completely disappears. Other times something gets priced out of my budget—I have very strict price guidelines. I used to buy metal lunchboxes; I thought they had great imagery on them,

> **People say, "Gosh, it's really *political* what you do: shopping at thrift stores. It's anti-'The System.'" In a way it is, because you're not buying what they're telling you to buy *now* . . . but I know I'll be buying it 20 years from now!**

and you could put stuff in them, plus there was that nostalgia from my childhood—whatever. But those became collectible, and now lunchboxes in thrift stores are $15. There's no way I'm going to pay that, so I don't *care* about lunchboxes anymore. Then I'm missing one need, so I have to come up with a new one! [laughs]

I'm extremely susceptible to other people's interests. Since starting *Thrift SCORE,* people have written to me: "Look at my collection of *this!*" and I've been completely converted on the spot. I never thought about belt buckles before, but somebody sent me a

> **There's this complete reverse snobbery: "I got this totally cool thing for no money, and the lady said it had been there for months!" The more discarded and cheap something is, the better the score in terms of bragging.**

photo of these bad, cheesy belt buckles from the '70s with bikers on them, etc, and I thought, "Those are so cool!" Now I regret all the years I *wasn't* looking for belt buckles, because I missed so many when I wasn't aware of them. Eight-track tapes and paint-by-number paintings are other recent "conversions."

I'm not a collector who's willing to pay whatever it takes to complete the collection—I can drop anything, anytime! My "needs" are completely artificial; I only create them in order to have a reason to go thrifting and in order to be sated. When I visit a thrift store, I have to leave with *something,* and I have to feel it's something I truly wanted and needed. So "the more you need, the more you buy; the more you buy—"

♦ **V: "—the happier you are!" Is that true?**

♦ AH: Absolutely. And the scary thing is: there's nothing "alternative" about this; this is what we're all conditioned to do by our culture. Advertising creates artificial needs that we buy into—we go purchase that thing, and we're "fulfilled." That's essentially the mind game I'm playing with myself. People say, "Gosh, it's really *political* what you do: shopping at thrift stores. It's anti-'The System.'" In a way it is, because you're not buying what they're telling you to buy *now* . . . but I know I'll be buying it 20 years from now! [laughs] I haven't shaken off that cultural training *to shop.*

I justify what I do by telling myself that it's pop culture studies, or I need something for researching an article. I'll rationalize: "It sat there for a month, and nobody else will buy it if I don't." I try to justify each purchase by making it serve some loftier purpose. But the truth is: I just like to buy things!

♦ **V: But you did successfully resist buying a shirt-ironing machine as big as a refrigerator—**

♦ AH: I didn't buy that because it was too big and bulky and weird. Besides, it was really my husband who wanted that, and I don't always play fair so I talked him out of it! He used to collect thousands of weird records and they were all over the house, so about five years ago I said, "That's it! No more weird records! You can only buy a record if you actually *play* it." Then, of course, *Incredibly Strange Music* came out and those records became worth a fortune overnight. He said, "All the people in this book are so cool. They're doing exactly what I was doing and you made me stop!" The funny thing is, after the books came out I became re-obsessed, and then *I* began buying records. They are still stacked up mostly unplayed.

♦ **V:** *Do you have a good turntable?*

♦ **AH:** I had my turntable from the '70s and thought, "I should get another one as a back-up, because I'm concerned they're going to disappear." I was looking at cheap ones in stereo stores for $100, thinking, "Next time I get a temp job, I'll buy one." Then I saw a beautiful Technics turntable at a thrift store for $40, and it looked absolutely unused. Forty bucks is a lot for me, but I was in a *mood* and I bought it. I ended up calling J&R Music World in New York and found out it was still in stock for $500! I went to a vinyl store to have the needle inspected, and the guy said, "This is a really expensive needle—just clean it." I didn't have the heart to ask how much a new needle cost, because I didn't know if that meant $20 or $200. And you can't buy those needles used.

♦ **V:** *You bought something high-tech—*

♦ **AH:** It was a good deal and a lot of my friends were envious. Envy is another big part of thrifting! Most people who thrift have friends that thrift, and part of the thrill is finding the cool things before they do, whether it's on the same trip (and you got to that part of the store before they did), or you went out on your own and got something. A lot of it is about gloating; there's this complete reverse snobbery: "I got this totally cool thing for no money, and the lady said it had been there for months!" The more discarded and cheap something is, the better the score in terms of bragging. It's the complete opposite of the guy who tells you how much his Lexus cost.

Most of my friends have similar tastes, so it's a friendly competition. It's a high compliment if you tell me about something you thrifted and I'm a little envious. It won't affect our friendship, but it's always there as an undercurrent! The first time I visited Lynn Peril's and Candi Strecker's apartments, I was going, "Oh, you have one of these? I have two of 'em." We talked about how many we have and how little we paid for them. After Lynn Peril and Johnny Bartlett got back from their honeymoon trip to Arizona, they invited me over to show off all the cool stuff they had found. I "oohed" and "ahhed" appreciatively—it's all part of the game!

♦ **V:** *They scored some "regional" finds—*

♦ **AH:** That's true; stuff does vary from place to place. San Francisco has a lot of souvenir shlock which people obviously brought back from the Far East, such as bad little plastic Chinese lanterns or weird sculptures carved out of this yellow-brown wood from the Philippines. Because of the large Asian community, people are going back and forth carrying souvenir gifts or presents for their families or whatever. You'd never see any of that in Pittsburgh because there aren't communities to support it. In California there are probably more Hawaiian shirts because there's a lot of vacation traffic between the two states. The Southwest offers more Western or cowboy stuff.

Big cities are not usually the best places for thrift shopping. On my last trip to San Francisco I hit a lot of thrift stores. It's sad—the Goodwills are trying to go upscale with lots of new merchandise, and the Salvation Army is, too. St. Vincent de Paul is still okay, but you really have to search every single section to find something—and usually when you do, it's in the wrong section! I did a lot better out in the suburbs.

♦ **V:** *What can you get in Pittsburgh that's special?*

♦ **AH:** Pittsburgh has amazing demographics for thrifting. It has had a very substantial, stable middle class for a long time. These people had disposable incomes; they were the first in their families to have any kind of money at all, and they bought a lot. As second-generation Americans, they wanted all the most "American" stuff, and in the '40s, '50s, and '60s they just stocked up.

Pittsburgh is full of enormous houses that people lived in their whole lives. They fill up their houses, then die or go to a nursing home, and their suburban kids show up and take everything straight to the thrift store. There's an incredible amount of domestic goods from bygone eras: curtains, kitchenware, furniture, and even clothing.

Pittsburgh has an aging population and all those people are dying right now! This is in contrast to a place like L.A. where people moved *to;* they tended to

Cover of Thrift SCORE #3

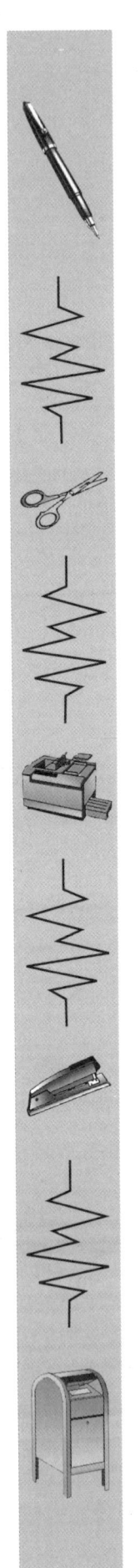

show up with just a suitcase or a car, leaving most of their stuff behind. They left it behind in places like Indianapolis or Pittsburgh or Iowa. A lot of other cities are more transient; people don't acquire a lot of stuff. I saw a statistic that said Pittsburgh has the highest percentage of "stay-put-ers" in the nation—on the average, people move to a house and stay there for something like *thirty-seven* years! And that's the *average!* So in that respect, Pittsburgh is a great place to thrift.

> **I think thrifting should be a democratic exercise that's about luck and fate. I have lucky days and unlucky days . . . It's harder for me to see someone buy something from underneath my fingertips when I know they're just going to resell it for a profit.**

There's no trendy scene in Pittsburgh. The hot cities have lots of hot people, all wanting the same thing. There'll be a million college kids all looking for gas station shirts; there'll be more vintage clothing stores, and there's more knowledge about all this stuff. Whereas here . . . sometimes when I think about trying to make a living by recycling stuff I find at thrift stores, a mantra goes through my mind: "If only I could get this to New York!"

♦ **V: But aren't there people who already do that—who sweep regularly through town and pick everything clean—**
♦ **AH:** I call them "pickers." I had a woman "picker" write me from Austin, and she was really smart about her justifications; she thought them all out. Sometimes pickers have their own stores or they work for the owner of a vintage store or even someone overseas. These people can walk into a thrift store and know what will sell in another place for considerably more money; a polyester shirt that sells for two dollars here can be resold in New York's East Village for $40. So they sell it to the East Village store-owner for $10, and everybody makes a profit.

I have a problem with this because I think thrifting should be a democratic exercise that's about luck and fate. I have lucky days and unlucky days, and if someone gets there before me, that's no big deal if I think they got something they truly *want*—that's fair, they got there first. It's harder for me to see someone buy something from underneath my fingertips when I know they're just going to resell it for a profit—they're not buying it for the actual love of the object itself or to *enjoy* the object.

What I particularly hate is people who negotiate with a thrift store ahead of time for a specific thing, with the result that the thing never makes it out to the floor. It may even be something they personally collect, but I still don't think that's fair! For a thrift store this means guaranteed sales; they're not stuck with something that may remain on the retail floor for months. They're in a weird business; they have incredibly high turnover—more so than a department store. They have to move stuff in and out fast. So if they can sell something out the back door, that saves them time and money. I doubt they care whether or not this is "ethical"; they're in business to make a profit or to raise money for charity.

I used to buy a lot of curtains at this one thrift store—almost every time I went, there'd be great curtains from the '40s and '50s. Then they just *disappeared.* I thought, "Maybe this is just one of those weird cycles," but I was still mystified—like I said, there's plenty of big houses with old ladies dying in them, and the curtains are the first thing to go. One day I was downstairs near the back door and I saw this guy who owns a vintage store walking out with an armful of curtains. Instantly I knew what had happened. All I could do was stare at his retreating back and put a hex on him!

♦ **V: Well, what else could you do?**
♦ **AH:** My only revenge is to not patronize those vintage stores, even if they have something I really want. I have my price limits and I won't exceed them. It doesn't make more stuff appear in the thrift stores, but that's all I can do. Then I get into "shifting ahead."
♦ **V: What does that mean?**
♦ **AH:** Vintage stores tend to stock things that have already been earmarked as "collectible." These things start back in antiquities and work their way up to the present; there's always a cutoff point where stuff is not considered collectible. Right now, depending on what city you're in, we're up to either the '60s or the '70s. In New York, stuff is already up to the '80s—maybe even the '90s! That's scary.

It's hard to stay ahead. If there are no more '50s curtains left, then fine—I don't have to have them anymore. I'll pick something else that I know I can still afford. I'm thinking of starting a Gulf War t-shirt collection because I know they're out there and nobody wants them right now. There are some completely insane ones that 10 years from now are going to seem amazingly weird. Something like that has *no* market right now, so I'll just "shift up" to them—*fine.* And it's not like I want to get it ahead of time so I can make a profit on it later, it's just so I can have something that's available to me. Again, it's that whole process of creating needs.
♦ **V: Well, if you spend too much money on something, you feel ripped off and end up feeling bad—**
♦ **AH:** Exactly—especially if you don't actually *need* the thing. The pleasure is in the hunt and in "How low can I get it for?" If it's a paint-by-number painting, I have no need for it, so it has to be priced low enough so that I essentially get it for nothing.

Al Hoff, age 11, in front of the Regency Theater, San Francisco

♦ **V:** *Surely you've been in a thrift store and spotted something: "So-and-so collects penguins; I'll buy that for her."*
♦ **AH:** Yes, I buy tons of gifts. I shop all year for people's birthdays and Christmas gifts! If I see something that a friend likes, I'll buy it and put it away, then dig it out at Christmas time and wrap it. And this is reciprocal—that's a *community,* and it's great. That's why you want to have friends similar to you—they understand your taste and what you want, but aren't looking for exactly the same things. This is another reason I like to shift to new things. Sometimes I'll be buying something and my friends will all get into it—then it becomes too competitive and I go, "Oh, forget it! I'm going on to something else."

This brings up questions about identity: part of your identity is bound up with things you buy that are different. It's always uncomfortable when suddenly everybody is buying the things that made you feel unique. That's another great thing about thrifting: you have all this freedom to recreate an identity. You don't have to answer to whatever the mainstream or "alternative culture" media say you're supposed to be wearing or buying this year. And it's so easy and cheap to be constantly shifting your taste.

♦ **V:** *Can you describe your past apartments?*
♦ **AH:** We had an apartment in a Washington, D.C. neighborhood that was "in transition," going from Middle-class Black to *Crack War.* We would often order pizza, and our front door opened into our living room which was just *packed* with stuff. Every inch of the wall had something nailed to it; shelves were overflowing; all the mannikins were dressed up. And the look on the faces of the delivery guys was always better than the pizza—they didn't know *what* to make of what they saw. They would ask, "Are you artists? Is this place a museum? What do you *do?*"

These were mostly young kids who hadn't had much exposure except to their own little circles. Not to wax sociological here, but people from lower-middle class or working class backgrounds are indoctrinated to strive toward some ideal "look" in home decor—perhaps the way things look on TV. Having matching furniture is *very* important! But none of our old furniture matched; there were all these kooky juxtapositions of objects. These kids didn't understand why, if you have a job, you don't have furniture that matches. They just wondered why you have so much *junk.*

My place is quite eclectic. I have admiration for people who can put together rooms with a theme or a feel; Lynn Peril's place is great. She and Johnny work with a 1945-65 time range, and they have little "theme" areas: a pin-up area, a little drag-racing area. They have a lot of different stuff, but it's arranged so there's a cohesive feel to the whole apartment. I was very impressed when I looked at all their little shelves and cubbyholes. Lynn was very specific when she told me, "We don't buy too many things past the '60s."

I, on the other hand, collect stuff from every era. There's cheap plastic things and nice furniture all mixed up. That's why it looks like *Sanford and Son;* it looks like you walked into a junk shop where everything's higgly-piggly. I'm not very good at arranging.

Actually, I think you should also give things *back* to thrift stores! . . . You should *never* steal from thrift stores. If you steal a tiki god, you're doomed!

Because I'm not committed to one time or look, everything is all mixed up. And I'm not very neat, whereas Candi Strecker is very neat—her place is spic-and-span. I try, but I just can't do that. I come home from the thrift store, take what I bought out of the bag, and find the nearest empty space—that's my Decorating in Action! Stuff gets lost; there's so much on display that you can't see it all. Friends will spot something and ask, "Oh, did you just buy that?" and I reply, "No, that's been there for two years."

♦ *V: That's selective perception—*

♦ AH: Probably sensory overload—your brain just can't take it all in! The main thing that's fun about doing my zine is getting complete affirmation of this aberrant behavior. People write me: "You *understand.* You're so cool; you're not insane. You're perfect." And they say this because they're essentially in the same position that I'm in. They write, "I thought I was insane; everyone who knows me thinks I'm insane. I can't tell you how glad I am that there are other people out there like me."

♦ *V: Thrifting is better than therapy, and cheaper too—*

♦ AH: Actually, it's not cheaper—readers are usually encouraged to go out and buy more! But instead of therapy, which goes up into thin air, they've got stuff left over—*souvenirs.*

One of my projected goals for the zine was to establish some kind of forum: I would be some sort of central clearing house of information for like-minded people. They could write and share their stories, and (like I said before) a lot of it is about gloating, boasting and being competitive. There's nothing like showing off (through the zine) in front of several hundred people and saying: "Look what *I* bought!" And people do write in and share information: "This is what I collect, and this is why it's cool. Here's how I got started . . ."

The main thing that's fun about doing my zine is getting complete affirmation of this aberrant behavior.

I get an amazing number of submissions and letters from people who are eager to *talk,* and I get these "therapy" letters where people start nine pages by saying, "I've never had anyone to talk to about this." Then follows page after page of descriptions of things they've bought. People send photos and I vicariously share their lives. I write back and say, "Good score!"— I'm going to have to trademark *that* phrase.

♦ *V: So what things did you start to collect after other people told you about them—*

♦ AH: Like I said, I recently started to collect belt buckles. Julee Peezlee sent me a photo of four of them laid out against black velvet, and they looked like nice jewelry or art objects. I had despised eight-track tapes my entire life, having grown up in the '70s when eight-tracks were these horrible, clunky things that had a million problems—songs stopped in the middle; they jammed. But I met Russ Forster, who publishes *8-Track Mind,* just because we had a common interest in going to thrift stores. When I sat down and read his zine I was instantly converted: "Ohmigod, you're right—eight-tracks are so cool!" I immediately went to a flea market (it was Sunday and the thrift stores were closed), found one of those eight-track players shaped like a dynamite detonator and a handful of tapes, and that was *it!*

♦ *V: You scored—those are getting hard to find.*

♦ AH: Wasn't that strange? That's weird *thrift karma!* I was so willing to "convert" that fate sent me that detonator for three dollars.

♦ *V: "Thrift karma"—that's another term for your* **Thrift SCORE** *Glossary.*

♦ AH: Actually, I think you should also give things *back* to thrift stores! Because then things come back to you. There's more to my code of ethics: you should *never* steal from thrift stores. If you steal a tiki god, you're doomed!

♦ *V: Do you plant objects back in the store?*

♦ AH: I usually dump them into the donations box. This reminds me—there's a guy who makes art and then sneaks it back into thrift stores. He buys the frames from thrift stores (keeping the price tag on),

Cover of *Thrift SCORE #4*

creates paintings and then puts them into the frames. He sticks a note in back (with a self-addressed stamped envelope) that says, "I made this art. Please write to me." Then he takes his art back to the thrift store and hangs it on the wall with the other paintings. This is the kookiest project—

♦ **V: That's certainly outside of the "fine art" economy—**
♦ AH: He's an art student at a well-known California art school. He actually sells work under his real name, so he does this giveaway work under a pseudonym in order to not devalue his own work. He also photographs his art when it's back hanging in the thrift store—that makes the project complete. A few people have actually responded to him. He's completely playing with the idea of what a thrift store is—its meaning and economy and purpose.

♦ **V: That's the opposite of Jim Shaw and his Thrift Store Paintings show and book—**
♦ AH: I bought his exhibition catalog and there's no text in it at all, just photos. I sent him some questions in care of his publisher and he graciously wrote back and answered them. I printed them in *Thrift SCORE*. His answers were great. He was very much aware that he was a trained artist and that this was a kind of art he couldn't even do himself (because he couldn't undo his training). And he had strict price limits as to what he would spend on paintings. He ended up being pretty cool.

I went to the library and could not find any background on Jim Shaw. I could find reviews of his exhibit (which were mostly incomprehensible; they didn't talk about where the paintings came from or why he was doing this; it was all: "In our post-Marxist society, the idea of art is . . ."). I asked him obvious questions like "When did you start buying them? Why did you start buying them? How much did you spend on them? If you go on a vacation, do you stop at thrift stores?" His answers were all perfect. Of course he had that dilemma: "I was doing this personally for years, and now that I've made it *public,* I've created this artificial market for amateur paintings. I've priced myself out of my own hobby! I've created a weird value problem that wasn't there before." I have a soft spot in my heart for him because *he wrote back!*

In Boston a *Museum of Bad Art* opened up which seems to be flirting with similar issues regarding good and bad taste. I read that they did a summer exhibit at someone's estate on Long Island and all the artwork was hung from trees.

♦ **V: But that sounds a bit self-conscious and ironic—**
♦ AH: "Irony is the curse of our generation"—that's a paraphrase of a line from an REM song: "Irony is the shackles of youth." At first I thought, "I never knew he was singing that—that's so smart!" Then I wondered, "Is he saying that ironically?" I got confused.

I know I'm an *irony victim;* I'm going to be cursed the rest of my life. My only justification is that I was ironic before it was "in." Irony is being mass-marketed now on TV, so there has to be a pendulum shift away from that. We'll be like those aging hippies sitting in a Berkeley coffee shop 10 years from now being ironic, and a table of 20-year-olds sitting next to us will be going, "Gawd, they're *so* outdated!"

I *try* to have genuine affection for things. I do buy things just because they're so unbelievably awful, but I try to take the approach of "Where do they fit into cultural history? What are they saying?"

♦ **V: Do you ever buy something because you think it's "cute"?**
♦ AH: To me "cute" is a negative word; people used it in high school and I had a lot of problems with it. It reminds me of walking into a Hallmark card store with someone's grandma—when she says something is "cute," you have to *lie* to agree with her.

♦ **V: I'm thinking of a ceramic statue of a chihuahua with big brown eyes, begging—**
♦ AH: I have one of those! I bought big-eyed dog statues for years, but now they're "in"—in fact, I just saw one of my sad-eyed dog figurines on MTV; it was behind the veejay. I thought, "Uh oh—time to take it to New York!"

Here's an example of how my irony has shifted around. I always bought those big-eyed things (mostly repro paintings of Keane, Gig, Eden, etc) just because of how they looked—they were absurd, but there was something so *great* about them. They've been piling up in corners for years. Our new house has this long narrow hallway you have to walk down to get to the bathroom, so you can't avoid it. I had an idea to line the entire hall with these paintings (and I always buy only the sad ones, not the happy ones) so it'll be a *Hallway of Sorrow* (like in *Night Gallery*).

One night I had this *epiphany* while staring at them: the saddest thing on earth is an "I Love You This Much" statue that somebody *threw away!*

Then I thought of those "I Love You This Much!" statues of people with their arms outstretched. They're about four inches high. There's a whole series of them: "World's Greatest Grandma," "World's Greatest Fisherman," and there's one of a guy with these beseeching eyes and arms outstretched saying, "I Love You This Much!" I see these all the time, and I thought of having a shelf of them at the end of the Hallway of Sorrow—you go through all this sorrow, and there's this embrace of love at the other end—this *antidote!*

After I started buying these "I Love You This

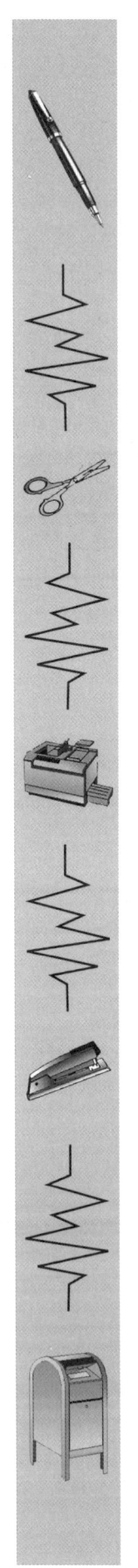

Much" statues, I discovered that there's an incredible diversity in them. Now I've got many variations of men, women, children and animals. One night I had this *epiphany* while staring at them: the saddest thing on earth is an "I Love You This Much" statue that somebody *threw away!* Here I was thinking this was going to be the *happy* part of the hallway, when in fact it was even *more* sorrowful. Imagine somebody giving you that as a gift, "I Love You This Much," and then you ditch it! So now I'm completely confused again.

♦ **V: *Objects do speak.***

♦ **AH:** I'm always wondering why things are, why they happened, where they came from, and who had them. I'm obsessed with *dead fads.* My new one is the Bicentennial; I'm stockpiling memorabilia from that. Obviously, I hated it when it came around the first time, but now I'm seeing it everywhere in thrift stores—there's so much of it and it all got ditched! It was pitched on TV as this great testament to democracy, and millions of people bought it, and now everybody is throwing it all away. They're looking at it, going, "This tin tray with the Bicentennial logo on it is just a *piece of shit*—it's not worth anything!" So now I'm interested in it, because next year is the 20th anniversary of the Bicentennial—I'm going to have a party, and I'll have all the stuff I need to celebrate the 20th anniversary of the 200th anniversary of this country.

♦ **V: *Talk about meanings collapsing in on each other: the postmodern condition—***

♦ **AH:** That's the old "Pop Will Eat Itself" line.

♦ **V: *What's your "take" on all this fashion which recapitulates the '60s and '70s?***

♦ **AH:** Retro fashion is a whole other area; there are blatant ripoffs of designs from the '60s and '70s, but they're all slightly *off.* At a certain Goodwill (which is in too good a neighborhood, therefore it doesn't have enough "junk" in it), a young girl/worker put together a "retro" rack so other kids could go directly to it and shop. I was flabbergasted at how ignorant this girl was. There was so much fake old stuff on the rack, like striped t-shirts from last year that were produced to *mimic* striped *Brady Bunch* t-shirts of the '70s. I thought, "Can't you even tell by the label, or anything?" There was also '70s clothing that our mothers threw away; I thought, "I know you weren't born then, but young people didn't *wear* this stuff!" (Like, your *aunt* wore this to the mall.) Not everything from the '70s has a cachet; if a garment is crappy, ugly, and poorly designed, just because it's made of polyester doesn't make it okay!

In the late '60s/early '70s polyester was a good word, then it became a bad word, and now it's a good word again. Five years ago I was in a D.C. mall, and I saw a young kid wearing a leisure suit. I'm one of those "Nothing can shock me; I've seen it all" types, but I did a complete double-take—I couldn't believe it. Suddenly I felt like I was getting old, because I just didn't *get* it. I had to overcome this urge to walk up to him and give him a lecture!

Imagine a *Mad* magazine theme park: "Come to *Real City* where you experience getting mugged and shot at—only at the end you get your wallet back!"

I try to be sympathetic, because I went through a lot of bad fashion phases, and I'm sure people felt the same way about me. But today the fashion industry is pretty scary in how it reproduces and recycles stuff. I have bowed out of buying new clothing; I just refuse to do that almost on principle. It's so expensive and so poorly made—I can buy 30 pairs of great pajamas for the price of one new pair. I can no longer justify buying something new. It's not a question of being stylish anymore—I *have* no style!

♦ **V: *But every time I've seen you, you have looked quite stylish—***

♦ **AH:** You saw me on two *special* occasions! My friends and I are trapped in what we perceive as the cool clothes of our youth, and we will continue wearing those. I'm not shifting "with the times." When I was in high school, I started to buy my own clothes, and they were in two categories: 1) punk or new wave or alternative, e.g.: tight black pants and mohair sweaters, and 2) mini-vintage-fashion: '40s and '50s clothing. And those are the same kind of clothes I still buy.

One of the highlights of my high school years was getting a pair of black jeans—I special-ordered them from a store, and my legs were so skinny that they weren't tight enough, so I spent an evening making them absolutely skin-tight. I still wear stovepipe black pants like every suburban mom—I'm trapped in that. If an occasion is "nice," I'll dig out a vintage dress and put it on. Also, in the early punk days people wore vintage dresses, sometimes with black tights and big clunky shoes. Three years ago, every teenage girl was wearing outfits like that, and so was I—I'd never stopped wearing 'em!

♦ **V: *These days, a lot of people wear Farmer John bib overalls—***

♦ **AH:** That's a new weird trend of the '90s: it's the "I want to look as bad as possible" fashion. Punk had elements of that, with clothes being ripped and torn, but

16

it had a certain panache. But kids today in these enormous clothes—*nobody* looks good in overalls. They are so unflattering; they're just work clothes that old guys wear.

I know—anti-fashion *is* fashion; I just have to accept that. I wish I knew more young people; sometimes I see someone in a thrift store and I want to go up and ask, "I don't understand why you're buying that; I wish you'd tell me. I want to understand why you're wearing that dress like my *aunt* used to wear."

♦ **V: *It seems like super-baggy clothes have been trendy for almost seven years, and that's a long time—***

♦ **AH:** I think they're finally on the way out. That'll be the next invasion of bad clothing into the thrift stores: that, and all those awful sports jackets bearing the names of college basketball teams. I'm afraid I'll be wading through all this stuff next year: extra-extra-extra-large t-shirts and enormous pants made for someone who weighs 350 pounds . . . and then 15 years from now some shop in New York will be reselling them for $150 to the *next* wave of kids who go: "Gawd, I wish I was young in the '90s—that was a really cool time!"

Retro-culture has very much become mass culture. Urban Outfitters—are they insane or what? I visited one in San Francisco and my head exploded—there was too much to think about, and I had to leave. Actually, they threw me out because I took a photo without asking permission. I was photographing this mannikin that was wearing $200 worth of clothing that I could have bought for $10: a polyester jacket from the '70s, a t-shirt and some jeans. That place is extremely strange: "We're gonna make this place look like a bomb hit it!"; it's filled with suburban kids trying to buy urban decay. That urban decay stuff—you can live it for a week and it gets old fast; there's nothing glamorous about it. But it's *sanitized* urban decay—it's Disney!land!

Imagine a *Mad* magazine theme park: "Come to *Real City* where you experience getting mugged and shot at—only at the end you get your wallet back!" Ana Marie Cox wrote a great piece on Urban Outfitters in her zine, *Noiseless*. I read her article, so I was kinda prepared when I went in, but nothing *really* prepared me for it in person. And it's expensive. What's even more upsetting was: that was where Woolworths was located, and I used to hang out there all the time—I *loved* that place. When you walked in the front door there was the most awful smell from the food counter with the popcorn and the weenies that rotate around and around. For a while it was the largest Woolworths left in the United States. I remember it so vividly, and now it's redecorated to look like it's deteriorating, with exposed beams—that's pretty scary.

There's still an old Woolworths-type store in Pittsburgh: G.C. Murphys. They sell really cheap underwear. They used to have a meat counter as well, and the smell of that as you were shopping for underwear was unbelievable! They stocked all these off-brands, including types of cereal you'd never heard of before: "Where did *this* come from?"

♦ **V: *Small change of subject: did you check out the Riot Grrrl zines when they were first happening?***

Cover of Thrift SCORE #6

Most popular music is just about the male experience, while the female experience is usually "I love him so much."

♦ **AH:** When I left San Francisco I was fed up with "alternative culture"; I was sick of all these *posing people*. I moved to DC where there was no youth culture, but I read about Riot Grrrl in *Sassy* and the *New York Times*—a completely *wrong* source—and thought, "Wow, I was doing that when I was a teenager, except we didn't have a name for it. Now these girls are organized and militant." I was interested in their ideas: "We're trying to establish a voice in the alternative culture which is so male-oriented. We don't want to be so-

and-so's *girlfriend;* we want to have our *own* band!" I was very encouraged by it. Since getting into the zine scene, I've had support from some of the Riot Grrrl zines. I think it's great; it's so much more amazing than anything that was going on when *I* was a teenager.

Now "alternative" has become "normal," and it's all a big mess. I respect the fact that zine people are able to network with one another and share similar experiences and disseminate them through zines or

It's empowering to shop at thrift stores. It's certainly *economically* empowering. You don't have to overspend; you can just buy what you want when the price is right.

the Internet. Fifteen years ago it would have been very hard for me to find 20 people across the United States doing what I was doing, or thinking about my particular interests. In '81 I worked briefly on *Idol Worship* (later *Beano),* an early zine by women who weren't trying to be groupies—just writing about bands they liked. Most girls I knew then wore short skirts and high heels and went to see alternative bands as members of the audience. Now girls have to *be* in a band, and god forbid anyone should try and pick 'em up!

I don't know if the relations between the sexes have evolved that much; I know they've changed. But I think that plenty of smart women still make really stupid romantic choices. However, I'm kind of estranged from contemporary sexual politics; I can observe them but I don't have to *negotiate* them anymore. So many things have changed; even acceptable meeting-and-greeting behavior seems to be different. If you say something, it can be perceived as harassment; if you compliment someone's hair, you're an evil male patriarch objectifying that person. None of these were issues for me; *I* would have felt flattered if someone said, "Your hair looks nice"—I would have written about it in my diary! But still, everyone's human; if you have a new sweater on and you've just done your hair, you're disappointed if nobody mentions it. [laughs]

♦ **V: *Riot Grrrl-influenced bands write about situations and points of view that have almost never been expressed in song before (or in print, for that matter)—***

♦ **AH:** I think it's great. Most popular music is just about the male experience, while the female experience is usually "I love him so much" or in the victim category. It used to be such a novelty to see a woman playing in a rock band, but the ability to play a musical instrument is not gender-based—all you need are basic motor skills and some imagination and creativity. There are thousands of all-girl garage bands now; in the future you won't even notice if a drummer is a woman or not. Girls will get arrested for throwing TV sets out the window of their hotel; the gender line will be completely blurred. They'll probably sell out to the major labels, too—just like the guys!

♦ **V: . . . *How have things changed since you started thrift shopping?***

♦ **AH:** I think more young men thrift now than ever before, and are far more conscious of filling personal space with stuff that reflects them. For teenage boys, there's no longer any social stigma about going to a thrift store and buying a bunch of paintings to hang on their wall. It's part of the "alternative as mainstream" trend, and much of this has been pitched to kids on MTV or in magazines. The earlier assumption was that men who cared about the interiors of their apartments were homosexual. Incidentally, my readership is split fifty-fifty between men and women.

When I started to thrift, as a teenager in high school, it was for clothing—that was a major empowerment about my own independence. It was *me* spending my own money (the little money I made from baby-sitting) and buying what I wanted—as opposed to my mother taking me to a department store and then having to *battle:* my mother saying, "Well, *I'm* paying for it so you're going to get *this."* Once you cross that line and say to your parents: "It's *my* money; I can buy what I want," then you can start establishing your identity. The girls in my high school wore Farrah Fawcett hairdos, designer jeans, and Candies (high-heeled mules with a strap across the toes—real "hooker"-looking, *not* a "classy" shoe); I purposely went out of my way not to look like them. I think I was identifying with the emerging punk subculture.

Q: "Do you think you'll be happy living in Pittsburgh for the rest of your life?" A: "Just as long as people keep dying and throwing things away!"

The next big change in life comes when you move out of your parents' house. You have this epiphany: "I can create my own space." What was so liberating about thrift shopping was: you're already completely out of the loop as to what the culture is telling you to buy. You can ignore the ads in the Sunday paper telling you how your bedroom should look, and give up striving for that. You can go to thrift stores and pick and choose among thousands of options. Suddenly you're aware that *there are no rules;* it's just about buying things you like. You put them together and get this incredible feeling: "This is *my* space that's unique to me." If you decorate out of thrift shops, there's no way anyone

The Andy Warhol Museum

[The Thrift Army gets up at 4:00 AM to visit the Andy Warhol Museum looking for "stuff."]

I don't know that Andy Warhol *thrifted,* but he was certainly an inveterate collector of "good" stuff and crap (this is important)—so we'll credit him *that* obsession. But look—we don't get many international high-art culturally bally-ho to-do's here in the 'Burgh, especially for the most famous person ever to leave Pittsburgh as fast as he could *and* the Museum was *free* for the first 24 hours.

We did a kinda SoHo Boho night owl thingie and hit the AWM at 4:40 AM. I envisioned that just the few of us would be rattling around the seven-floor museum in the still of the night. WRONG! Let's talk GEN-X-Plosion! Wall-to-wall flannel, carefully designed facial hair, docs, and lots of "Andy-homage" look—silver hair, tin foil accessories, Warhol-related T-shirts, sunglasses and cross-dressing. After about 15 minutes (really!)—most of 'em cleared out and we could browse in relative peace.

With over 500 pieces on display, there's bound to be something for everybody—mylar balloons, 30-foot tall Mao, homo-erotic art, cute kittie drawings, Jesus punching bags, black & white, color, 3-D and all the "famous" stuff—Campbell's Soup, Elvis, Marilyn—actually on the wall and not just 3″ x 3″ on the pages of *Vogue*.

We were psyched to check out the "stuff"—the AWM is the repository of all Warhol's time capsule boxes—cardboard boxes into which he just threw stuff and sealed when full. Only one was emptied and on display—and it did appear to be full of the flotsam and jetsam of his NYC life. You can peer through a glass divider in the library to this *wall* of time capsule boxes. Some of us salivated openly at the thought of all that undiscovered "stuff."

To represent all that Warhol collected in his life (a lot got auctioned after his death), they had a glass case full of goofy metal windup toys—none played with and some still in boxes. Another case had a random sampling of collectibles—Fiesta plates, feathered fan, cookie jars, jewelry and a Howard the Duck watch (still in packaging). Another case had about 40 fabulous women's shoes from the '50s and '60s (which had been used in a painting, but then Warhol had a "shoe thing" too). The creepiest was the glass box full of Warhol's wigs. Ick.

Overall Grade: B (Missing a certain weirdness factor and a sense of humor to make it an "A"—it was a little museum-y)

The Andy Warhol Museum, 117 Sandusky, Northside/Downtown, Pittsburgh (412) 237-8300. Not a huge museum (one to two hours visiting time), research library (make something up), film theater, photo booth (make your own art), coffee bar, gift shop (which was curiously NOT open), restroom, water fountain, leather sofas, white walls, etc.

—from *Thrift SCORE #2*

---

else in the whole *universe* can have the same room as you! It's completely about *you.*

It's empowering to shop at thrift stores. It's certainly *economically* empowering. You don't have to overspend; you can just buy what you want when the price is right, and save an amazing amount of money. I'm shocked when people buy things new, like sofas that cost $400. Saving money is *always* empowering! And you're out of the fashion loop. There are fashions in how we live our lives: "You should dress this way, your house should look this way, your car should look this way." The manufacturers constantly change these rules so they can sell more stuff. Once you leave that behind—that's *it;* you're free! You can sit through the TV commercials knowing they're not going to affect you.

♦ **V:** *So you watch TV—*
♦ **AH:** About six or seven hours a week—that's channel surfing time, not including videotaped movies. I'm an amateur student of pop culture, so I have to occasionally be tapped into mainstream media: "You have to know the enemy!" I read *People* magazine and enjoy it without any guilt—I *want* to know what happened to Kevin Costner's 20-year marriage (it was an age-old story; he lost it to some hula dancer). If you're going to be in a thrift store rescuing past trends, or re-appreciating a Keane painting, then you need to be tapped into mainstream culture. You should know why stuff disappeared, where it went, what took its place and what could be coming. If you understand how pop culture works this year, you can understand how it's always worked.

If you understand that there are fashions for certain things—be it patriotism, colors, or cartoon characters—then you'll be a much better thrifter. The more knowledge you have about a subject, the more you'll appreciate it. For example, the more I know about the Bicentennial, the more amazing the "Bicentennial TV" becomes—the TV had a woodgrain finish with signatures from the Declaration of Independence etched into it! If you dropped in from planet Mars and saw that, it wouldn't mean anything to you, but the more you know about our culture, TV, the Bicentennial and how horribly commercialized it got (just how *absurd* it got), then with each bit of information, that TV becomes a more amazing artifact. The fact that somebody would etch the signers of the Declaration of Independence onto a *TV* . . . and with no irony? Somebody did that seriously, and you were supposed to feel good about your country when you bought that!

♦ **V: Do you think you'll be happy living in Pittsburgh for the rest of your life?**
♦ AH: Just as long as people keep dying and throwing things away! Who knows where a person will end up? I decided that it's too much effort to live in a big city. It's not as hard as it used to be to live in more obscure places, because information and other things are more widely disseminated now. I lived for years in San Francisco and didn't have many friends, but now that I've left, not only do I have better friends there (we have stronger connections and much more in common) but when I go back and visit, I have two weeks of quality time with them.

With e-mail, I speak to John Marr and Candi Strecker and Lynn Peril almost every day and it's weird—after the course of a year, I *know* them. I corresponded with Candi and Lynn before I ever met them; John Marr and I met back in '81. He took me thrifting in Oakland and turned me on to pulp paperbacks; we've been friends all these years. In the insular world of zines, my biggest claim to fame is the fact that I know John Marr!

♦ **V: Why did you change your name to "Al"?**
♦ AH: I just hate the name Alison; I never liked it. It didn't suit me; it seemed like a Laura Ashley flowery dress/flowing hair kind of name. When I first put out the zine people got confused about my gender (like it really mattered?) but that seems to have cleared up. I still get mail addressed to "Mr. Al Hoff" but it's not an issue to me. And if people think you're a guy it's no loss—guys always get more authority and credibility.

There's a lot of log-rolling in the zine community—that's a term I read in *Spy* magazine. You know those recommendations you read on the dust jackets of books? *Spy* would find a quote from Kurt Vonnegut saying, "John Updike's new book is the best novel of the year!" Then they'd find a matching quote from Updike: "Vonnegut's book is the best I've read all year!" It's mutual back-scratching or *quid pro quo*. A lot of that goes on in the zine scene: "This is my friend's zine and it's highly recommended!" But that's how the world turns.

I have my own standards; I won't give anyone a plug unless I can stand by it. (Of course, if someone wants to give me a plug for no reason, that's okay!) But it's not such a big deal—at the very worst, someone sends somebody else a dollar for a zine and they're disappointed. This is such a small risk compared to all the fun and insight you can get from reading a zine which you know has only been printed in a few hundred copies, collated and stapled by hand with love and care, and sometimes even hand-colored. It's like belonging to a very special secret society! **V**

USE this for THAT

Old camera cases from Polaroid Land Cameras and others make great purses and/or carrying bags. They're already designed to be sturdy, fit comfortably 'round your neck or over your shoulder, and to fasten shut securely. They come in different sizes and in nice neutral colors like black, brown and tan. Definitely a unisex look to assuage anyone with unresolved gender-identity issues. People might actually think you're a photog/artiste! You'll find them very reasonably priced—even with a camera in 'em. Sometimes the cameras still work, so it's like getting a free gift!
—from *Thrift SCORE #2*

You don't have to be an old lady to spend some time in the Linens section at your thrift. Look for great old bedspreads from the '40s, '50s, '60s and '70s. Besides being bedspreads (duh!), you can use them for decorating—slacker style. Throw 'em over an ugly chair, thumbtack them over a window, give to the dog for a cool bed, toss 'em over that ugly mess in the corner, cut 'em up and use the fabric to make things (if you're domestic scientist) like book bags, pillow covers, clothes, whatever.
—from *Thrift SCORE #1*

PETROLEUM IS OUR FRIEND, TOO . . . Synthetic Fabrics

If a fabric sounds like it came out of a chemistry lab, it probably did . . . The bold names are generic terms; trade names are also listed [in italics] here since fabrics may be identified by them. These are trademarked terms for fabric *inventions*.

Nylon—first true synthetic fiber—in 1938, DuPont mixed together petroleum, natural gas, air & water and used to make hosiery. Fabric proved terrifically popular—easy care and durability—and the rest, as they say, was history. *Antron, Enka, Qiana.*

Spandex—developed during WWII to take the place of rubber. *Lycra, Elura, Clospan, Numa, Spandelle, Vyrene.*

Acrylic—made from coal, air, water, petroleum and limestone. *Acrilan, Creslan, Zefran, Orlon* (the oldest acrylic introduced in 1952 by Dupont).

Polyester is technically the generic term for fabrics manufactured from coal, petroleum, air and water, but has become the de facto generic for any synthetic fabric. *Dacron* (first polyester made by Dupont in 1953), *Encron, Fortrell, Kodel, Trevira.*

Modacrylic—a fake fur made from natural gas, coal, air, salt & water—*Dynel, Elura, Verel.*

Vinyl—derived from ethylene, often used in place of leather.

Latex—rubbery elastic material in older clothes and newer sex toys; spandex is now used in place of latex in clothing.

—from *Thrift SCORE #5*

CAN '70S CLOTHING *HURT* YOU? Our Expert Says YES!

POLYESTER SHIRTS—What were they?
Made from 100% synthetic materials designed to simulate satin, silk, and even cotton (albeit with a slimy and slightly spongy feel), these shirts were *de rigueur* for many men *and* women. They had wide, long lapels and the really scary ones were cut to fit close to the body. The most memorable polyester shirts screamed with outrageous multi-colored patterns—swirls, paisleys, Egyptian, Roaring '20s, Bicentennial and nature motifs, photographs and neck-to-waist full landscapes. People knew the wearer was Mr. Casual or Mr. Swinger or Ms. Kooky. Oh, and they *were* wash-n-wear. **Danger Element:** Highly flammable, would melt upon contact with flame, hangnails would snag easily on fabric, did not "breathe" as natural fabrics do, often reducing Mr. Swinger to Mr. Sweaty-n-Stinky.

ELEPHANT BELLS & FLARES—What were they?
The '70s saw the '60s bell bottom refashioned with a looser thigh and increasingly wider pants leg. Also, by the mid-'70s, the once "outré" bell-bottomed look of the '60s had been toned down, and flares were worn by suburban moms in polyester knits (like Mrs. Brady) and natty pin-stripe lawyers in suits. The early '70s bells featured a do-it-yourself trend where swatches of groovy fabric could be sewn into trouser legs to give them even more dimension. As high heels became standard, the bells grew wider and longer to cover the increasingly high shoes. **Danger Element**: It was possible to trip *inside* your *own* pants leg, you could trip over the flap of your *other* pants leg, they got caught in bicycle chains.

TIGHT JEANS—What were they?
Jeans for men and women were to be worn TIGHT at the waist, hip, buttocks, crotch and thigh. Ideal tightness revealed all that nature had intended to remain secret and mysterious. **Danger Element:** It was hard to sit down, and once seated, you were apt to be very uncomfortable with coarse denim seams digging into your soft thighs and genitals, zippers often gave up under duress and split (if worn without underwear, the functioning zipper presented other hazards). It was discovered (and widely reported and apparently largely ignored) that men wearing tight clothing about their reproductive area increased their body temperature in "that area" and consequently had markedly lower sperm counts. Women, too, were prone to "female trouble."

SPANDEX DISCO WEAR—What was it?
This shimmery shiny stretchy fabric was fashioned into shirts, halter tops, tank tops, trousers (with a discreet flare) and full body suits for the disco/roller disco set and prostitutes. Though an early relative of the ubiquitous "body/exercise wear" of the '90s, this fabric came in a few colors (red, black, white, blue, glitter) and was considered evening wear. **Danger Element:** All the inherent dangers of a synthetic fabric (see POLYESTER SHIRTS) and too tight clothing (see TIGHT JEANS).

HOT PANTS—What were they?
These arrived as a "fashion sensation" in 1971. They were super short tight shorts worn bare-legged, with knee socks or with tights in the winter (!). They were manufactured from many fabrics including denim, silk, satin, wool, mink ($195) and were often adorned with patches, embroidery, rhinestones and glitter. They were considered liberating for women (and we can assume, for the few men) who wore them. "They are an expression of the female's new freedom and they mean she is no longer willing to be submissive to convention. They also show that she is on a serious mission to relate to other people—especially men. She may not be wearing them just to be sexually provocative, but because she desires to get attention as a prelude to a genuine relationship."—Dr. Jason Miller, NY psychiatrist. Short shorts persevered throughout the '70s especially in the form of jean cut-offs. The convergence with athletic wear-as-fashion and the roller-disco craze gave a late '70s rebirth to satin tuxedo-style hot pants, with a stripe down the side. **Danger Element:** See TIGHT JEANS for physical hazards and reflect quietly to yourselves about social and aesthetic lows of hot pants (Hint: both Sammy Davis Jr. and Liberace performed in hot pants.)

BRA-LESS TOPS—What were they?
Tank tops (with teeny straps), halter tops (made from tied bandannas or scarves) and tube tops (a band of stretchy knit fabric) meant school's out and summer's here! The basic design of these garments precluded the wearing of any bra (this was before flaunting your underwear was fashionable)—and ideally exposed a lot of skin about the shoulders, back, midriff, and breasts. **Danger Element:** The potential for social embarrassment was extremely high, given that many of these garments were flimsy, really small and slipped or shifted when one moved. Some men perceived these garments as open invitations to pinch, squeeze, or expose breasts. The fabric would chafe. Fuller-figured women were naturally uncomfortable. There was an increased risk of sunburn.

BIKINI STYLE UNDERWEAR—What were they?
Tiny underpants with the elastic "waistband" straddling (and usually pinching) the middle of the buttocks. This created a new hallmark of fashion disaster—the VPL or Visible Panty Line. Though more popular with women than men (we're guessing), '70s men did take up this "French-styled" brief. **Danger Element:** Enormously irritating to have one's buttocks bisected by elastic, see also dangers associated with POLYESTER SHIRTS and TIGHT JEANS.

SHOES—What were they?
There *were* shoes in the '70s, thank god, after all that free-love barefooted nonsense of the '60s—but many of the shoes of the '70s proved to be as dangerous, if not more so, than barefootin'. Shoes continued to be made from synthetic material—leading to increased foot odor and fungal infections. In women's shoes, there was a tendency towards "open toe"—ouch! which hurt a lot if your dude trod on you with his Frye boot. There weren't many flats for women (or men!) either—thick heels and platform soles of the early-mid '70s gave way to ankle-strap, super-high-heel, street hooker sandals by the disco designer jeans era. For those who shunned high fashion and wanted a more macrobiotic look, there were of course the short-lived Earth Shoes (1970-1977).

—from *Thrift SCORE #1*

Beer Frame

One of the best-publicized zines is *Beer Frame*—the name is derived from a bowling term that indicates the point when bowlers stop to take a beer break (editor Paul Lukas loves bowling). Subtitled "The Journal of Inconspicuous Consumption," the zine focuses on product reviews, ranging from the Dial-a-Pick toothpick dispenser to musk-flavored Lifesavers produced in Australia. Issues #1-6 are $3 each ppd (no subscriptions; make checks payable to Paul Lukas) from 160 St John's Place, Brooklyn NY 11217 (e-mail: krazykat@pipeline.com). An anthology of *Beer Frame* material is forthcoming from Crown Books. (All photos from *Beer Frame* by Jasmine Redfern.)

♦ **VALE:** *Can you describe* **Beer Frame?**
♦ **PAUL LUKAS:** *Beer Frame* is about closely examining products and services that are either so weird and obscure that we rarely see them, or so ubiquitous and in-our-face that we've essentially *stopped* seeing them. I came up with the concept of "inconspicuous consumption" a couple of years ago. I had done another zine which was your basic music zine with hundreds of record reviews—the same kind that everybody does. As a joke, I included a page of product reviews; I thought it would be funny to apply the same critical standards to a box of cereal or a cat toy. I got good reactions and realized I was enjoying this more than writing music criticism. I had gotten burned out on all the bullshit of the music scene.

I stopped doing my music zine for a few years, and decided to do a new zine which was all about products. Musical coverage, if any, would be conceptual at best. In *Beer Frame,* the record reviews are about anything *but* the music: how heavy is the vinyl, how intriguing is the packaging. A review of a live show covers anything *but* the performance: how I found parking that night, and what brand of beer I sneaked into the show. This was a way of thumbing my nose at conventional music criticism. The rest of the zine is about products—looking at products and services in excruciating detail.
♦ **V:** *How do you do the research?*
♦ **PL:** Basically, it's a matter of having my radar turned up high enough. Most consumer culture is right there in front of us, but we haven't stopped to think about what we're seeing. The prototypical object of inconspicuous consumption is the Brannock Device—that chrome-and-black gizmo used by shoe salesmen to measure our shoe size. Most people don't know what it's called, but *everyone* knows what it is. And when people pause and really *see* it, they usually go, "Yeah—that's really cool; I just never thought about it before."

We're assaulted by all kinds of products everywhere we go, and I manage to stop and think about them a little more than most people. I'll see something and wonder, "What was the board meeting like when they were launching this? How did they decide on the package design? What product names did they reject before they settled for *this* stupid name? How much stupider were the rejects?" I enjoy imagining this behind-the-scenes process, and every product has its story.

Also, my readers are incredible—total strangers send me groceries, canned foods, antiques and artifacts from all over the country, usually with a note: "I saw this and thought of you."

22

♦ **V:** *Can you describe some of these?*
♦ **PL:** They're all over my house. I'm staring right now at several brands of Kraut Juice (sauerkraut juice), a bottle of snake-oil cold remedy called "666," a can of corned mutton, a drink mixer called Creamy Head, a Japanese version of Gatorade called Pocari Sweat (it replaces the essential minerals you lose when you sweat), a bag of clam jerky (it's just what it sounds like, and is *really* disgusting), plus other bizarre foodstuffs. My Brannock Device is also within easy reach.

I have a love-hate relationship with capitalism because it presents us with all these incredibly bizarre objects.

♦ **V:** *Where can you buy one?*
♦ **PL:** That was the very first object reviewed in *Beer Frame*. I called the company and they were really nasty: "No, you're not a shoe store!" and they hung up on me. It took several tries before I found a shoe store willing to order one for me. Since then, I was interviewed by a magazine, and the reporter heard my story and called up the company in Syracuse, New York: "Why wouldn't you sell Paul Lukas a Brannock Device?" It turned out that the woman I had spoken with had been fired, and they'll happily take anyone's money now ($48 plus tax and shipping from 509 E. Fayette St, Syracuse NY 13202).

♦ **V:** *Has the manufacturing of that device changed?*
♦ **PL:** It was invented in the '30s by Charles F. Brannock—he died in 1994—and is still being manufactured by his company. That's all they make.

It's beautifully engineered; I think it's spectacular. The early ones were considerably heavier; they were probably made of stainless steel. Now they're made of aluminum and are lighter. Don't worry—they're still sturdy.

The *New York Times* printed a review of an industrial design exhibit that included the Brannock Device. They received a letter from a man who had been Charles Brannock's roommate in college. He wrote: "While the rest of us were out chasing girls and getting drunk, Charlie was fiddling with that damn invention of his. We made fun of him then, but I guess he has the last laugh!" He said that Charlie was always waking up at 4 AM to jot down notes: "I just had this revelation—I don't want to forget it!"

♦ **V:** *I wonder if he's an unknown Thomas Edison-type with thousands of ideas in his notebooks—*
♦ **PL:** He died in 1994. He was a lifelong bachelor who was "married to his invention." His father had been in the retail shoe business. As to whether he invented anything else, I think that one invention on the level of the Brannock Device is probably enough—I know that would satisfy me. *Everybody* comes into contact with a Brannock Device; when you think of the impact that man has had on contemporary America—well, find me somebody who *hasn't* had their foot in one! It can't be done.

♦ **V:** *So . . . why did you start publishing a zine in the first place?*
♦ **PL:** In college I ran a record store and this allowed me to get tons of free records. After that job ended, it seemed like the easiest way to keep getting free records was to do a zine. That zine was a way to let off steam, but it wasn't very good; *Beer Frame* is much better. I do it for the same reasons most zine editors would tell you: it's an *imperative.* You don't have much of a choice; there's this thing inside you that you've gotta do.

♦ **V:** *You've also changed the perceptions of your readers. Now they notice things they never noticed before, and a small percentage actually send them to you—*
♦ **PL:** And that's pretty cool. My only real goal is to inspire people to think a little. I may not be able to give "The Answer," but I can raise a lot of questions. Some people have accused me of celebrating capitalism too much and not being critical enough. They say I don't have enough of a political angle, and that by documenting and analyzing consumer culture I'm giving a *de facto* endorsement of capitalism. Frankly, I would

Paul Lukas at the Grand Canyon. Photo: Bonnie Schwartz

hope that anyone possessed of a more subtle intelligence could see an implicit political critique in everything I write about.

♦ **V: I like your slogan: "A service economy is a servile economy."**

♦ PL: I think that capitalism is really weird and kinda fucked. I have a love-hate relationship with capitalism because it presents us with all these incredibly bizarre objects. While this is really exciting, it's also something we should be suspicious of. I'm not trying to hit anybody over the head with an agenda, I'm interested in pointing out certain contradictions or ironies while raising questions.

♦ **V: What is "inconspicuous consumption"?**

♦ PL: That's a hard question to answer. There was a supreme court justice who said, "I may not be able to define obscenity, but I know it when I see it!" Inconspicuous consumption is like that. Here's what it *isn't*: it isn't kitsch . . . something that is just really tacky or ridiculous or that doesn't make me think that hard. I'm more interested in things that have one foot in the cultural mainstream and one foot in the bizarre.

Antiques are not "inconspicuous consumption," either. I happen to love antiques and collectibles—I've got a lot of them in my apartment—but I don't write about them. Occasionally I write about an artifact that makes me think about the people who were once connected to it, but in general I don't want inconspicuous consumption to be about nostalgia. If I wanted to do an antiques zine, it wouldn't be *Beer Frame*. We can definitely learn from what the consumer landscape *used* to be, but that's a different issue.

♦ **V: Give us your critique of nostalgia—**

♦ PL: I'm not against nostalgia *per se*. In my apartment I have a 1930s barber chair, an old fare box from a bus, a 1950s parking meter, a '50s pay phone—I've got all these old things that I love. But I'll never write about them in *Beer Frame*. Nostalgia can be a dangerous trap: if all you see is the way things "used" to be, that's very limiting. The past definitely affects how I look at the world, but I like to keep it in its place and look at the present as well.

♦ **V: Nostalgia has been critiqued as a very superficial emotion, and a conservatizing force—**

♦ PL: It usually involves some artificial concept of romance: some "romantic past" which was a crock. The '50s were not this blissfully innocent time and neither were the '20s—

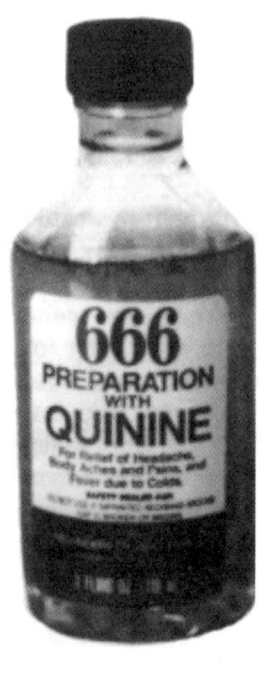

there was a lot of crap going on to be really critical of. To just focus on the pleasant, romantic aspects ignores—

♦ **V: —the homophobia, sexism and racism going on. Nostalgia is a marketing device . . . Earlier, you mentioned clam jerky. Obviously, somebody thought it was a great idea and a real inspiration—**

♦ PL: Actually, that's a Japanese product. In their culture, clam jerky may not be so unusual. A lot of people don't like raw clams because they're too slimy or gelatinous. Somebody probably thought, "This is the ideal product to turn into jerky." I thought it was brilliant to take a food like clams and transform it into something exactly the opposite. Perfect for somebody who thought that regular clams were gross!

I'm more interested in things that have one foot in the cultural mainstream and one foot in the bizarre.

♦ **V: They removed the chief repulsive qualities of clams—**

♦ PL: —and added some new repulsive qualities, too!

♦ **V: You're like a Sherlock Holmes investigating the mystery behind products—**

♦ PL: I like to call the companies involved and chat with them. Again, I prefer to write about products that are available now. If you're going to write about consumerism, the whole point is that you can consume it.

♦ **V: So you provide the addresses of products you review?**

♦ PL: Definitely. That's a play on zine culture. Music zines review indie records and give a mail order address because you'll never find that record at your regular record store.

♦ **V: You're spotlighting a panorama of ready-made pop art objects, available through the mail—**

♦ PL: Usually people describe *Beer Frame* as "an alternative *Consumer Reports*." I don't quite agree with that. It's more of an aesthetic, personal and situationist project . . . it's more about *me* and my reaction to these products. Consumerism is an incredibly personal experience. We all have very strong associations with the Brannock Device and with our favorite cereal or toothpaste. Readers seem to connect with the idea of having a personal association with certain products—acknowledging or *bonding* with their "inner consumer."

In *Beer Frame #5* I did a piece on the distinctions between Hydrox and Oreo cookies (these are chocolate sandwich cookies with a cream filling), and how everyone in the world is either a Hydrox person or an Oreo person. Hydrox pre-dated Oreos; they were invented in 1908. Oreos ripped them off in 1912.

Hydrox are made by Sunshine, the same people who make Cheese-Its. They've got national distribution, but they're nowhere near as big as Nabisco. Jewish families and vegetarians often prefer Hydrox, because they're kosher—Oreos used to have lard in them, although not anymore. The cookies look almost identical, so a lot of people think that basically they're the same thing.

I also wrote an obsessive piece on the new M&Ms color. They added blue, but didn't tell anyone this meant they were eliminating tan—which had been my favorite color! Consumers had been invited to vote on blue, but they didn't say they were going to eliminate a color—I regarded this as a kind of election fraud. I spoke with a lot of people in their office about this.

♦ **V: Do you buy things just for the packaging?**
♦ PL: Sometimes. I've definitely bought something on the basis of packaging—because it was particularly beautiful or particularly bizarre. I love going to supermarkets. You can separate that word into its component words: *super market,* and people forget that. That's a case of "inconspicuous word derivation." By definition a supermarket has an incredible selection of products laid out for our consideration and approval. In New York City, real estate is so expensive that nobody can afford the square footage it takes for a really excellent supermarket. So whenever I travel I seek them out—suburbs are the best.

When I enter a supermarket, I ask myself, "Is there some interesting aspect I've been overlooking about a normal product I've seen my entire life?" I like to

When I enter a supermarket, I ask myself, "Is there some interesting aspect I've been overlooking about a normal product I've seen my entire life?"

monitor familiar or iconic brand names like Heinz or Colgate, and note when they make subtle alterations in their logos. I'll wonder, "What was the point of this? How many board meetings did it take?" I try to suss out what was behind that change. I've had some interesting epiphanies lately.

♦ **V: Tell us about one—**
♦ PL: Recently I needed some toilet paper, and Scott is my brand.
♦ **V: Single-ply or double-ply?**
♦ PL: I don't know; I guess I really ought to notice! I buy individual rolls which come wrapped in paper with a bows-and-ribbons design. I was looking at this wall of toilet paper, unable to find my brand, when I realized I was staring right at it—the design had completely changed. Up in the corner was a "burst" (an exploding word balloon with pointy edges) that said, "Still the Original!" And it showed a tiny illustration of the old package design.

I thought this was amazing. Obviously someone had thought, "We're going to change to a more modern design; try to attract some new consumers and lower the demographic. But at the same time, to make sure our old consumers aren't disaffected, we're going to include a reproduction of the previous design." They were trying to have their toilet paper and eat it too!

I called up the company's "800" consumer number and a woman came on the line. She explained that Scott had expanded into several foreign markets and "wanted a uniform design worldwide, like Coca Cola has for their products." The bows-and-ribbons design was working fine in America, but it wasn't going over well overseas, so someone in the corporate hierarchy had decided they needed a more streamlined design. The new typography is much more "clean" and modern-looking—actually, it looks more generic and boring. Eventually they'll phase out the little "burst" and it'll be gone forever, so I'd better start hoarding 'em now.

♦ **V: You used the phrase "lower the demographic"—**
♦ PL: That's a magazine-industry phrase, or at least that's where I learned it. Basically, if the people buying your product are aging, eventually they'll all die out and you won't have a market anymore. If you want to "lower the demographic," that means you want to lower the average age of the people consuming your product. For one thing, old people don't spend as much money, and if you're a magazine, you want a market of big spenders to attract advertisers who'll pay more. Often the process of lowering your demographic means you offend or lose some of your more traditional readers—that's a calculated risk.

A prime example is the *New Yorker,* which for years was getting old and stodgy. The owners brought in a new editor, Tina Brown, to lower the demographic. In the process, they totally pissed off people like my parents who had been loyal *New Yorker* readers for decades. I remember my father saying, "I'm going to cancel my subscription because there's nothing in here for me." I told him, "Frankly, they don't give a shit if you read it. It's not for you anymore because you're not spending enough money on the products their advertisers are offering. They're quite willing to lose you as a reader if they can gain *me* as a reader." I'm worth more because I'm younger and supposedly have a lot of disposable income.

BEER FRAME

THE JOURNAL OF INCONSPICUOUS CONSUMPTION

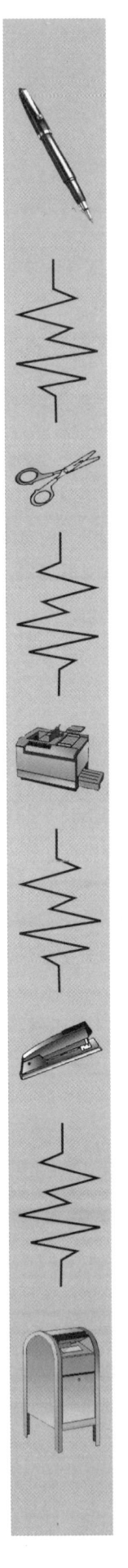

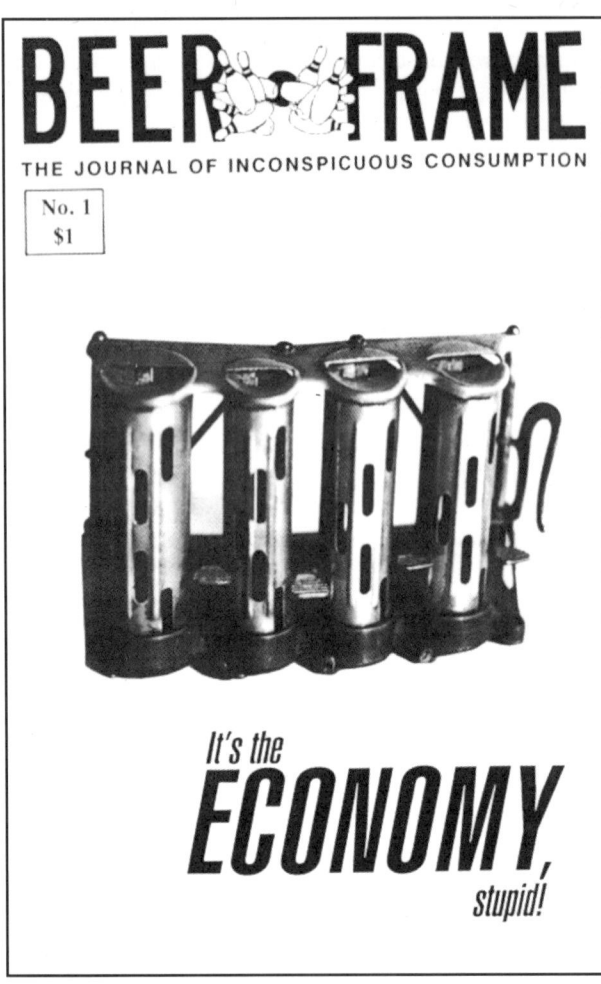

No. 1
$1

It's the ECONOMY, stupid!

Cover of Beer Frame #1

♦ **V: What's the demographic of Beer Frame?**
♦ PL: Almost anybody can understand what I'm writing about; that's probably why I've gotten a lot of attention. Consumerism is a pretty universal concept. Other zines can be about sex or rock music or gay/lesbian issues or whatever, but consumerism is universal. *We are all consumers, whether we want to be or not.*

Consumerism transcends age; my parents can understand what I'm writing about just as easily as my friends can. So my content is not generational; it's not limited by age or gender. I wasn't planning this when I started the zine, but that's what happened.

♦ **V: Have you studied advertising?**
♦ PL: I'm not an authority like those people who do *Adbusters;* I'm obsessed with the *objects.* I'm just a guy who buys a lot of stuff and who tends to think about this process a little more than most.

♦ **V: Have you always been this way?**
♦ PL: Sometimes if you close your eyes, you can remember specific incidents, like being eight years old and reading a certain box of cereal. I remember very clearly being about six years old and looking at a thermostat on the wall of my parents' house. It was this gadget with all these knobs and dials on it (I'm really into gadgets) and actually, I think my idea of "inconspicuous consumption" was being born at that *exact* moment when I was staring at this thermostat for five minutes. That was a *formative consumer moment.*

♦ **V: Remember that Morton's Salt ad, "When It Rains, It Pours!"? Here this girl is skipping along, gaily letting the salt pour out—just wasting it. This challenged any childhood upbringing which emphasized being thrifty—**
♦ PL: Excellent; I never even thought of that. You just provided me with an epiphany. It's drummed into all of us to "Be thrifty; don't waste anything!" (especially after the '70s and the Vietnam War when the whole economy went down the toilet). You weren't allowed to be "luxurious" anymore; you bought the economy car, not the Lincoln Continental. And here's a product whose icon is that you're *wasting* it. You just had an "inconspicuously consumptive" revelation!

♦ **V: Well, you brought it out. One of my favorite Duchamp lines is "the spectator completes the work of art"—**
♦ PL: Have you seen the film, *Money Man?* It came out in 1993. It's about an artist, J.S.G. Boggs (he considers himself a fine artist) and all he makes are reproductions of currency. He never pretends that it's anything other than a reproduction; he doesn't say, "Here's my $20." He says, "Here's my art which *looks* like a $20 bill." And it's not fully "art" until he can convince a vendor or a retailer to take it . . . then he wants *change!* He'll take the change and the receipt for the product and then sell those as other pieces of art—it's totally brilliant. Talk about the spectator completing the piece—this is it!

Boggs went to a bank with 20 of his own bills and said, "I want to open up an account with my bills." The bank manager said, "No, we can't take them," and they went back and forth on this point. Finally Boggs said, "When I close my account, I wouldn't mind if I got back these *exact same bills.*" Then a light bulb went on over the bank manager's head: "Oh—you don't want a savings account; you want a safety deposit box." Boggs said, "No, I don't want a safety deposit box—I want *interest.*" [laughs] It was fantastic; he was making a statement: "What is 'real' money? It's this paper which we choose to believe has value. Here's my art: it's paper. *I* say it has value; why can't you agree with me?" Conceptually this was really brilliant.

> **Consumerism is universal.
> We are all consumers,
> whether we want to be or not.**

♦ **V: Secret Service agents nabbed Boggs for counterfeiting, but I don't think the charges stuck. I clipped a newspaper article on him that said, "Courts in Great Britain and Australia agree with** *artist J.S.G. Boggs that the drawings of money he makes and 'spends' are art . . . His bills say Pittsburgh, Pa., instead of Washington, D.C., and carry Boggs' signature and the line 'The Unit of State of Bohemia.' 'I've consciously made my bills different enough that you can't fool somebody with them,' Boggs said. He doesn't sell his art. Instead, he spends it in a sort of performance in*

If you can fool the *parents,* you've got the next generation locked up.

which he explains to waiters and clerks that he is an artist and wants to exchange his art for goods or services."

♦ PL: When I was a kid, my father used to tell this joke which I never fully understood until I saw *Money Man:* "A man walking down a street sees a guy on the corner with a sign, "DOG FOR SALE: $1,000" (and it's just a mutt, a mongrel). He asks the guy, "A *thousand dollars?"* The guy says, "Yeah!" He says, "Well, good luck—I hope you sell the dog." A few days later he walks down the same street and sees the guy and asks, "Hey, did you sell the thousand-dollar dog?" The guy says, "Yeah, I traded it for two $500 cats!" The point is that *value is whatever we agree it is.* And this certainly plays into consumerism: what we're willing to pay and what the market will bear.

♦ *V: That's what perfume makers, cigarette manufacturers and Coca Cola are selling: illusions and images. They're not selling intrinsic value—*

♦ PL: They're not selling value in terms of practical utility. But one might say that if someone is willing to pay $1,000 for a dog or 75 cents for a can of Coke, then by definition it is worth it. I think it's ridiculous that a can of Coke costs 75 cents, because I know what it costs to produce: fractions of a penny. But I do occasionally pay that because I like the product. And I vastly prefer it to Pepsi, not because it tastes better, but because I identify more with it as a product. I'm able to suspend my disbelief regarding their corporate atrociousness, yet I'm not able to do that with Pepsi.

♦ *V: Faced with buying Coke or Pepsi, I usually choose the underdog—*

♦ PL: Wow—if you usually go for the underdog, you've definitely got to buy Hydrox! They are the underdog to Oreos all the way; you have to *search* to find them. The whole concept of brand loyalty is weird; some of it is just *imposed* on us by circumstance. Maybe it's because of a strong association: your mom bought Hydrox instead of Oreos, or Coke instead of Pepsi. Of course, the corporations know this, so a lot of kids' marketing is actually pitched more at parents. If you can fool the *parents,* you've got the next generation locked up.

♦ *V: Although . . . I recently saw a kids' Saturday morning cartoon show, and all the commercials included animation. It was hard to tell where the program left off and the commercial began—*

♦ PL: If they were different, the kid wouldn't pay attention . . . There's a good book on the history of package design in America: *The Total Package* by Thomas Hine, published by Little-Brown. The subtitle reads: "The evolution and secret meanings of boxes, bottles, cans and tubes." It's interesting and insightful.

♦ *V: Tell us about your favorite failed packaging—*

♦ PL: [laughs] A recent fad has been "ice beer"—everyone's selling one now. When I first saw an ad for Coors' "Artic Ice" beer, I didn't notice the misspelling, but when I did, I called up their "800" number. The first girl gave me an honest answer (I don't think she was supposed to say this): when Coors found they couldn't trademark "Arctic Ice" (it's public domain), they did a quick variation on it and removed the "c" to make it "Artic Ice."

Coors has gotten a fair number of calls about this, mainly from grammar teachers and proofreaders. When I called a second time, a different woman gave

Cover of Beer Frame #5

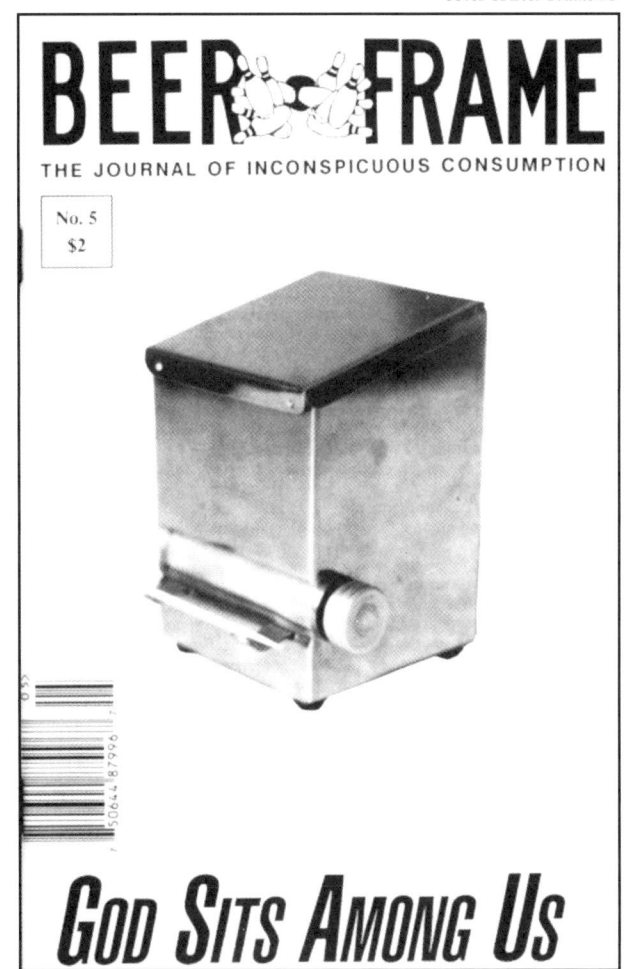

27

me their "party line": "We were just trying to be *playful,* and enjoy a pun on words. There are all these other products that have misspellings, like Nestle's *Quik* or *Kix* cereal, and we're just following in that tradition."

But Coors doesn't seem to get it: *Quik* and *Kix* are obviously *intentional* misspellings. *Quik* has a "Q" and *Kix* has an "x"—those are what I call "gadget letters." (If you play Scrabble, those are the most highly valued letters; they're worth the most points.) Whereas "Artic Ice" has no gadget value whatsoever. And it's subtle, so that when you *do* notice it, it seems like a mistake instead of something intentional. As far as I'm concerned, they've totally blown it and made themselves look like *morons.* At the moment, this is my favorite failed package.

♦ **V: There are so many typos and misspellings everywhere, even in magazines like the New Yorker and the Sunday New York Times Magazine. That reminds me—there have been quite a few mainstream press articles on zines—**

♦ PL: And most of them are not very good—big surprise! A lot of times it's obvious that the writer hasn't a *clue.* And even when a writer is bright, then the piece can get butchered in the editing process.

Kraut juice is probably the most disgusting product I've ever encountered; it's really, really *foul*—I can't even be in the same room with an open can.

The problem with most mainstream media coverage is: it's done for an audience that doesn't know much about zines—therefore the piece is done in a spoonfed kind of way: "Ohmigod, have you *heard?* There are these things called 'zines'; it's self-publishing. What a concept: people actually publishing their own magazines! Oh!" In this approach, the article has to go so far back to Square One that it's kind of pathetic.

Media people tend to look at things in a media-centric way. It's hard to get somebody to write an article about zines unless it's also about the mainstream media. Far too often, the articles focus on which zines are trickling down (or up) into the mainstream, or how Madison Avenue is looking to co-opt them.

I have a book deal with a major publisher to anthologize all the *Beer Frame* material into a trade paperback. This invariably gets mentioned in any coverage of *Beer Frame.* Frankly, I don't think this matters much, yet it's always mentioned as some sort of *validation:* "You can take this more seriously now—in fact, that's part of why we're writing about this: a major publisher has given its stamp of approval. I guess it's a news story now." Or, "Paul Lukas has been on NPR and ABC TV News. I guess what he's doing is newsworthy." I say, "Fuck that!" What I'm doing should be judged on what it is, not on how major media institutions have chosen to interact with it. It doesn't need that kind of validation—yet that is invariably what major media articles tend to focus on.

Of course, I can understand the viewpoint of a writer trying to sell an editor on a story: "Let's do a story on these zines." "Yeah, but how many copies are printed?" "Not many." "Can our readers actually go out and buy them?" "Well, they're hard to get hold of; they're underground." The editor goes, "Well, because there are so few copies of them, and they're such an underground subculture, it's almost like they don't exist." Then the writer goes, "But *look*—this guy has a book deal! That person was mentioned in *Newsweek!* This group has a popular website!" The editor responds, "Well, here's how you're going to write this story. You're not going to write about these zines; you're going to write about how some of these zines are gaining mainstream acceptance."

To get something into print, you almost *have* to pitch a story that way. But it seems to me that the ultimate standard of newsworthiness ought to be *quality*—if something is *good,* what could be a better standard of newsworthiness? Of course, if you think what I do is not good, that's fine—I have no problem with that. But to say that it doesn't matter until it's validated by something bigger is a crock. That is the problem with most coverage of what we all do.

There's another factor here, too. In any major newspaper book review section, Little-Brown can take out a big ad that a small publisher can't afford. They'll claim otherwise, but that's exactly what it's about.

♦ **V: "I'll scratch your back and you scratch mine—"**

♦ PL: Yeah. That's totally what it's about, and why *Rolling Stone* won't review certain records, although that's changed a bit. Every critical institution is usually in bed with whatever it's covering.

♦ **V: Let's get back to packaging—**

♦ PL: There are some packages I just consider beautiful. The cover of *Beer Frame #3* features a can of Meeter's Kraut Juice. Kraut juice is probably the most disgusting product I've ever encountered; it's really, really *foul*—I can't even be in the same room with an open can. I tried to taste it and couldn't get past the smell; I was rushing to the window to puke—it was so gross. Nevertheless, this particular brand (Meeter's, a small Wisconsin company) has an incredibly beautiful label design. A friendly-looking glass of green kraut juice is posed against a yellow background. The Meeter's logo is in white type on a blue banner, and the words "Kraut Juice" are in red against a yellow background—it's all primary colors. If I saw that product, I'd buy it in a second! (As it turns out, somebody sent it to me.)

I did buy Corned Mutton at a nearby supermarket. In the canned goods aisle (always a good section, with Spam, deviled products and other weird offerings) I saw this huge display of a new product: Corned Mutton. The can has four horizontal bands of color: red, white, blue and red. The first red band bears the company name, "Guycan" above "Corned Mutton." In the white band is a photo of an incredibly pissed-off-looking sheep staring at you with this look that says, "Go on—buy the fuckin' can and eat me!"

When I first saw the can, I was in hysterics over the packaging—plus the very concept of "corned mutton" is bizarre. When I looked closely at the can, the ingredients list delivered the knockout blow: it said "cooked mutton, mutton." Why the separate listings? Also, it comes in one of those great trapezoidal cans.

I also like the package design of Creamy Head, a foaming agent which you put in a mixed drink to produce a lathery head. Under the name it says "for a creamy head on cocktail shaker drinks"—in other words, "Creamy Head for a creamy head"—they couldn't think of anything less redundant. I guess when your product name is Creamy Head, you want to repeat that as often as possible.

♦ **V: There are obvious softcore implications to that brand name—**
♦ **PL:** Exactly. It should have said "Creamy Head . . . for when you want some good head!"

Here's an interesting package which is personal to me. Somebody gave me a container of a seasoning powder called "Super Lucas"—my last name is Lukas. (The fact that it says "Super" kinda makes up for the not quite correct spelling.) This made me think a bit: if your last name is McDonald or Colgate, you see your surname constantly in consumer culture—you're

If I saw that product, I'd buy it in a second!

practically bombarded with it. What do other people named Brannock feel about the Brannock Device, especially people unrelated to the inventor?

♦ **V: Maybe everybody should release some product named after themselves—**
♦ **PL:** We were discussing validation, but if *I* put out a product called "Super Lucas," it's not as satisfying as if somebody else does! I get a kick out of seeing my name in a newspaper byline—I wish I could say it doesn't matter, but it does.

♦ **V: Only if you do your own zine do you have the freedom to include an article about products named after your own surname—**
♦ **PL:** Actually, we could discuss something related to this. Now I merchandise *Beer Frame* products. I do t-shirts (big deal; everybody does t-shirts), but I also do *Beer Frame* beverage coasters, wristwatches, keychains, bowling shirts and refrigerator magnets. I thought, "If I'm going to be documenting consumer culture, I should also be participating in it."

♦ **V: How did you figure out how to do this?**
♦ **PL:** There are companies that will put your logo on just about anything—they'll even stamp it into a chocolate bar. But usually you have to order very large quantities or spend at least $500. I had 2,000 coasters made for about $400—I decided that was worth it because they're really fun. When you think about it, 20 cents each is actually a lot for a fuckin' coaster (although the first order includes all these start-up charges; the next one will be cheaper). Also, I did two-sided coasters, and that made it more expensive. But bowling shirts—you just go down to the same place where bowlers get their shirts made and order a dozen.

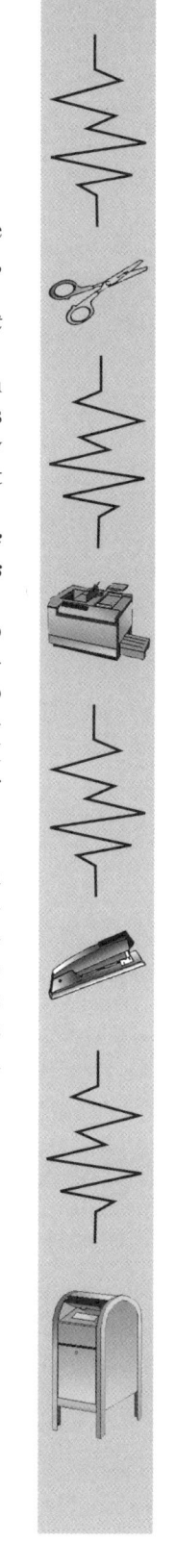

I found a place in Seattle that would custom-make refrigerator magnets for a minimum order of only $100—that's not much. If you ever read the in-flight magazine on an airplane, you'll find at least four or five companies that will put your logo on a wristwatch. They usually have an introductory offer of 2-8 watches for a fairly low price, like $14 per watch. I wrote all the companies and got 6-8 watches from each. I used the introductory offer from each company, got a bunch of watches, and now they're all sold out.

I also found a company that will cast your logo in metal; they produce metallic products like keychains, cufflinks, money clips and paper weights. They had an introductory offer, too, so I ordered a bunch of *Beer Frame* keychains. But if I'd wanted more, the price would have gone up. There are many companies out there; you just have to snoop around. In this department, my readers have helped me a lot.

Personal product marketing raises a number of issues. Brand loyalty is about being loyal to a *logo*. It's not to an actual product; your association is with the logo or the package design. Sports fans aren't loyal to the actual *people* in the uniform; they're loyal to the uniform itself! If different players are traded, it's not like you suddenly root for them on their new team—no, you root for whoever's coming in to wear the same uniform you've always rooted for.

By putting the *Beer Frame* logo on a product line to which people can have brand loyalty, I'm having fun,

Van Dyke Supply Company

Face it, you need a new hobby. That stamp collecting thing is getting a bit old, don't you think? And please, enough with the gardening, woodworking, painting, knitting, hiking, model making, boating, whittling, and photography—totally passé, each and every one of 'em. You need something new. You need something exciting. You need taxidermy.

Don't laugh. Skinning and mounting a dead animal might not sound like your idea of fun, but a good 75,000 or so professional and amateur American taxidermists would disagree with you, and the number is growing. That information comes from L.J. Van Dyke, and he oughtta know—his mail order operation has been servicing the trade for 45 years.

Face it, you need a new hobby . . . You need something exciting. You need taxidermy.

The Van Dyke Catalog, which runs nearly 300 pages, is practically an education in taxidermy. The company stocks all the necessary materials for you to create your own taxidermed menagerie. Step right up and name your animal—chances are Van Dyke's carries a sculpting form for it. In addition to the obvious deer and moose, they'll also fix you up with everything you need to work on a warthog, antelope, seal, wildebeest, raccoon, otter, porcupine, caribou, armadillo, lynx, beaver, wild hog, or kangaroo, among scores of other possibilities.

The most spectacular items in the catalog are the dozens of glass eyes, which are available for a multitude of mammals, birds, fish, reptiles, and amphibians. The most obvious comparison would be marbles, but these genuinely beautiful orbs, many of them sparkling and shimmering, really deserve to be in finer company than that; they're more like jewelry. And at prices averaging only a few bucks per pair, you can buy a pile of them just to keep around the house.

Less beautiful than the eyes, but every bit as interesting, are the other assorted artificial body parts that Van Dyke's sells: noses, antlers, whiskers, claws, mouth/jaw assemblies ("Look at the throat muscles in these jaw sets!" says the catalog), ears, tails, etc. The idea behind all this is apparently that you can never be sure just which part of your four-legged trophy is gonna be destroyed or damaged by the buckshot, but I see other possibilities. With this much animal anatomy available, there's really very little need to go hunting—you can create your own beast from scratch.

Just in case you don't already have your own set of taxidermy equipment, Van Dyke's handles a wide variety of highly specialized tools of the trade. An electric gizmo called a "bird and small mammal degreaser and flesher" will run you $139.95, but the hand-held ear opener ("Greatly improved!") is only $9.45.

Interestingly, Papa Van Dyke finds taxidermy uniquely suited to today's ecologically and environmentally sensitive times. "People are more conscious of wantin' to preserve things," he told me, with absolutely zero hint of irony. "Years ago they'd just eat the damn thing and forget about it." I considered suggesting that perhaps the best way to preserve a deer, bear, moose, or whatever would be to avoid shooting it in the first place, but something told me I wouldn't get the most appreciative response, so I let it slide.

Okay, so let's say you like the sound of all this, but you have no taxidermy experience and don't know where to begin. No problem—Van Dyke's even has the training materials to get you started, from instructional manuals (*Fish Mounting, Oily Skinned Varieties,* $9.95) to books (*Taxidermy Pricing Workbook,* $39.95) to videos (*Skinning and Prepping a Small Mammal for Mounting,* $24.90). Your cats might not be too thrilled about this new hobby of yours, but they'll probably stop scratching up the furniture once they realize what could happen to them if they don't behave. (Van Dyke Supply Company, P.O. Box 278, Woonsocket, SD 57385; 605.796.4425)

—from *Beer Frame* #4

plus I'm raising questions about the whole concept: "Is this a better shirt because it has a *Beer Frame* logo on it? How do certain values transfer from one product to other spin-offs?"

So, does putting a *Beer Frame* logo on a bowling shirt push my readers' buttons in the same way? Obviously there aren't millions of people running around wearing them—just a few dozen. You could get one because it's "hip," but by wearing it, you're helping to advertise *Beer Frame* for me—you're a

Sports fans aren't loyal to the actual *people* in the uniform; they're loyal to the uniform itself!

walking ad. If the product's considered hip, then you're saying, "This makes *me* hip." But you're also helping to institutionalize a brand name—which is something we associate with big corporations, not little fanzines. You could say, "That's the irony of it, man! This hip little zine is doing this big corporate thing!"

♦ *V: There are layers of irony here—*
♦ PL: I think this process feeds upon itself. When does this stop being hip and start being dangerous? Maybe the corporation was being hip and ironic too! These questions about *context* are all interesting.
♦ *V: You're raising an issue of empowerment here: the little guy can use the same marketing techniques as the big corporation and enlarge the sphere and impact of his own influence—*
♦ PL: Envision this unlikely scenario: *Beer Frame* explodes and its circulation grows to 500,000; it becomes part of mainstream media. Everybody knows about it and it's no longer this hip little thing. At that point, does a *Beer Frame* bowling shirt suddenly stop being hip? Does it become evil, and a symbol of my greed—spinning off my corporate logo and trying to further capitalize and merchandise? Does it become a symbol of everything bad about mainstream publishing? Do people start saying, "Yeah, I have a *Beer Frame* shirt—but I bought it *years* ago! That was when that Paul Lukas guy only did a few dozen of 'em—when *Beer Frame* was still *cool*."

Firefox Enterprises

Hey there, you say you need a 100-pound drum of magnesium? Or maybe 40 gallons of HX-878 propellant bonding agent, direct from NASA's surplus stock? How about a few dozen plastic spherical shell casings? And have you checked your supply of isophorone diisocynate curing agent lately?

Whatever your pyrotechnic needs, you'll probably find what you're looking for in the pages of Firefox Enterprises catalog. Primarily serving a market of special-effects professionals, magicians, state and local police departments, rocketry clubs and, one imagines, arsonists, Firefox has just about everything imaginable for any application that involves touching a match to a fuse, from custom-milled oxidizers and propellant resins to ignition materials and, my favorite, smoke mixtures.

None of which is to suggest that Firefox will just blithely sell you the ingredients to create your own private stock of M-80s. Unless you have a Federal explosives permit, they won't ship combinations of chemicals that are "obviously intended to be used for constructing flashpowder and/or exploding fireworks devices ... and other illegal audible effects devices." They'll also check your ordering history to see if you're trying to assemble a munitions depot on the installment plan. On the other hand, while Firefox is obviously concerned about running afoul of assorted governmental regulations, they're also keenly aware that an explosives-happy public is good for their business; with this in mind, they tell you exactly how to apply for the necessary Federal permit, and if you're approved they'll "furnish chemicals and materials in any quantity or combination you may require." *Now* we're talking.

While this is all plenty of fun, it's worth noting that Firefox's appeal ranges far beyond the pyromaniacal. The company stocks a wide variety of rocket and missile supplies, including motors, tubing, aerodynamic fins, and recovery parachutes. In addition, they carry assorted tools and supplies, laboratory equipment, and "exotic hardware," the latter of which is best exemplified by a pest-control grenade launcher. Really. They also offer a literature section, featuring such titles as *Deluxe Bottle Rockets* and *Smoke Generation*: *Tactical/Survival/Civilian*, although it's hard to imagine any of this printed matter surpassing the catalog itself. Even if you're not equipped or inclined to use any of Firefox's wares, some of the descriptions alone are priceless. I'm sorely tempted, for example, to drop $33 on a 30 meter roll of Thermalite igniter cord, available in three different burn rates (16, 8, or 5 seconds per foot) and described as being ideal for rocket motor ignition or "general-purpose use." Uh, right.

Despite all the stern language in the catalog about the company's refusal to ship incendiary combinations of materials, at least one chemistry-minded Firefox customer, who happens to be an acquaintance of mine, has had little difficulty obtaining the proper components to make his own DIY illegal firecrackers. Wanna get in on the fun? Send two bucks for the Firefox catalog. (Firefox Enterprises Inc., PO Box 5366, Pocatello, ID 83202)

—from *Beer Frame #3*

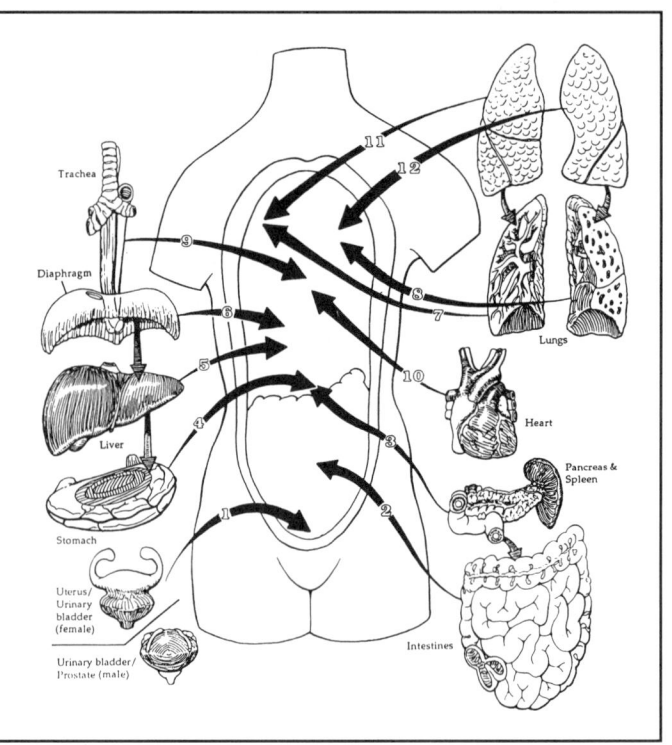

♦ **V: Now, the ads try to get the viewer to think they're smarter than the advertisers—that's the best way to sell something. The way to fool people is to let them think, "I know I'm being fooled." How many copies do you sell?**
♦ PL: *Beer Frame* now sells 3,000 copies, and that's as much as I can handle. And I'm such a lousy collaborator that I prefer to work alone. If I'm going to keep it just *me,* I don't think it can get much bigger. Actually, *Beer Frame* is a spinoff; my product reviews run first in an "Inconspicuous Consumption" column which I get *paid* for writing. The column came about because the people at the *New York Press* (an "alternative" weekly) liked my first issue. Ever since, all subsequent issues of *Beer Frame* have been compiled from the columns that have appeared in the *Press.* Now the column has moved to *New York Magazine,* a slick weekly with a circulation of over 400,000.

♦ **V: You're having your cake and eating it too!**
♦ PL: Yeah, I get more than a typical zine editor would get for his or her work. I've also gotten a book deal, and there's more brewing. I didn't plan any of this when I started the zine, but I have no problem with any of it, either. No one has asked me to do anything other than what I already do.

This raises another issue: I was described in a mainstream article as "bursting to sell out." Personally, I'm happy to get attention and have somebody write about me. When CNN called and asked, "We're wondering if you might be a news story—are you?" I replied, "You bet I am!" But I don't consider talking to major media as "selling out." To me, *selling out is when you change what you do for money.* I don't feel guilty about selling my columns to *New York* mag-

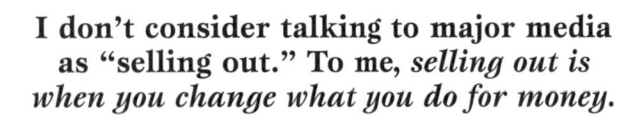

"Sweet Sue" female torso from the Anatomical Chart Company, from *Beer Frame #1*

> **I don't consider talking to major media as "selling out." To me, *selling out is when you change what you do for money.***

azine or getting a book deal—all that makes me feel *great!* But if I had to change *anything,* or water it down, that would be very different. Nobody's asked me to do that yet.

What would happen if *Beer Frame* did achieve a circulation of 500,000 but remained basically the same magazine? Then a *backlash* would occur: suddenly you're not cool because you're so popular. People get pissed off when they're no longer one of the 5 people who know about you; now they're one of the *5 million* who know about you. That mainstream writer thought I was "bursting to sell out" because I was talk-

ing to *him!* Maybe I would have had more "integrity" if I had said, "No, man, you're the fuckin' big media—I won't talk to *you* because you're evil, in your big tall building. I'm not going to cooperate with your agenda." As far as I'm concerned, if he's interviewing me, he's advancing *my* agenda.

♦ **V: Every mainstream article on anything "underground" always includes something pejorative, no matter how positive they pretend to be—**
♦ PL: I think they're always a little jealous. They have to remind us that we're not really "professional": "Zine publishing—the production values range from the slick to the embarrassingly amateurish." Phrases like that remind the readers that these zine people don't really know what they're doing (unlike the "professionals" who are writing the story). There's always a bit of condescension.

The mainstream media are extremely reluctant to *challenge* the reader—they prefer to spoon-feed instead. They have to make sure that we appear non-threatening.

♦ **V: Well, if there were any threat at all—**
♦ PL: There'd be a riot! A fucking urban riot, wouldn't there?

I'm starting to get more media interest from magazines I would never actually *read.* You know, I don't think *Beer Frame* will sell 500,000 soon. Actually, it's important to keep it small. The same material may appear in a mass distributed format, but I want to maintain *Beer Frame* as a non-mass distribution publication to reach people who would not read the awful slick magazines. I like the sociability of zines; I like getting just enough mail so that I can answer it *all.* ▼

Frigid Fluid Company

The deathcare business, as they say, is pretty much recession-proof. Death, after all, is a fact of life. In fat times or lean, you don't need to check the actuarial tables to know that loads of people are going to be kicking off, keeling over, buying the farm, rendezvousing with the Grim Reaper, snuffing it—in short, lots of our fellow citizens will be *dying*—and that someone's gonna have to handle the burial, the cremation, the funeral, and what have you.

Which is where trade publications like *American Cemetery* [see *Beer Frame* #1] and firms like the Frigid Fluid company come in. Frigid Fluid, a Chicago outfit specializing in embalming fluids, was brought to my attention by my Chicago-based pal Bettina, who learned of them while rooming with an aspiring mortuary cosmetician (yes, someone who applies makeup to the corpse before an open-casket funeral). According to Bettina's roomie, who'd visited the company's offices, the Frigid folks even had a bumper sticker that read, "Get Rigid with Frigid!" So when I zipped out to Chicago for a mini-vacation this past summer, a field trip to Frigid HQ was definitely on my agenda.

With Bettina navigating and my friends Tim and Elena along for the ride, we drove over to Frigid's digs, located along a pleasingly industrial stretch on Chicago's West Side. The building itself was unremarkable: a simple office with what looked to be a small-ish manufacturing and/or shipping operation out back. None of it looked particularly inviting, and I had a feeling that factory tours were not part of Frigid's community-outreach program.

I led the way in and was greeted by a very uptight-looking receptionist, about 60 years old, who viewed us with considerable alarm. In retrospect, this was probably understandable. Lost in the carefree euphoria of my vacation, I'd neglected to consider how unbusiness-like we looked: we were young; the temperature was around 90, so we were all wearing shorts and tank tops; two of us were prominently tattooed; and upon glancing over my shoulder, I noticed that Elena had chosen to sit on the reception-room floor, rather than on the couch. We were not exactly swimming in professionalism. if you know what I mean.

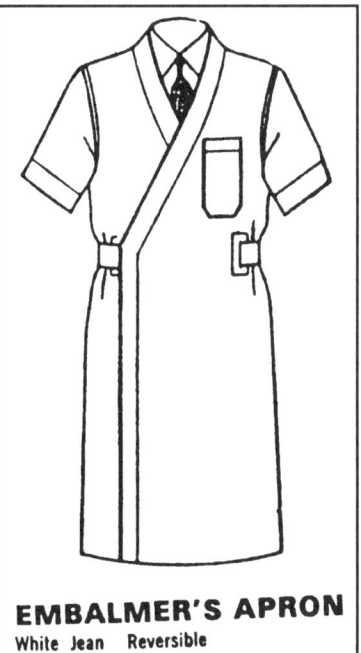

No matter. I launched into my writer's shtick—*Hi, I write about specialized products and services, and wouldn't it be great if I could help give your firm some free publicity, and hey, here's a chance to help the general public understand your industry so maybe they'll stop making jokes about you all the time,* blah-blah-blah—and motioned for the others to stop giggling while we waited for the receptionist to consult with her boss.

"The foreman's out today," she eventually announced, "so you can't have a factory tour. And the company president is too busy to speak with you right now." It sounded like a dodge—the president, I suspected, would end up being "busy" all week. Out of force of habit, I asked if any promotional materials were available.

To my surprise, our receptionist suddenly perked up and brightened, as if she'd just been infused with premium Frigid fluids. "Here," she said, "you can have this."

"This" turned out to be Frigid's catalog, a 96-page curiosity that proves death is still alive and kicking. The first several pages are devoted, predictably, to embalming fluids, including X-20 Arterial Fluid ("Produces desired firming action and a natural, life-like base for cosmetic application"), 36 Plus (Incorporates new penetrants for abundant drainage"), Flo-Tone ("Completely different!... Try it with your more difficult cases!"), Frigid Special ("Should be kept on hand at all times for frozen or refrigerated bodies"), Cavity King ("The Undefeated Fluid of a Hundred Uses...For cases where circulation is destroyed, bodies posted, mutilated, diseased, crushed, dismembered"), Eotene (Highly recommended for cases that require cross-country shipment"), 5-Purpose Cavity ("A powerful deodorant against putrefaction, gangrene, and other body odors"), Solvol ("Recommended for embalming infants"), Natural Tone ("Produces 'Living Skin' qualities"), Stop Fluid ("Destroys maggots, lice, and vermin"), and the enticingly named Premium Jaundice (don't ask).

But fluids, as it turns out, are only a small part of Frigid's distribution business. The rest of the catalog, one section of which is playfully entitled "Sundries," is a motherlode of funeral and cemetery supplies, including such specialized products as facial-expression formers, jugular drain tubes (manufactured, I swear, by a company named Slaughter), caskets, urns, "Reserved for Funeral" road cones, mortuary cots, funeral home registers, burial suits and undergarments, and a *lot* more. The most entertaining bit is on page 71, which features four wall-mounted crucifixes, one of them stamped "DISCONTINUED," a reference that presumably applies to the specific ornament shown, not to Christianity itself.

Unfortunately, no prices are listed. When I requested a current price sheet from the receptionist, her cheery mood quickly evaporated: "You don't need that; you're not going to be buying anything." And with that she whooshed us out the door, before I could even ask for one of those "Get Rigid with Frigid!" bumper stickers. (Frigid Fluid Company, 465 N. Desplaines St., Chicago, IL 60610)

EMBALMER'S APRON
White Jean Reversible
No. 4306—

—from *Beer Frame* #5

Crap Hound

Sean Tejaratchi publishes *Crap Hound,* "a picture book for discussion and activity." Far more than a counter-culture clip art resource, this publication embodies razor-sharp graphics, sardonic social criticism, and humor of the subtlest degree. A sample issue is $6 (cash preferred—otherwise send a check payable to Sean Tejaratchi, PO Box 40373, Portland OR 97240-0373).

♦ **VALE: Why did you choose the name Crap Hound?**
♦ SEAN TEJARATCHI: Another name possibility was *Clip Rat,* an anagram of Clip Art, but *Crap Hound* covered more facets. It also has a potty word in it, so it sells well to grade school kids—*just kidding.*

♦ **V: Crap Hound—*is that like "Bullshit Detector"? With the variety and quality of graphics provided, your publication seems like a real public service—***
♦ ST: I don't think I'm doing a Mother Teresa act; my reasons for publishing a zine are as selfish as anyone's. I love doing it, it's a great deal of fun and it's a nice middle finger to a bunch of things in society that I hate. It gives me a chance to make a commentary on a number of things that frustrate me. The payback is immediate in that I look at it and like it. And it's nice to have a place where I can experiment and make decisions without fear that some committee will screw it up at the last minute.

I have an urge to document and catalog. As a child I was prone to collecting: stamps, shells, insects, rocks—anything. I want to look at the present as if it's already happened. In an antique store or thrift store, it's always the everyday things that I find striking. Everything around us will be gone some day—just like every other time period, this civilization is on its way out. Today's trash is tomorrow's nostalgia.

I love to look through old books and wander aimlessly around town keeping my eyes peeled. I started collecting graphics to make posters with, so now I have a lot of weird stuff to choose from. I've learned where to find things and they usually aren't where you'd imagine. It gets easier as I go.

♦ **V: What are your work habits?**
♦ ST: Right now I go to bed about 6:00 AM and get up at about three in the afternoon. I run errands, come home, sit in front of the computer for awhile, and work on various projects. It's a good way to keep your overhead low: stay up all night and sleep all day—nothing to buy! Except for some books, everything I own is in one room. I end up going to Powell's Books [largest bookstore in the USA] a lot, and that's always nice. On my current schedule, I can't go to as many thrift stores and garage sales as I'd like to.

♦ **V: Describe your resource library—**
♦ ST: It's not all that impressive. The vast majority of images come from active searches and contributions. I have one file drawer of clippings in manila folders that are all color-coded. Different colors designate different topics; for example, deep red signifies violence/murder/crime/judicial/vice. Anything from the "natural world" is green, like plants and farm animals. Sports is grouped with Weapons and Warfare. This filing system only has to make sense to *me!*

♦ **V: Where would clowns and devils be?**
♦ ST: Stage/Theater/Performance/Circus and Western Religion. I'm organized as a matter of necessity—I live and work in one room and couldn't last five minutes without some order. Anything I bring in either goes somewhere or sits on my bed until I find a place for it. It's a matter of survival.

♦ **V: What else is in your room?**
♦ ST: A desk, which is a door resting on two 2-drawer

legal-size file cabinets. There are two metal cabinets filled with everything I need to make a publication: pens, pencils, scissors, postage, drafting tools, rubber stamps. There are graphic supplies such as tape, *Pantone* books, and drawers full of stick 'em notes, power tools and household supplies.

My room is a rectangle with a narrow corridor down the middle; a Macintosh and a scanner occupy the far corner of the room. A light table for layout is at the other end. I don't use the computer for layout of the pictures. Computers are great but they have their place; *Crap Hound* would look tremendously different (and I think much worse) if it were done on a computer. I use wax and an X-acto knife for paste-up. I love working this way and I wouldn't trade.

♦ *V: Do you do a lot of reduction or enlargement?*
♦ ST: The graphics I work with aren't instantly malleable or sizable. If I have a picture of a certain size, I can take it to the copier in the next room and re-size it, but I'm much more likely to search for a place where it fits. Things fit together like a puzzle. Nothing is sketched out beforehand; it's much more trial and error. For the most part, pictures stay the same size. I'm becoming much better at problem-solving spatially.

♦ *V: So what were your objectives in starting* **Crap Hound***?*
♦ ST: I wanted to do something with all the graphics I had been saving. I was getting paid corporate wages working at Adidas, I didn't have an extravagant lifestyle, and I wanted to do something worthwhile with my earnings. I love things that are practical. If I'm going to write something, I don't want it to be self-obsessed poetry; if I'm going to paint something, it can't be something that no one will ever comprehend. So if I was going to do a zine, I wanted it to be something useful and relevant.

It's a good way to keep your overhead low: stay up all night and sleep all day—nothing to buy!

I started out calling it clip art, but it's changed—my motives are now officially different. However, the same desire persists: to do something practical. That's why the images don't get shrunk down too much; I want things to be *clear.* There definitely wasn't a plan; I didn't say, "I want to do a zine—what could it be?" I think my first idea was to do a zine of typefaces. Then I realized it wouldn't be terribly exciting. I thought about combining type with clip art, and it went from there. This entire chain of thought occurred as I was walking down a hallway; by the time I reached the end, things had pretty much fallen into place.

Sean Tejaratchi. Photo: West Armstrong

♦ *V: But you don't just provide clip art; you're critiquing society and culture—*
♦ ST: A lot of it *is* criticism, with me shaking my head in disbelief. As an everyday person walking around with some knowledge of how advertising and propaganda work, I look at what's out there and get disgusted and amazed by the blatant manipulation and twisted logic. It's really satisfying to vent my feelings in a coherent way . . . in a format where the images are out of their original context and made much more revealing simply as a result of placement.

As I was laying out *Crap Hound #4* I realized all these images of Ronald McDonald are set up to look exactly like Jesus. It was so nice to put those two together—they reflect badly on each other! In general, I try not to come off as strident or ranting; the juxtaposed images hopefully speak for themselves. I just hope that people see what I see; I'm up in the middle of the night laughing and I want other people to laugh as well—to see it for what it is.

♦ *V: You're very critical of religion—*
♦ ST: Well—what's *not* to hate?! Religion's an old joke, but it's still funny. The Ronald/Jesus connection is just another revealing coincidence. When your eyes start to blur from looking at all these pictures, you start to see oblique connections you may not have suspected before. All these little *windows of clarity* open up.

♦ *V: Where did you get the "Size of Vaginal Orifice" graphic?*
♦ ST: [laughs] Actually, that was given to me as an *enlargement*—I couldn't tell how big it was supposed to be; there was no scale! I wanted to reprint it at the

35

Cover of Crap Hound #1

right size, and when it came to reducing it I kind of *estimated* from personal experience . . .

♦ **V: Where did you get your glossaries of slang synonyms for words like "penis" and "vulva"—**
♦ ST: They were lifted straight out of sex education books—scanned and slapped down. With found text I try to use the original typesetting when possible. If I re-typed something, I don't think it would have the same impact. The original typeface has its own "voice," and when you reset the type, you lose that. Most of the graphics are the same way—reprinted in the condition I found them.

The quality of my life is largely measured by the number of fun projects I'm able to do.

♦ **V: Some of the captions you reprint are amazing—it's hard to believe they were written without a trace of irony . . . Your publication is subtle; to fully appreciate it, the reader has to do some work and make deductions—**
♦ ST: I think having fun and gradually noticing things is an underrated part of the reading experience. Juxtaposing the "fresh water mussel" next to a human vagina—well, there *are* correspondences! I don't think I'm saying much in *Crap Hound* that's really new—I'm just presenting it a little differently. If this has all been said and it's just sitting unseen in boring academic journals, then it's not doing much good, is it? Sometimes I don't even notice certain coincidences until the issue has been printed. Pictures are much more open-ended than words, so there's a lot more opportunity for accidental connections.

The way I keep track of pictures when I'm building an issue also lends itself to combinations. Once the images are copied and cut out, I paste them into a "halfway" book. That way I'm no longer sorting hundreds of little pieces of paper—I'm just turning pages looking for the right image. When I'm assembling the halfway book I just slap things down anywhere, but later I'll realize there are some coincidences that are hilarious. In that form it's something like a flip book, with images overlapping and combining, blurring into one another.

♦ **V: Tell us about your background—**
♦ ST: My father is Iranian and my mother is Irish-American. I grew up in Los Angeles. When my mother remarried I spent a lot of time at a ranch in the mountains near Bakersfield, California; it was a good thing to experience living without electricity. My stepdad had been a drill sergeant, so I learned how to shut up and work hard, which was a pretty important thing for me. When I was 16 I moved to Eugene, Oregon to live with friends of the family because I hated L.A.

Despite spectacularly low grades, I finished high school in Eugene, and managed to weasel into the University of Oregon, but I dropped out after something like 12 hours of classes. I repeated this at a community college. After 12 years of school I didn't feel like being bossed around anymore. I moved to Portland and worked at cafe jobs and Kinko's and did paste-up for local newspapers. I did odd graphics projects for fun, and designed fonts. In 1992 I joined my friend Mike King, making posters for the exciting low-budget world of rock-n-roll. I got hired at Adidas to deal with and design alphabets and patterns and I ended up staying there for about three years, eventually doing small graphics projects.

♦ **V: But you weren't a "company man"; you wanted to do something else—**
♦ ST: The quality of my life is largely measured by the number of fun projects I'm able to do. Losing my job was pretty great, actually. I have a very strong work ethic, but I want to be able to respect what I'm doing and take pride in the finished product. I'd rather be making less money doing things I love, than spending my time and energy helping to strengthen some faceless corporation who doesn't give a shit about me or anyone else.

♦ **V: I think you're doing reference-quality work that will be influential years from now—**
♦ ST: Twenty years from now I really hope some kid digs through his dad's boxes in a garage, sees *Crap*

Hound and goes, "Wow . . . cool!" I would love that. I'm trying to be critical and irreverent toward everything. In the "sex" issues, I tried to maintain steady levels of both ridicule and acceptance. I didn't want any one particular group to feel too smug just because they had the more common fetish or were screwing the right demographic. When you look at things with a dispassionate eye, *everything* starts looking sort of idiotic. So if I were going to make homosexuality look stupid just because of the graphics I found (guys hanging out in their socks with huge boners), I had a duty to make heterosexuality look equally ridiculous!

I'll get the graphics from love-forsaken teen magazines and a million other sources—"Unhappy People" is a goldmine waiting to be excavated!

♦ **V: Have people sent you images?**
♦ ST: A handful of people consistently send stuff, and I'm very grateful for them. Like I said, my files aren't that big, and what I've saved over the years accounts for a fraction of each issue. *Crap Hound* is composed almost entirely of additions, as opposed to a single central piece. The final product becomes more than the sum of its parts. In particular, the Clowns/Bait/Devils issue was the result of contributions. Some people just sent a single picture. It still helps. I've started announcing future topics, and I think this will increase contributions.

I think a lot about topics before finalizing anything. "Sharks and Insects" was a good pair, but it lacked that magic third ingredient. "Sharks, Insects, and Unhappy People" was a possibility, but that would have been overwhelming. At the last minute my friend Chloe suggested "Bones" and it was decided right there.

There's really no rhyme or reason to the topics: why I chose *this* over *that*. But when I chose "Devils and Clowns," there was a weird harmony. It could have been "Clowns and Weapons" but that didn't seem as satisfying. Right now, "Unhappy People" is a special category that I'm savoring—I want to do that one *right*. I'll get the graphics from love-forsaken teen magazines and a million other sources—"Unhappy People" is a goldmine waiting to be excavated!

I've already noticed that each era uses a few particular images to represent generic "trouble." In the '50s it was a child getting bitten by a dog, or children burning themselves. It's weirdly consistent throughout each period. Unhappy people today are depicted in relation to money, and the effects of emotional stress, like anger and confusion. It's obvious how some images emerge—during the Depression, empty pockets stood for unhappiness, but the '50s image of kids being bitten by dogs—how the hell did that get chosen?
♦ **V: "Unhappy people"—you could use graphics from headache remedy ads—**
♦ ST: —upset stomachs, families staring at their burning homes from insurance ads, furious bosses—the possibilities are endless. I also can't wait to do "Anthropomorphic Animals and Objects." In Japan they have this urge to anthropomorphize everything. Whether it's a bowl, a piece of driftwood, or a piece of candy, they can't resist the urge to give it a pair of eyes and have it saying something cute. Japan takes Americana and pumps it up to an incredible degree and makes it their own: it's *hyper-America*.

I love strange pictures, and now I get to see them all the time. There's so much bizarre stuff out there and it's a pleasure to keep discovering it. Like finding the "pigs eat sausages" graphic—it's common knowledge that there's nothing a pig likes more than to sink its teeth into its own flesh!
♦ **V: Where did you find this article of a former McDonalds clown speaking out against meat-eating?**
♦ ST: *Newsweek!* It was pure luck. Someone had left an issue behind at the bus stop, and when I saw that, I thought, "Aha!" and tore the page out. I eat meat, so this isn't my personal anti-meat-eating statement, but I don't like being lied to, and I don't like McDonalds. My attitude is, "How dare they inflict all this propaganda on kids?" It's creepy.
♦ **V: I just noticed that McDonalds has trademarked the term "McMemories"?! What a horrible concept—**

Cover of *Crap Hound* #2

#34

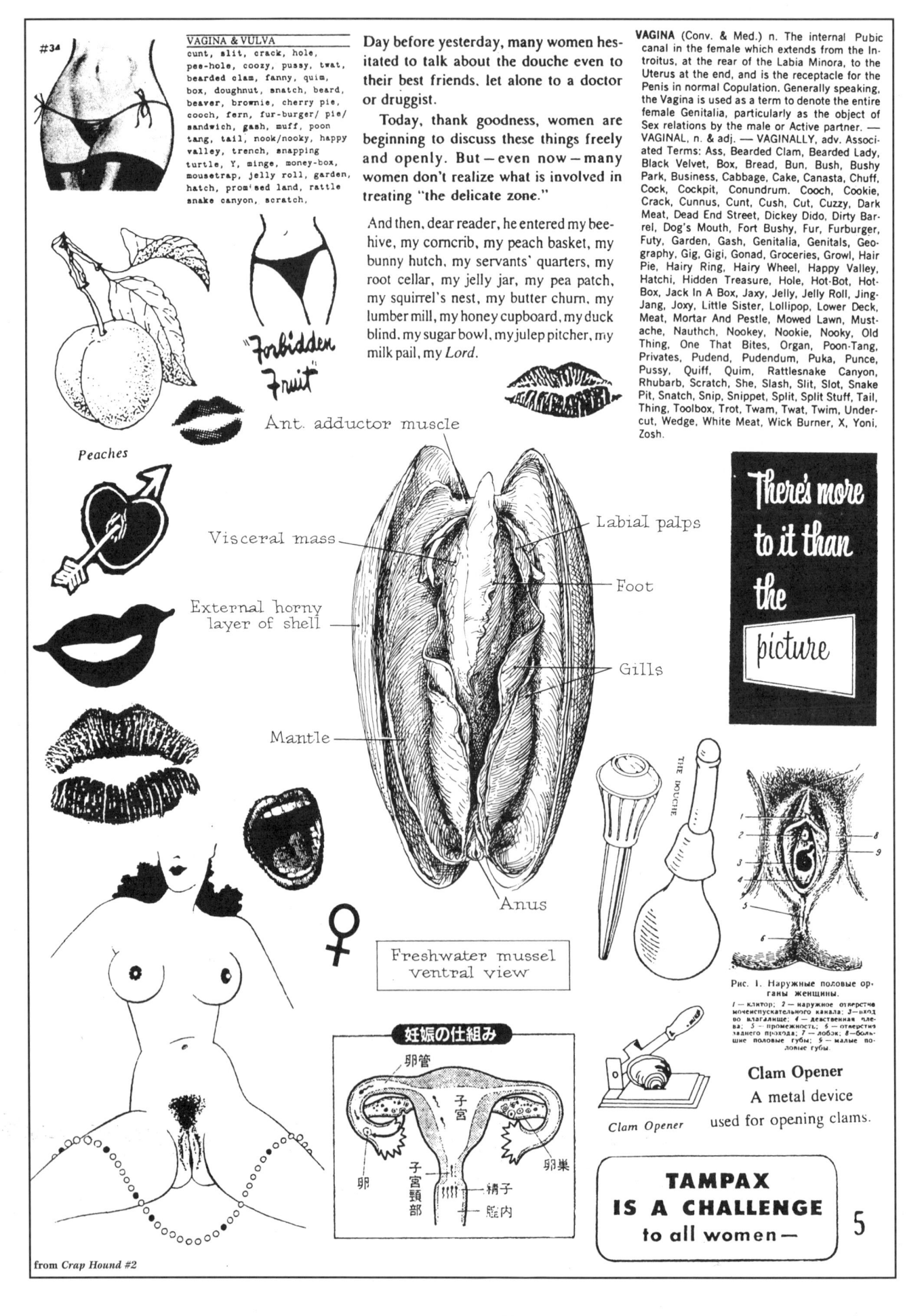

VAGINA & VULVA
cunt, slit, crack, hole, pea-hole, coozy, pussy, twat, bearded clam, fanny, quim, box, doughnut, snatch, beard, beaver, brownie, cherry pie, cooch, fern, fur-burger/ pie/sandwich, gash, muff, poon tang, tail, nook/nooky, happy valley, trench, snapping turtle, Y, minge, money-box, mousetrap, jelly roll, garden, hatch, promised land, rattle snake canyon, scratch,

Day before yesterday, many women hesitated to talk about the douche even to their best friends, let alone to a doctor or druggist.

Today, thank goodness, women are beginning to discuss these things freely and openly. But — even now — many women don't realize what is involved in treating "the delicate zone."

And then, dear reader, he entered my beehive, my corncrib, my peach basket, my bunny hutch, my servants' quarters, my root cellar, my jelly jar, my pea patch, my squirrel's nest, my butter churn, my lumber mill, my honey cupboard, my duck blind, my sugar bowl, my julep pitcher, my milk pail, my *Lord*.

VAGINA (Conv. & Med.) n. The internal Pubic canal in the female which extends from the Introitus, at the rear of the Labia Minora, to the Uterus at the end, and is the receptacle for the Penis in normal Copulation. Generally speaking, the Vagina is used as a term to denote the entire female Genitalia, particularly as the object of Sex relations by the male or Active partner. — VAGINAL, n. & adj. — VAGINALLY, adv. Associated Terms: Ass, Bearded Clam, Bearded Lady, Black Velvet, Box, Bread, Bun, Bush, Bushy Park, Business, Cabbage, Cake, Canasta, Chuff, Cock, Cockpit, Conundrum, Cooch, Cookie, Crack, Cunnus, Cunt, Cush, Cut, Cuzzy, Dark Meat, Dead End Street, Dickey Dido, Dirty Barrel, Dog's Mouth, Fort Bushy, Fur, Furburger, Futy, Garden, Gash, Genitalia, Genitals, Geography, Gig, Gigi, Gonad, Groceries, Growl, Hair Pie, Hairy Ring, Hairy Wheel, Happy Valley, Hatchi, Hidden Treasure, Hole, Hot-Bot, Hot-Box, Jack In A Box, Jaxy, Jelly, Jelly Roll, Jing-Jang, Joxy, Little Sister, Lollipop, Lower Deck, Meat, Mortar And Pestle, Mowed Lawn, Mustache, Nauthch, Nookey, Nookie, Nooky, Old Thing, One That Bites, Organ, Poon-Tang, Privates, Pudend, Pudendum, Puka, Punce, Pussy, Quiff, Quim, Rattlesnake Canyon, Rhubarb, Scratch, She, Slash, Slit, Slot, Snake Pit, Snatch, Snip, Snippet, Split, Split Stuff, Tail, Thing, Toolbox, Trot, Twam, Twat, Twim, Undercut, Wedge, White Meat, Wick Burner, X, Yoni, Zosh.

"Forbidden Fruit"

Peaches

Ant. adductor muscle

Visceral mass

Labial palps

Foot

External horny layer of shell

Gills

Mantle

There's more to it than the picture

Anus

Freshwater mussel ventral view

THE DOUCHE

Рис. 1. Наружные половые органы женщины.

1 — клитор; 2 — наружное отверстие мочеиспускательного канала; 3 — вход во влагалище; 4 — девственная плева; 5 — промежность; 6 — отверстие заднего прохода; 7 — лобок; 8 — большие половые губы; 9 — малые половые губы.

Clam Opener
A metal device used for opening clams.

Clam Opener

妊娠の仕組み
卵管
卵巣
子宮
卵
子宮頸部
精子
膣内

TAMPAX IS A CHALLENGE to all women—

from *Crap Hound #2*

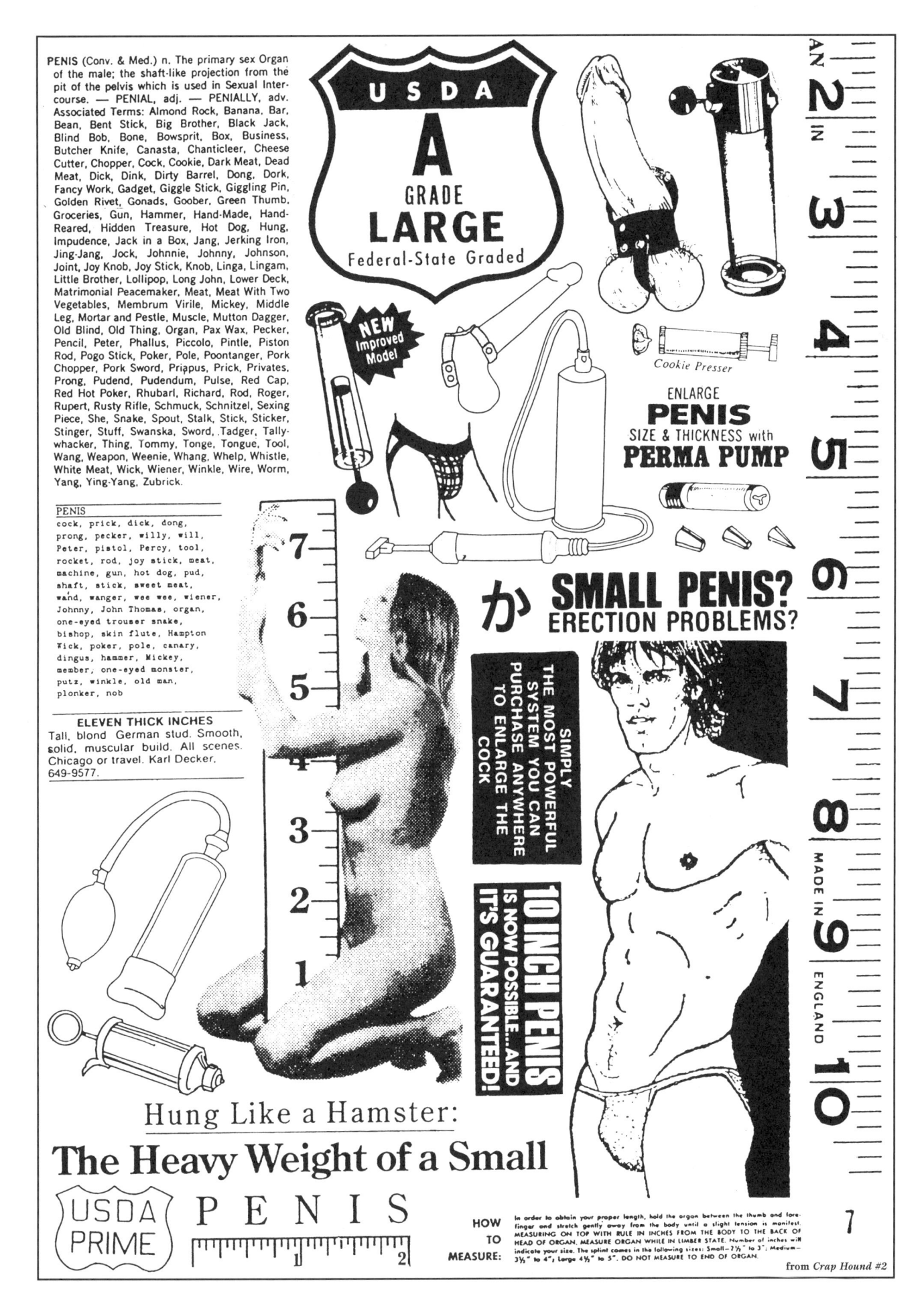

PENIS (Conv. & Med.) n. The primary sex Organ of the male; the shaft-like projection from the pit of the pelvis which is used in Sexual Intercourse. — PENIAL, adj. — PENIALLY, adv. Associated Terms: Almond Rock, Banana, Bar, Bean, Bent Stick, Big Brother, Black Jack, Blind Bob, Bone, Bowsprit, Box, Business, Butcher Knife, Canasta, Chanticleer, Cheese Cutter, Chopper, Cock, Cookie, Dark Meat, Dead Meat, Dick, Dink, Dirty Barrel, Dong, Dork, Fancy Work, Gadget, Giggle Stick, Giggling Pin, Golden Rivet, Gonads, Goober, Green Thumb, Groceries, Gun, Hammer, Hand-Made, Hand-Reared, Hidden Treasure, Hot Dog, Hung, Impudence, Jack in a Box, Jang, Jerking Iron, Jing-Jang, Jock, Johnnie, Johnny, Johnson, Joint, Joy Knob, Joy Stick, Knob, Linga, Lingam, Little Brother, Lollipop, Long John, Lower Deck, Matrimonial Peacemaker, Meat, Meat With Two Vegetables, Membrum Virile, Mickey, Middle Leg, Mortar and Pestle, Muscle, Mutton Dagger, Old Blind, Old Thing, Organ, Pax Wax, Pecker, Pencil, Peter, Phallus, Piccolo, Pintle, Piston Rod, Pogo Stick, Poker, Pole, Poontanger, Pork Chopper, Pork Sword, Priapus, Prick, Privates, Prong, Pudend, Pudendum, Pulse, Red Cap, Red Hot Poker, Rhubarl, Richard, Rod, Roger, Rupert, Rusty Rifle, Schmuck, Schnitzel, Sexing Piece, She, Snake, Spout, Stalk, Stick, Sticker, Stinger, Stuff, Swanska, Sword, Tadger, Tally-whacker, Thing, Tommy, Tonge, Tongue, Tool, Wang, Weapon, Weenie, Whang, Whelp, Whistle, White Meat, Wick, Wiener, Winkle, Wire, Worm, Yang, Ying-Yang, Zubrick.

PENIS
cock, prick, dick, dong, prong, pecker, willy, will, Peter, pistol, Percy, tool, rocket, rod, joy stick, meat, machine, gun, hot dog, pud, shaft, stick, sweet meat, wand, wanger, wee wee, wiener, Johnny, John Thomas, organ, one-eyed trouser snake, bishop, skin flute, Hampton Wick, poker, pole, canary, dingus, hammer, Mickey, member, one-eyed monster, putz, winkle, old man, plonker, nob

---

ELEVEN THICK INCHES
Tall, blond German stud. Smooth, solid, muscular build. All scenes. Chicago or travel. Karl Decker. 649-9577.

USDA A GRADE LARGE Federal-State Graded

Cookie Presser

NEW Improved Model

ENLARGE **PENIS** SIZE & THICKNESS with **PERMA PUMP**

か **SMALL PENIS?** ERECTION PROBLEMS?

SIMPLY THE MOST POWERFUL SYSTEM YOU CAN PURCHASE ANYWHERE TO ENLARGE THE COCK

10 INCH PENIS IS NOW POSSIBLE...AND IT'S GUARANTEED!

Hung Like a Hamster:
The Heavy Weight of a Small

USDA PRIME PENIS

HOW TO MEASURE: In order to obtain your proper length, hold the organ between the thumb and fore-finger and stretch gently away from the body until a slight tension is manifest. MEASURING ON TOP WITH RULE IN INCHES FROM THE BODY TO THE BACK OF HEAD OF ORGAN, MEASURE ORGAN WHILE IN LIMBER STATE. Number of inches will indicate your size. The splint comes in the following sizes: Small—2½" to 3"; Medium—3½" to 4"; Large 4½" to 5". DO NOT MEASURE TO END OF ORGAN.

from Crap Hound #2

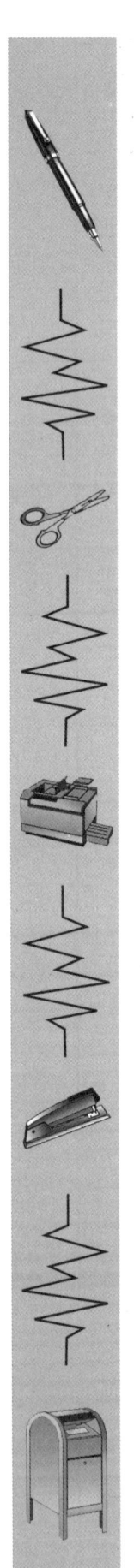

♦ ST: I'm very glad you noticed the horror of that. On one of the "devil" pages there's a list of satanically-inspired activities, and I had a good time inserting "McMemories."

♦ V: *That's creepy, because I think that's what most people have: McMemories—a pastiche of "virtual" experiences mostly derived from television and* People *magazine type media.*

♦ ST: [mockingly] "I felt just like Tiffany on *Days of Our Lives*—it was the exact same thing! I can't believe Bob would do that to me! He was acting just like Sterling!"

♦ V: *I love this page: "What is more fun than a circus?"*

♦ ST: That page resulted from a very happy accident. The headline came from an old kid's activity magazine. I took it to the copier to reduce it. The wall behind the copy machine is completely covered with clippings and pictures, continually mutating. Come to think of it, this wall has probably had a huge influence on *Crap Hound.* Anyway, when I closed the lid I found

I like to see people doing zines—it demystifies the process for others.

myself staring at this list of child behaviors: "Is Your Child In Trouble? If your child displays any of these activities, send for our free booklet!" It was one of those perfect moments. If I had made it up, it wouldn't be nearly as funny, interesting or poignant.

♦ V: *Your "Devils and Clowns" issue treats evil as banal, in a way that parallels most people's superficial engagement with religion. To most people, committing to a religion is like buying a super-cheap, shoddy life insurance policy—the kind you purchase out of a vending machine five minutes before your plane takes off. People actually believe that if you commit a sin, no matter how vicious, all you have to do is go and confess to a priest and you'll be forgiven!*

♦ ST: One-stop shopping! "I have to run some errands now—get the laundry, run to the drugstore, and if I find a place to park I'll have just enough time to be absolved of all my sins!"

♦ V: *Did you have any particular religious background?*

♦ ST: No particularly horrific religious upbringing—no one convinced me of anything.

from Crap Hound #4

My mom was a teacher, and it wasn't enough to just learn at school; every summer I had to pick something to study. I remember her taking me to a teacher's supply store one summer where I chose this book with a title like *Teaching Kids About Advertising*. My god—the things I learned stuck with me forever! I'd look at a church pamphlet and go, "Oh, that's a *bandwagon approach* . . . That's a *testimonial*." I was able to recognize and name all these different advertising techniques, and I'm sure this protected me from a lot of stupidity as I was growing up. It was just a simple workbook; a very straightforward primer on ad techniques aimed at little kids. If I were in charge of the universe, I'd slip this book into every grade school desk! Knowing how advertising works takes care of a lot of problems . . .

♦ **V: *It would be good schooling to teach kids to manipulate images like those in* Crap Hound. *Kids love to cut up things and paste them down—***

♦ ST: That would be squashed like a bug by all these corporations who want their images left pristine: "You don't fuck with that, sonny! Stay away from Ronald McDonald!" Nowadays corporations like Dow Chemical are sponsoring classroom science programs. Children are taught from grade school that big business is their friend. But imagine teaching kids that nothing is sacred—imagine a little kid given free reign with a disembodied Ronald McDonald head—copyright infringement with safety scissors! It'll never happen.

♦ **V: *Did you draw as a kid?***

♦ ST: Yes; my dad is an artist, a sculptor and painter. There was no hardcore drive to make me do art, but I was always encouraged, and I definitely liked making things. Early on I wanted to be a craftsman and an illustrator—those words suggested something more practical to me.

♦ **V: *One of my favorite "artists" actually was classified as an illustrator—Charles Addams. He could pretty much do what he wanted; he had a wide influence and was engaged in a critique of society. He also made enough money so that he could collect all the weird objects he desired.***

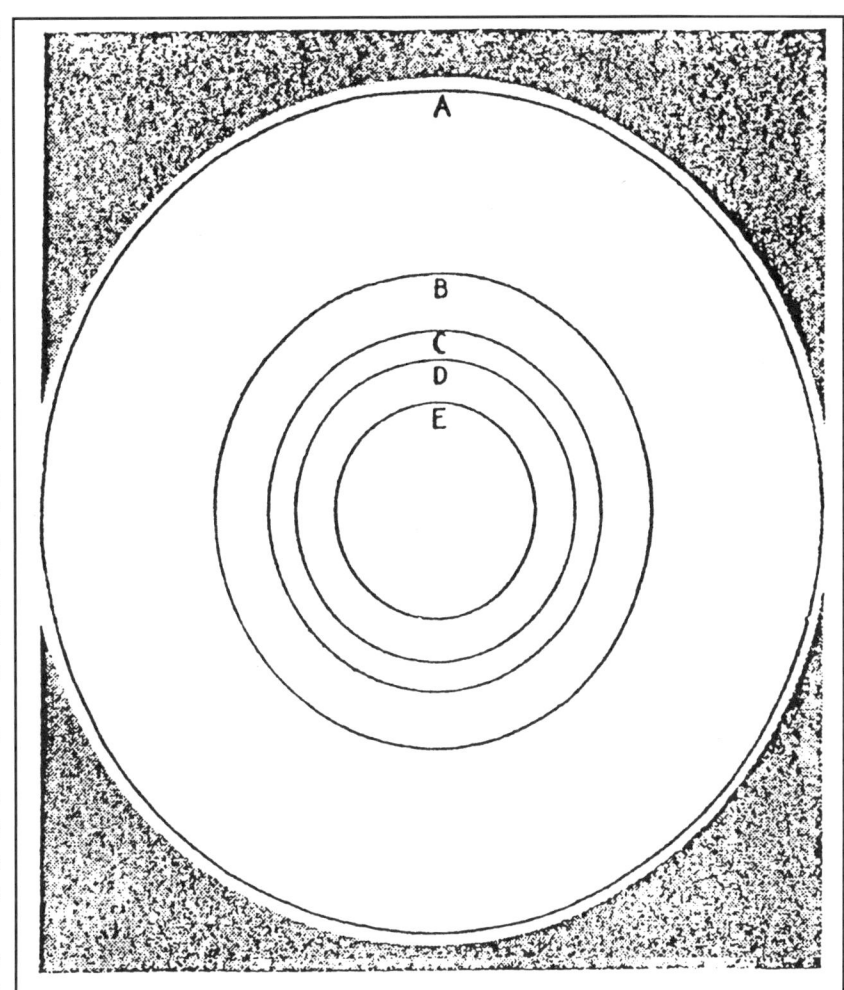

SIZE OF VAGINAL ORIFICE

These are approximately exact sizes of the degrees of expansion in the female vagina.

A During passage of infant's head at birth
B Orifice of woman who has given birth to one or more children
C Orifice of woman who has had intercourse but never became a mother
D Average diameter of male penis
E Average diameter of virgin vagina

from *Crap Hound #2*

♦ ST: I've never geared anything I've done, *Crap Hound* included, toward being in a gallery. The world of fine art is pretty thoroughly divorced from reality. Even as a kid it always seemed fake and whiny to me. Making *Crap Hound* look nice is tremendously important to me, but I refuse to think of it as a "work of art." I hate that. It's just that if I'm going to call all the shots, I'm not going to let it look like shit. I screw up every now and then, but I do my best. It's a matter of taking pride in one's work.

I try to keep my comments to a bare minimum and let context do its work. I selected all the graphics, however, and I did it with bad intentions! I'll admit to that. Maybe all I'm succeeding in doing is making people

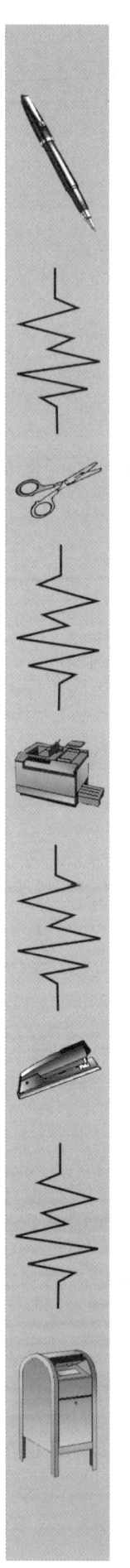

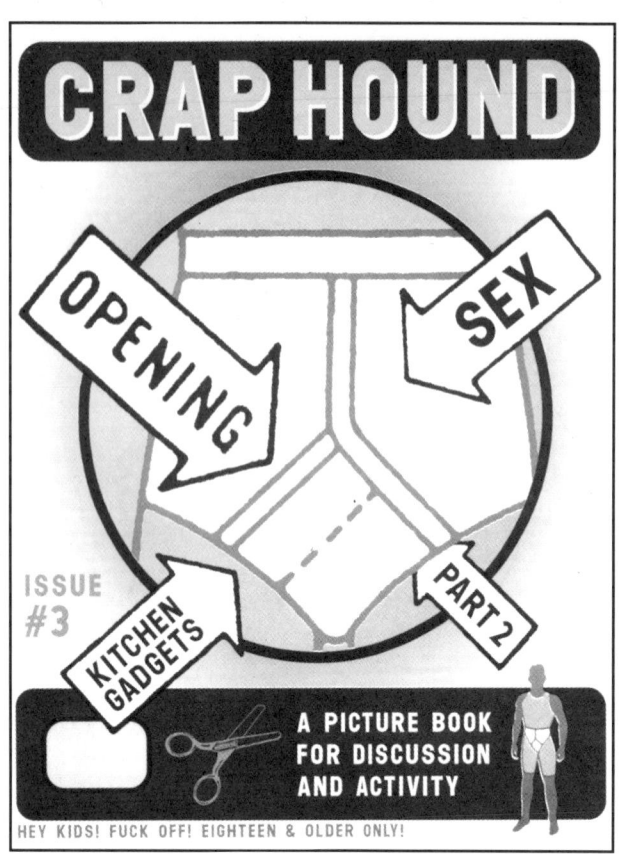

Cover of Crap Hound #3

"*C'mon clowns, c'mon you pussies!*"
♦ ST: [laughs] That's really just me laughing. I think everybody wants to goad clowns and push 'em over the edge a bit to see what happens.
♦ V: *Tell us why you plugged the band Chumbawamba—*

I love it when darker things appear— it's like truth dares to show its face for an instant. Again, it's like a window of clarity.

♦ ST: They're an English band, very political and very entertaining. They make these beautiful pop songs with some of the most evil, subversive choruses imaginable. They showed me that it was possible to be fiercely critical and extremely entertaining at the same time—they made me think more than any huge protest march ever has! Their extensive liner notes also introduced me to historical events I wouldn't have known about otherwise. They exposed me to a lot of ideas at once and made it all so palatable. Their music is well-produced—not to the point of Barry Manilow, but they take care and pride, and they're excellent musicians.
♦ V: *In a way, what you're doing is a visual correl-*

laugh, or preaching to the converted. That's okay, too. I don't mind. The converted still need entertainment!
♦ V: *I like this article about a professional clown who allegedly wanted his wife killed—*
♦ ST: He offered the hit man a microwave oven! And above is a conspiracy letter from this guy who says that the federal government is run by Satan, and they have microwaves "with which they manipulate and torture others!" Makes you think!
♦ V: *I like the "Clown's Code of Ethics"—here, you're using their own material to hang them. Like, this is an "ethic": "I will appear in as many clown shows as I possibly can"? Talk about self-promotion: "Notice Me!" These days everybody wants to be on Oprah; they all want their 15 minutes of fame—*
♦ ST: Sooner or later Oprah will have used up the entire population. Who will be left to care?
♦ V: *This article is amazing: "In the eighth century, Muslim hordes overran the Moroccan city of Fez and butchered 50,000 Christians. The streets ran red with blood."*
♦ ST: That's from a Jack Chick booklet. It was shocking: the whole fez-Shriner-clown-devil muddled mess. Clowns are really devils and the devils are clowns and the Shriners are smack in the middle of it all. Violence and ugliness swirling just below the surface allegiance to stupid religious ideals . . . I love it when darker things appear—it's like truth dares to show its face for an instant. Again, it's like a window of clarity.
♦ V: *Did any clowns respond to your challenge:*

Cover of Crap Hound #4

42

ative to what Chumbawamba does—

♦ ST: I don't think I'm of the same caliber. That's like saying to a doctor, "Jesus healed the sick—so do you!" In terms of copyright terrorists, I also like what Negativland did. They reach into this constant stream of media and advertising and rearrange what they find, turning it all on its head simply with rearrangement and context.

What's frightening is how little they have to change to make it sinister. They do with sound clips what I would like to do with pictures. Negativland was sued for plagiarizing a U2 song, and they documented their ordeal in a book, *The Letter U and the Number 2*. They claimed that all this music and all these sounds are swarming through the air as radio waves among us—they're *completely public.* The powers-that-be can pump as much sound as they want at us, but *we* can't pluck anything out and use it ourselves. Media bombardment is a very one-directional process.

♦ *V: They don't like it when you turn their own emissions against them—*

♦ ST: That's why I didn't mind calling *Crap Hound* "social criticism." If it were called "clip art," it would be a dangerous thing to put Ronald McDonald in there. *Crap Hound* was originally subtitled "Encyclopedia of Clip Art." But after receiving a threat of lawsuit by a creep who shall remain nameless, I changed the subtitle to "A Picture Book for Discussion and Activity." It has a nice ring to it, and the shift in focus and intent has made what I'm doing a little safer.

♦ *V: You certainly maintain the quality standards of any commercial clip art source—*

♦ ST: A few people have commented that *Crap Hound* looks too slick. But what does that mean—that it looks nice? Does the Do-It-Yourself ethic have to include sloppiness? If you learn to write well, it's understood that you're able to communicate your ideas more effectively. But if you spend time on layout or presentation, it's often considered insincere or "slick." I think publications are more effective when they look better. I

If you just want to produce a visual piece, great—hang it on your wall! But if you're a designer, make a decision: are you trying to communicate something or are you just jerking off?

don't feel I'm lazy or unfocused, but I'll work only so hard to read something, and if a publication is too illegible, I'll probably abandon the effort. On my list of important things to do, "struggle to read a paragraph" ranks pretty low.

♦ *V: I also hate the "cutting-edge" computer*

No Comprende

♦ *VALE: Tell us how you produced* **No Comprende**—

♦ R. COLLISION: First of all, I started producing zines in 1981, while I was living in Portland: *Slug Fest, Propagandada,* and *TOWNdowner.* I included articles like "Beautification of Billboards," which gave advice on billboard modification, "Media Murders: 20 Years of Pulling the Trigger on TV," a lengthy John Waters interview, plus collages and news articles which provide their own commentary (e.g., Brooke Shields and her mom taking a week-long make-up seminar). These were mostly distributed for free in the Portland area.

Then I moved to San Francisco and started working at a photocopy shop in San Francisco's Castro District. Customers would bring in the most lurid and bizarre images you can imagine, and naturally I'd copy as many as I could get away with. Medical photos, mug shots, vintage American advertising, horror movie material, sexploitation—I accumulated quite a collection of amazing images.

In June, 1988, the A.T.A. (Alternative Television Access) Gallery sponsored a five-day "Plagiarism Festival" that I contributed to, along with hundreds of others. Actually, this inspired me to publish *No Comprende* as an anti-copyright project. From the graphics I had accumulated at work, I decided to publish an image compilation book which would say "Recycle This" on its cover, and began copying as many pages as I could at work. Eventually I had enough sheets to publish 200 copies of a 300-page book. I called it *No Comprende.* It took a week to collate; I hand-screened the covers and had the book perfectbound. Eventually all the copies sold out.

In June 1992, along with Daniel Wylie I started *Filth,* a cooperatively-produced satirical tabloid which is distributed for free in San Francisco. Topics have included conspiracy theory, sex, meat, crime, etc. Local advertising enables us to barely break even. I consider this a zine of sorts; it's put out by a group of self-publishing junkies who need a bimonthly fix. Our latest issue is #20. (Correspondence to R. Collision, 984-A Harrison St, San Francisco CA 94107).

43

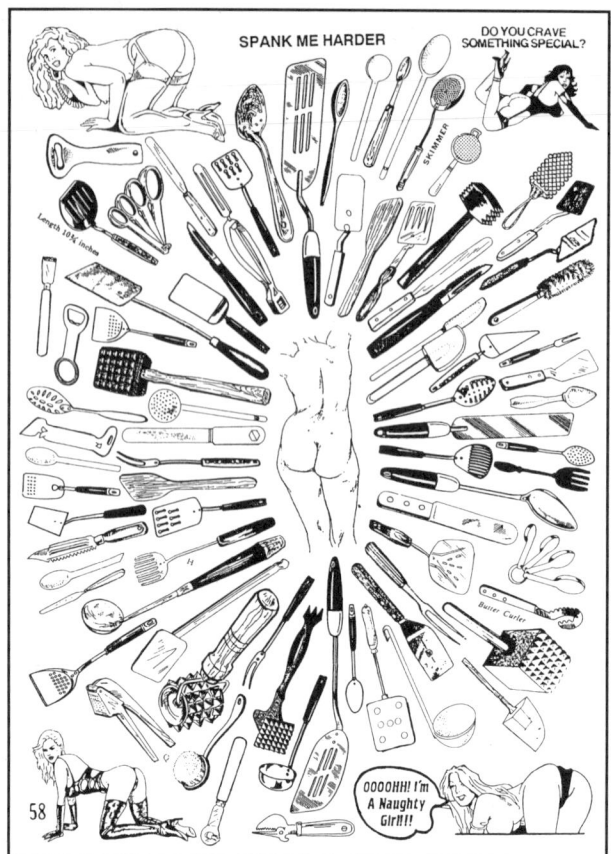

from Crap Hound #2

graphics in magazines—the kind that feature green type against a red background, for example. Out of frustration you end up reading the advertisements, just because they're at least legible— come to think of it, that was probably the intention.

♦ ST: If you just want to produce a visual piece, great—hang it on your wall! But if you're a designer, make a decision: are you trying to communicate something or are you just jerking off? When I see layouts like that I'm reminded of the doors on modern buildings, the ones where you can't tell whether to push or pull, or even which side you should try. Some "architect" thought it would be visually striking—never mind that people would actually have to *deal* with his brilliant idea. The priorities are all screwed up, maintaining surface style while being functionally retarded. One defense of high-tech annoying text is: "It's only a matter of getting used to it." Designers point out that people 500 years ago used to read black letter calligraphic script with ease. Well, people used to wipe their asses with bark, and with practice I'm sure they can still do it, too!

♦ **V:** *You included instructions on how to capture black-and-white artwork from a full-color original. This is very useful information—*

♦ ST: It's great; it helps people steal!

♦ **V:** *You also included some fonts you designed.*

♦ ST: I've been making fonts for awhile, and I've been putting a few in each issue of *Crap Hound*. This amazing type designer, Dan X. Solo of Oakland, California, has been putting out Dover alphabet books of copyright-free typefaces for decades. He's sort of a secret hero. I wonder if he knows what he's contributed—all these kids in the '80s made punk rock posters using his alphabets, including people like ART CHANTRY. He basically threw all these alphabets out there in a very egalitarian manner. If you had six bucks, you had 100 alphabets. Nowadays some jackass would put them on CD-ROM and try to make you pay for the privilege of browsing through them. The fonts in *Crap Hound* are a throwback to Dover Books. Not everyone has, or even wants to use a computer. There's nothing wrong with scissors and glue sticks.

♦ **V:** *By reprinting the work of forgotten commercial artists, you've given their art a new lease on life—*

♦ ST: A lot of completely unknown people have contributed to our culture—especially those in the fields of commercial art. All these artists worked for businesses and art houses, and the credit was usually absorbed by the company. They left behind a record of their world as they saw it. Recent technology makes it very easy to gather this stuff up and either reprint it or alter it. I don't think it's stealing, not in the negative sense. It's taking things apart and making something new from the pieces. Things mutate, nothing gets lost. Copyright enthusiasts love to blather on and on about the consequences of this kind of use. But what they're trying so hard to avoid has already happened in certain areas.

There's a renaissance going on in type design, thanks largely to the Macintosh computer and new graphic arts software. You can take any typeface and pull the leg of the "R" a little wider, and that's it— you've technically made a new typeface. You can name it anything you want and no one can stop you. You can take a typeface that someone has spent a decade developing, and in three seconds make your own from it.

> "Anyone who's vaguely dissatisfied will finally have a way to express themselves!" I sincerely doubt the computer scientists or the people at Xerox were thinking about this —but it's too late now!

That's incredibly lazy, but it's completely possible and legal. I think it's quite interesting that the world of typography hasn't withered and died, which is exactly what copyright enthusiasts would predict in this situation. But when there are billions of dollars to be made in royalties and copyright infringement lawsuits, it's not terribly surprising when the laws come down on the side of restrictions and so-called "intellectual property."

Some Things I've Discovered about Clowns

THE DISCOVERY It happened halfway through the assembly of this issue, while reading *Brewer's Dictionary of Phrase and Fable*. I made the discovery that would open my eyes to the stinking, ancient evil that lurks underneath the powdered face of clowning. I had inadvertently confirmed something millions of children already know, and that I should have realized long ago.

"**The clown of circus and pantomime, in his baggy costume, whitened face, grotesque red lips, and odd little tuft of black hair, is probably a relic of the Devil, as he appeared in medieval miracle plays.**"

A friend pointed out that I must have been subconsciously aware of this when I chose Clowns and Devils, and perhaps he's right—it's too perfect. Clowns and Devils are both archetypes, occupying space in our minds whether we want them there or not, from Tarot cards to Batman and Joker. Some people believe there's no such thing as coincidence, and in this case I'm inclined to believe them.

A SORDID PAST . . . While laughter has always been central to clowning, it's important to remember that brutality and death have always been right there alongside it . . . Clowns have been tidied up like fairy tales, the blood washed away and a happy face slapped crookedly on them. Themes of decapitation, dismemberment, and random violence were common, and still are just below the surface. A famous skit features a clown barbershop, into which a terrified clown customer is dragged and held down as several huge, nicked, straight razors are produced. And what child doesn't squeal with delight when an argument between two clowns escalates into a full-fledged riot once the clown cop and his nightstick arrive? It's just like real life! The traditional Punch and Judy show revolves around beatings and murder, including a wacky infanticide. Bloodshed—it's clowntastic!

A FEEBLE EXCUSE . . . Clowns are quick to defend their existence with tales of countless visits to bed-ridden, swollen kids in hospitals. Well, it figures. I'm sure being terminally ill might take the edge off an encounter with a clown. If I were facing a horrible, wasting death every day, I might even be able to look a clown in the face and smile. Anyway, it's not as if these kids are going to leap up and run away. They're a captive audience! In fact, I'd like to present the theory that the entire Shriner Hospital organization exists to furnish clowns with a perpetual audience of sick and dying kids.

DANGER! Finally, a word of caution. When approaching a clown, remember that you are walking toward an adult, most likely a man, who likes nothing better than to disguise his face and shoot the shit with pre-adolescent children. Clowns are not on a first name basis with reality. I've met a few clowns out of makeup, and they set off mental alarms all over the place. I know there's a Portland chapter of the Kooky Klown Klub, or whatever it's called. Maybe they'll find this issue of *Crap Hound* and feel outraged enough to write. Oh well. Clowns are fuckers and perverts and I take nothing back. Come on, clowns! Come on, you pussies!

—from *Crap Hound #4*

I love the fact that the whole zine world is an unforeseen by-product of technological innovation. I don't think anyone sat around and thought, "Hey, people will start making thousands of different publications! Anyone who's vaguely dissatisfied will finally have a way to express themselves!" I sincerely doubt the computer scientists or the people at Xerox were thinking about this—but it's too late now! When new technologies are being evaluated, scientists always seem to underestimate the urge to communicate. They make predictions without factoring in human desire or dissatisfaction.

♦ **V:** *Today it's so cheap to get an entire computer set-up, especially if it's a few generations old and not state-of-the-art—*

♦ **ST:** Not only that, it's the *copier* that changed the equation. Copiers are so common we forget how significant they are. I laugh when I hear people complain that there are too many zines. Are they going to use up all the good words? Everyone can speak, too, and that doesn't cheapen powerful speeches or good conversations. I certainly wish some people would stop publishing zines, just as I wish certain people would die and shut up forever. But overall I think self-expression is a good thing. I understand the frustration of having to wade through a stack of crappy zines to find something you love, but somehow people miraculously manage to deal with a similar crisis each time they enter a record store. The weekly press run of your newspaper's ad inserts probably outweighs all the crappy zines you've ever read. If you don't like it, don't read it. Give it a bad review and tell the world exactly why it's stupid.

With *Crap Hound*, I hope that people start to think about the mechanics and ploys of advertising. The supermarket, the Pope and the government are all using the same techniques.

I like to think that when authorities are getting serious about censorship, trying to shut people up, the experience of having done your own zine makes you a lot less likely to remain ambivalent. After you've experienced the thrill of publishing something you've really wanted to say, you're more likely to take it personally when someone tries to restrict freedom of the

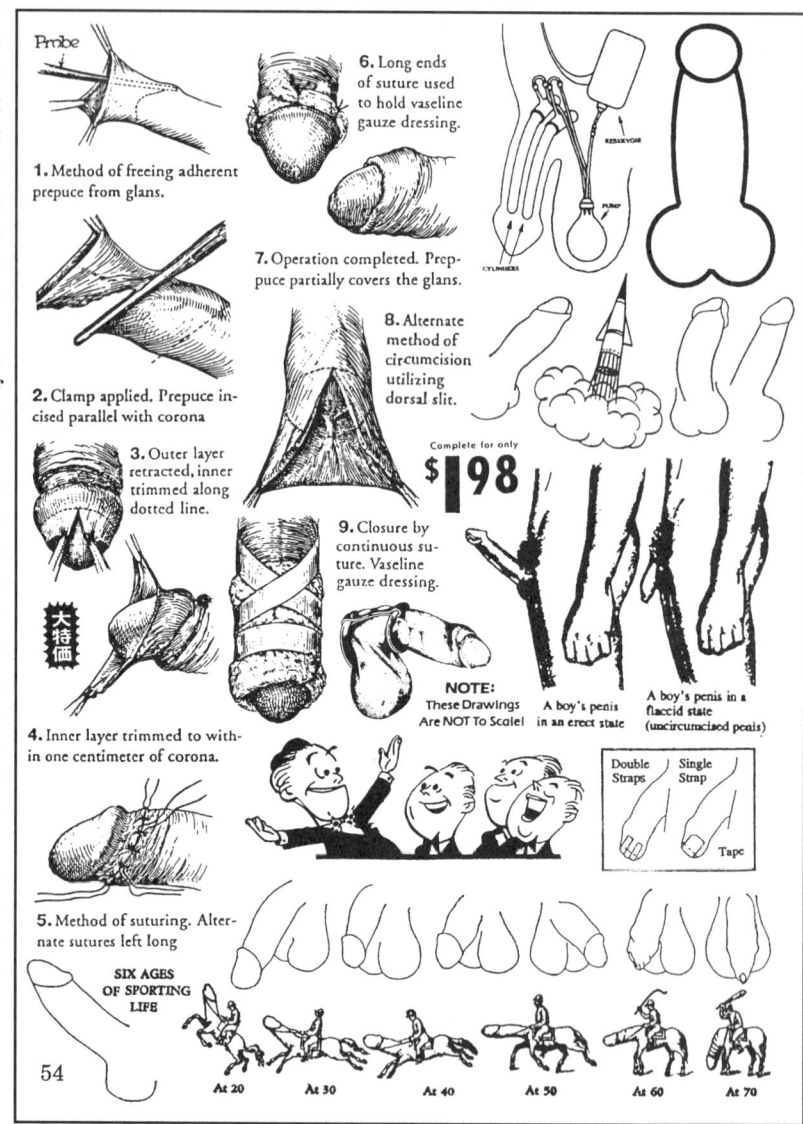

from Crap Hound #3

press. So when someone comes in and says, "This is obscene!" and *you* don't consider it obscene, you feel *involved*. It's not an abstract notion any longer.

♦ **V:** *Can you live off publishing* **Crap Hound***?*

♦ **ST:** No, but it might have swerved close to breaking even. Now that the Adidas gravy train has been derailed, the future's a bit more uncertain. I've stopped taking subscriptions for awhile, so I don't have this group of subscribers continually hanging over my head. Paper costs are always increasing. Between October 1994 and December 1995 the cost of standard paper rose 75%. I've been looking into hemp paper. Right now it costs three times the standard rate simply because raw hemp has to be imported. The technology already exists, and the market already exists. It's fucked-up and stupid that something that works so well is so hard to get.

46

The timber shortage is presented as this major crisis, with the timber industry pitted against the environmental movement. Meanwhile there is a virtual monopoly in the paper industry. They own the forests, the mills, the distribution—they run the show. It's in their interests to keep things just the way they are. Alternatives and innovation cut into their profits. They've created a state of perpetual crisis that sends the prices up and benefits no one but themselves. I love when paper companies put out their token "green" or recycled line of paper and then use half of it patting themselves on the back. If they're so fucking eager to help the world out, why aren't they lobbying for domestic production of hemp?

♦ **V: Who inspired Crap Hound?**

♦ **ST:** A friend in San Francisco named R. Collision, who's now involved in publishing *Filth,* a free satirical tabloid now up to issue #20. In 1989 he published a 300-page renegade clip art book called *No Comprende.* I realized I could publish something like that as a *periodical.* As far as ideas and philosophy go, Chumbawamba was an inspiration, like I said. Mike King, whom I met in Portland, had a big effect on the overall aesthetic—he's the one responsible for most of the wall behind the copier in the photo of me. Also, what might have also been an influence is Tuli Kupferberg's *1001 Ways to Make Love;* I reprinted some slang terms from it. He used to be in the FUGS.

Just being around friends who did zines here in Portland was very important. I was around *Snipehunt* and *Nosedive!* here in Portland, and being around people who were unapologetic and unafraid to make their own decisions was amazing. They were not trying to produce a homegrown version of *Rolling Stone.* If you're exposed to that for awhile, you begin to realize you don't have to wait for other people to do things for you, or make things you want to see. You realize it's possible to get exactly what you want without waiting in someone else's line. That's another reason I like to see people doing zines—it demystifies the process for others. I would never have started *Crap Hound* if I hadn't been around my friends and seen them working.

Crap Hound also provides a place where I can experiment in useful design, in a medium where other people actually look at it. I've accepted that it's not going to make money. With that out of the way, I can pay attention to other goals. I can rethink things and make mistakes and learn. I could be spending tens of thousands of dollars at school, going into debt, getting told what's right and wrong and becoming like everyone else. And I would have nothing but a piece of paper to show for it.

With *Crap Hound,* I hope that people start to think about the mechanics and ploys of advertising. The supermarket, the Pope and the government are all using the same techniques. If I can show you a sexually charged image, maybe you'll look more favorably on the

from Crap Hound #4

> **Enough tricks and you've got someone with a completely idiotic message sounding like a completely rational person.**

How to capture B&W art from color

I've developed a secret trick that I'll share with you, the careful reader. It's a method for capturing the black and white artwork from a full color original (e.g. a comic book), or anything copied on colored paper. Take your picture to a color copier, and get a big sheet of opaque white paper. Set the copier for a regular full color copy (turn off the goddamned *original recognition* setting). Place the paper on the glass, right where your original would go. Leave the lid up and press start. The color copier works in four passes, Cyan, Magenta, Yellow, and Black, each time scanning for one of the colors. Watch as it scans only the paper for the first three. As the scanning bar draws back, getting ready for the fourth and final pass (Black), quickly remove the white paper and slap your original down in its place. The final pass will capture only the black in the image, with all the color completely missing. Note: this is different then just setting the color copier to "Greyscale." If you do that, the copier simply turns the colors to shades of grey, leaving you with a murky piece of shit. With this method, the colors are gone completely, since the copier didn't see any on its first three passes. This trick takes a bit of timing and practice to do it fluidly. I've learned to set my original in place above the white paper, yanking the paper out of the way in time for the fourth pass.—**from *Crap Hound #4***

product sold along with it. In politics, if I can make you fear for your safety and security, then you stand a better chance of approving and obeying my new laws. And if I can convince you that another group of people is evil and somehow threatens your big chance at an eternity in paradise, you'll do what it takes to silence them, convert them, or kill them. These tendencies aren't necessarily weak or evil or stupid, they're simply part of being human. We recognize and work around built-in behaviors in other animals, but we imagine ourselves to have evolved above and beyond all that . . .

I want people to be aware of the inherent biases, patterns and switches *hard-wired* into them.

I think of all this in terms of *emotional reflexes.* Certain responses are more likely than others. We do not treat all information equally. For example, false information given beforehand can profoundly affect our opinions, even when contrary and convincing information comes later. What's interesting is that in experiments, the only defense against this phenomenon is awareness of it. Reason and intellect are not the only factors operating here, and knowing this allows us to compensate for it.

Outlawing something is always such a chickenshit way of facing perceived problems—plus, it never works.

I read about an experiment testing people's suggestibility. A group of people are sequestered in a room, and the administrator says, "The man who's about to fix the water cooler is a child molester. Don't say anything even jokingly that might make him feel worse for what he is." Then the man comes into the room, and he acts perfectly normal—he doesn't scratch himself where he shouldn't, or mutter to himself—he acts like a perfectly normal guy who has shown up to do a repair job. He leaves. The group has to fill out a form rating him on his appearance, behavior and speech, and their scores are very low. In their estimation, he couldn't do *anything* right—things that would have been ignored (or barely noticed in the first place) are given a new significance.

Fifteen minutes later, the administrator of the experiment says, "I was lying earlier; this man *isn't* a child molester." The same man is brought in to check the water cooler, and even though people know they had been lied to, their scores aren't much higher. Finally, the subjects of the experiment are informed as to how this parlor trick works (feeding people erroneous information that remains influential, even after conflicting information is given). Then they're given the test again—only then do their scores *begin* to approach what would have been a "normal" test result.

Guilt, sex, self-image, the desire to conform and even *logic* can be exploited if you know how. It's not like people are all idiots, but there are a lot of simple tricks that convince people *beneath* their level of awareness—there's more to an argument than what is being argued. If someone says something forcefully, you're probably going to think it makes more *sense* than if it's spoken haltingly. Enough tricks and you've got someone with a completely idiotic message sounding like a completely rational person. If you photographically enlarge the pupils of a woman in an advertisement, you make her look more attractive. Unless you know that trick, you might not be able to figure out why an ad appeals to you. Certain *colors* impart certain feelings; a small change in the position of shapes on a page can produce a distinct impression. We absorb much more than we realize.

48

Advertising, religion and government have either been deliberately studying these psychological tricks or have passively discovered them over time. They've had centuries to perfect them, and they're getting better all the time. They know what it means to be *human,* oddly enough. They know our fears, hopes and desires, regardless of what we feel comfortable admitting to. The current world has been built by people who have no qualms about using this knowledge. They have no reason to fool themselves, so they're much more successful. There's a saying, "Liberals understand Christmas, but conservatives understand Halloween." I think that goes a long way toward explaining a lot of things.

I want people to be aware of the inherent biases, patterns and switches *hardwired* into them. Yet people won't take the trouble to find out what their little switches are. We like to pretend we're these perfectly rational beings of ethereal intellect—minds without bodies—and that we have no inherent urges or biases. While we're congratulating ourselves for being so brilliant and savvy, the political leaders, churches and advertisers know better. *They know more about you than you know about yourself.* They smile, nod and say, "It's great you're so together! Here's a beer made especially for people like you, who really know what's going on!"

Control systems take advantage of our *emotional reflexes.* Just as if I tap your knee, your leg jerks—if I show you a woman with big breasts, you may desire the product associated with her. In politics, if I show you a picture of a foreigner, your immediate reaction will be distrust—that's hard-wired into your body— even though that could be someone who saved your parents' lives.

I hate the idea of people trying to outlaw and regulate the ad industry out of existence. Outlawing something is always such a chickenshit way of facing perceived problems—plus, it never works. People are getting off really easily when they go, "Oh, these advertisers are showing us beer and naked women together; I've just *got* to purchase some Budweiser now. I really don't have a choice; I've been manipulated by an evil ad agency!" This is absurd.

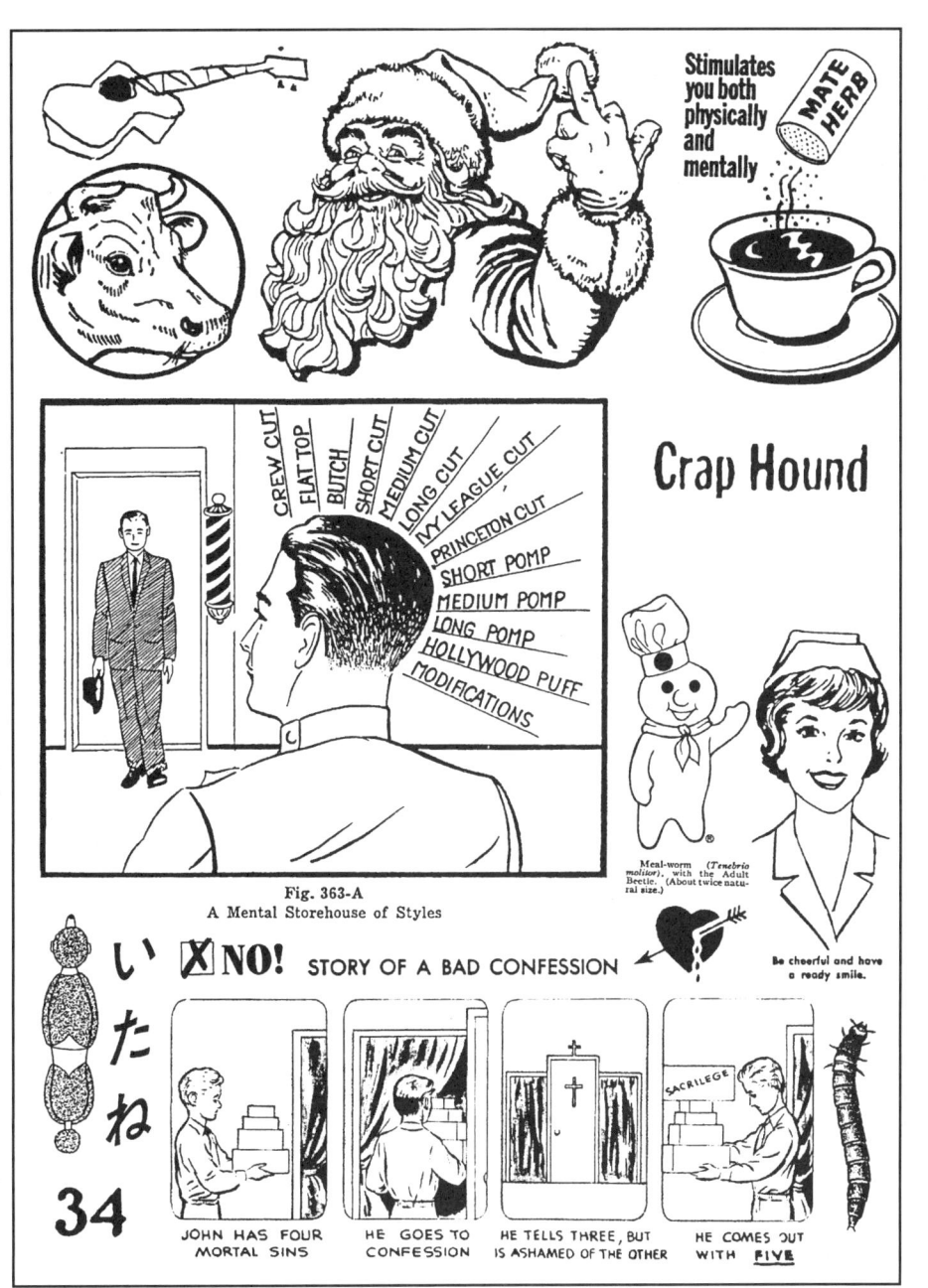

People need to take *responsibility* for their actions, get to know themselves, and become more aware of what makes them work. People have to make themselves aware of the mechanisms that motivate them. It's one of the best reasons to be honest with yourself—familiarity with your own feelings provides a great deal of immunity to exploitation of your fears and desires. You can't outlaw people who try to be convincing, like advertisers. So we all have a *job* to do: to figure out the mechanisms inside us that are affecting our perceptions and our behavior, whether we know it or not. You *can* learn to see through bullshit. ▼

Housewife Turned Assassin

Housewife Turned Assassin was first published by Sisi and Dani in Los Angeles in July, 1993. Subsequently they helped form the Revolution Rising collective, which has produced zines, a documentary, bumper stickers, t-shirts, photo and magazine collages, a spoken word compilation tape, art shows, benefits and fund-raisers—all toward the goal of social change. For a sample copy of *HTA* send $2 cash plus 2 stamps to *HTA*, PO Box 914, North Hollywood, CA 91603.

♦ **VALE:** *When you started publishing* **Housewife Turned Assassin,** *were you motivated by a feeling of indignation?*
♦ **SISI:** Definitely—that's a lot of it. The premise behind a zine is often anger, frustration and maybe the bits of happiness that sometimes happen. Doing a zine is like an inexpensive form of therapy. It's a very cathartic process.

When I started going to RIOT GRRRL meetings, that's when I found out that people were putting out their own zines. I would read them and be very inspired, or think, "Fuck that—that doesn't relate to *my* life. Why don't I do my own and maybe someone could relate to it." We're not eloquent, but we wanted to voice our *own* opinions in our own way. We want to talk about our experience, since everybody's experience is unique. We feel, "Hey—what if someone else could relate to what *we're* trying to say, or the shit we go through . . ."

For the most part, people invest a lot of time, effort and (sometimes) heartache to put out their zine because they have to put all their money into it—unless they get lucky and find some friend who'll print it free of charge. Some people use newsprint because it's cheaper in the long run, but initially they need a large amount of money. We didn't go that route; we saved up some money and then photocopied *HTA* and sold it. We don't make any profit and often don't break even because the postage is so expensive. Sometimes we get lucky and a friend copies an issue for free—it depends.

♦ **V:** *Tell us your background—*
♦ **S:** I grew up in the San Fernando/Pacoima area in the San Fernando Valley, a barrio-type area where a lot of Mexican immigrants live. Both my parents emigrated from Mexico. My dad immigrated here in the late '50s; my mom immigrated in the late '60s. My mom came from a little ranch in Durango, Mexico where electricity and running water were not available. My mom has had a very tough life. She lost two children in Mexico; one to malnutrition and the other because it was a premature birth, leaving a surviving twin. She came to the U.S. with her son in hopes of getting work and a different quality of life.

The premise behind a zine is often anger, frustration and maybe the bits of happiness that sometimes happen.

My mom had quite a trip to make it to the USA. As it is with many immigrants, she couldn't legally come into this country. She eventually made it by borrowing a Mexican passport from a relative. To get to the border from Durango, she took a train and also arranged a ride through relatives. She couldn't figure out why they (the ones she was riding with) kept stopping and switching cars, until later she realized they were transporting pot. Needless to say, she made it. A little later she met my dad. Now I have two brothers and three sisters.

My mom worked in factories, and once she was able, she sent for my grandma. It usually happens that a relative will come here, and little by little send for more family members as money permits.

♦ **V: What kind of factories did your mom work at?**

♦ S: In North Hollywood she had a job at a bottle labeling factory making $1.47 an hour. As a result of working with cleaning agents and paints, her asthma got so severe she had to stop. For the past 25 years my dad has been employed at an aerospace company; he's a highly skilled machinist. He got his machinist's certificate at Los Angeles Valley Community College.

There are a lot of little enclaves of Mexicans and African-Americans here; in the communities we live in one doesn't feel so alienated. There are other people who speak Spanish so you don't feel like, "Fuck—I can't even communicate." A lot of people don't understand how trying the Chicano/Mexicano experience is. It's weird. You're born here (or come when you're very young) and you don't realize how misplaced you feel in society and institutions until you confront yourself with questions like "What am I, Mexican or American? Why do some people treat me like shit?"

I was born in 1973 and grew up speaking both languages, although I learned Spanish first. It was definitely a Chicano community where I lived; I grew up surrounded by people who had similar problems and experiences. None of my immediate family got involved in gangs (because I'm sure my parents would've kicked our asses if we had), although some of my extended family have had the misfortune of drugs and gangs. When you don't have a supportive family, you try to fill the void through joining gangs.

My mom really pushed to get us into better schools,

Sisi by the sea. Photo: Fred

and managed to put us in the Magnet program, which offered better classes. I was one of about three Mexicans in my class; the rest of the kids were White and Asian. It was difficult; all of the other kids were wearing brand-new clothes and we were wearing hand-me-downs or thrift shop clothes—and not by choice; that's all we could afford. Kids would tease us because of the way our hair was fixed. Up until the sixth grade my mom brushed my hair into tight braids. She would try to keep us as neat as possible, but it wasn't the fashion to be this way—we were caught in this time warp of polyester, corduroy and flooding pants, and kids would tease us. Kids aren't blind; they know when you're poorer than they are and they make sure you know it.

♦ **V: Did you keep a journal?**

♦ S: I've kept journals since I was maybe twelve; I still continue to do them.

♦ **V: Did your mom encourage you to keep them?**

♦ S: My mom has always been very supportive of all of my endeavors. I was always the black sheep of the

with a lot of shit! She always tells me really sad stories about her childhood and when she first got pregnant—just the weirdest, wackiest stories, like when she would go to these dances with her girlfriends. One time there was this man who would not stop harassing her. He kept trying to touch her, so she just grabbed a chair and smashed it over his head!

She's just that kind of person; she doesn't allow herself to be abused. People think that Mexican women fall into one of two categories; you're either an aggressive, man-stealing slut or you're totally submissive—just a little wifey. My mom doesn't fall into either category; she's very strong-willed and does her own thing.

♦ **V: Is that unusual in the Mexican community?**
♦ S: I think a lot of women fall into the trap of being very religious and subservient to their husbands. I think this is changing now. Many people believe in the stereotype of the Mexican man as being macho and having no respect for women, but I've met just as many men from other cultures who have distorted views about women. I don't think a disrespectful attitude towards women is unique to the Mexican male. I think that the more men and women communicate and try to understand what's up with one another, the easier it is for both genders to find their commonalities and a mutual respect. I see a great change taking place in the community because both genders are more aware of their rights and both feel empowered by this.

I think activism has a lot to do with this change. There was momentum in the '70s when the Chicano Moratorium happened. It died down a lot in the '80s when everyone was assimilating and trying to become as Anglo-cized as possible. But things are changing. Although they don't have Chicano studies classes in high school, in college you can start learning about your culture's accomplishments and gain a sense of self-worth and motivation.

I learned that back in the '30s there were mass deportations of Mexicans who were actually Americans. They were called "repatriations." The U.S. sponsored these *bracero* programs in which a lot of Mexicans were recruited to come to America and work in the agricultural fields and other cheap labor industries. The time came when people thought, "There's too many Mexicans here; let's round them up and ship 'em back." So the police would just collar anyone who had a brown face and ship them back to Mexico—some of whom couldn't relate to what was going on in Mexico because they had been *born* in America. So they had to find their way back, usually without money. It's remarkable how this history has been suppressed.

♦ **V: You have a supportive community now—**
♦ S: I'm surrounded by very creative people. My friends who do zines like Debbie and Tye, Dani and her photography, Fred, the all-around artist, Sergio

Cover of *Housewife Turned Assassin #2*

family, but she never suppressed my need to express myself. As insignificant as it may seem, I wanted to have my hair black because I went through this whole Gothic stage. And then when I got pierced, and when I got a tattoo, she would always just shake her head and say, "You're expressing yourself in that way—that's fine. But whatever you're going to do, just don't get involved in drugs."

> **People think that Mexican women fall into one of two categories: you're either an aggressive, man-stealing slut or you're totally submissive—just a little wifey.**

♦ **V: She sounds smart—**
♦ S: She is. She was only able to attend school to the eighth grade. Most education comes from your experience, not from what you learn in school. My mom's a very tough, strong-minded woman—she's had to deal

and his spoken word—I could go on and on. Dani and I are involved in a collective called Revolution Rising which we helped start. It started when about five women got together; we all wanted to start up a new group. We had been part of a Riot Grrrl group until it fell apart. We were doing our own thing and occasionally we would call each other and say, "We really miss having those meetings—that support of whatever it was we were doing." We wanted to incorporate emotional support with being creative.

> **Back in the '30s there were mass deportations of Mexicans who were actually Americans. They were called "repatriations."**

I don't want to misrepresent what other people might feel the Revolution Rising collective is about, so I'll just describe what we've done so far. We put on a free art show where we invited artists to participate. We had a mailing list and sent out postcards saying, "Bring your art, display it and it's free." We got a lot of really cool art. There was no theme; people brought mannikins' heads and wire structures and photography and paintings. Later, there was a spoken word event where people read their poetry and short stories. We've put on fund-raising shows and benefits. We also produced a spoken-word compilation tape, and we produce a zine, *Revolution Rising.* We've done five issues so far.

My friend Tye (who's in Revolution Rising) had the idea to do a documentary on body image—not expressly eating disorders, but how we feel about our bodies. We produced a documentary using a Fisher-Price pixelvision camera (which uses a standard cassette tape; years ago it was sold at Toys R Us). She interviewed men and women and edited the tapes; it's called *Good Enough to Eat.* It's a very poignant film, about 13 minutes long. We look ghostly in it because of the graininess of the pixels.

Through the years we've done our own zines, but in *Revolution Rising* we invite anybody to contribute. We sell zines at shows. Recently there was a big show at the Palladium with Sonic Youth, Bikini Kill, and the Amps, where we had a booth. It was a successful evening in that we distributed a lot of material to people who might not have had access to it; usually we do small shows. People were really psyched buying t-shirts and zines and getting free condoms and free literature. However, the Palladium wanted us to give them 30% of our earnings! The tickets were $25 each, so why did they need to make more money off *us?* We're just a little collective that hardly makes any profit, and any profit we make gets plowed back into making more t-shirts, zines, etc.

Also, they told us we couldn't sell stickers, and we love selling stickers—it's such an easy and powerful form of activism to sticker an offensive billboard or bus stop ad. I imagine this policy was to prevent vandalism. We decided to sell stickers anyway. The owner of the Palladium came to our booth and picked up a sticker and said, "What's this?" We said, "Oh, it's between bands and we were just organizing our stuff." He started screaming at us: "I'm not used to repeating myself! I said NO STICKERS!" He was very abusive, getting in my face, yelling, "I want you out of here now! Get the hell out!" He tore a sticker in half and grabbed a handful of flyers and threw them at me. I was thinking, "Fuck, I can't take this abuse!"—he was so mad. His face was red and he was hovering over me. He picked up the table and leaned it over, then something came over me. I looked right at him and said, "Don't yell at us! We're not stupid! Stop being so abusive!" He had been completely unreasonable and very physically threatening, but he backed off and then we got kicked out of there.

♦ **V:** *You got kicked out?*
♦ **S:** Yeah, and we had to hang around the parking lot for two hours because our car was blocked in—they had crammed in as many cars as possible, even at $7 per car. In a way we got screwed, but we did sell stickers, we didn't give them their 30%, and we didn't have to pay to get in, so we got a little bit out of the experience. And I stood up to this jerk. But it was very emotionally draining for me. I'm not a wimp, but it was very weird to stand up to him—he was really big and overbearing. He reminded me of a school administrator, because that kind of thing used to happen to me in high school.

The Revolution Rising collective has women and men involved. It was started by women but our intentions were to have anybody and everybody who was interested involved. There's a good variety of people as well; we try our hardest to be approachable.

♦ **V:** *What bands played at your benefits?*
♦ **S:** A band called Tummy Ache, Crown for

Illustration by Sheryl from Revolution Rising #5

Athena—those are all-women bands. Lucid Nation is a co-ed band. The Fondled, Still Life, Casper Spook, and See Saw have played at Revolution Rising benefits. We've done spoken word shows. We've also had booths at shows by Heavens to Betsy, Excuse 17, Switched at Birth, Spitboy, Bikini Kill, and FYP. At every show we collect items such as food and blankets for the homeless and give them to those who want it.

♦ **V: *That's definitely active—***

♦ S: Sometimes we get stagnated by our personal lives, but we still keep going.

♦ **V: *Tell us about your involvement with Riot Grrrl—***

♦ S: I had read about it in the *Noise,* an L.A. high school underground newspaper, and in the *L.A. Weekly,* and my involvement started off small. First I took Danielle and another friend to a meeting in L.A. Then I met Dawn who was having meetings in the Valley.

Previously I had had a lot of misconceptions about Riot Grrrl, like: "Are you all straight-edge? Are you all vegan?" I had stereotypes in my head about it, and I went to one meeting in L.A. where Danielle and I were the only people of color there—we felt kinda uncomfortable. But soon afterward we met Dawn and went to a meeting at her house, and that's when I started feeling safe and happy for having found them. It was interesting; our experiences were very diverse and each meeting was a great learning experience. Many of the girls were very young, starting at age 14.

♦ **V: *What was discussed?***

♦ S: We talk about everything: our lives at home, our lives at school, our lives at our jobs, the way things affect us. People tell stories; they talk about oppression or problems they've faced, and other people offer suggestions. We talk about issues; sometimes it was very activist-oriented. Sometimes they were support-group meetings; sometimes they were taking-care-of-business type meetings, like if we were going to have a booth at a show next week.

We love selling stickers—it's such an easy and powerful form of activism to sticker an offensive billboard or bus stop ad.

The reason I was disappointed by some of my experiences in Riot Grrrl was—everyone tried to create this *utopia:* "We should all love each other 'cuz we're girls. It doesn't matter what class, race or religious background we have, because we all share in common the fact that we're girls." I think that's a self-defeating, ignorant view to adopt, because it's just not true. There *are* disparities between us; there are differences. At meetings I'd feel like addressing race, or talking about how we feel about race regardless of background. But whenever these issues were brought up for discussion, they were disregarded by some individuals as not being part of the premise behind Riot Grrrl. That's a bunch of shit—Riot Grrrl's not supposed to have such an exclusionary agenda! There's not supposed to be this set of restrictive standards; it is about a common goal of female empowerment. We do have to talk about race and class issues. Regardless, I left with some disappointments, but a lot of wonderful friendships.

Revolution Rising started after I met people at Riot Grrrl who wanted to do something different since the group fell apart. But actually, Riot Grrrl's coming back; I've heard of four conventions planned for the summer, including one in Seattle and one in Santa Barbara. I'm so glad there are still people who want to do something about it, and who want to disprove that it was

Sisi. Photo: Danielle

just a flavor of the month activist group making fashion statements. It has been and will continue to be a very strong movement.

♦ **V: It's very important to have woman-only spaces and meetings—**

♦ S: At a 1995 Riot Grrrl convention in Pomona (near L.A.) I talked about how I felt a bit ostracized, and that a lot of people did not want to address issues of race, class, religion—everything that's diverse about us. Some people didn't get it, but a lot of people did. I had some really cool conversations about this taboo. Some people want to make it seem like everything's wonderful and great and we all love each other. But it doesn't happen that way. We have conflicts; we're all human. It's unrealistic to think that the girls in these collectives are all supposed to like each other.

♦ **V: But I think that women have a less macho or aggressive way of talking with each other—**

♦ S: I don't know if I could say that. Women *do* sometimes get aggressive and are not very nice to each other. You *can* get intimidated. I don't think that communication conflicts are automatically easier to solve just because you're talking with a woman. I feel like a movement that concentrates on helping women gain strength through each other is necessary, but it is just as necessary for both women and men to communicate with each other for a more mutually progressive means of coexistence. I go about doing that through zines, spoken word and Revolution Rising.

♦ **V: To begin with, it's really important to have these meetings—society doesn't tell you to have them; you have to do this for yourself.**

♦ S: Yes, and it's very tough getting people together, especially in Los Angeles—we're so spread out, sprawled everywhere, so you have to make it a very widespread network. Some of the L.A. Riot Grrrl meetings were huge—there were like 50 women! It was amazing—there were so many people interested.

The majority of people who go to Riot Grrrl meetings are girls and women who listen to punk music. But there are a lot of girls out there who listen to Top Forty or hip hop. And maybe they feel they can't relate to people who dress a different way and listen to different music. If that's the case, that's kinda fucked. I think that's why there aren't as many people of color at meetings; they have trouble relating.

♦ **V: But you crossed over. How did this happen?**

♦ S: Like I said, I've always been the black sheep. I've always listened to music that had messages. I didn't like the trendy music; I searched out music that addressed issues both emotional and critical about society. I clung to Danielle; both of us were pretty much outcasts in our school. We didn't feel we had barriers keeping us from listening to whatever we wanted to listen to.

♦ **V: That's what it takes—**

♦ S: Just one other person—a partner in crime!

♦ **V: You started employing not just the medium of the zine, but also bumper stickers which are definitely an activist medium of communication.**

♦ S: I made up a lot of stickers with my boyfriend Fred; we would give them to people and pretty soon they were everywhere! We'd even make band stickers; when Bikini Kill came to play we gave them Bikini Kill stickers we had made—we weren't making money off them, we were just giving them out, just because we wanted to say, "This is the kind of music we listen to and are motivated by, and we're happy about it." Now it's a lot more common to see this, but back then it wasn't as common.

♦ **V: How do you make a bumper sticker?**

♦ S: It's easy; on a computer graphics program you use a certain font for what you want to say, print it out and get it copied on label paper. You could do it more expensively and get it printed on plastic, but I never did that. You can just go to Kinko's and they already have the label paper there.

♦ **V: This is a pretty inexpensive way to communicate and do something—**

♦ S: Oh yeah! Revolution Rising put out a spoken word cassette; that's pretty cheap to do and people can buy it for $3. It's all about being self-sufficient and doing it yourself; it's about not waiting for something to come along and give you a break. Also, people hinder themselves with rules and regulations, but we don't—we do whatever we want to. We just take it upon ourselves to do things. And there's always people who are interested in it.

The motivation and momentum that Riot Grrrl gave me helped me put out my own zine and start a collective.

♦ **V: How do you find other kindred spirits?**

♦ S: For us, it was at shows. When we have a booth with all this stuff, people approach us and say, "Oh, this is really cool—how can I get involved?" They'll leave their addresses; we have a voice-mail telephone and people leave messages on it and we'll contact them. That's how we get other people involved. Our intention is *not* to create branches of Revolution Rising everywhere; it's more: "If you want to start a collective, then start it! You don't have to have someone else validate what you're doing."

♦ **V: This energy is obviously fueled by anger. Things still happen to you—**

♦ S: Oh yeah—all the time! Even in the job market, Danielle and I constantly have to compromise ourselves in the way we look and who we work for. We don't want to dress in nylons and suits. It's so hard to find a job that actually accepts you in the way you

Cover of *Revolution Rising #5*

want to look. I've left a lot of jobs because I felt I was compromising myself too much, or because they just wouldn't accept me: "Either change or get out!"

Right now I work as a bilingual teacher's assistant for the Los Angeles Unified School District. It's a three-hour-a-day position during the day working with bilingual kids. Danielle works as a biller, and she's also a photography student—we're both students at community colleges.

♦ **V: It would be ideal if you could somehow manage to live off activism—**
♦ **S:** Yeah, that would be really cool—I'd love to live off publishing zines for the rest of my life! I would like to do some kind of non-profit work where there would be a space, and you would provide people with job leads, and if people didn't have a place to stay they could stay there, and you'd provide training and workshops on different subjects. The collective has talked about putting something like that together, but that takes a lot of money and time and dedication. We're all dealing with our own lives, and it's hard to dedicate yourself to a project as big as that. Although there sure is a need for it—especially around here.

♦ **V: You've taken ideas inspired by Riot Grrrl and mutated them in your own directions—**
♦ **S:** Oh yeah—that's what you should do with *anything*. You shouldn't just follow blindly; you shouldn't wait for something to give you direction. You take what you want from something and you use it for your benefit. The motivation and momentum that Riot Grrrl gave me helped me put out my own zine and start a collective. Having other people around to support you and say, "Yeah, I want to do that too!" has helped so much.

♦ **V: Have you encountered a lot of prejudice in your life?**
♦ **S:** Oh yeah—a lot of prejudice in school and at work. At school both Danielle and I encountered discrimination; kids would tease us because we weren't white. They thought our ultimate goal should be to act and look as white as possible, but we didn't want to be assimilated into American "culture." My culture is so much a part of me, and I cherish that.

I once worked at a pest control company, and I would always vocalize my disappointment if I wasn't happy with something. A lot of people liked to fuck with me because of that; they liked to push my buttons. I'd be sitting overhearing co-workers talking in the background: "Oh, don't get Sisi mad—she's got that *Latina* temper!" They were constantly making jokes about Mexicans and would get annoyed if Spanish-speaking customers would call: "Why don't they just learn English?"

More recently, when I was a clerk at a bookstore, I was ringing this man up on the register and he looked at my name tag and tried to pronounce my name. "Hmm—Arseeleeah—what are you, Arabic?" I told him my name was Arcelia and that I was Mexican. So he asks me, "Do you have problems with La Migra [the U.S. border patrol]?" I didn't really know how to respond so I just answered, "No." I think his strange question had to do with the current anti-immigrant sentiment and his assumption that Mexican equals "illegal." Fuckin' moron—*whatever!*

♦ **V: These people think they're being funny when nothing's funny at all.**

I would *love* to start a band that addresses the Chicana struggle.

♦ **S:** People will crack jokes, thinking it's okay with you: "You're not like those *other* Mexicans, because *you* speak English."
♦ **V: I looked up Lupe Velez in a dictionary of film, and she was described as "the Mexican spitfire." Where does that come from?**
♦ **S:** It's so weird. There are so many stereotypes about Mexican women. She was supposed to be this funny little hot-tempered Mexicana—you better not

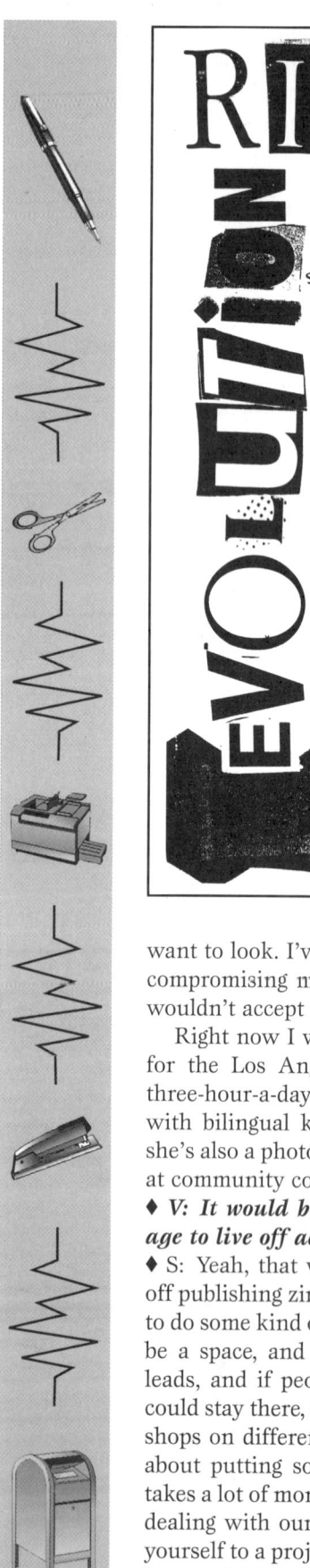

set her off! She was like a cartoon character. I don't know where that stereotype came from, but people still believe it. They use stereotypes to wrap you in a neat little package: "I know who you are; I know what you do, because you're from this race or culture."

♦ V: *So you were in the punk rock scene—*

♦ S: We go to punk shows; I've gone to shows for a long time now. I don't go as frequently anymore, and sometimes the only reason we go is to have a booth or table. Not enough interesting bands come through. What initially attracted me to punk was the message.

♦ V: *Are there any Chicana bands?*

♦ S: No, but there are Chicano punk bands like LOS CRUDOS—they're wonderful. I would *love* to start a band that addresses the Chicana struggle, but I'm not disciplined enough to start a band. I've tried to learn the guitar; Danielle and I aspired to start a band, but we just never did it—we got wrapped up in other things that were easier for us to do. But there is definitely a need for women of color to get out there and say their piece.

The most approachable band I've ever talked with is Los Crudos. They are amazing; they're very nice. At shows they always pass out lyric sheets and zines with lyrics and articles that the singer, Martin, writes. They are a very big inspiration—I'm so happy they exist. Every time they come to town I make an effort to see them play and talk with them.

♦ V: *What did you think of the movie* West Side Story?

♦ S: They used Puerto Ricans as background actors, and Rita Moreno. But the main actor, Natalie Wood, was white. Hollywood still does this. Antonio Banderas is a Spaniard playing a Mexican in the sequel to *El Mariachi* called *Desperado*, which originally starred a Mexican actor. Banderas is the stereotype of the swarthy Latin lover. There are plenty of Mexican and Chicano actors out there waiting for work besides bit parts as maids and cholos.

♦ V: *Are there any mass media role models out there for you?*

♦ S: You know, I can't think of any. I could appreciate that film *Mi Familia,* even though it was very romanticized. It was kinda corny, but it was good—finally there's a representation of what a Mexican family is like! There are wonderful Chicano writers out there that are not really mass-media role models, like SANDRA CISNEROS (who just put out an amazing poetry book, *Loose Woman*) and MARISELA NORTE. She does spoken word, and has a spoken word CD out on SST. She's from East L.A. Also, former *L.A. Weekly* journalist, author and spoken wordist Ruben Martinez.

♦ V: *What do you think of Edward James Olmos?*

♦ S: I think he's cool. He's done things that I haven't agreed with, but he's done a lot of cool things like *Zoot Suit*—that was rad! He directed *American Me,* which was well made but I'm tired of seeing all the negative shit about my culture. Similarly, the only films made for

Page by Dani from *Revolution Rising #3*

I WOULDNT BE THIS FUCKED UP IF MY DAD HADNT BEEN SUCH A DICK TO ME HE SAID AGAIN TODAY. SHUT UP SHUT UP SHUT UP!!!!
WHY DOES EVERYONE INSIST ON BLAMING EVERYONE ELSE FOR THEIR FUCK UPS?? COME ON, WERE ALL ADULTS NOW, SO LETS PLAY THAT WAY! I COULD EASILY USE THAT EXCUSE..IVE BEEN ABUSED BY MY BROTHER, BEATEN BY MY FATHER, IGNORED BY MY MOTHER, ISOLATED BY MY PEERS, AND WATCHED MY FATHER DRINK HIMSELF INTO HIS GRAVE. BOO HOO CRY ME A RIVER. ITS ALL IN THE PAST NOW!I DO NOT CHOSE TO LIVE IN THE PAST. AWAY FROM ALL THOSE SITUATIONS, I DO NOT CHOSE TO DWELL ON THEM ANYMORE.
DONT GET ME WRONG, I AM OVERWHELMED WITH COMPASSION FOR ANYONE WHO HAD A FUCKED UP CHILDHOOD!! I JUST DONT WANT US TO CONTINUE THE CYCLE AND LIVE FUCKED UP LIVES AND KEEP BLAMING OUR PASTS. I AM FAR FROM WITHOUT PROBLEMS OF MY OWN, AND I TOO CRY AT NIGHT, BUT I AM TRYING REALLY HARD TO FACE THIS SHIT AND TO ACCEPT RESPONSIBILITY. I JUST DONT WANT US TO HOLD OURSELVES BACK AND TIE OURSELVES TO THE MYTH THAT WE CANNOT MAKE A DIFFERENCE.
TURN AROUND, TAKE A HARD LOOK, CRY, WIPE YOUR TEARS, AND THEN TAKE A STEP FORWARD.

African-Americans seem to be gangsta films—although a few good ones have come out, like *Poetic Justice.* I think a lot more needs to be done in film. My boyfriend wants to make films that portray the Mexican experience and not tokenize it, and I know he will.

As a kid I grew up listening to a lot of Mexican and Latino pop music like Tatiana, Menudo and Timbirichi. Today I listen to a lot of different types of music like jazz and roc en español (which is "alternative" music in Spanish). Some of those bands are Maldita Vecindad, Tijuana No and Caifanes. There's also a Mexican punk scene with bands like Attoxico and Masacre 68, plus there's other bands like Empirismo, Huasipungo and Dogma Munditas who are from the U.S. but talk about issues relative to the Chicano struggle.

In high school Danielle got me into Goth music. Maybe I was into it because you could dress up and pretend you were some Romantic or tragic figure. Going to a Gothic club was like being at a fashion show, and it was funny the way people would stare each other down with a look of approval or a look of disapproval, or a look of total envy because you're more gothic than they are! It was about pretending you were experiencing something else; trying to forget about your humdrum life.

The roc en español scene still sucks because there's a lot of accepted genderism: the whole "boy in the pit" thing. Once in a while there's a girl in the pit, but it's rare if she has a cool experience there. Strangely enough, I've never been at a Bikini Kill show where there wasn't slamming; actually, I've never seen people quiet and peaceful at a Bikini Kill show. It's so weird—

♦ DANIELLE: Because we're not in the '80s!

♦ *V: That doesn't seem appropriate, and Kathleen Hanna has spoken out against that—*

♦ S: I saw Bikini Kill at a big Rock for Choice show in '93 at the Palladium. It was an awful experience. People didn't know who Bikini Kill were back then, and the crowd was waiting for Bad Religion to come on. Bad things happened; a man hit this woman with a stick, and a few girls filed a report that there was a man masturbating in the pit. People were sexually assaulting women in the pit—grabbing them. Kathleen Hanna tried to "let the girls come up front," but nobody let them. She was trying to get people to be less violent, but it didn't work out—sometimes it just doesn't.

I saw Bikini Kill at Las Palmas Theater and it was awful. Some "punks" came and started yelling "Feminazi" and "Man-hater" and other bad shit at Kathleen. There were girls there who yelled, "Shut up!" and "Let us watch the band." But obviously these people just came to harass her and the fans.

A boy will say that Riot Grrrls are man-haters, and I'll say, "Have you ever *been* to a Riot Grrrl meeting?"

Revolution Rising had a booth there, and some girl started harassing me. She kept passing by the booth and asking, "Do you sell little barrettes?" and we just ignored her. "Do you sell little shirts that say 'Whore' and 'Slut' on them?" I assumed she was just making fun of the whole Riot Grrrl thing. Pretty soon she just came up and said "Riot Whore!" right in my face. I just thought to myself, "Whatever!"—I didn't want to get into more trouble than I was willing to deal with.

♦ *V: How would you ideally deal with that?*

♦ S: I don't know. You could try to argue, but she looked like she could potentially get her friends to kick my ass or whatever. Even though she was messing with me, I thought it was better to ignore her. It is sad, but there are a lot of girls who feel that way.

♦ *V: They're fighting against their own best interests—*

♦ S: It is weird. They just try to pigeonhole you into some category. It sucks; I hope I never see her again. Kathleen invited all the girls up on the stage, and pretty soon the stage was ready to collapse because there were so many onstage who had felt threatened down below. I didn't want to go up onstage, but I felt like I was alone down on the floor. I tried to prevent some girl and boy from fighting, and the girl got annoyed with me: "Fuck off!" Then she apparently fell down, and in falling grabbed the front of my shirt, exposing my chest to the world. She wouldn't let go—I don't know what she was trying to do. That was a very bizarre evening.

Dani and Sisi. Photo: Tye

A lot of people already have an opinion about Riot Grrrl. A boy will say that Riot Grrrls are man-haters, and I'll say, "Have you ever *been* to a Riot Grrrl meeting? Do you really know what Riot Grrrl is about?" "No." "Then why are you telling me this? I've been to meetings; if anyone should say anything it should be me, not you." But people feel they have to say their piece. Just like those articles that came out in *Seventeen* and *Newsweek,* with that girl Jessica talking about Riot Grrrl. I feel very bad for her because she probably wanted to vent and not hurt anyone, but instead the articles came off diminishing Riot Grrrl to the stereotype of: "They're a bunch of girls and they all have bad haircuts because they all cut each other's hair, and they all wear Doc Martens and messed-up dresses and they all write on each other"—and it's like, "What?!" "And they're all middle-class white girls." Well, I'm not! I've met other Riot Grrrls who weren't white—what about *them?*

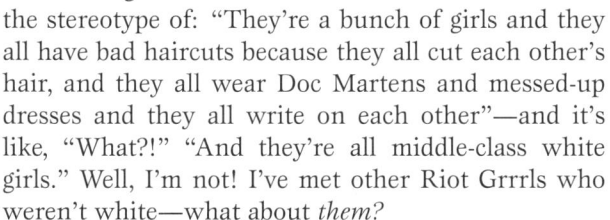

♦ **V: *The mass media obviously doesn't want social change to happen. I still think Riot Grrrl is one of the most important social change movements of this century; it has yet to fulfill its potential—***

There's always something to do to express your disapproval of social norms: through zines, activism or music.

♦ S: Riot Grrrl's coming back. Its "disappearance" had a lot to do with the media and how they portrayed it, and not enough women had the chance to go in there and actually see for themselves what it was about. And even if it's not Riot Grrrl, even if it's just a support group of friends who get together and talk about things that pertain to being a woman, or talk about things they want to do, like activism—like they hate a billboard because it's really degrading—then it's up to them to get together and go, "Let's fuck it up! Let's spray-paint it or put some sticker on a strategic place." There's always something to do to express your disapproval of social norms: through zines, activism or music, it's communication that will help us improve our relations with each other. But no one's gonna do it for you. Being active in any manner can create positive change—I really believe that.

Cover of *Housewife Turned Assassin #3*. Artwork: Fred

REFERENCE: Lists by Sisi

Bands
Bikini Kill, Chumbawamba, Crass, Los Crudos, Dead Kennedys, Digable Planets, Disposable Heroes of Hiphoprisy, Fugazi, F.Y.P., The Gits, Heavens to Betsy, Honey Bane, Life But How To Live It, Lois, Operation Ivy, Raooul, Sleater-Kinney, Spitboy, Subhumans, Tummyache, X-Ray Spex, The Yeastie Girlz

Books
Anaya, Rudolfo: *Bless Me Ultima*
RE/Search: *Angry Women*
Burciaga, Jose Antonio: *Drunk Cultura*
Cisneros, Sandra: *Loose Women; Woman Hollering Creek*
Friday, Nancy: *My Secret Garden*
Hurston, Zora Neale: *Their Eyes Were Watching God*
Moraga, Cherrie & Gloria Anzaldua: *This Bridge Called My Back: Writings by Radical Women of Color*
Morrison, Toni: *Sula*
Viramontes, Helena Maria: *The Moths*
Zinn, Howard: *The People's History of the U.S.*

Zines
Alien c/o Witknee, 17337 Tramonto #306, Pacific Palisades CA 90272
Cometbus c/o Epicenter, 475 Valencia, San Francisco, CA 94113
Function c/o Dawn, 390 61st St, Oakland CA 94608
I'm So Fuckin' Beautiful c/o Nomy, 1505 N.W. Groves Ave, Olympia WA 98502
No Fun c/o Ralf, 965 Johnson Ave, San Diego CA 92103
Pocho c/o Esteban & Lalo, PO Box 40021, Berkeley CA 94704
Slave Goddess c/o Debbie, 501 N. Venice Blvd #13, Venice CA 91307
Sweetheart c/o Princess Robin, 6505 Esplanade #1, Playa Del Rey CA 90293
That Girl c/o Kelli, PO Box 170612, San Francisco CA 94117
Too Far c/o Adrienne, PO Box 40185, Berkeley CA 94704
Wrecking Ball c/o Mary & Erika, 1573 N. Milwaukee Ave #473, Chicago IL 60622

Collage from *Housewife Turned Assassin #1*

INTERVIEW WITH DANI

♦ **VALE: Tell us about growing up and going to school—**

♦ DANI: I grew up in North Hollywood with my mom, dad and brother. When I was five, my dad lost his job due to his inability to function in the real world as a result of alcoholism. (He died four years ago of cirrhosis.) We were on welfare for a few years but I was too young to notice or care. At least we were always fed, clothed and had a home. Luckily, our uncle sold us the house we were living in for next to nothing.

My mom had a few jobs before she found the job she's at now (15 years later). My brother and I were forced to take care of the house and our father at a young age. We were still pretty poor then. In the sixth grade I had five pairs of corduroy pants and five shirts to wear for the year. My peers were sporting *Guess* clothing (I didn't even know what that was). Needless to say, I was made fun of. I shopped at thrift stores long before it was "cool" and used to lie about where I bought my clothes.

My parents never let me go out or go over to friends' houses or have friends over. This left me a bit of a loner. I was not allowed to wear dresses or shorts, either. To add to the pre-teen insecurity I already felt, I had several issues with my appearance. I hated my looks and body. But I was pretty lucky because I went to a Magnet elementary school. This is an integration program—they bussed in kids from everywhere and it was very diverse. I really wasn't color-aware until I got to junior high. Sisi [see preceding interview] and I went to the same junior high, and there were very few Latinos. I am Mexican and have some German and Japanese in me, and I had a friend who, when she introduced me to someone, would say, "She's only *half* Mexican."

♦ **V: I guess that was to rationalize being seen with you—**

♦ D: Exactly. Today I cannot believe I tolerated that. I maintained this friendship for years, but finally I realized, "I can't take those comments anymore." Toward the end of our relationship she would spew out racial slurs about African-Americans or Asians or people of other races, and I would say, "That offends me." She would say, "I don't understand why that would offend *you*" (the implication being that she wasn't talking about someone of *my* race). Needless to say, this friendship is over. I have a much better group of friends now.

I grew up in L.A., but my parents grew up in Colorado and were very big on assimilation. They didn't teach me Spanish. In junior high there was a group of girls who would try to pick fights with me because I didn't know Spanish—I had it from both directions, and really didn't know where the hell I fit in.

In high school Sisi and I were different from most of the kids there. At lunchtime we would have to pass this group of kids at the cafeteria and they would shout "Beetlejuice!" at us *every day*—they never got tired of it (in the film there's a girl who's very morbid and wears all black). People would throw stuff at us and ask us, "Who died?" In the eleventh grade people would fuck with us all the time. It's funny; we weren't very strong women yet, but we became stronger because we were forced to!

I was part of several minorities; at *that* high school if you were Mexican you weren't part of a minority (that was the local community), but if you were anything but trendy, that was taboo, and we were going through a little Gothic phase. My parents forbade me to wear black—I was very suicidal and they connected the two, yet one had nothing to do with the other. They gave me a lot of shit, but that has passed, fortunately.

> **I had a friend who, when she introduced me to someone, would say, "She's only *half* Mexican."**

♦ **V: How did you get over being suicidal?**

♦ D: It was a hell of a process. I was serious about it and had made some very serious attempts. After that, in high school, I went to several counseling groups, talked to a lot of people, and came to terms with it. Things were bad once, but they aren't that bad now.

♦ **V: *You must have been filled with despair and hopelessness—***
♦ D: I just didn't want to look ahead. I was dissatisfied with my life; I really felt I didn't have the energy to deal with anything. I'm making it sound like it was nothing, but that's the way I deal with really intense things: I talk about them casually. But I feel I've gotten over this, and it doesn't pain me to look back on it. I didn't have much personal strength; I had closed myself off to all my friends. I was feeling very alone and disconnected from my family and everybody else, so I didn't feel I had anybody to turn to. Even though there were people there, I didn't realize it. I was just very miserable.

I think that my generation went through a phase of hopelessness, where we just didn't really see anything to look forward to. I see that changing. At the time, I really felt an apathy among my peers as well. Even now, a lot of my peers aren't doing a helluva lot with their lives. The economy's bad, and there's no emphasis put on education whatsoever. There's no money anyway—where are the resources with which to educate people? There's definitely a problem, and it's not the kids—it's society. If there's any hope at all, education is the way out.

Sisi and I used to fantasize about opening an alternative school where people could learn at their own pace, study what they were truly interested in, and learn practical skills. Then we'd have the dilemma of not wanting to turn anybody away! I see many people slightly older than me already at the stage of simply "accepting" everything and giving up on the possibility of social change. But personally, I cannot see myself just accepting bullshit! I never have.

I have suffered discrimination over my facial piercings on many occasions. I was a manager at a coffee bar, but after I got a lip piercing they were going to fire me. They didn't mind my nose piercings, my eyebrow piercing or my tattoos, but they would not tolerate the lip piercing. I had worked for them a long time, and didn't realize there was a problem, but one day out of the blue they said, "Either you take it out or you're fired!" They knew I was a good worker, and knew that legally they'd be in trouble if they fired me, so they decided to make me so miserable that I'd quit. They did a really good job at making me miserable.

The job I have now is pretty cool. Job hunting was hell, and to get hired, I took all my piercings out. After

Dani. Photo: Tye

Free to Fight! "an interactive self defense project" was produced by Candy Ass Records (P.O. Box 42382, Portland, Oregon 97242). $12 ppd

I got the job, slowly but surely I started adding things back, and they never said anything. I guess they know what a good worker I am. I got lucky, because it's a big corporation—a suit-and-tie place and I am allowed to look so different. Also, I'm fairly computer-literate; I work in *Excel* and *Word* daily—I'm a biller and do accounts receivable and accounts payable. I'm studying photography in college and I've studied film.

♦ **V: *What was your earliest rebellion?***
♦ D: At a young age I went through a school-ditching, drug experimenting alcoholic phase. I had a major chip on my shoulder and everyone I encountered felt the brunt of it. I got a fake I.D. and checked out the "Goth" scene and fell in love with it. I loved the clothes, the make-up and had already fallen in love with the music. But it's a very high-maintenance scene! It's such a fashion show about who's cooler than who, and I'm not into that. But it was a way of making myself different from the norm. I started going out and lying to my parents about where I was ("I'm staying overnight at a friend's house"). I was a big Bauhaus and Sisters of Mercy fan; I loved Joy Division and Siouxsie and Alien Sex Fiend. We saw Nine Inch Nails at Helter Skelter before they became famous. I still like the '80s new wave scene with Nina Hagen, Marc Almond (Sisi and I went through a phase where we had posters of him all over our walls) and Gary Neuman.

♦ **V: *How did you get into Riot Grrrl?***
♦ D: It was Sisi. She would always talk about it. She asked me to go to the first meeting, and I went. We met Tyc there (who's in Revolution Rising), and the three of us clicked instantly—that was nice. I thought it was great to see all these girls supporting each other and standing up for themselves. It was a large group and I didn't really express myself; when I'm in smaller groups then I'll talk. We wanted to put together a public-access cable show—that didn't happen, but we still had this desire which became the basis for Revolution Rising. We planned a lot, talked a lot, but never really did anything. I was very discouraged and disappointed that nothing happened—

♦ **V: *Although, I think it's amazing that women can have these meetings—***
♦ D: Oh yeah—I was amazed at how many girls would turn up, all of us with very different backgrounds, sitting in a circle, *connecting.* It was a great thing. I'm sorry that the meetings fell apart, but I hear they're coming back. I don't think Riot Grrrl should ever die; I think it has the potential to be a great vehicle for social change.

> **"Take a stand against records, movies and magazines that put women down and say it's okay to be abusive to women."—HTA #3**

I think the mass media destroyed the L.A. chapter meetings of Riot Grrrl. There are a lot of people who don't want to let the ideal die, and I think they should

Primary Targets diagram from the *Free to Fight!* booklet

totally close themselves off to the public media. They're all smart women; they should do their *own* media—get a camera, get on the radio—just get out there themselves and do something. That's the policy of REVOLUTION RISING. We're very private. We were interviewed by another zine, and we've been on a radio show, but it was college radio and the interviewer was a friend we met through Riot Grrrl. So of course we felt safe there, but that's been the extent of it, because we really want to protect ourselves.

♦ *V: The mass media are pure parasites. They need you so they can create a steady flow of sensational stories, but they never pay you anything or benefit you in any way. They always misrepresent you—that's guaranteed.*

♦ D: If we feel we want to get something out there, we'll get it out ourselves. I remember the meeting when we all sat around trying to decide on a name. Revolution Rising was the most powerful name we could think of; I think the name itself is empowering. We've had pretty good luck; whenever there are problems, we're able to work through them. This is hard when you have a group of people. We've been pretty lucky in terms of getting over conflicts. At that huge

You CAN defend yourself: no one's gonna do it for you! Flyer by Sisi, reprinted in *HTA #3*

YOU CAN DEFEND YOURSELF

The potential 4 being attacked is very much there. Stop feeling like a prisoner in your own body by learning how to use it. It (you) CAN save your life!

You have some options of how you can learn & practice self defense: a training school like (aikido, judo, tae kwon do, kickboxing, etc)/wommin's groups who conduct their own classes/D.I.Y w/ sum friends, grab a book w/ techniques & practice.

• Things to remember: if you choose a training school it will probably be expensive. Make sure the school doesn't cheat you by providing watered-down versions that stress get-away tactics and allow no bodily contact.
• If you start training with friends, practice. Take turns on acting as the attacker and the attacked. Get comfortable with hitting, kicking, punching, etc. Learn the use of your body's motions and potential.
• Physical training is not the only thing you have to practice. Mental/psychic exercises are just as important. Start knowing that you have the power to hit someone. Act confident when you're on the street.
• To lessen the chance of panic and fear, 'cuz these emotions may impair you from remembering what you are capable of. You are less likely to be attacked if you look alert.
• Think of stuff you're wearing to use as makeshift weapons: belt buckle, heavy purse, heavy or sharp shoes, keys, pen, umbrella, etc.
• Or carry something intended for defense: spray bottle with lemon juice, vinegar, hairspray, etc. Be quick to use so attacker won't use it against you.
• If you consider using other weapons like: a gun, knife, or pepper spray, these items may require training as well as licensing.
• A hard and fast knee to the groin (if attacked from the front) is always effective.
• If you get in a bad situation and you feel you are unable to defend yourself, RUN! Go to a well-lit area where there may be people.
• If grabbed from behind move hips to jab elbow into their stomach and follow up by a punch to the back of head.
• If arms are free, chop or punch at their temples, eyes, under the ears, at mouth or nose.
• While you counter-attack, let out a yell (not a scream for help) but a loud battle cry. This will scare the attacker and help you get into a defensive mode.

These are some suggestions that I hope will motivate you.

Bikini Kill show, I was really proud of Sisi when she stuck up for herself when we were caught selling stickers and got kicked out.

♦ **V:** *What are the goals of Revolution Rising?*

♦ **D:** We've had a lot of different goals. Initially we wanted to start a monthly public access TV show, but we got sidetracked doing projects like photo essays, photo projects and films. But it's the goal of the group to still do it, and have programs available on videocassette. We want to be eye-openers, using different media to get people to think twice about things. At least that's a personal goal for me—I don't want to speak for the group. Also, we try to be supportive of artists or anyone who needs a place to display their work—or the encouragement to do it.

Riot Grrrl was encouraging people to express themselves in every medium: "You've never done a zine before? You can do one!"

♦ **V:** *Some informer sneaked into a Riot Grrrl meeting and then viciously defamed it—*

♦ **D:** Yes, and I was there at that meeting, and to this day I don't know who that girl was! It was so frustrating; there were a lot of girls there. It was so awful of her; she's a total traitor to her conscience. How could you be in a group where everybody's gut-spilling and then go report on it in such a negative way? If she had told us who she was, then it would have been up to us to allow her to stay. Personally, I couldn't imagine disrespecting a group like that.

♦ **V:** *That's because you're a decent person.*

♦ **D:** How could she gather such an opinion out of just one meeting? It took me a number of meetings to understand and fully appreciate what Riot Grrrl was all about. I don't know how you could attend just one meeting and know everything about the movement.

Riot Grrrl needs to come back in full strength, because the ideas are so inspiring: having women-only meetings (although I feel that the need for men and women to meet and discuss, understand and destroy the division between them is just as important!) and supporting each other, providing that safe space. There was always talk of starting workshops on self-defense, classism, racism, etc. When we went to the Riot Grrrl convention last summer there were workshops on self-defense and class, and they were so inspirational. We women need to take control of our lives and start learning how to protect ourselves. A friend of mine is trying to get a law passed for elementary school where girls are mandatorily taught self-defense as a P.E. (Physical Education) class. Unfortunately, I really believe this is necessary.

♦ **V:** *It's part of reclaiming and regaining power, not to oppress others with, but to defend the space you're entitled to—*

♦ **D:** Exactly. The "Free to Fight" demonstrations were amazing. At that show we were selling stickers of a woman's symbol combined with a fist, and a man approached and asked what it meant. I said that it basically meant female empowerment. Immediately he snapped, "At the expense of men?"—he was ready to attack! I said, "No, that's not what we're about. It's not about raising yourself up at the expense of another person." Certain people are threatened by a group of strong individuals—that's an idea that will never die out of Riot Grrrl: the strength people give each other.

Also Riot Grrrl was encouraging people to express themselves in *every* medium: "You've never done a zine before? You can do one. You've never been in a band before? You can learn an instrument and be in a band. You want to make a film? Just get a camera and do it."

♦ **V:** *In one zine, I read an article calling for more women to get jobs at music equipment stores, because the men who work there act so superior and unwilling to share information, especially with women. There are so many details to work out in trying to improve life—*

♦ **D:** Every day you have to work on this. Our friend Tye is very sensitive to issues of authoritarian language and verbiage in general. She has taught us a lot. As opposed to "feminist" she calls herself an "equalist"; as opposed to "sexist" she prefers "genderist."

Old Riot Grrrl flyer by Sisi and Dani

♦ **V: And let's face it—the white males have had their day—**
♦ D: Just turn on the TV or look at billboards or print media and there is a desperate need for more people of color everywhere. It's slowly starting to happen. All of my photography and filmmaking has involved diversi-

Housewife Turned Assassin **has gotten letters from Canada, France—all over. It's so amazing how something spreads.**

ty. In all my endeavors I have tried, and will continue to try to include a whole variety of people of color, ages and sizes. Also, it needs to be said that both women and *men* are just as beautiful, and people with different body sizes are also as beautiful. I really feel the need to express the fact that there is no one "beauty"—that *everyone* is beautiful. There's a need to do this in a way that isn't tokenized.

On many occasions Sisi and I have felt like we were being tokenized. We produce one of the few zines that discuss color issues, and we have gotten a lot of letters about this. Although it is nice to receive this feedback, it also makes us feel a bit pandered to. This is a grey area to me: how to tell when you are being tokenized and when you aren't. It's *very* subtle, and it's hard to call people on things—sometimes you don't even realize until *after* it happens—in fact, for me, that's usually

Flyer promoting Housewife Turned Assassin

Sisi's Story

Finally I've seen the obvious. I have been touched by the truth, I have not always been able to say that I love who I am . . . that is, a Chicana/Mexicana/Pocha girl. I looked down upon my heritage, culture, language and customs. Growing up I thought that white was the rightest, smartest, cleanest & best. I couldn't understand why I was cursed with the tight braids, hand-me-downs and imperfect English—I could never explain myself without using my Spanish (it was warm, comforting and seemed almost like a sweet secret).

Everything has been a secret in my life. Don't talk of home or family or you will embarrass yourself. My family's apartment was a pink rough boxed-in thing with our assigned letter "G." I lived in "G," I was lucky that we lived across the street from the park where every summer we went swimming in the lice-infested pool and got our free lunch—stuffed extra milk and napkins in our pockets. I lived in a 2-bedroom space with 7 other people, until my dad got us a 2-bedroom house in Pacoima. Soon our family increased to 9 people—usually we had around 12 people all together. I really felt that our money troubles were inherent in our color and language. It scared me that I felt so much self-hatred and that other people chose not to talk to me because I am a smelly Mexican in their eyes.

I never talked about my living conditions and I was in constant fear that the kids at school would find out stuff like that my dad drinks a lot, my mom doesn't know English, and that my sisters and I had to share clothes. When people asked to come over my house, I would lie and choose from the selection of circumstantial untruths of why they couldn't. "Why did we go to Tijuana so much?" was another constant question. I couldn't say, "Well, it's because my aunt-cousin-grandma-friend needs us to smuggle them across this weekend because they can't afford a coyote." [a coyote is a person you pay hundreds of dollars so they will smuggle you into the U.S.] Harbored secrets. I will give them to you for understanding and self-inspection. This hurts me: I always lied and stretched the truth to my White, Asian & Jewish etc friends. Cuz to be Mexican was a dirty word, an unglamorous culture. I felt spurts of cultural self-acceptance sometimes . . . like when I was in a Mexican dance troupe in elementary & I danced a Norteña (like a country dance) with my sister at an assembly in school. My comfort and smiling heart were crushed. People laughed and called me a beaner and thought it was funny that I wore those clothes and danced that hard and smiled so beautifully while I did it.

—Sisi from *HTA* #3

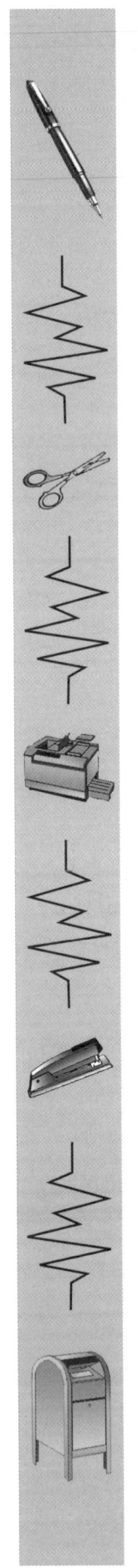

> **RIOT GRRRL IS . . .**
>
> Women who have come together to create a sisterhood designed to support each other & to build a strength that aims at bringing a long overdue change for our equality. It is women who are aware that we are by no means men's "compliment" or a secondary human form which exists to be subjective to men. It is going to build awareness that our place is not in the home but rather our place is out in the world making a difference. Most importantly it is women fighting for women, women helping women & no longer competing with women.
>
> —Dani from *Sheila-Na-Gig*, an L.A. Riot Grrrl zine, 1993

how it is. Afterwards you realize, "I should have said *this*!" I really hate it when I don't react as I should have.

♦ **V:** *Why do you think the ideas of Riot Grrrl haven't reached more people of color?*

♦ **D:** Because musically it's considered a punk rock thing. Yet there are so many girls out there who aren't punk rock, like "151" [young rapper from Portland, featured on the *Free to Fight* compilation CD]. These people have a lot to say and can offer support—maybe they need support as well. But they don't feel like they fit into the punk rock scene. I really hope this changes.

The "Free to Fight" tour featured more spoken word or folk music (like LOIS) than punk rock. But overall, Riot Grrrl is punk rock. That happens to have been where it started, but I think it's been around long enough to branch out. A lot of the punk rock scene is socially aware—that's what makes them do what they do. I just think there are a lot of girls out there who could use the empowerment who aren't necessarily into punk rock. There is some diversity in Riot Grrrl, but it's not as broad as it could be. Actually, there was a lot of diversity on the "Free to Fight" tour.

During the women-only self-defense workshops, we were all able to take turns practicing moves, and this was very helpful. It makes you feel like you can *do it*—you *can* fight back. I just wish more girls would look into learning self-defense, because it's so necessary. It might actually save you, because if you walk with confidence ("Yes, I can stand up for myself")—well, people are animals and they can *read* that.

♦ **V:** *At the heart of Riot Grrrl is the empowerment that "you can do it yourself—in fact, you* **have to**.*"*

♦ **D:** The gist of it is the strength of standing on your own and taking action.

♦ **V:** *How do you actually produce* **Housewife Turned Assassin?**

♦ **D:** So many people asked who wrote what that we started putting our initials in the corner. Of the two of us, Sisi is the better writer—if anything's great, she probably wrote it. We just write whenever we feel inspired—when something pisses us off, or when we want to say something. We start pasting down what we have; we don't necessarily write *for* the zine, we just write, and some of it ends up making it into the zine.

♦ **V:** *That seems quite natural; it doesn't sound contrived. Do you use a manual typewriter?*

♦ **D:** Sometimes—it depends on where I'm working! It is important to not have our zine be contrived. That's why our last zine took over a year to put out. We were not about to put out a shitty zine just to get it out. Some people have the energy to publish regularly, and I say, "Lucky them!"

♦ **V:** *Tell us more about Revolution Rising; it seems like a natural extension of the rebellious spirit you encountered in Riot Grrrl—*

♦ **D:** We started with a small group and didn't want to exclude anybody. Some people have come and gone, and contributed a lot while they were part of the group. We don't want to be this exclusive little club; we want to have open energy and not shut anyone out for any reason. We're not hierarchical.

We just write whenever we feel inspired—when something pisses us off, or when we want to say something.

Some people have written asking how to be a part of Revolution Rising, or how to start a branch of Revolution Rising, and we just send them all the literature we have, all our zines, and tell them, "This is what we do. You can do whatever you want. If you feel power using the name, then use the name. We just want to encourage you to do this yourself—not necessarily to join *our* group." It's a lot easier to do something when you have more people involved, like to make t-shirts or produce stickers or zines—all that is time-consuming and it's nice to have help.

Housewife Turned Assassin has gotten letters from Canada, France—all over. It's so amazing how some-

> **Catcall Retaliation Ideas**
>
> 1. Make funny faces: stick your tongue out, cross your eyes, etc
> 2. Fart (if you have the enviable power of farting on command) or carry a stink bomb. Let it off and run very fast.
> 3. Spit out a huge loogey, while making lovely noise to disgust them further.
> 4. Stare at their crotch and laugh.
> 5. Shout "Suck My Dick!"
> 6. Start singing show tunes (anything from "The Sound of Music" loudly).
> 7. Just yell the first thing that comes to mind (e.g., "Yeah, well you look like Mick Jagger!" or try this one, "I think I hear your mother calling."
>
> —Kristen (Bomb) from *HTA* #3

thing spreads. I think it's incredible that somebody across the world is inspired by some tragedy in your life, or some venting of your anger, and it gives you a good feeling—it was well worth it to do all the work of putting out a zine. Zines go all over the place—we get them from all over, too—and I think it's a great little community of people who communicate this way, educating each other.

♦ **V: One purpose of a zine is to share experiences—**

♦ D: We've heard some great stories. It helps us with our problems—to know that somebody else out there had to deal with them, too. Have you read *I'm So Fuckin' Beautiful* by Nomy Lamm—she's great. Apparently she's gotten a ton of feedback from girls who can relate to her problems. She's sarcastic and funny as she deals with body issues and the fucked-up way she's been treated. She has reached so many girls who are afraid or embarrassed to talk about these issues. I think it's so great that she has the courage to say, "This is how I am and this is what I've dealt with and this is how I'm going to deal with life now." I admire her for doing that.

♦ **V: How do you deal with harassment?**

♦ D: I'm not a violent person and I've been lucky—I haven't been too fucked with physically, at any rate. Sisi and I were chased once by some guys, but it's strange—I can't remember why this happened. I've had to run from men several times; one time it was when I was walking to my car late at night.

As for verbal harassment—that's happened many,

Drawing by Sheryl, from *Shelf Life* PO Box 91260, Santa Barbara, CA 93110, reprinted in *Revolution Rising* #5

"No one can make you feel inferior without your consent."
—Eleanor Roosevelt, 1937

many times. Now *that* is a fact of life; that is a daily occurrence. And the wittier you are, the more you frustrate the hecklers and make them feel stupid. In *HTA* #2 we printed a section on catcall retaliation, and a lot of girls sent us their suggestions which we printed in *HTA* #3. There are some pretty funny ones—I've actually used a few myself!

I hate to see people sit around and complain about things in their immediate life; I always think, "Then do something about it!" I think a lot of people don't realize the power that they hold. They have *voices*, for godssake. Anybody can do something and make a difference. I think more people need to realize that they alone have the power to make a difference. It's just a matter of doing it. ◆

REFERENCE
Recommended in *HTA*:

Books
The Complete Guide to Women's Health
Our Bodies, Our Selves
Take Care of Yourself
The Wellness Encyclopedia

Information
Open Magazine Pamphlet Series, PO Box 2726, Westfield NJ 07091. Any of this pamphlet series such as "Reproductive Freedom: Our Right to Decide," by Marlene F. & Loretta Ross; "Women & Abortion: The Body as Battleground," by R. Baxandall; "Gulf War Policy," by Noam Chomsky; "Compassionate Society," by Helen Caldicott; "Black America," by Manning Marable, etc.

More Books
Acuna, Rodolfo: *Occupied America, A History of Chicanos*
Barbach, Lonnie: *For Yourself: the Fulfillment of Female Sexuality*
Barnes, Djuna: *Nightwood*
De Leon, Arnoldo: *They Called Them Greasers*
Friday, Nancy: *Women On Top*
Gornick, V. & Barbara M.: *Women in a Sexist Society*
Kuhn, Annette: *The Power of the Image*
McCullers, Carson: *The Ballad of the Sad Cafe & Other Stories*
Melamed, Elissa: *Mirror, Mirror: The Terror of Not Being Young*
Melville, Margarita: *Twice a Minority*
Plath, Sylvia: *The Bell Jar*
Portillo, Estella: *Day of the Swallows*
Root, Jane: *Pictures of Women: Sexuality*

Films
El Norte
Roger & Me
Who Killed Vincent Chin

Meat Hook

Tye publishes *The Meat Hook*. In '87 she began producing newsletters ("pre-zines") as well as feminist short films. After an involvement in Riot Grrrl she helped found the Revolution Rising collective. For a copy of *The Meat Hook,* send $2 to TYE c/o Revolution Rising, PO Box 2743, Los Angeles CA 90078. Voicemail for Revolution Rising: (213) 368-4630.

♦ *VALE: When did you first put out a zine?*
♦ TYE: In 1987, when I was twenty, I started putting out *newsletters.* That's what I called them; it was before I'd ever heard of "zines." They weren't punky because I missed the whole punk rock scene.

After high school, I went to film school from 1984-88 because I thought it would be fun and creative—and not boring. I made some films, and every single one of them either dealt with rape or being stared at on the street—just being exploited, basically. All my school papers were about either eating disorders or being violated as a woman.

The summer before my senior year I was depressed. Then I thought, "I have to do something with my energy and my anger. What would make me feel better? If there were a group of people who could work together on gender issues, that would make me feel better." When school started, I received a $1,000 grant from school to fund regular discussion group meetings. That was when I started mailing out newsletters. I had this mailing list of about 200 names, and every other week I'd produce something and send it out. I'd put up equalist-issue flyers that said things like, "What's wrong with this picture?" Students would write cruel things on the flyers—like "Nothing but what an ugly dyke feminist would mind."
♦ *V: You recently did a documentary with a pixelvision camera—*
♦ T: It's a Fisher-Price $99 camera that was sold at toy stores. It uses standard audio cassettes. You shoot the "film" and hook the camera up to a TV to see the images. You can transfer and then edit, just like editing a video.

My aunt sent me the camera, which was broken, but my best friend fixed it in five minutes—basically, the batteries were corroding and he cleaned it out. Revolution Rising raised $150 so I could make this documentary. I shot 20 hours of footage, interviewing my friends, Revolution Rising members and my family. A friend has an editing studio, and I worked the bar at his shows in exchange for free editing time.

The documentary started off being about eating disorders but ended up being about body image as well. I edited it down to 13 minutes, but I'm going to make a two-hour version. Hopefully I'll keep on interviewing people forever and just have different installations featuring the newest footage. It's black and white and very gossamer-looking—it looks a bit like Super 8. The sound is really clear because it's recorded on an audio tape.
♦ *V: This seems like the cheapest filmic medium to work in—*
♦ T: I don't know why they quit making the cameras. Lately there's been this big resurgence of interest in them, and I've heard rumors that a new and improved version will come out. But really, the original camera is the "raddest," because it's so funky. Jean Cocteau said, "Film will become an art when its materials are as inexpensive as pencil and paper."
♦ *V: Where did you get the impetus to produce work on feminist issues?*
♦ T: Just living my life. But what I just thought of

when you asked was: maybe it had something to do with an early babysitter. He was a 17-year-old teenager. When I was about six years old I remember asking him, "Hey, how come women are always on the covers of magazines? Why are their breasts always showing?" He said, "It's because we like it, and it looks good." I said, "Oh—okay." I don't know if he molested me or my brother, but I do know that he used to get us to take showers with him and I think weird things would happen. I wonder if *this* had an impact on what I did later? [laughs sardonically]

I've had to work through some fairly common difficulties. When growing up I remember being obsessed with movie and TV stars like Jean Harlow, Cher, and Marilyn Monroe—all these sex symbols. As I became an adult I was bulimic from ages 15-23—I was really into trying to control my weight and look a certain way. But I knew this was crazy. I once read in a book called *A Feminist Dictionary* [Cheris Kramarne & Paula A. Treichler, Pandora Press, 1985] that bulimics are actually very angry—every time they throw up, they're throwing up their anger and resentment at society. I tried to meet the social ideal of thinness, but in the process of trying to make myself "perfect" I chose a very violent way to express my resentment.

I know I still internalize this because sometimes I don't want to go out and function in the world because I feel that I'm too ugly. I feel that I'm too fat. I don't have the money to buy the clothes others have. I feel like I don't look the way I should, and there are all these women who do, and who the hell am I to go out there in the world and function? Which I know is *irrational,* but sometimes that feeling is so strong, it takes everything I have just to show up at work and earn a living, just so I can pay my rent and not be homeless.

I thought, "I have to do something with my energy and my anger. If there were a group of people who could work together on gender issues, that would make me feel better."

I really believe that all work is the same work. I was waiting tables in a restaurant and the dishwashers earn the least. Which to me made no sense, because if those plates weren't clean, what would customers eat off?

♦ **V: Work is part of the whole enormous oppressive system. One thing everyone can do is to become sensitive to the language they use—**

♦ T: I used to say "Hey, man" a lot—similar to "Hey, dude, guys, brotherhood." So I quit saying it. I used to use the word "genius" all the time, but I was reading this book on the Guerrilla Girls and they don't use the word "genius" because it derives from a Latin word

Tye (right) with Dani from the Revolution Rising Collective. Photo: Sisi

which means "testicles." Isn't that intense? Language totally reflects and shapes our thoughts—

♦ **V: —and restricts our thoughts—that's the scariest thing of all. These days people are very conscious about resisting labels and categorizations—**

♦ T: Language needs to change so much. It is heavily weighted in favor of men and patriarchy, and against women and children. Notice the priority implied in the standard phrase "men, women and children." But take this word "genius." How many people know that it's derived from "testicles"? If so many people don't know, is using the word a problem?

The reason I started using the word "genderist" rather than "sexist" is—to use the word "sexist" is to talk about sex. When we use the word "sexism," generally we think about women. But really, there's another word that's just as good, and it's "gender." The word includes both women and men, and doesn't have any confining associations with sex and sexuality.

I don't use the word "feminism" either, I use the word "equalist," because to me "feminist" is another way of separating women. I think both genders are oppressed, so I don't see any service in separating them and saying, "Women Power." It's about people having equality. It's about all living beings, including the planet, having equality—

♦ **V: I don't know if "equalist" will catch on. It seems that until recently a lot of women were ashamed to call themselves "feminists." Now people are reclaiming that word . . . A key feminist idea that was adopted by Riot Grrrl was the necessity for women-only meetings in a women-only space—**

♦ T: It's important for women to have a safe space; historically women have not had this. But we have to move toward women and men being able to meet in a safe space and create communication and understand-

Cover of *The Meat Hook* #4

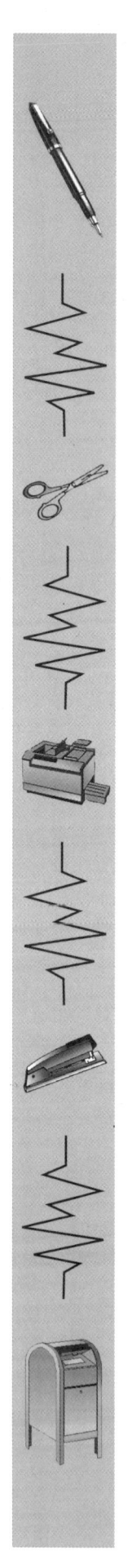

ing. In *You Just Don't Understand,* Deborah Tannen writes about how men and women communicate differently and therefore messages get crossed.

♦ **V: A Woman's Guide to the Language of Success** *says that in power negotiations women often say "I," which signals indecision, while men say "we." There are so many subtle codes to uncover which reinforce hierarchy and status. As we uncover them, we can spread the word about them—*

♦ T: —literally!

♦ **V:** *Imagine little groups of people scanning and dissecting all language for anything that reinforces hierarchical relationships. This kind of speech works most successfully when we're the least aware of it—that's scary. Small change of subject: did you feel excitement when you first heard about Riot Grrrl and went to meetings?*

♦ T: Total and complete excitement; I couldn't wait. I read an article about them in the *L.A. Weekly* and thought, "Ohmigod!" Kathleen Hanna from Bikini Kill was quoted as saying, "Because I live in a world that hates women and I am one who is struggling desperately not to hate myself, my whole life is felt as a contradiction." [*Jigsaw* fanzine quote reproduced in *L.A. Weekly*] I thought, "That's how I've been feeling my whole life. That's so articulate; it's exactly how I feel." After I became abstinent from bulimia and drinking, I would cut myself and hit myself—I think that was my "next" way of trying to hurt myself. I don't know if it was because I "naturally" hate myself, or because the world hates me, or because the world hates women, or the world hates everybody (and I don't do that anymore, by the way). I think it's important to be honest about this, because I think there are other people out there who have bulimia, or who are alcoholic, or who have cut themselves and hit themselves. I think it's important to get out there and talk about it. I liked what Kathleen said, so I was totally excited to get into Riot Grrrl.

The first meeting I went to was awful, but the second was one of the most amazing meetings I'd ever been to. There were all kinds of women, all ages, nationalities, all different body sizes and body types, mostly different clothing styles, and they were all aware and smart and sexy and beautiful. I thought, "Wow—who are these women? Where do they come from? This is great!" And they had zines—something I'd been doing. It was raining outside; I love the rain. We met at somebody's apartment and we talked about important issues, and it was just totally empowering.

♦ **V:** *That's an archetype to always keep in mind: no one's telling these people to get together, or paying them to get together, but these women are getting together to discuss issues related to social change—*

♦ T: Exactly. That's how I felt when I first read a Riot Grrrl zine, before I went to the meeting. It was a tiny zine from Olympia, Washington, filled with all these contributions from different Riot Grrrls about whatever they wanted to say. One of the most amazing statements I read was by Allison from BRATMOBILE: "Riot Grrrl, to me, is about us grrrls taking over the means of production together to create and recreate actions and images which actively challenge the status quo in our lives; to utilize the means of production accessible to us in a manner which challenges dominant standards of professionalism, due to who I am as a non-adult white-anglo bisexual punk rock new wave middle-class girly-girl." She was talking about using sound equipment, music equipment, film equipment, video equipment, computers—anything that a woman might be afraid to use. And who cares if you don't do it like a fuckin' genius! Just do it.

Jean Cocteau said, "Film will become an art when its materials are as inexpensive as pencil and paper."

That's when I started realizing how great "punk" was, because punk had just passed me by—I thought it was goofy. But now I realize how amazing the punk rock ethic is: "You just do it yourself." And that's what Riot Grrrl represented to me: just doing it yourself,

> **Language needs to change so much. Notice the priority implied in the standard phrase "men, women and children."**

but with a more specific application. Music, films, and creativity in general is powerful—it moves you, it makes you feel good and it's a tool for social change. Punk was the first time I actually saw women making powerful music—before that, it was mostly just women doing folk or pop or sex material. There's nothing wrong with being sexual or having fun, but there's something really great about being angry, screaming, or even not being angry but screaming anyway.

♦ **V: The Riot Grrrl records are a genuine musical breakthrough. These kinds of thoughts and lyrics have virtually never been expressed in songs before—**

♦ T: The whole Riot Grrrl music phenomenon is amazing . . . I felt strong hearing Seven Year Bitch—they blew my mind. I saw them with Tribe 8—the lead singer took off her shirt and I thought, "That is so cool." But then, someone said onstage (I don't know whether they were talking about Tribe 8 or Seven Year Bitch), "They're great; they have the best tits in town." I thought, "Once again, we're talking about tits, and which women have great tits," and it pissed me off—I fell into the lonely place in my brain where I feel no one sees what I see, or feels what I feel. Is this just one more example of women having to show their bodies? And then get *judged* on their bodies?

♦ **V: That was a very reduc-** tionist remark, and it's not funny. Onstage Tribe 8 are wild (or even threatening to some people)—no wonder someone tried to cut them down. Besides, Lynn Breedlove [lead singer] taking off her shirt is breaking a taboo; why is that illegal? A man can take off his shirt in public; why should it be illegal for a woman to do that?

♦ T: One of my favorite songs by Fugazi, "Suggestion," asks, "Why can't I walk down the street free of suggestion?"

♦ **V: One of the Riot Grrrl arguments is: "I have the right to dress sexy, or any way I please, and you do not have the right to interpret this as 'I am making myself available to you.' "**

Illustration by Tye from The Meat Hook #4

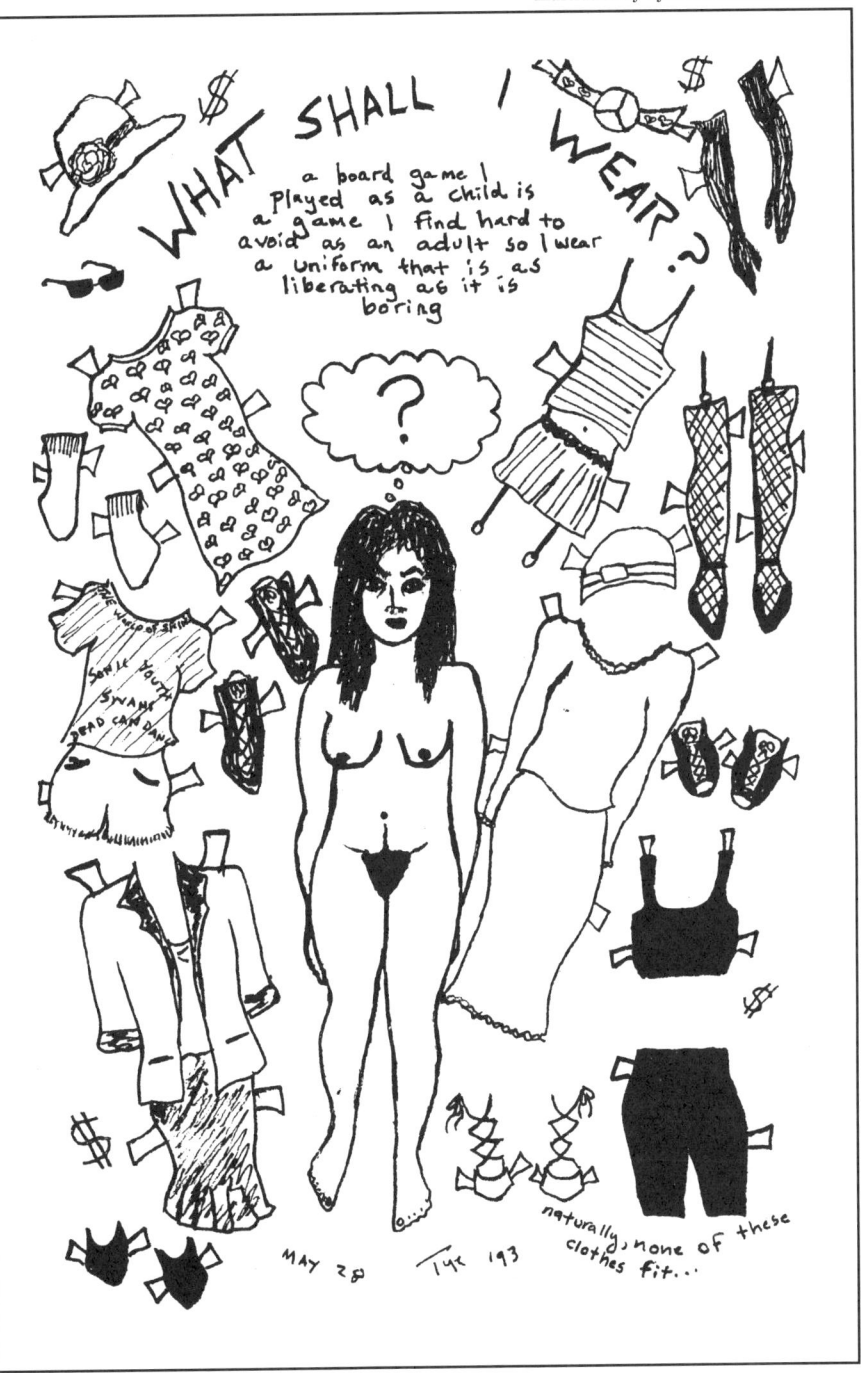

♦ T: People used to say to me in college, "How can you be a feminist—you look like such a slut!" I used to wear fishnet stockings and mini-skirts and high heels because I felt insecure and also because I wanted to feel like a female, but I also thought, "Why can't I wear what I want to, without having people make these judgments?" Truthfully, I know the reason I dressed that way was because I *did* want to look attractive by society's standards, but later I dressed that way to prove my point: "I can wear whatever the hell I want, and it's not an invitation." I still believe that.

Anyway, the second Riot Grrrl meeting gave me a glimpse of *what could be,* whereas the first Riot Grrrl meeting gave me a glimpse of *what could be that I wouldn't like.* And that's what Riot Grrrl was—it was a mixture. I remember one girl didn't want to discuss race at all; she thought gender was the issue—which *I* took issue with, because race and gender and economics are all related.

♦ ***V: An "issue" means that something's not resolved—that it remains confusing. I still think Riot Grrrl represents the future, because it springs from deep-seated needs which have definitely not been fulfilled.***

When something bothers you, you don't know every nuance and every causal factor involved, but you know something's wrong, and the cause is usually complex. It takes a lot of time, effort and discussion to even shed a small amount of light. So to treat Riot Grrrl as some flavor of the month, as the media tried to do, completely denies the fact that it arose because there was a true need for it to arise. Riot Grrrl may be a label, but the reality behind it means a lot, and that reality won't go away. Why should anyone allow mainstream media to denigrate it?

When someone announces a Riot Grrrl Convention, you know exactly what you're going to get: rebel-feminist music, self-defense workshops and lots of discussions dealing with sexism, racism, classism, homophobia, ageism, job oppression—everything that's wrong with society. And hopefully you'll get to meet like-minded souls. That Riot Grrrl "label" still attracts people who fervently desire social change. The media tries to dissipate anything that could possibly function as a focal point or magnet for sustained rebellion by reducing it to some "fashion" that can then go "out of date"—

♦ T: Exactly; I agree. And that's also why we're stuck in mindless jobs, or jobs that pretend to give us a purpose—to prevent a revolution. Until we all stop participating in the oppression we call our lives—work, bills, marriage, lots of kids, cars, so-called property, and our mass-addicted consumerism—we will never know revolution. If we stopped, just stopped this stupid race for a glossy lie, we would know freedom . . .

Kathleen Hanna from Bikini Kill was quoted as saying, "Because I live in a world that hates women and I am one who is struggling desperately not to hate myself, my whole life is felt as a contradiction."

There's a debate about the word "grrrl" in Riot Grrrl. Some people say they're reclaiming the word "girl" and other women say, "I'm too old to be called a *girl*." However, my mom and I are doing a zine together (she's 51) and I know she loves the idea of Riot Grrrl! In a way I think it's really great—it's taking back the word "girl." I think little girls are anarchists, but at the same time I'm thinking, "We're women, not girls; that term will alienate a lot of women."

♦ ***V: But if anyone chooses to be alienated by the term, it's her loss—she hasn't had firsthand experience of going to a meeting and feeling the support and empowerment. It's not like women have had all their rights restored to them. Riot Grrrl is about reclaiming rights—not privileges, but just plain rights. Again, everyone owes it to herself to be exposed firsthand to the sources: go to a meeting and read an original zine, not a mass media distortion.***

♦ T: I'm 29. When I first heard about Riot Grrrl, I thought it was a *miracle* (I was 26 at the time). When I got my first Riot Grrrl zine, I thought it was totally cool. A lot of zines I've gotten have been doodled with flowers and hearts (Gloria Steinem, in her book *Revolution from Within,* talks about the meaning of the heart and how it's actually a procreative genital symbol, a female version of the phallic symbol, a symbol of female power. She realized this when looking at photos of prehistoric archeological finds).

Sometimes I felt extremely alienated because I was older and didn't wear these cute little punk rock out-

Cover of Revolution Rising #3

fits, and because I didn't go to a lot of shows, and because I didn't shave my head or dye my hair purple. A lot of girls didn't really pay attention to me because of that, which made me think, "Gee, that's the problem with a group that's associated with a look." And I don't know if that's the media's fault or what. But I stuck with Riot Grrrl because I believe in the *ideals,* and I met a few women like Sisi and Danielle— the three of us look completely different. Danielle looks like Goth trash, Sisi looks like punk trash and I look more like slutty trash! [laughs] We're really different and we all have different musical tastes, but we *connected* through Riot Grrrl. Which is why I like what you said: "If you can remember the meeting that was great, then you have a vision of what it could be." And that's what keeps me around.

Tye, January 1996. Photo: Sisi

♦ V: *Times are so tough that we hold onto any little glimmers of the future to sustain us. It is vision that creates the future, yet it's easy to lose that vision because it's so hard to survive—you're constantly being brought down to these mundane, grubby levels of preoccupation. Society's brutality forces people to do all these horrible things just to pay the rent or get by . . . Anyway, you've gotten involved in Revolution Rising—*

"Riot Grrrl, to me, is about us grrrls taking over the means of production together to create and recreate actions and images which actively challenge the status quo in our lives."

♦ T: Revolution Rising is pretty cool. There've been some fights and arguments and times when we all wanted to quit, and I'm sure this group means something different to everybody, but we've been together for two years. A few people have left and a few new people have joined, but it's pretty cool. We've done every kind of project together; we've done quite a lot. And the important thing is: we raise funds for people who would otherwise have no funds with which to create.

I remember how bad I felt after Sisi and Danielle and I quit going to Riot Grrrl meetings. About six months passed before we all got together just to save our asses and do something creative. And it evolved into a group. I can't speak for everybody, but I know that the three of us still believe in the Riot Grrrl ideals—they mean so much to all of us. So Revolution Rising gives me a specific focus with a creative outlet. Actually, Revolution Rising and Riot Grrrl are very similar; the only difference is that men are involved. Everything else is almost identical: the ideals of equality, the collective, creativity, personal and societal evolution, revolution, empowerment and change. And no *hierarchy.* V

REFERENCE

Non-Fiction
Berger, John: *Ways of Seeing*
Doane, Mary Ann & Patricia Mellencamp & Linda Williams, eds: *Re-Vision: Essays in Feminist Film Criticism*
Kaplan, E. Ann: *Women in Film Noir*
Kuhn, Annette: *The Power of the Image: Essays on Representation and Sexuality*

Fiction
Atwood, Margaret: *Cat's Eye; The Handmaid's Tale*
French, Marilyn: *The Women's Room*
Piercy, Marge: *Woman on the Edge of Time*

Films
Barfly
Dog Day Afternoon
Maya Deren's *Meshes of the Afternoon*

X-Ray

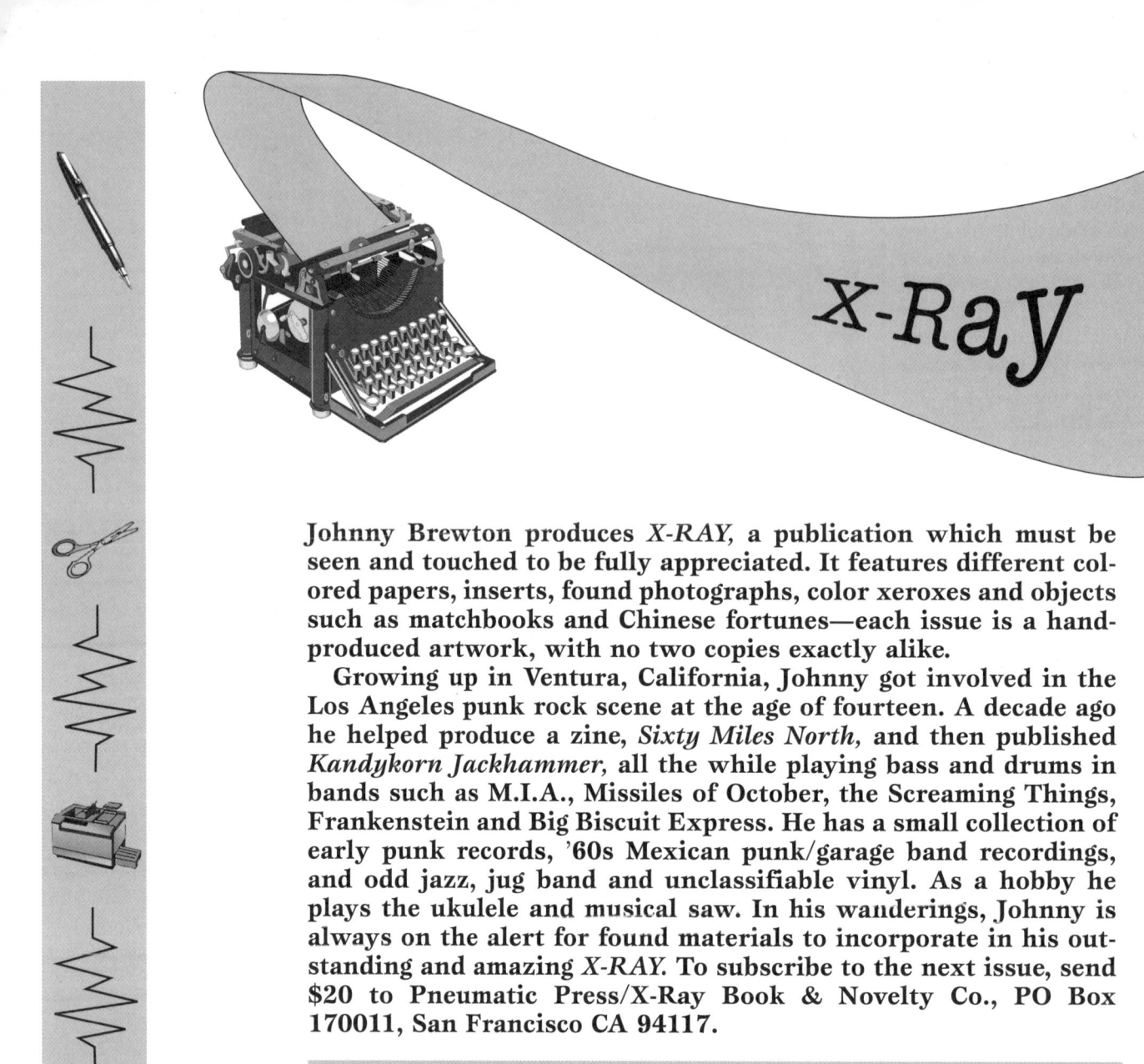

Johnny Brewton produces *X-RAY*, a publication which must be seen and touched to be fully appreciated. It features different colored papers, inserts, found photographs, color xeroxes and objects such as matchbooks and Chinese fortunes—each issue is a hand-produced artwork, with no two copies exactly alike.

Growing up in Ventura, California, Johnny got involved in the Los Angeles punk rock scene at the age of fourteen. A decade ago he helped produce a zine, *Sixty Miles North*, and then published *Kandykorn Jackhammer*, all the while playing bass and drums in bands such as M.I.A., Missiles of October, the Screaming Things, Frankenstein and Big Biscuit Express. He has a small collection of early punk records, '60s Mexican punk/garage band recordings, and odd jazz, jug band and unclassifiable vinyl. As a hobby he plays the ukulele and musical saw. In his wanderings, Johnny is always on the alert for found materials to incorporate in his outstanding and amazing *X-RAY*. To subscribe to the next issue, send $20 to Pneumatic Press/X-Ray Book & Novelty Co., PO Box 170011, San Francisco CA 94117.

♦ **VALE: Can you describe X-RAY?**
♦ JOHNNY BREWTON: It's a literary and an assemblage magazine, but it isn't snooty or arty. It incorporates comics, interviews, film transparencies, tickets—all kinds of found objects. Maybe it's easier if someone else describes it. The *International Directory of Little Magazines and Small Presses* wrote: "*X-RAY* is a literary and art magazine. Recent contributors include Charles Bukowski, Neeli Cherkovski, Jack Micheline and Hunter S. Thompson. Correspondence artists are encouraged to contribute. Accepting short fiction, poetry, erotica, prose, found poems, found objects, assemblage, original art, comics, interviews, photography, etc. Materials range from a Chinese telephone directory to sheet music from the early 1900s to hemp and colored kraft paper. Every page is a different paper. Chapbooks can be found within the pages stuffed into envelopes and fold-out broadsides also grace the pages. When sending original art keep layout to the right of the binding edge at least 1½". Use permanent adhesives and pigments. Size is 8½ x 7" exactly. Send one completed piece for approval. After approval, send at least 226 pieces as the edition is limited to 226. Publishes 23% of manuscripts submitted. Payment: one copy."

I try to include content that is relevant, with an emphasis on ideas. One issue was on the theme of "chance" and included an interview with John Cage.
♦ **V: On this theme, Buckminster Fuller had the idea of constructing a school without walls, so if you're taking a class on one subject, you're able to overhear other classes and possibly make connections between topics not usually associated.**
♦ JB: I also included some found poetry, a fortune suggester, and someone sent a painting cut into 226 pieces and glued to the pages.

I try and keep a good balance going and not use too much assemblage or poetry. People will read an inter-

Johnny Brewton. Photo: Robert Waldman

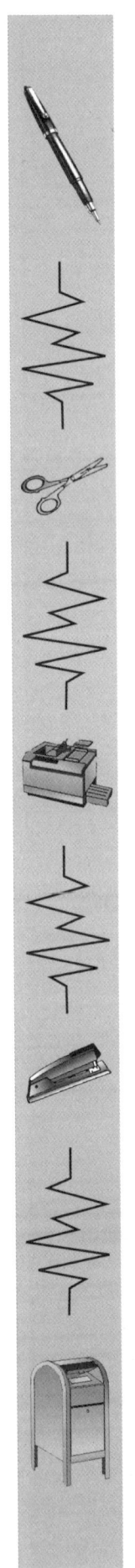

view for awhile, put it down, pick it up again and look at the comics . . . it's not so exhausting. If you see a big thick book of poetry, I think it really wears you out. But if you bump into a poem, you might actually read it.

♦ **V: What's the size of X-RAY?**

♦ JB: My publication is 8½x7˝. I chose this half legal size because there weren't too many magazines that size out there. This size is problematic since manufacturers don't make really nice paper in legal size—if they did, we could just fold it or cut it in half. So we have to work with letter size 8½x11˝ if we want a nicer paper, which leaves us with 4 inches to either discard or print a broadside with. I try and put everything to use.

♦ **V: You produce the most beautiful hand-made zine on a no-money budget. What were your influences?**

♦ JB: The Lujon Press, which produced *The Outsider* (1963), has been a big influence on my hand-made limited editions. It's self-described as a "book/periodical," and the issue I own, No. 3, is pretty rare. It has a lot of different types and textures of paper, and is rubber-stamped "printed by hand in New Orleans."

♦ **V: Bukowski is on the cover, and inside there's a great series of photos of him at the typewriter, cigarette dangling from his mouth. This copy of The Outsider contains an interesting W. S. Burroughs piece: "Take it to Cut City, USA: the area of Total Pain, Total Alert, Total War" . . . Who else influenced you?**

♦ JB: My dad taught me how to read with *MAD* magazine. Art Spiegelman's *RAW* was influential: cardboard cover, trading cards inside. Black Sparrow Press's limited editions are another influence—they use expensive papers, letterpress and produce some beautiful books, chapbooks and broadsides—great design work. I have the Black Sparrow bibliography and there are some amazing Bukowski books listed, as well as books by Wanda Coleman, Paul Bowles, Creeley, etc. But for someone like Rexroth to say that Bukowski's books were *too* nice for his work is bullshit. Just read *Crucifix in a Deathhand* (Lujon Press) and tell me this wasn't written by a man possessed with pure genius. A lot of people think of him as just some womanizing beer-drinker, but he sure had some nice books published during his lifetime.

Another influence was this PBS documentary on a painter, which I saw when I was 7 years old. I had to do some research to find out who he was, but this show completely changed my life. There was this bald guy with a cigarette throwing paint—it turned out to be Jackson Pollock. He blew me away; that was probably my earliest influence. When I think about it, the hair on my arms stands up.

♦ **V: Just seeing him do this anarchic display—**

♦ JB: He had such style doing what he did. I don't know why, but that documentary hit me like a ton of bricks. I *had* to find out more about his work, so I went to the library and read all these books and word-of-mouth biographies (the kind where people talk about having known him). He was very serious about what he was doing, and didn't know if his work would be accepted or not. It happened to be accepted, but that was just what he did. I liked his outlook and his determination.

♦ **V: X-RAY is definitely an unusual concept. You've taken zine publishing far away from conventional xerox production values. Yet you probably had very little capital to begin publishing with—**

♦ JB: When I started I had nothing at all. I'd just moved to the Bay Area and didn't even have a bank account. I started out doing a little bit at a time, and gradually accumulated enough sheets to produce a small number of books. I did a limited edition because even though my budget was non-existent, I could still make something really nice if I only did 200 copies. In order to mass produce something beautiful, you need a lot of money.

♦ **V: I see you as an anachronism—in a good way, of course. What you're doing is radical: taking all these found materials and incorporating them, but not just any found materials—you're very selective—**

♦ JB: I'm influenced by a lot of things: this city, what I come across on my way to work, the people, the noise, the crime—everything goes into the pot. *X-RAY* includes a variety of found materials. I like to number them with old coat-check tags. I incorporate carved rubber stamps and an embosser to add to the handmade feel. The title page always has an overlay of vellum. I like this page to look like it comes from an old book: the kind with marbled papers that you might find in an antiquarian bookstore. The title page also has a different icon for each issue. The fifth issue I'm

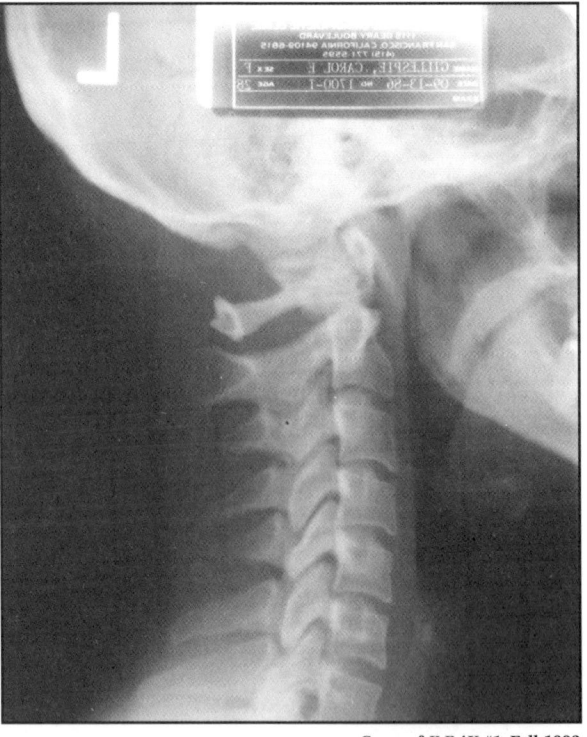

Cover of X-RAY #1, Fall 1993

working on now will use this drawing of a gorilla at a typewriter I found years ago.

Handwork is the main quality. I wanted to create something that was *not disposable*—something that people would keep and show to their friends. But it takes a lot of work; plus I like to embellish things and go the extra mile. When I wanted to have a real x-ray cover, I went to a metal-reclaiming junkyard, dug through all these bins and managed to pick out a few hundred x-rays. When Mark Van Slyke contributed a few hundred tiny cards that said things like "I saw you masturbate" or "I'm retarded—please give what you can," I searched until I found some tiny envelopes that fit them perfectly, then glued them onto old sheets of accounting paper that were probably from the '50s. I like old weathered paper.

♦ **V: *Each contributor gets paid in one copy, so this isn't exactly done for profit—***
♦ **JB:** No. Out of the 226 copies printed, I only have 160 to sell; the other copies go to the contributors. I have to pay for various print jobs, such as the one done for Hunter S. Thompson. He wanted to contribute, and I suggested the cover. He wasn't sure what he wanted to do, but he wanted to incorporate his gun and shoot something. We agreed on the photo of Marilyn Chambers as the Ivory Snow girl, and I had about 300 printed and mailed to him. He kissed a number of them (that's his lip print there; he put on lipstick and kissed a few). The photos were in stacks of 25, and he shot bullets

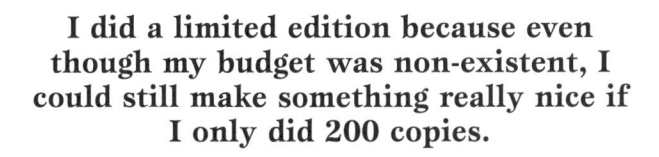

Cover of *X-Ray #4*. Postcard with lipstick mark and bullet hole by Hunter S. Thompson. Note embossing.

I did a limited edition because even though my budget was non-existent, I could still make something really nice if I only did 200 copies.

through each stack. The ones at the top were really nice—they had powder burns. He was great to work with; I hope to do something with him again.

When I sent Hunter Thompson his copy I included a switchblade letter opener that I bought in Chinatown. He was on the speakerphone and was really excited about getting his copy; he was saying these great things about it (and it was encouraging to hear this from a guy that I've read and respected for years). Then I heard him flicking the switchblade out, and his secretary saying, "Hunter . . . Hunter, no . . . Hunter—*don't*, it's not funny!" It sounded like he was jumping up on furniture making these gorilla noises and flicking the switchblade in and out: "C'mon! C'mere! I'm gonna cut you!" Then he would come back to the speakerphone: "You still there?" [laughs]

♦ **V: *How did the idea for X-RAY come about?***
♦ **JB:** As corny as it sounds, it came about over drinks. A friend, Francis Kohler, and I sketched it out on cocktail napkins. We really wanted to make something different. We decided on the name *X-RAY* and started getting it together. Another friend, Delia Shargel, is a contributing editor—she's a good poet, too. It was my idea to get people to contribute handwork on 226 pages. This was to encourage assemblage and handwork. There are 200 copies plus 26 copies numbered "A-Z"—that's an homage to an old small press literary tradition. The lettered copies are signed by the cover artist and certain big name contributors. They sell for a little more.

♦ **V: *I'm sure you'll have imitators—***
♦ JB: I hope so. This isn't about competition—I have nothing to prove to anyone but myself here. With some publications, you contribute a poem, your work is accepted, you finally receive your copy—and it's *crap,* not fit to wrap fish with. Experiences like this drove me to want to produce something exceptional.
♦ **V: *Why did you name your press "Pneumatic Press"?***
♦ JB: My first magazine was titled *Kandykorn Jackhammer,* so Pneumatic Press was in reference to the jackhammer—I thought it was funny, I guess. In Ventura, I worked in a warehouse with my friend Dave Holifield and in the monotony of pulling orders we came up with these ideas for a magazine. Another friend, Bruce Brink, would come up with these weird random word combinations, and one day out of the blue he announced, "Kandykorn Jackhammer." I thought, "That's a perfect title for a magazine!" Dave and I started writing articles under pseudonyms; we called our friends and hustled submissions and began "publishing," just to have something to do. Ventura was so boring, and we wanted to create some kind of oasis. I think we succeeded for a while.

Kandykorn Jackhammer contained comics, poetry and interviews. I hand-painted one of the covers; I was leaning toward doing handwork even back then. It was just a basic zine, really. We did three issues and each one got bigger. Though it was just a folded-and-stapled thing, it was really important to a lot of the people around us. They had a place to put their writings and drawings—it was a good outlet.

The first issue had a photograph of a midget wrestler on the cover. I got a lot of hate mail for the midget photo; also the back window of my Comet was shot out. I wondered if there might be some short bastard with a gun lurking around. Included in the first issue was a poem I wrote about my best friend hanging himself in Cemetery Park, a wrestling quiz by a noted Doctor of masked grappling (I used to go to the Forum and watch wrestling; I'd see Stan Lee from the Dickies there, and other musical personalities). Also included was a humorous comparison by Starch Carmichael titled, "Jesus Christ vs. Billy Barty."

I did a Robert Williams [painter] interview for *Kandykorn Jackhammer,* and that was an *experience.* He was really irritated because Dave and I were late. He gave these complicated freeway directions, telling me to get off at a certain point and go "north." Of course I went south and ended up calling him from a phone booth. He said, "Better get your ass over here; I don't have a lot of time, kid!" We finally showed up and I immediately had to use his bathroom: "Oh, all right—jesus!" On the tape he really didn't warm up to me for quite a while. [laughs] He gave "yes" or "no" answers, there were a lot of heavy silences—god, that was my first and last interview. But then he opened up and was really fun to talk with.

I got a lot of hate mail for the midget photo; also the back window of my Comet was shot out.

♦ **V: *How did you first get submissions for* X-RAY?**
♦ JB: I wrote to a few friends and considered getting a fourth issue of *Kandykorn Jackhammer* together, but thought I'd leave the past behind and start on something else. I asked Charles Bukowski if he'd be interested in contributing something. I wrote him on a Monday and got an envelope containing some poems on Saturday—not even a week had passed. At this point I knew I had to get this idea of a magazine together. I was amazed at how generous he was—he really *gave back* a lot and supported small presses; he taught me a lot about professionalism and deadlines. He was always on time.

Even my dad contributes to *X-RAY.* I found a poem in my mother's garage he wrote years ago, and put that together as a little chapbook insert titled, "Outrun the Blast," about an incident that really happened to him: his stepdad tried to blow him up with dynamite! I included a mugshot of him circa 1955 (he looks like a real fifties Juvenile Delinquent). He's a natural poet.
♦ **V: *What's your background?***
♦ JB: I grew up in Ventura, which is a scenic retirement community between Santa Barbara and Los Angeles. It's right off highway 101 on the coast, quiet, pretty—and when I lived there, there was less than nothing to do. You can't get food after 9 o'clock; everything shuts down. It's a nice place but I had to get away. I met Jaime Hernandez and his brother Ismael there at Arthur Treacher's Fish & Chips around 1979 or '80.

Cover of Kandykorn Jackhammer #1

78

We'd go there after school; we knew the guy who managed the place and he'd give us free food. I must have been about 14—I still had a paper route; that's how young I was. There was a good connection between the Ventura punks and the Oxnard punks—no territorial bullshit. We had this bond since it seemed like the rest of the world wanted to kick our asses for the way we looked.

When I first met the Hernandez Brothers, they hadn't published anything yet. We'd all go to our friends Art and Joey's house and they'd be there drawing comics on the kitchen table. There were great versions of punk Archies: Jughead with a leather jacket playing the bass, Archie flipping off Mister Weatherbee. They did this almost too well. Then *Love & Rockets* came out and that was inspiring. They did it themselves, didn't have to answer to anybody and did a real professional job. They brought copies to Art and Joey's and we read it—no one said a word—we were amazed at the quality. We thought, "These guys will go somewhere; this is real talent."

♦ **V: How did you learn drums?**
♦ **JB:** My sister's friend Joe Lopiano was a drummer but his neighbors would never let him play. They'd call the cops, so my mom let him practice in our garage. Since the drums were there just gathering cobwebs he told me, "If you wanna mess around with them, go ahead." Joe was cool—he'd turn me on to these obscure records. He also got me into collage and spray

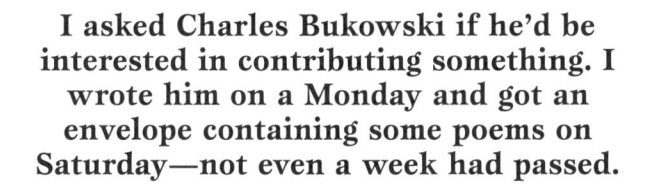

A page from X-RAY #3 by Mr. Frankenstein

I asked Charles Bukowski if he'd be interested in contributing something. I wrote him on a Monday and got an envelope containing some poems on Saturday—not even a week had passed.

can art. Anyway, I taught myself and put a band together and started playing. My band M.I.A. appeared on a compilation LP with the Germs, Minutemen and the Bags called *Life Is Beautiful, So Why Not Eat Health Food?* Our song was titled "Last Day at the Races."

From there I got into graffiti art. I made elaborate stencils and would go on freeway underpasses and paint something like Johnny Rotten's face belching "Anarchy!" I suppose I was trying to get a message out. I also did t-shirts with spray-paint and stencils.
♦ **V: Why did you make t-shirts? Most kids just go out and buy them.**
♦ **JB:** Well, if you wanted a Chiefs or a Weirdos t-shirt—those bands were so new that they weren't that popular yet. You couldn't buy one, so you had to make your own. The Rotters (who recorded "Sit On My Face, Stevie Nicks") were friends of mine—I played drums with those guys in later incarnations, the Wuffie Dogs and the DeSotos. We actually started a magazine together called *Sixty Miles North*—I shouldn't say I started it, but I helped out. That was my first hands-on experience with publishing.

Eventually I got my own apartment. I worked as a shipping clerk in a warehouse off and on for ten years. I was a carpenter, a sign painter; I also worked putting toys in those crane vending machines. I took a few junior college courses but it seemed like the long way around. I kept playing music but the whole scene just changed and went sour. When punk first started, you could be walking down the street and see someone with spiky hair or a handmade Cramps t-shirt and have this immediate bond. A lot of people today don't

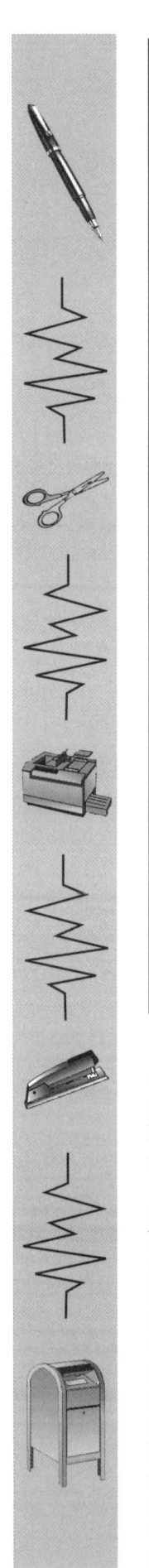

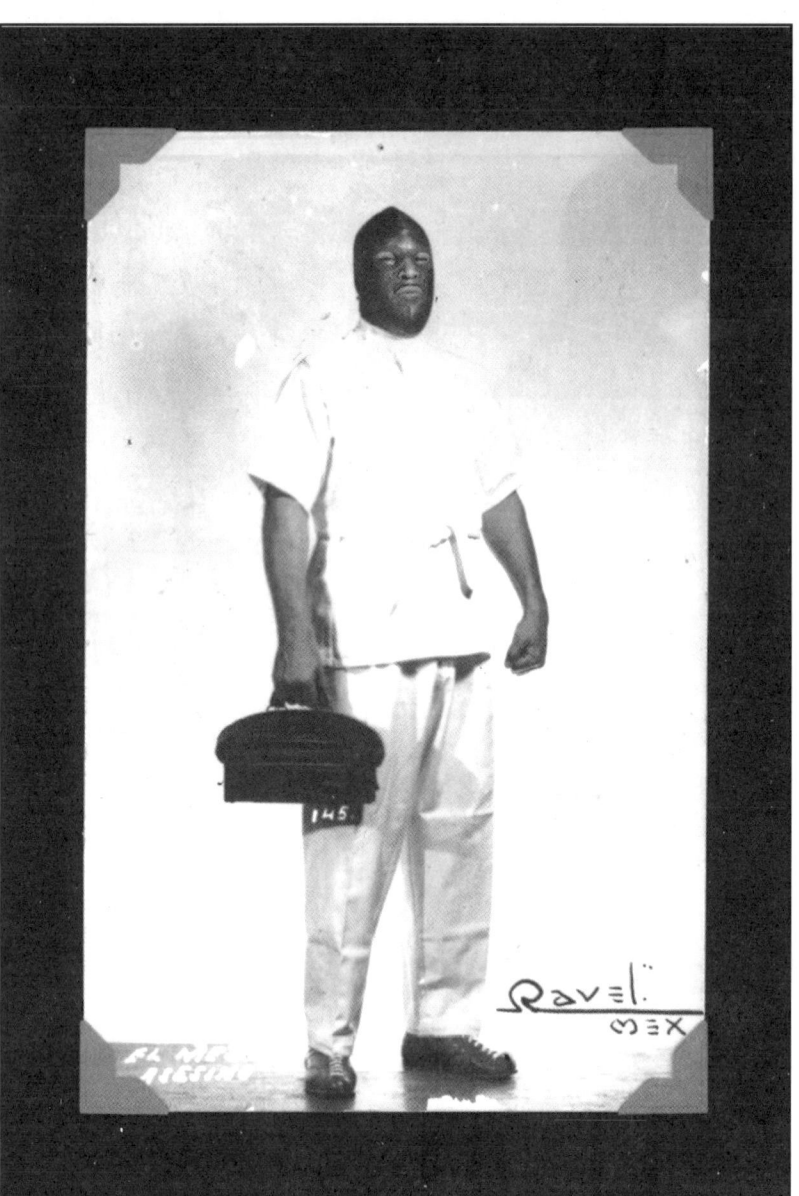

X-RAY #3: each copy had a different found photograph on the cover

understand that. I wouldn't call what's going on now *punk* but since that's what the media is calling it, I'd have to say it's a shame the way it's been marketed, mass-produced and abused.

I was planning to attend the S.F. Art Institute. I had moved away from home and was living on my own, but I felt, "I've got to get out of Ventura! Maybe I should go to art school—I could use their equipment." I came to San Francisco and got a room with these cretin-subnormal art enthusiasts. What a dull bunch—white trash, they lived in complete squalor. I ended up going to these art school parties with them, and I've never seen so many homely people in my life. Horn-rimmed frumpy girls with their gas station attendant-looking yellow-haired boyfriends. If I had to be around these people every day I'd wind up in prison for beating someone to death with an easel or something. So at that point I gave up the idea of attending art school, and fueled with this hatred and rage began work on the first issue of *X-RAY*.

♦ **V: There's a "street" edge to what you do that keeps it from evaporating into something arty and pretentious—**

♦ JB: I think not going to art school really saved my ass! I think that would have completely drained any ounce of creativity out of me.

I also thought that doing a magazine would be self-educating, and I'd be learning as I went along. Since I wasn't going to school, I thought, "If I do a magazine it'll keep me on track, and it'll keep me in publishing and design. As long as I stick with it and stay on that road, it might eventually lead to something."

♦ **V: Were you doing mail art?**

♦ JB: I've been doing mail art for about ten years now. I was writing letters to people and decorating them and I didn't know there was something called "mail art." Then someone said, "Oh, you're into *mail art.* Let me give you so-and-so's address." I started getting lists of exhibits and things like that.

Mail art is a lot bigger in other countries. I really appreciate galleries that will showcase art that people can relate to and be a part of. And anybody can be part of a mail art exhibit; they don't reject anything! Everything is accepted, as long as you follow the theme. That's really nice; it gets a lot of different people to participate. I think that if you like to make things, mail art is the thing to do. For someone who doesn't have time to make a magazine, when they feel creative they can say, "This exhibit is coming up; here's the deadline. I'll work on this little postcard until then."

♦ **V: There are so many personal touches in X-RAY, like a lock of pubic hair—**

♦ JB: I met that guy and he was bald. He told me, "I do all these projects with my hair. I'm waiting for it to grow back so I can do another one." He kept eyeing my hair; I think he had a pair of scissors in his pocket.

♦ **V: Here's an overlay by Carey Calter showing a woman in underwear: you turn the clear page and she's nude underneath—that's nice.**

♦ JB: I like to keep some xerox inclusions so it doesn't get too slick. One contributor, Alice Borealis, xeroxed and *hand-colored* 226 sheets of "Dadapost" stamps, and each one is perfectly done. It was amazing. When I saw it I couldn't believe it; I wanted to bind all of them *together* because they're all done in different colors. Another contributor from England, Patricia Collins, sent 226 pairs of cardboard glasses with real x-rays as the "lenses." Each one was assembled by hand—that was a lot of work!

The next issue will have interviews with Susie Bright and Jim Carroll, some letterpress printing, three more poems by Bukowski, and a stencil submission. Billy Childish submitted something too—I'm doing a chapbook for him next year. He's been in bands like the Pop Rivets, the Milkshakes and Thee Headcoats. He probably has *fifty* books of poetry out—he's really prolific, to put it mildly.

♦ **V: You finally put your Robert Williams interview in X-RAY—**

♦ JB: That hung over me like a huge black turd for five years. I thought, "This man invites me to his house. I do the interview, and I don't publish it." I talked to him a couple times, and he always asked, "When you gonna get that thing together? What are you gonna do with it?" When I finally sent him a copy, the first thing he said was, "Johnny, I'm really proud of you for this." It was a big relief to finish it after all that time.

♦ **V: Well, who wouldn't be proud of it? How much did you charge for the first issue?**

♦ JB: Seven bucks. I told everybody, "I don't know what to charge for this." I wanted it to be affordable—something that *I* could afford to buy. Then they sold so fast that I realized, "Shit, I should have charged

Cards by Mark Van Slyke from *X-RAY #3*

thing into their piece. Like Julee Peezlee's checks which say: "Pay to the order of Greed. Devastate to Liberate." We got to know each other through mail art. She published *No Poetry* and is very active in the zine and mail art scene. She would drive up and visit when I lived in Ventura.

I called up Timothy Leary and asked if he would contribute and he said, "Sure—that sounds great!" He was very enthusiastic: "Send me a copy and we'll work it out!" I sent him a copy and received a call from his secretary, "Mr. Leary has to charge one dollar per word for articles and stories—are you sure you want to do this?" I said [casually], "Oh yeah; that fits my budget perfectly. I'll buy one word!" She said, "Which word do you want?" I said, "I don't know—have Mr. Leary decide." She said, "Tim, this is kind of weird . . ." and I overheard him saying, "That's *great!* Yes! I pick the word 'Chaos'—that's my piece!" I called his contribution "A one word dosage from Dr. Timothy Leary," printed the word "Chaos" on a little card and put it inside one of those pill envelopes from a medical arts press.

Here's a Ray Johnson page; shortly after he sent this, he killed himself . . . Here's a booklet from John M. Bennett—he's a poet and is in a lot of small press publications. Neeli Cherkovski produced a tribute to

> **I think not going to art school really saved my ass! I think that would have completely drained any ounce of creativity out of me.**

more"—not so much to make money, but in order to do *another* one. I barely made back the money I put into it.

Another thing—I hand-type letters to people on the mailing list. I want it to be personal. And it takes me two weeks to collate and bind each issue; I do it all myself with a used Gestetner binding machine I found for $100. In the past, people tried to help, but they did things like leave a page out, or grab two sheets of the same page, so I ended up a page short and had to search all the copies to find the missing sheet! (Then I had to unbind the copy, and rebind it.) It's easier to do it all myself. I'd hate to inflict this tedious job on anyone else.

♦ **V: With no money, a person can put together something exceptionally beautiful, partly by getting other people to contribute—**

♦ JB: The nice thing is that people really put some-

Cards contributed by Mark Van Slyke to *X-RAY #1*

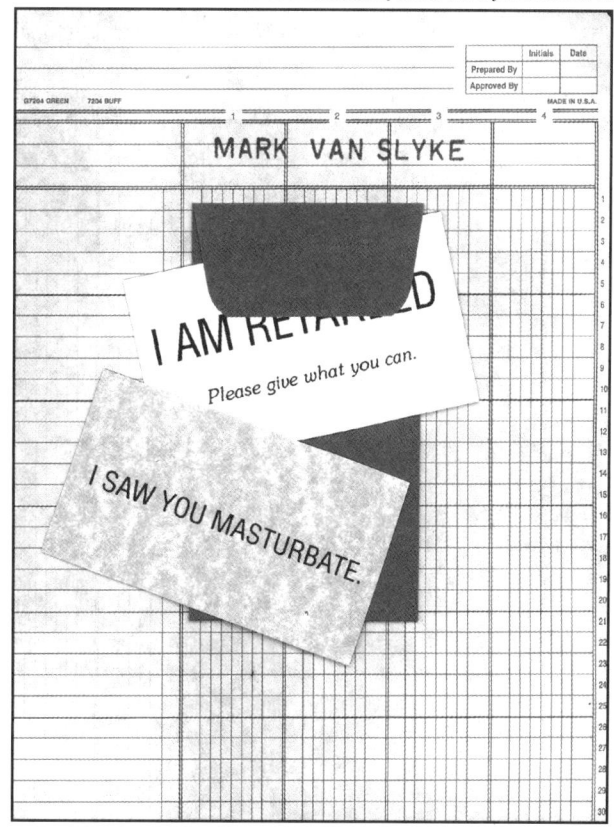

Bob Kaufman [beat African-American poet] which is really nice. Have you ever seen Neeli's drawings or paintings? I like abstract primitive art, and what he does is great. He sent me a poem and I made a small chapbook out of it and that's in #4.

♦ **V:** *How do you do the production?*

♦ **JB:** For chapbooks, I typeset on a Macintosh in Microsoft *Word,* do the layout in *QuarkXpress,* buy a ream of good paper, cut, fold, staple or sew. That's it. A toddler is capable of running a small press!

I really try to convey that it's not a snooty, arty thing.

♦ **V:** *X-RAY has so many different paper textures and colors and is so palpable, with overlays, little booklets bound in, cards inside little envelopes pasted on a page, and even cloth sewn onto a page, contributed by a quiltmaker. More than any other publication I've seen, you're tapping the dimension of touch—*

♦ **JB:** [laughs] I really try to convey that it's not a snooty, arty thing. Even my step-grandmother who's in her 80s loves it. Maybe there's something for everyone. And people add things sometimes, like one poem had a band-aid attached. All this kind of personalizes it somehow. If something is so sterile and so arty and so held above everybody's head, then who gives a shit about it?

The Cooper-Hewitt Museum (Smithsonian Institute's National Museum of Design) is doing an exhibit next year which will feature *X-RAY.* They asked me for a copy to put in the show, and I thought, "Wow!" The show is called "Mixing Messages: Graphic Design in Contemporary Culture." The J. Paul Getty Library ordered a "lifetime" subscription—I couldn't believe it. Various universities including S.U.N.Y. at Buffalo's rare book department and the University of Wisconsin have also ordered lifetime subscriptions. I'm honored that they have done so. I think it's amazing that this kitchen table project has blossomed into this *thing.*

♦ **V:** *Have you ever approached a major publisher?*

♦ **JB:** Someone told me: "You ought to go to Chronicle Books and see about doing an *X-RAY* annual that's mass-produced with less hand-work." I had meetings with the editors, but they weren't interested unless it had more "20-something" appeal, like a catchy Generation X title. I didn't pursue it with them after that. I wouldn't want to live with sacrificing *X-RAY.* I'd rather call the shots—that's what small presses are all about.

♦ **V:** *They want to put their own stamp on it; they don't want you to have total control—*

♦ **JB:** I talked to John Martin of Black Sparrow Press about doing a large-scale production, and he said, "It's a pretty big dream. We'd have to rent a *warehouse* to assemble it." I said, "That's nothing! I could get people to do that—that's easy." He was saying, "I don't know, I don't know. It sounds crazy to me." It's funny, because I was inspired by the things *he* did a long time ago. I'll keep going; I'll keep doing it on my kitchen table.

♦ **V:** *Again, X-RAY has to be seen and felt to be fully appreciated. It's fueled by the principle of doing something just to please yourself—*

♦ **JB:** I'm certainly not being paid to do it. It would be nice, but . . . I always want things to be more than they appear to be at first glance. For example, the front cover on my new issue is a foldout cover by Jaime Hernandez; I wanted it to be interactive. A lot of my covers have things attached to them. Since it was a drawing, I wanted it to move. It shows this Superhero-type woman with her hand outstretched and there's something bubbling or smoking out of her hand. When you turn the flap, whatever it was has landed on the floor and turned into this big fish handing her flowers, holding a heart-shaped box of chocolates under his fin. It was screen-printed by Chuck Sperry of The Psychic Sparkplug; they do the best poster art in town.

♦ **V:** *What's heartening is that so many people are willing to put a lot of effort into their contributions. Quality attracts quality—*

♦ **JB:** *Factsheet Five* has been a major help bringing it together. If you do a magazine and don't have that directory to be listed in, you're only going to distribute it to your friends and possibly some stores in your neighborhood. But you can send it to *Factsheet Five* and somebody will review it and people will order or contribute to it. With *Kandykorn Jackhammer,* that's how I hooked up with a lot of people. They saw my review and sent poems, comics, etc. and I would contribute to *their* magazines. *Factsheet Five* is really indispensable.

Factsheet Five died for awhile after Mike Gunderloy quit. I thought, "Man, where do you go now?" Seth Friedman has done a really good job of bringing it back to life. He selected the first issue of *X-RAY* as an "Editor's Choice"—we were off to a good start.

♦ **V:** *I think X-RAY gives people a high set of standards. Hopefully some people will take more care in*

Reproductions of original linoleum cuts by Generic Mike, X-RAY #3

their productions—

♦ JB: —and try and do something more permanent, not something that's disposable. If I ever get a bigger budget, I'll put it into some nice detailed production values. I don't want to produce something and have it be crap. I want people to look at it, especially if they've never heard of it. I want it to grab their attention just because of the design; I want them to say, "What's this?" I don't want them to think, "This looks like everything else!" and toss it away.

♦ *V: You juxtapose sophisticated typography and design with raw pages done on a manual typewriter. Yet somehow the typing looks basic and classic, whereas if the whole publication were like that, it would look crude. You use all these contrasts to your advantage—*

♦ JB: I do. The pagination is really important. I'll go over and over what page goes next to what. I want all the articles to complement each other, and even suggest something with just a color. For example, I try and make sure that the pages, even though created by different people with different ideas, complement each other. This is where that contrast and color scheme comes in. People might not notice that immediately, but if and when they do, I hope they appreciate it.

I like to break everything up. I don't group all the poems together or the neat handmade pages all in one place. On Hunter's contribution, he sent me this fax and I thought, "If I typeset that, it's gonna lose a lot. It won't be nearly as interesting." So I thought, "I'll print it just like it was received." But I did it on nice paper with thermography, and all that brings it to *life*. Also, I design the title page in a slick *old* book style. I could maintain that sensibility throughout the entire book, but that wouldn't be nearly as much fun. It would look too slick.

♦ *V: What you do gives people something to aspire to—and again, it takes very little money.*

♦ JB: I think it's important for people to look at what they're throwing away, and what's around them. You can recycle so many things and make something else out of them.

♦ *V: Most people would just throw away those old coat check tags—*

♦ JB: You can go to flea markets and find things; the ephemera at flea markets is usually pretty cheap. That bag of raffle tickets from the '50s I found was five bucks. It was a huge bag, and you know they're all losers! It took decades, but finally those old losing raffle tickets are good for something. Pages from old magazines can be your "paper" to mount something else on; you can take them to Kinko's and get them chopped down for a dollar a cut. That's what Francis Kohler did with these yellow pages from a Chinese phone book—just the fact that the printing is Chinese makes it special, although thousands of these directories get thrown away in Chinatown every year. The point is: there are all these resources available for next to nothing, and people should take advantage and use them.

Found Shopping Lists contributed by Elyse Kutz in *X-RAY #3*

I found a box of hundreds of old photos at a flea market, so every copy of the third issue of X-RAY had a different photo on the cover. Actually, it was a lot of work to precisely glue down the four green triangular corners holding each photo in place. But I love found photos, so it was worth it.

I think it's important for people to look at what they're throwing away... You can recycle so many things and make something else out of them.

♦ *V: I think you have to keep raising your prices. Maybe some day you'll make a quarter an hour—*

♦ JB: You never ever get paid for your time. In the meantime I'm getting a lot of computer experience, and I have an excuse to use it. When I first got the computer I didn't take it out of the box for two weeks because I was so intimidated. I'm used to a typewriter; I like the feel of the key striking the paper and I like the way it looks. I still don't write letters on a computer because it feels too impersonal. Anyway, I finally took the computer out of the box and had no idea what to do. But once I got going I realized, "God, it's *made* to be easy." It really is. The Peachpit Press books, especially the Visual Quickstart series, are

fortune suggester

HOW TO USE IT:
Take the suggester out of the pouch and position your index fingers and thumbs beneath it in a way that allows you to open it like a puppet mouth. Find someone who is willing to play along. Begin with the suggester closed. Ask your volunteer to pick an object/word that appears on the outside. Spell that word out loud while opening the "mouth" in alternating directions for each letter. Ask them to now pick an object /word that appears on the **inside**. Repeat the above process. Now ask them to pick a final object/word. Lift the flap and read the fortune that appears underneath. For entertainment purposes only. No gambling please.

Fortune suggester by Francis Kohler from *X-RAY #2*

great. That's how I taught myself *QuarkXpress*.

♦ **V: I like the fact that you haven't gone into trendy topics. You've stayed away from serial-killer chic and shock-for-shock's sake, which is the content of so much of today's "art"—**

♦ JB: Although I went through a phase . . . I remember getting autopsy trading cards from Julee Peezlee and thinking they were so cool: "Check these out—not when you're eating, but later!" I have letters from John Gacy. My friend Todd from the Angry Samoans used to write to Gacy; he gave me the address and said, "Just write him and see what happens." I went through a phase of reading about serial killers, reading books with letter bomb recipes—I got all these books and plowed through them, thinking "My god, humans are such sick animals!" Then at a certain point I'd seen all this twisted stuff and realized, "I've had enough. Argggh! Take it away!"

♦ **V: There's more to life than that.**

♦ JB: When I had the space I would paint more often. People would look at most of them and think I was disturbed: "Johnny . . . are you feeling okay?" I'd have this black background spattered with cigarettes and ashes—dark, grim visions. When I did *X-RAY,* it was the first time I'd created something and had people say, "That's *beautiful.*" I just wasn't used to that reaction. I guess there's another side to me after all. Might keep me from being committed to an asylum. [laughs]

♦ **V: *X-RAY* is not simplistic; there's a huge emotional range—**

♦ JB: That's another part of doing a magazine or drawing a picture or having a band or writing a song or making an omlette: you've got to have some kind of *outlet,* otherwise you'll crack. You may as well do something with that energy and create something with it. And it doesn't have to be angry, angst-ridden energy; it can be very positive. I'm sure some people go in their rooms and *try* to feel tortured, and then they get bored: "I guess I'll go out and call somebody." There's a widespread mythology perpetuating that kind of "tortured artist" role-playing. Either you're tortured or you're not.

♦ **V: That mythology perpetuates what the status quo wants artists to be: self-destructive freaks. Society doesn't want people to grow up and be artists, even though—**

♦ JB: —everybody is, in a sense—or that's what they say.

♦ **V: Retarded people prove that—you don't even need to have a normal IQ to be able to produce art.**

♦ JB: Some of the nicest art I've seen is by retarded people, because it's so honest. There's no pretension, it's just completely pure soul and honesty. This kid—I think he's seven years old—did 226 drawings for an issue of *X-RAY*. He wasn't drawing to meet women, he was drawing the pictures because that's what he wanted to do! [laughs]

I'm used to a typewriter; I like the feel of the key striking the paper and I like the way it looks.

I first started playing music when I was pretty young. I did it because I loved music and wanted to be playing and creating it. Then I met these assholes who played guitar just to meet girls. I thought, "That's bizarre"—I hoped everyone was playing music just because they loved it.

♦ **V: You're lucky to have been in that early punk scene. Then you kept going, transmuting your energy into producing something unique—**
♦ JB: I remember going to the opening of the Decline and Fall of Western Civilization [Penelope Spheeris's punk documentary] in Hollywood. The street was packed with people with blue and cropped hair wearing black leather, spikes, combat boots, kilts, mohawks and sneers. In the middle of the street the police had a barricade and they were all in riot gear. On the other side of the street a crowd of "normal" people were gawking at us. Back then it was rare to see someone who looked like a punk—that was when it was great; when everything was so new and honest.

I was lucky to have met Jaime and Gilbert when I was so young, too. They encouraged me to draw and play music . . . to create. Besides having creativity, they had a huge sense of humor. Just being around them was really inspirational. When I met Jaime and his brother Ismael, he had a mohawk and Ismael had a jacket that said "Weirdos" on the back. I had black eyes and a fractured jaw and contusions and lacerations on my head because I'd been beaten up by this guy with an ax handle just for being a punk.

I had a few run-ins with the law, although I didn't really do anything too criminal. My band played a party that turned into a riot; the newspaper headline read, "Rock and Bottle-Throwing Melee at Punk Rock Party!" When I was 16, I got arrested for nothing in front of Ben Frank's. The charge was "suspected armed robbery," and I went to jail where they took mug shots and took my fingerprints—the whole thing. I remember I was wearing a Motorhead "On Parole" t-shirt! [laughs] They kept me for two days and I was acquitted.

♦ **V: You got into punk before it got self-conscious; before all the jocks came in who just wanted to slam dance and hurt people—**
♦ JB: Yeah. I think this jackass from Suicidal Tendencies was responsible for a lot of that "gang" mentality. I remember going to see Bad Religion. Before the show, me and about five friends went to the store to get beer. On our way back, we walked into the middle of a gang fight. We were caught in the middle of a street with this guy and his gang on one side, and these San Fernando Valley guys on the other. One of the guys from the Valley side grabbed a friend of mine and pressed a broken bottle against his throat. It was really terrifying; we didn't know what to do. I said, "He's no one to you—c'mon, man." I was trying to talk him out of slitting my friend's throat. They finally let him go and then they got into their fight and we got out of their way. It really made me sick to see that. What were they fighting about—territory or greed? Nothing. What did they accomplish? Nothing—who knows.

The punk scene changed when all these rednecks and assholes and jocks came to the clubs and started plowing into people, just hitting them. But I remember going to punk shows when slamming wasn't like this [imitates a guy charging with his arms in front], it was just chaotic, with people jumping around and bouncing off each other. Then it turned into a washing machine of people who always went in the same direction. One time I fell over and my shoes were knocked off, somehow. I just remember that one guy helped me to the edge of the pit and another guy handed me my shoes!

♦ **V: That's the way it should have stayed—**
♦ JB: It was so great. The kind of people who first liked punk rock didn't want to hurt people. The way I see a lot of kids acting now is: they act like the way

You've got to have some kind of *outlet*, otherwise you'll crack.

punks are portrayed on TV. I see those shows and think, "Nobody I know does or says those things!" [exasperated] Like, "Society doesn't understand us, man!" Yeah, I've seen that episode of Quincy.

♦ **V: Do you still play drums?**
♦ JB: I sold my drums to Jaime. Actually, I play the ukulele these days. Recently I went to my dad's house and he gave me a violin and a bow in a case. I got an idea; I went to his workshop and picked up a saw: "Man, I'm gonna try this." In about five minutes I had figured out how to play musical saw. [Demonstrates playing the saw with a violin bow]

Cover of X-RAY #2. Each copy included a real compass on a string.

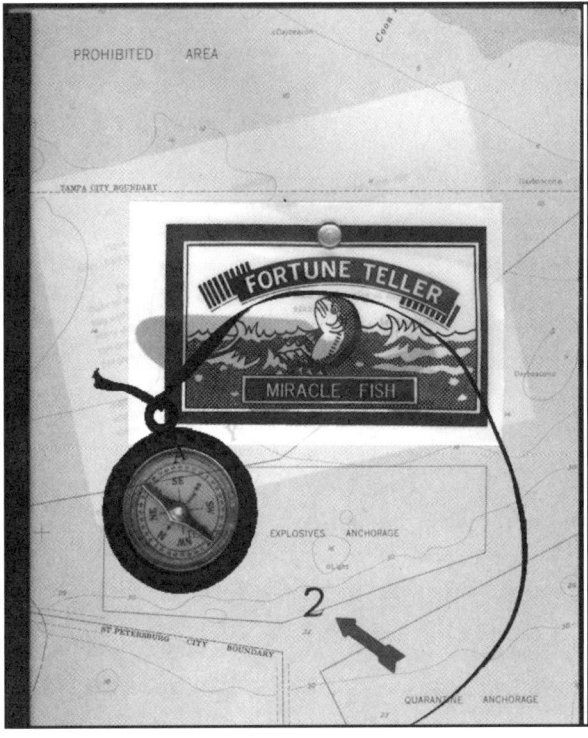

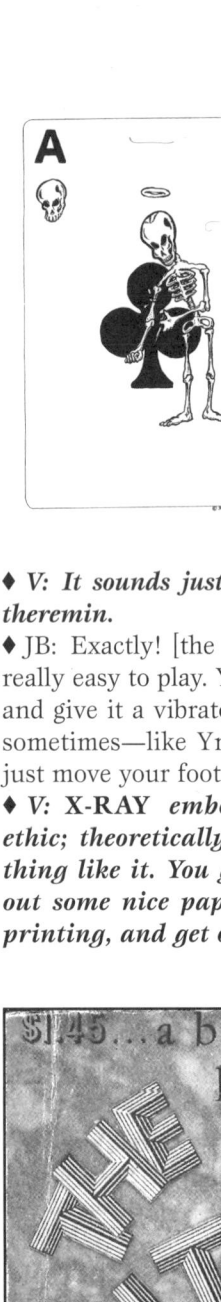

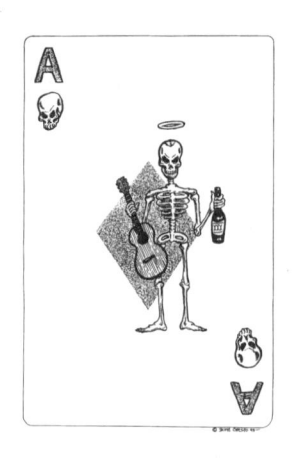

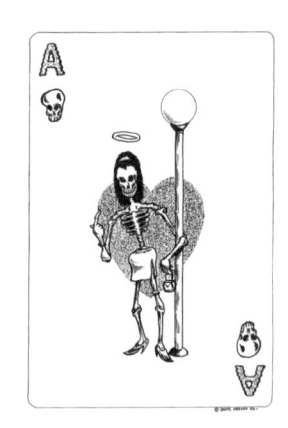

♦ **V:** *It sounds just like a theremin! It's a low-tech theremin.*

♦ **JB:** Exactly! [the sound whistles up and down] It's really easy to play. You put the saw between your legs and give it a vibrato. It sounds like a woman singing sometimes—like Yma Sumac. To get the vibrato you just move your foot up and down like you're nervous.

♦ **V:** *X-RAY embodies the Do-It-Yourself punk ethic; theoretically almost anyone could do something like it. You go to a paper supplier and pick out some nice paper, learn a little bit about fine printing, and get other people involved—*

Cover of *The Outsider #3*

♦ **JB:** For example, you can staple a booklet together, or you can take a bit more time and sew it by hand, throw some paint on it, etc. I think a lot of people

I like to take something out of its context and bring *new life* to it.

don't know they can do that. It'd be nice if people were doing finer productions. There's always something to learn and something to try—why limit yourself? That's what I like about publishing: it's limitless. There are so many possible topics and materials; it's a lot of fun.

♦ **V:** *The way you do it, it's also a recycling project. Doing X-RAY has expanded your awareness in that you keep your eyes open for anything that could possibly be included. The world becomes more alive—*

♦ **JB:** Yeah, it does—that's a good way of looking at it. I mean, things that I would have thrown out before... For example, if I'm in a parking garage, I pick up those ticket stubs with the big bold numbers on them, and someday I'll have enough to do something with them. And they have this certain *life* to them. It may be a footprint, or it may be the fact that they've been driven over so many times that there's the imprint of the gravel below. I really appreciate the fact that it has lived! And now it's retired, but it has its little place.

Some of my best contributors are people who wouldn't normally contribute to a regular magazine. They say, "Oh, but I'm not an artist." I say, "But you make things." They say, "Yeah, but that's just for fun." I guess it all goes back to that honest "real people who are just *doing* it" feel.

♦ **V:** *There's a definite spirit of play, involving chance elements and found objects—*

♦ **JB:** I like to take something out of its context and bring *new life* to it. ▼

The Man Who Loved Chicken

At approximately 1500 hours, V Smith saw a male (suspect M__) out in front of his house, inside the horse paddock. The victim had seen the suspect before, when he was in the company of Thomas L__, the man who boards two horses at the victim's house. The suspect was tending to the two boarder horses and since the victim saw that everything was all right he discontinued watching.

A short time later, the victim heard a chicken scream. He immediately thought that the dog (a German Shepherd) that had accompanied the suspect was killing one of his chickens. He went to a window overlooking the paddock area.

The victim saw the suspect (whom he described as male, 5´8˝, thin, muscular, wearing lt.-colored Levis, red shirt, cowboy hat & boots, with a moustache) facing away from him, holding onto a chicken. A child was walking by the front of the property. The suspect turned away from the child, which positioned him to be facing the victim's location. The victim was appalled to discover that the suspect was having sex with the chicken.

The suspect was holding onto the chicken by the wings. He moved the chicken back and forth as he moved his penis in and out of it. After a few moments, the chicken ceased to struggle and its head hung limply as the suspect continued. When the suspect finished, he pulled the chicken off himself, exposing his uncircumcised penis to the victim. The suspect proceeded to pull feathers and debris from his fly area. He brushed himself off a little and secured his fly. (He threw the chicken's body in the feed bin.)

As the suspect straightened up, he appeared suddenly startled (the victim thinks the suspect saw him) and ran across the paddock. He jumped over the fence, got on his black beach cruiser bike and rode away. He had left his dog behind in the paddock.

The victim said he was stupefied. He didn't know what to do. He went to his phone and began to call the police, then decided they would think he was crazy, so he hung up. He then decided to call Mr. L__ to tell him to get his horses off his property. The phone was busy. He went back to the window and looked out. The dog was now gone, too.

The victim then called several friends. Through their collective advice, he decided to call Norton Sheriff's Station for assistance.

The victim showed me the chicken (EV.1), which I took into evidence. I decided to go to the home of Mr. L__ to see if he knew anything more about the suspect since the victim had seen the two together before.

I knocked on the door of 13285 Greenaway. A little girl answered the door and I asked to speak to Mr. L__. As I was waiting for Mr. L__ to come to the door, I saw a man fitting the suspect's description sitting on a couch. When Mr. L__ came to the door I asked him who the man on the couch was. He told me he was his brother-in-law. I asked if I could speak with him and his brother-in-law outside because there were so many children present (at least four that came near the front door). They both stepped outside. I asked Tom if he or his brother-in-law had been to tend their horses today. Tom asked his brother-in-law and told me that yes, he (the suspect) had been to see the horses. Based on the brother-in-law's physical description matching the suspect's and his statement that he had been around the horses, I detained the brother-in-law for a field showup.

Assisting unit 46K2 Dep. Clancy (#269975) advised the victim of field showup procedures and transported the victim to my location. The victim immediately stated, "That's him," when I had the brother-in-law stand up in front of the lights of 46K2 vehicle.

I advised the suspect he was under arrest for 597(a) PC and 286.5 PC. I transported and booked the suspect at Norton Station with the approval of Sgt. Smith and Watch Comm. Lt. Lance.

I took a Polaroid photograph (EV.2) of the chicken at the station.

—ACTUAL FOUND POLICE REPORT from *X-RAY #1*

REFERENCE (Some of Johnny's Books)

Acme Novelty Library: *Jimmy Corigan, The World's Smartest Kid*
Berman, Wallace: *Support the Revolution*
Brautigan, Richard: *Sombrero Fallout; Loading Mercury with a Pitchfork*
Broonzy, Big Bill: *William Broonzy's Story*
Bukowski, Charles: *Crucifix in a Deathhand*
　Genius of the Crowd
　Poems Written Before Jumping Out of An 8-Story Window
Cherkovski, Neeli: *Hank* (bio of Charles Bukowski)
Coleman/Young: *Mingus/Mingus*
Crespo, Jaime: *Narcolepsy Dreams* (comic)
Fante, John: *Ask the Dust; Dreams from Bunker Hill*

Fluxus Codex
Fuller, Buckminster: *I Seem To Be A Verb*
Gonzales, Babs: *I, Paid My Dues*
Guralnick, Peter: *Lost Highway*
Hernandez, Jaime: *Whoa Nellie; Penny Century; The Death of Speedy* (comics)
Kleinzahler, August: *Like Cities Like Storms*
Novello, Don: *The Laszlo Letters*
Pocho ($3 to PO Box 40021, Berkeley CA 94704)
Runyon, Damon: *Runyon, First & Last*
Saroyan, William: *The Man with the Heart in the Highlands*
Thomas, Piri: *Down These Mean Streets*

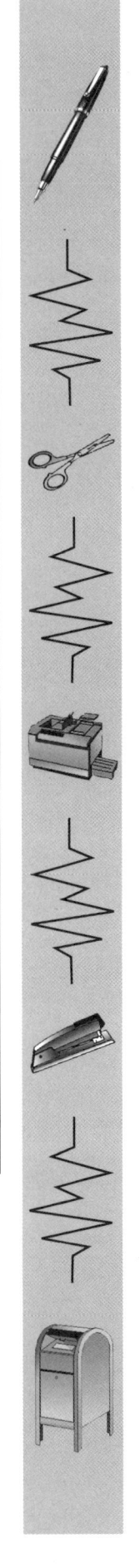

Mystery Date

Lynn Peril publishes *Mystery Date*, a zine drawing on diverse sources such as '50s home economics textbooks, etiquette manuals, dating manuals, biographies of stars and starlets, as well as rereleased films and educational videos. She grew up in Milwaukee, Wisconsin and in the '80s moved to San Francisco, where she lives with husband Johnny Bartlett of the Phantom Surfers (who showed up at the end of the interview). For a sample copy of *Mystery Date,* send $3 (cash only) to PO Box 641592, San Francisco CA 94164-1592.

♦ **VALE: Tell us how you started Mystery Date. For source materials, you draw on these older—I hate to say out-dated—etiquette books?**
♦ **LYNN PERIL:** They're often frighteningly up-to-date.

I had wanted to do a zine for a really long time. I had a couple of false starts. An original zine title that I came up with around 1988 was *Bookhead*. It was going to be about used books or books I liked, but that never really got off the ground. I have a folder full of ideas for that project.

Meanwhile, I have always been interested in popular culture—particularly how it pertains to women. I was inspired to collect etiquette books by reading Johnny Marr's "(Anti-) Sex Tips for Teens," a one-off issue [1988] of his zine, *Murder Can Be Fun* [three dollars cash from MCBF, Box 640111, San Francisco CA 94109]. It's great; it goes the whole nine yards from the 19th century forward.

Everything finally reached critical mass, and I put out the first issue of *Mystery Date*, back in 1994.
♦ **V: You must have been incubating for years—**
♦ **LP:** I *was* incubating for years and years. I remember reading punk rock fanzines in the late '70s and wanting to do writing for them, or produce my own. But I never wanted to do a music-only zine.

Actually, when I was a little kid I used to write my own books—about the neighbor's cat or something like that. My friends and I were all into the soap opera *Dark Shadows* and we wrote a *Dark Shadows* newsletter.

When I moved out here, I had a boyfriend who worked at Subterranean Records. His employer kept every music zine that had ever been sent to him. There were boxes full of them under the counter space; I used to sit there and go through them and think, "*I want to do this.*"
♦ **V: How old were you when you did the Dark Shadows newsletter?**
♦ **LP:** Eight. It was just an activity for a rainy afternoon done mainly for pleasure. I still have my boxed set of *Dark Shadows* novels that I got for Christmas one year. I'm bummed because when my mom moved she threw away my Barnabas Collins game. That newsletter was hand-written and was not something we mailed out.

Now I have a Mac computer and it's great. If you make a mistake on a typewriter, there's no going back. Also, typing is incredibly labor-intensive.

I'm impressed that so many young kids—14- and 15-year-olds and even younger—are out there writing and editing zines. If only I had had the gumption to get it all together sooner!
♦ **V: The urge to publish a zine isn't just born out of collecting etiquette books; it comes out of your entire life—**

Lynn Peril. Photo: Robert Waldman

♦ **LP:** And a large desire to get mail—I *love* getting mail! Creating a zine is the *best* tactic for getting mail. I have been known to get extremely upset—even *outraged*—if I come home to an empty mailbox. Sometimes I'm convinced it's the end of the zine and no one's going to buy another copy. Then someone will send me the greatest stuff. I know I should say I have loftier aspirations, but I think my number one goal is to get mail. [laughs]

♦ **V:** *It's because people turn you on to things—*

♦ **LP:** People send me all kinds of great books and videotapes.

Another inspiration was a book called *High Weirdness By Mail,* which came out in 1988. It made me think about all the wonderful stuff you can get *only* through mail order, and influenced me to send away for more things. This book is not purely about publications; it also lists organizations like the Flat Earth Society that have a particular "take" on subjects. It made me realize how much fun could be had through the mail.

♦ **V:** *When did you first start mail ordering?*

♦ **LP:** As a kid, I was really into horses and bought all these horse magazines. I would write away for all the free advertising material. I owned boxes of *stuff*—which is kind of like my life right now! [laughs] Very early on, I knew that mail had potential.

♦ **V:** *That's smart—especially if you have no money—*

♦ **LP:** Exactly. You can make collages—cut out the ads, paste them up and do your own rearranging if you want. The ads provide fantasy material—

♦ **V:** *But you didn't have a horse back then?*

♦ **LP:** No, and I don't have one now, either. I sublimated on cats—which I do to this day. I have two of those—but maybe someday . . .

♦ **V:** *Did you have an allowance that enabled you to do this mail ordering?*

Creating a zine is the *best* tactic for getting mail. I have been known to get extremely upset—even *outraged*—if I come home to an empty mailbox.

♦ **LP:** No, it was always free stuff—pure advertising: "Hi! I saw your ad. Send me your brochure; I want to know all about the bridles you make." I enjoyed coming home from school or work and finding our mailbox crammed full of mail for *me*. Nowadays I'm a lot pickier; junk mail isn't enough anymore.

♦ **V:** *Did your mom encourage you? She must have given you stamps—*

♦ **LP:** Well, I always did get my stamps. I certainly don't remember her discouraging me.

♦ **V:** *What were your earliest collections?*

♦ **LP:** I've always been a collector, but I don't remember specifically when that started. I remember collecting objects I liked, without being able to explain why I liked them or was attracted to them. But I've been a book person—*always*. *Mystery Date* is basically about a particular subgroup of books. Book-collecting and reading are two of my favorite activities.

I had my box full of horse stuff—I wish I still had it. I used to go to riding camp in the summer and we would have a horse show at the end. Everybody would put braids in their horse's mane, and I kept some of the braids in my horse box.

♦ **V:** *What did your parents do for a living?*

♦ **LP:** They had a hardware store; they were self-employed.

♦ **V:** *Where did this passion for books come from?*

♦ **LP:** My parents read to me practically from the time I was born. I was never taught to read; I simply woke up one day and discovered I could. I remember going downstairs and telling my mother, "Hey mom—I can read!"

I also had an uncle whose room at my grandmother's house was just this tiny closet entirely surrounded by

Cover of Mystery Date *#2*

books. He died when I was six years old. When my aunt moved out of the house, she had all of us nieces and nephews take what we wanted. They're all amazing books! It's really wild to go to Acorn Books [antiquarian bookseller] down the street and be able to say, "Hey, I have that book." My uncle read books by Eugene O'Neill, Flannery O'Connor, and Nabokov. They were all first editions because he would run out to buy the newest releases from these authors. He also had rare editions by authors like Jean Genet that were privately published or in limited editions. Acorn Books was asking five hundred dollars for one book that I owned.

♦ **V:** *That was really special—that your parents read to you.*
♦ **LP:** Oh yeah, you gotta read to the little bambino. It's very important.
♦ **V:** *What was the $500 book?*
♦ **LP:** A Flannery O'Connor first edition of *A Good Man Is Hard To Find*, with dust jacket. Only some of my books have the original dust jackets, but most of them are in pretty pristine condition, nonetheless.
♦ **V:** *What are some of your favorite "normal" books?*
♦ **LP:** *Lolita* is bar none my favorite. I love the *language*, of course, and the story is blackly hilarious, a great caricature of fifties Americana revealing all the seamy stuff underneath the surfaces. The movie's great—I love James Mason—but the book is just the best. I like other Nabokov books too, like *Pale Fire*. He's such an amazing writer, especially considering that English was his second language (he was a Russian-nobility immigrant). This is one of my favorite passages from *Lolita:* "Has she already been initiated by mother nature to the Mystery of the Menarche? Bloated feeling. The curse of the Irish. Falling from the roof. Grandma is visiting. 'Mister Uterus' (I quote from a girls' magazine) 'starts to build a thick soft wall on the chance a possible baby may have to be bedded down there.' The tiny madman in his padded cell." I love those last two lines.

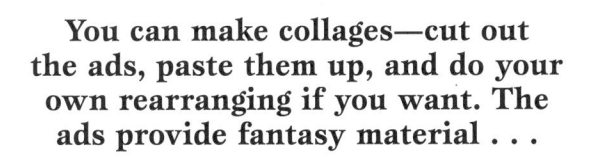

You can make collages—cut out the ads, paste them up, and do your own rearranging if you want. The ads provide fantasy material . . .

Another early influence was the Scholastic Book Club—I think it's a subsidiary of the *Weekly Reader*. Every few weeks you would receive a little newsprint flyer advertising books you could order.
♦ **V:** *Through the school?*
♦ **LP:** It starts in grade school. You would study these

Cover of *Three's a Crowd*

flyers and then ask your parents for the money to order the books, bring the money to the teacher and two weeks later, you'd come in and there would be this stack of books on your desk. It was the best thing *ever!* They offered all kinds of books: on sports, animals, teen romance novels (as students got older)—just about everything.

I have a bunch of late '50s teen romance books published by Scholastic that I want to write about in a future issue of *Mystery Date*. I really love the covers. One, *Three's a Crowd*, is about these twins that fall for the same guy. The cover shows the twins looking at each other with this perplexed-looking guy in the background. I swear to god, the way the girls are looking at each other it looks just like some lesbian novel. They look like they're saying: "Forget you, guy!"
♦ **V:** *The subtext—*
♦ **LP:** Yeah—that's what I like to do in *Mystery Date:* talk about the *real* subtext of books.
♦ **V:** *Can you describe the content of your zine—it's not just critiques of old etiquette books?*
♦ **LP:** No, although those are some of my favorite books to look at. A lot of the same attitudes prevail in more recent etiquette books of the '70s, '80s and '90s, but the authors have learned to be more careful—they try not to say anything outright sexist. But you'd

be surprised what they *don't* consider sexist... I also have tons of old home ec [home economics] textbooks.

I like the look of books from the '40s and '50s because the printing process is so saturated with color. Those textbooks have that in spades! Charm and beauty books are really great, too. Of course, teen sex books are good—not erotic novels, but sex education and dating advice books. I'm still looking for more of those pamphlets they gave to girls in school about menstruation. It was a horrifying time in my life, as I recall, but now I'm fascinated by it.

In the zine, I also talk about games that teach the same kind of value system. The objective is usually dating or getting a guy. Of course, the larger context involving gender roles and popular culture is always lurking in the background. Though I haven't really discussed this much in my zine, I think the roles set up for men are just as restrictive as those set up for women.

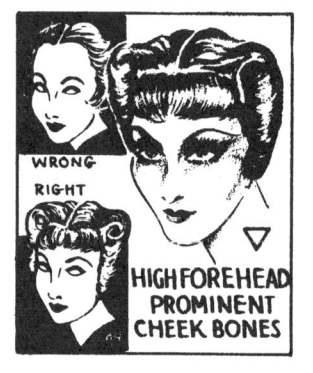

Up until the '70s when there was legislation prohibiting sex-segregated classes, girls were expected to take home ec and boys were expected to take shop. Occasionally people would switch. In some of the post-'70s home ec textbooks, the introduction carefully acknowledges that it may be a mixed class, but then the rest of the book is definitely geared to female students.

At a garage sale I found a shop textbook and looked at it carefully, and it was so *boring!* The home ec textbooks go beyond sewing and cooking; there's a heavy dose of moral teaching: "What you should be like as a woman, wife and mother"-type advice. Whereas the shop book is just about "how to make a table"—it doesn't say *anything* about how to be a man or a father; it doesn't say anything about what your morals should be. It doesn't tie making a good table with being the right kind of man, or intimate that women might not like you if you don't know how to use a band saw properly.

I also like books that are eccentric or written by eccentric people. Privately-issued books are usually grand fun. Celebrity dirt written by relatives of celebrities or people who dated celebrities are fabulous. I have one written by a woman who swears up and down that she was Liberace's girlfriend. It's self-published, too!

♦ **V: Maybe he had that closet side of himself—the closet inside the closet... Your zine also discusses some films—**

♦ **LP:** Yeah, there were so many great classroom films. A friend sent me a videotape of instructional films from the late '40s through the early '60s, and one is literally called *What To Do On A Date*—just in case you had any questions! There are also a couple of interesting juvenile delinquent films on this tape, particularly one about how necessary it is to have youth clubs—because otherwise "boys play with knives." It's narrated by Richard Widmark and features a very young Chuck Connors as "the adult who gives a damn."

There are some unbelievable classroom films, like *Boys Beware* [see excerpt], which is about the dangers posed by lurking homosexuals. It's pretty scary; it's about a boy who is seduced by this older, leering man. In the end, the boy goes to his parents and they turn the guy in; the guy goes to jail but the boy is put on probation. It's odd: the boy has been victimized, so he's put on *probation?!* Of course the whole subplot is that homosexuals prey on innocent young boys, "initiating" them into the gay lifestyle. I was completely shocked the first time I saw *Boys Beware*. It's one of the vilest pieces of anti-gay propaganda I've ever seen.

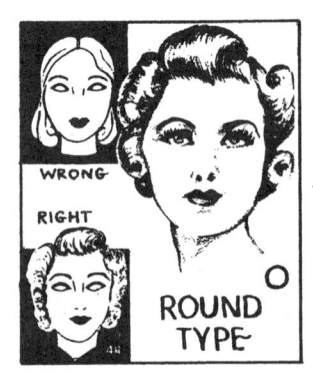

Alpha Blue Archives released a compilation called *Pink Slip,* which contains excerpts from late '60s and '70s menstruation films. One is supposed to be a teen anti-smoking film, but it's actually a how-to-smoke film. A girl and her cousin get together: the girl is mousy and boring, and her cousin has breasts, wears make-up, is hip and smokes. There's actually a scene where her cousin teaches her the mechanics of smoking: "No, you hold it *like this.* No, draw it into your lungs *like this.*"

One amazing film is *Facts About Menstruation,* made for mentally retarded girls. It stars a girl with Downs Syndrome, her older sister and their parents—it's a family. The most fascinating part is when the older sister goes into the bathroom and says,

Illustrations on this page from *"Lady, be Lovely"* by Anne Rodman, 1939.

"Come on, Jill, let me show you how I change my pad." She pulls down her pants, sits down on the toilet and takes her pad off; there's red ink on it (or something). It's astonishing, especially compared to the Disney-produced films (supposedly made for "normal" viewers) that sugarcoat everything. Whereas this film for retarded children is so much more honest. Of course, that makes it completely shocking; you're thinking to yourself, "Ohmigod! I can't believe she just did that on film!"

♦ **V: How did you find these videos?**

♦ LP: My husband gave one of his friends a copy of *Mystery Date*, and she sent the tape to me. The other tape I bought from Alpha Blue Archives, which sells a lot of older porn. The proprietor also has a lot of instructional films. He read *Mystery Date* and wrote me a letter, "Hi, I read it and really liked it. Here's a catalog of what I put out . . ."

♦ **V: Not too many people have thought of collecting "home ec" books. The sexism and attitudes they display are completely unselfconscious because they have this other purpose they're trying to communicate—**

♦ LP: Someone wrote me who was fairly young (judging by the fact that the letter was written on a sheet of paper torn from a three-ring notebook): "I really like *Mystery Date*, but is this really relevant to today? You're just discussing these products of the '50s and '60s, but what does it have to do with *now?*" This person had missed the whole context. It struck me that most of our political leaders come from an era when "girls go to home ec and guys go to shop." Those classroom textbooks and films were the propaganda they were raised with. I think that they're now trying to get back to this past that never truly existed.

Home ec books rarely let up on the "this is what you as a woman are supposed to be" moralizing. But sometimes the attitude of an author will completely knock me out, because I'm not expecting to find anything progressive. Candi Strecker gave me a book called *The Bride's Primer* as a wedding gift. It's about how to schedule your housework on a timetable, and is pretty exacting. The author also talks about when you have kids, and says: "Don't just ignore your sons. Boys enjoy cooking, too; they enjoy playing in the kitchen just as much as girls do. Don't ignore them or push them out." An attitude like that from the past surprises me—maybe I'm just too cynical. It's a reminder that all people didn't necessarily cling to conservative views in their daily lives. It's important to remember that prescriptive literature like this doesn't necessarily mirror real life, and vice versa. What fascinates me is the overlap between the two.

♦ **V: When you were growing up, were you taught to cook?**

♦ LP: Oh, I love to cook. I love to eat—if you love to eat, it only makes sense that you love to cook.

♦ **V: You had a traditional upbringing, yet... what made you different? Were you ever ill for a long time—**

♦ LP: Are you saying that illness causes difference? [laughs]

♦ **V: No, but there's a theory that anybody who's unusual has had some experience prior to the age of ten that somehow set them apart. Like, perhaps they were ill and missed school for a month—**

♦ LP: There were probably some incidents, but nothing I'm willing to talk about publicly.

♦ **V: Okay. So did you have a pretty traditional upbringing?**

To You Girls (advice book) 1961

♦ LP: No, not entirely. My parents ran our hardware business, and they ran it side-by-side. It wasn't like dad went to work and mom stayed home; mom worked her butt off, too. I also had an aunt who never married—she worked all the time. So I had strong female role models whose lives weren't necessarily situated in the domestic sphere.

When I was ten my dad had me putting together lawn-mowers and bicycles. I liked that. This experience never panned out into any kind of extensive mechanical knowledge on my part, but I always enjoyed doing it.

I remember one day, when I was in my teens and working at the store, the phone rang. A guy came on the line and I asked him if he needed any help. He immediately said, "Is there a man there? Can I talk to a man, please?" My dad was doing something in the back, like having lunch, and I had to go back and tell him, "Dad, this guy wants to talk to a *man*." My dad just said, "Why? You help him—what's his problem?" However, the guy refused to talk to me, so finally my dad spoke to him. It turned out that the guy just wanted to know if we had a yardstick—something really lame! My dad got really pissed at the caller (this was before sexism or gender issues were widely recognized)—he couldn't believe how stupid the whole thing was.

> **One amazing film is *Facts About Menstruation*, made for mentally retarded girls. The most fascinating part is when the older sister goes into the bathroom and says, "Come on, Jill, let me show you how I change my pad."**

♦ **V:** *That's a good example.*
♦ LP: Oh god, it was so ridiculous. What he was asking for was so trivial.

I think a lot of other people have a much more difficult time with their parents, who demand that they follow in more traditional roles.
♦ **V:** *You survey these pop culture sources to see how they reflect actual morals and attitudes, some of which are pretty excruciating—*
♦ LP: Right. What I hope comes across in *Mystery Date* is that I am ultimately serious about everything I write. However, a lot of the material is just hilarious—unintentionally so. I want to communicate that there's more there than meets the eye, but I have no desire to over-intellectualize about popular culture. I prefer to make people think while they laugh.
♦ **V:** *[picks up a book] Ah—*The World of Modelling. *Finally, books are coming out that give the real dirt—*
♦ LP: I want to read that new one by Michael Gross: *Model: The Ugly Business of Beautiful Women*. The one you're looking at is a swingin' '60s, English model, "how-to-be-Jean Shrimpton" type of book. It was written by Lucie Clayton, the woman who actually used to run the modeling school that Jean Shrimpton went to.
♦ **V:** *Is that another type of book you collect: on fashion?*
♦ LP: I love fashion. It's an interesting topic; it's definitely a future *Mystery Date* issue. I've been collecting books on the fashion world for awhile. There's a great one from the '60s called *Beyond the Looking-Glass: America's Beauty Culture* by Kathrin Perutz, who in 1969 wrote a fascinating article on attending the Miss Teenage America pageant in the same week that the Vietnam War Moratorium was held. It juxtaposes this very patriotic, prim and proper girl event with more "counter-culture" teenagers in a Texas town who wanted to participate in the moratorium. It's an excellent article.

I try to read at least a little bit of everything I get, but there are some books I buy just for the covers. I also have a tremendously huge backlog.

I've heard of at least two men who collect menstruation-related material. I have pretty liberal attitudes, but I think that's *twisted*. On the East Coast, there's this guy who runs a menstrual museum, and there's another man who's always looking to buy used kotex machines. I just don't understand why *men* would be interested in this; I understand why *I* would be, but even I don't want a kotex machine or care about how menstrual belts have changed over the years. I just want the texts; I want to know the didactics of menstruation over the decades.
♦ **V:** *There used to be ads: "No more belts or pins!"*
♦ LP: Before tampons you had this little garter belt with plastic or metal clips that would clamp onto the pad, like garter fasteners. But if you didn't have the stupid belt, you could use pins. I remember way back when I started menstruating, the vending machines

Cover of *The World of Modelling*

would give you the pad and two safety pins—you'd pin them to your panties.

Whoever invented the tampon was a genius—that's all I have to say!

♦ **V: There's been a lot of opposition to tampons, involving toxic shock syndrome—**
♦ LP: Yeah, but who leaves them in for eight hours? And it's mainly those super, ultra, heavy-duty plastic ones that cause problems. I think tampons are a by-product of World War II, by the way—at least the modern tampon.

If you're female, there's two days in your life that are supposed to be special: getting your period and getting married. Obviously, getting your period is a milestone in your life, but to imagine that it's somehow the gateway to the mysteries of womanhood and that it's so wonderful because you can give birth is bullshit.

♦ **V: It used to be common for women to learn typing in school. Did you?**
♦ LP: No. I'm a professional typist *now*, but I didn't really learn how to type until I got a job that demanded I know how. I took typing in high school, but I was really bad at it. All of the little books I did when I was a kid were handwritten. When I was in grade school I had this teacher who made us write stories—it seemed like we were constantly writing. Every week we made covers for our little story booklets.

♦ **V: Didn't punk rock emerge about the same time you were in high school?**
♦ LP: Yeah. I was a junior in high school when I went to see Iggy Pop and the Dead Boys in 1977. This was the first punk rock show I ever saw. Just walking in, I realized it had incredible meaning to me. It was the coolest thing I had ever seen in my entire 16 years!

♦ **V: How did you get in and who told you about it?**
♦ LP: It was at a theater, so it was an all-ages show. I had a "bad girl" friend who told me about it. But at that point in time we didn't know the Dead Boys from Donny and Marie [Osmond]; we just walked in and said, "Ohmigod! This is amazing!" After that we tried to see everybody who came to town, and hopefully they weren't in clubs—we were notoriously chicken about trying to get into the over-18 clubs. My friend had a great mom who let us stay out late because she knew we didn't drink and weren't doing any drugs—we just wanted to see bands. I'd always tell my parents I was staying at her house, and then we'd go out.

♦ **V: Weren't there punk zines back then?**
♦ LP: There were just one-sheet publications. The one I remember the most was a local effort called *Autonomy*. Somebody else did the first really professional-looking zine I ever saw: *Crush On You*. Whoever published it did this completely fake scene report about this town in Iowa that didn't exist, and this scene that didn't exist—it was great! Those were the earliest two that I remember. There was another zine from 1980 that I recall: *See Hear*. It was produced by a neopsychedelic band called Plasticland who actually

from "The Adventures of Honey West" book series (early '60s)

had a nationally and internationally-known "underground" press.

♦ **V: Did you obtain these zines at the local punk rock record store?**
♦ LP: Probably. Although it wasn't what I would call a "punk rock record store"—it was called Jack's Record Rack.

♦ **V: It used to be difficult to find punk rock material, even in San Francisco—**
♦ LP: Well, there wasn't that much out there to begin with. Do you remember *Punk* magazine from New York? Unfortunately, I sent them money for a subscription just as they went out of business. There used to be slick glossy magazines like *New Wave* and *Punk Rock Spectacular* for sale. We would cut pictures out and put them up in our lockers.

♦ **V: People weren't putting out zines like they are now—**
♦ LP: When I think of early zines I think about British ones, like *Sniffin' Glue*. *Autonomy* was the Milwaukee version of that.

One reader told me that he really loved *Mystery Date* because it reminded him of *Bikini Girl*, a zine out of New York that ran from the late '70s to the early '80s. However, the only real similarity is: they're both

Cover of *Bikini Girl* #4

by women, and they both have covers printed in black ink on pink paper. I have a friend who has a whole file of *Bikini Girl,* and it was really interesting to see them because in one of my Milwaukee zines there's some little gossip comment that reads: "Was that Vicky, Milwaukee punk, in the latest issue of *Bikini Girl* magazine?"

Vicky was the first person I ever saw with green hair—she was "Miss Queen of the Scene" in Milwaukee. However, that didn't mean I wasn't above snubbing her on her 21st birthday by telling her I had turned 18 three days before: "Oh, you're 21? That's *so old!*" I was *awful*; just think of the snottiest 18-year-old you can imagine and that's who I was. Anyhow, it was cool to see those zines that I had read about so long before, and open up a copy and see this photo of Vicky. At the time she must have looked really avant-garde, but now she would just look like someone in a mall with her mom—in fact, someone's mom from the suburbs looks just like that now.

♦ V: *What's the best thing anybody sent you?*
♦ LP: I received a letter from a man named Dewey Webb, who works for the *New Times* in Phoenix, Arizona and is a big fan of *Mystery Date*. He wanted extra copies to give to friends. I should also say that Dewey's the person responsible for me owning an autographed copy of *That Girl in Your Mirror*, which is a teen advice book written by the 1965 Miss America—Vonda Kay Van Dyke (whom I'm also writing about in an upcoming issue of *Mystery Date*). Anyway, one day I went to my mailbox and got this huge package from Dewey's friend Paul Wilson. Inside was a sweet letter about how he liked my zine. In addition to the written letter, he sent me a "video-letter" where he takes me on a tour of his house in Phoenix and shows me some favorite things in his collection.

In one hilarious part of his video he says: "Well, in *Mystery Date* you talk about this Franciscan Starburst tea-and-toast set" (Starburst being one of the most famous of the 1950s dinnerware produced by Franciscan, a California pottery-maker). I had a home ec textbook with a picture of this tea-and-toast set in Starburst which I had never seen before—not in a thrift shop or a collector's show. In the video, Paul says, "Well, I read about that and I thought, 'Let's see.'" Then he walks over to his shelf and takes out the same home ec book I had and says, "Why yes, here it is."

Not only did he have that book, but from what I could see on his shelf, we had at least eight or ten books in common. This guy and I were obviously on the same wavelength. Then, in the video he proceeds to show me all this other cool stuff he has, like these wonderful records on sex education—including one on menstruation facts for *boys*. (By the way, his whole house is done circa 1955.) Then he said, "I'm also going to include my videotape homage to *Mystery Date,* the game" (which he had done independent of me producing the zine).

Paul is so talented! He basically took the soundtrack from an old *Mystery Date* commercial and made this wonderful black-and-white commercial of his own, featuring himself in drag playing *all* of the little girls playing the *Mystery Date* game. He also plays all of the dates behind the doors! At the end the dates run off together, leaving the little girls very perplexed. It's incredibly well done, in black-and-white and synched perfectly with the soundtrack, and looks like it was really shot in the early '60s. At the end of the videotape, he says, "Oh, I'm coming to San Francisco and

One of the most rewarding aspects of doing a zine is getting to know all of these really great people. If you're lucky, you get to meet them face-to-face.

I'd like to meet you, but I know that you don't really know me," etc. Of course, I wanted to meet him.

We all met at the Tonga Room when he was in town with his boyfriend, Al, who it turns out grew up within a three-block radius of where my parents had their hardware store in Wisconsin. All of us really hit it off. On our honeymoon, Johnny and I went to visit him. Paul took us thrifting to every place in Phoenix, from eleven in the morning to eight at night. He showed me his room which is like *my* dream room. It's jam-packed with vintage women's clothing and shoes; everything is absolutely gorgeous! The best part of the night was when he had a stack of clothes for me to take if I wanted them, because he had just started seriously getting into drag and didn't have his sizes down. He had bought clothes that were too small, so he gave them all to me. He's wonderful.

When we went to visit him this summer, he had just won an M&Ms video contest. A couple of months ago I got a letter from him with a big clipping from the Phoenix paper because he had just won the Twinkie 65th Anniversary Video Contest!

One of his art projects is this photo album with a family he's totally created. The album starts with the parents' wedding; he's really good at making fake documents, so there are newspaper clippings from the society pages announcing the marriage. Of course, he plays everybody: the mom, dad, kids, etc. There's a big blank spot where the children's childhood photos were stolen or burned up in a fire, because he couldn't recreate *that*. When they come in as teenagers, they're living the lifestyle these books would have you believe everybody led. There's a photo of the family on sex education night. Paul's dressed as the mom who's teaching the kids with a very professional-looking dummy—

♦ **V: *How does he do all that?***

♦ LP: He poses, then cuts things out and pastes them all down, xeroxes it and then does more. He calls his make-believe family "The Kimballs." There's a picture of the family at the Tonga Room. He loved that place so much that he and Al went back the next day and talked the management into letting him take photos for the background before the place opened.

♦ **V: *What's the Twinkie film about?***

♦ LP: It tells how the Kimballs get caught in an atomic attack and have no Twinkies because they're trapped in the house and it's not safe to go out yet. They try to make their own Twinkies—a hideous failure. Pretty soon, the coast is clear to leave the house; Mrs Kimball goes to the corner store and comes back with three-foot-long Twinkies because they've all been radiated. What I think is amazing is that the Twinkie people went for it—this is what they picked! Paul got something like $6,500 as a prize. He's going to be famous, I'm sure.

♦ **V: *He's pretty young—***

♦ LP: He's about 30.

♦ **V: *If his house was built in the '50s, he was barely born then—***

♦ LP: What's interesting is that it used to be his parent's house, then his parents sold it and bought the house next door. The new owners put it up for sale and his brother bought it and moved in. Then his brother sold it to Paul. So Paul lives in the house that he grew up in, next door to his parents. But Paul realized that moving back into his old room would be a little too Freudian, so he lives in another room. He's absolutely, without question, the most interesting person I've met through *Mystery Date*.

One of the most rewarding aspects of doing a zine is getting to know all of these really great people. If you're lucky, you get to meet them face-to-face.

♦ **V: *You also collect other artifacts—***

♦ LP: Yes, of course. I try to write about those, too: games, records and whatever else I find.

I got the best thing at a flea market recently: a 1955 Frederick's of Hollywood catalog. It is so cool! I want to do an article on the brassieres that Frederick's of Hollywood sold, and that whole side of the female experience: breasts. People give me things now and then because of the zine, and somebody gave me the Joe Bonomo course for bust beauty; the actual title is "Figure Ritual for Beautiful Bust Contour." It's this little booklet with all these exercises in it.

"Sharing the Facts of Life" from So You Want to Raise a Boy?

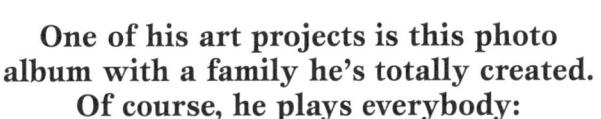

One of his art projects is this photo album with a family he's totally created. Of course, he plays everybody: the mom, dad, kids, etc.

♦ **V: *And this course was written by a man . . . some famous bodybuilder?***

♦ LP: He was. I also have another booklet by him which is a glamour and beauty course. He branched out, publishing little booklets on everything from physical beauty to anti-drug propaganda—I have a xerox of one called *Don't Be a Dope*. Another reader

Cover of Joe Bonomo's bust development course booklet

sent me a gorgeous pink and black Bonomo publication called the *Bonomo Original Hollywood Success Course*. It contains lots of information on charm and personality (two words that tend to be synonymous in self-improvement lingo), plus how to choose your "type": are you an Exotic Woman or a Gamine? And, to top it off, it's autographed by Joe Bonomo himself!

♦ **V: *Are there etiquette books aimed just at men?***
♦ **LP:** Yes. Any book published by *Esquire* from the '50s or '60s is worth having—I have one called *What Every Young Man Should Know*. Basically it's all about how to pick up girls. The book offers manly advice on "beefing up" your image, as well as practical advice on cars (e.g., how to properly drive a stick-shift), how to choose a fraternity, etc. It describes this life that really doesn't exist anymore—except perhaps in the ivy leagues, which I know nothing about.

There's advice on how to plan your college weekend (if you go to a boy's school and she goes to a girl's school, it tells how to plan a weekend for when she comes to your campus). It's definitely about a particular kind of man. It's not purely about being rich; it's about knowing more esoteric skills like how to mix drinks properly or how to choose a sports car. You have to know this etiquette, otherwise you're going to be a complete *boob*.

That's what you would read back then if you were in high school or starting college. Then you'd graduate to *Esquire's Handbook for Hosts*, which is all about mixology—all the proper drinks to make—and how to barbecue properly, and how to play party games. The editors define etiquette as "the art of eliminating friction from daily living." This is the kind of "inside" male knowledge that I don't think guys are required to know anymore.

♦ **V: *Thank goodness—***
♦ **LP:** There's an *Esquire Etiquette* book *still in print*, although I have the 1960 version. The 1953 edition has an entire section on "Your Wife and Work," and it advises, "Keep her *out* of it, if you can."

When you were growing up, do you remember seeing those little films on telephone etiquette? They gave lots of tips like, "Don't breathe too heavily into the phone." You were supposed to answer a call with, "Peril residence, Lynn speaking!" One etiquette book I have devotes *eight pages* to phone manners. I think this is something that has disappeared—a lot of old mannerisms just vanish over time.

♦ **V: *Don't you also collect old cookbooks?***
♦ **LP:** The *American Woman's Cookbook* is a good example of what I like: the endpapers have one of those glorious color photos (of petit-fours, no less), and I'd sure like to know what Freud would say about this amazing appetizer which uses deep-fried zucchini sticks speared through onion rings. I think the folks at the test kitchen were going a little bit crazy, and this was their joke on the rest of us. Either that, or they were seriously repressed and didn't realize the symbolic meaning of their "creation." But I prefer to imagine a bunch of test kitchen hussies hopped up on cooking sherry having a good giggle.

> **Do you remember seeing those little films on telephone etiquette? They have lots of tips like, "Don't breathe too heavily into the phone."**

It's interesting to look at all these complicated concoctions now, because who has *time* to make any of them? Who has time to individually deep-fry zucchini sticks and onion rings and then place the zucchini sticks through the center of the onion rings? Some of these presentations are huge! I think the advertising of the day equated self-worth with complexity of food arrangement.

Another thing I'm starting to collect more of is promotional booklets of almost any kind, as well as travel pamphlets. I always feel extremely sorry for people who don't read—people who say they don't *like* to read, or who think that books are boring. Obviously somebody's been slipping them misinformation, because books are so cool!

♦ **V: Do you collect books on child-raising?**
♦ **LP:** I have an unbelievable one called *The Mother's Book*. I think it's a 1921 edition, but the copyright information goes back to 1907. I love the chart dealing with "proper discipline." There are three columns: the middle column is the transgression, the left column is the improper way of punishment, and the right shows

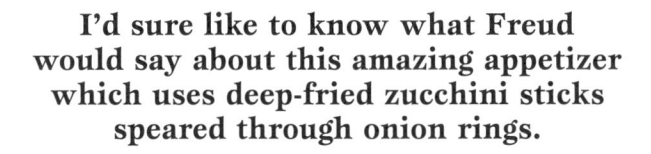

> **I'd sure like to know what Freud would say about this amazing appetizer which uses deep-fried zucchini sticks speared through onion rings.**

the proper way. A particularly memorable sin is "running away": the wrong way of punishment is beating or whipping, but the really advanced, liberated form of discipline is: *tying your child to a tree!* Is your child playing with matches? The new, "progressive" way to teach your child a much-needed lesson is: put your child's fingers in the flame!

I have a couple of other books from the early part of this century that are about health and body issues associated with raising children, and the way they deal with sex education issues is by good old-fashioned denial. A fun one is called *So You Want to Raise a Boy?* It traces a boy's development in year-by-year chapters such as "Anarchy at Eleven," and then deals with "problems" such as stealing, alcohol, narcotics. The chapter "Sharing the Facts of Life" contains such gems as, "Every boy should know that masturbation may be the first step toward homosexuality. What is a homosexual? This is a person who tries to get sexual satisfaction from someone of the same sex. Frequently it starts out with masturbation, and then the individual seeks a partner for mutual sex play. These practices are destructive to the personality, and frequently this type of individual disintegrates to the point where he becomes involved in various types of sex crimes. In fact, the moral degenerate is responsible for some of the most vicious and sadistic sex crimes on record." A solemn warning indeed.

Jumping back to menstruation, *The Mother's Book* has a great section on this topic. The book advocates telling girls straightforwardly about menstruating, and offers fairly clear advice. What's hilarious is the descriptions of consequences if you *don't* tell them. There's a description of a girl who wasn't adequately prepared for her menstrual period—she was taken by surprise, took a cold bath, caught pneumonia and died. There's another tale about a girl who became hysteri-

cal because she hadn't been warned about menstruation—she was put in an asylum for three years. This is another thing I love: ludicrous warnings surrounding sexual behavior.

I also have a number of 19th-century sex education and marital advice books. Those contain the most incredible misinformation you can imagine. One book states emphatically that the consequences of masturbation are: blindness, death, and softening of the brain!

Religious books can be interesting, too. I have one called *Teenagers Today By a Friend of Youth*. It's published by St. Paul Editions, so it's pure Catholic screed. One of my favorite sections concerns what could happen if you engage in "loose behavior":

"There was a certain young girl, very attractive and extremely popular with her friends. She went to a parochial school and then to a good high school. There she unfortunately began to relax some of her religious practices. She skipped weekly communion, grew careless about her prayers and rarely went to the Sodality meetings. She was growing up and wanted to taste the joys of adult life. She began traveling in fast company and didn't let her parents know because they would object. They were old-fashioned, she told herself. She was becoming indifferent. Sin no longer held the same horror it once did. The conviction that she was strong made her careless. Then she learned how weak she really was.

"One night, leaving home on the pretense of going to another student's house, she met a boy who moved

Cover of Joe Bonomo's *Success Course*

in fast company. She thought he was great fun. They went for a drive; after a while they parked. The spot was well-known, but now deserted: 'Lover's Lane.' The night was cold. Only two sounds broke the silence: the drone of the heater and the radio turned low so that they could talk. Then the boy began making passes at her for an innocent embrace, harmless in itself, yet dangerous. Under repeated invitations from the devil, the girl soon grew tired of resisting the boy's uninterrupted advances. She gave in and consented.

"About twenty hours later, a curious passer-by found the couple locked in death's embrace, apparently victims of carbon monoxide poisoning. That young girl had a beautiful funeral. She was radiant in white; in her hand she held a mother-of-pearl rosary and two white orchids. Of course the neighbors could not see her soul! This story sounds very dramatic, doesn't it? Yet such tragedies can and do happen every year."

Do you know when this edition was published? 1980! The thing is, if these guardians of public morality *really* wanted to warn kids about the dangers of pre-marital sex, they should just talk to somebody who had a baby when she was 16 and kept it—just let her talk about how hard parenting is. I can't think of anything better that might keep teens from having sex—or at least *unprotected* sex. I would certainly be the first in line for some kind of contraceptive after seeing or talking to someone who had endured a teenage marriage, or had to deal with child-raising at the age of 14 or 15.

Actually, in *Mystery Date #1* I discussed a book called *Riding in Cars With Boys*. It was published only a few years ago. The author, Beverly Donofrio, wrote about her dreadful teen marriage that she endured in the '60s, and how hard her life was. If more teens read books like these or talked to people who had endured teenage pregnancies or marriages, they might think twice before they did anything, or at least take precautions. Of course, in the area of sex the religious moralizers don't want you to *do* anything. They have one-track minds that constantly repeat: "The wages of sin is death."

♦ *V: No one's going to believe absurd stories about carbon monoxide poisoning.*

♦ LP: I love how all these celibate priests and nuns write books advising you about your sex life. One favorite book is called *To You, Girls;* it's published by the Daughters of St. Paul. The cover has a very '50s-looking girl inside a pink heart holding a soda and looking cheerfully at the camera. It's from 1961 and it's fiction—but the *proper kind* of fiction. This is how one story starts:

"What's your term paper on, sis?" Jean looked up at her brother and replied, "Oh, I guess I'll write something about Pope Pius XII's remarks to a large gathering of young girls about the mistake of exploiting their beauty in any way that detracts from their human dignity." That'll show those secular humanists a thing or two!

Cover of *Coronet*, November 1952

♦ *V: That sounds just like the youth of today talking.*
♦ LP: These religious books are funny in how they drastically mislead people. They're more dangerous than the behavior they allegedly want to curtail—mainly because they lie to people.

An important part of producing *Mystery Date* involves categorization: I like to make lists and piles of things. Home ec books go here, religious books go here, teen sex-ed books go there, etc. When preparing the next zine, I take one of those stacks and start writing. At least the books in a pile relate to one another.

♦ *V: Categorizing can drive a person nuts—*

♦ LP: That's why I do my categorizing *on paper*, because in my house and on my bookshelves everything's all mixed up! One of my housekeeping books suggests categorizing books by color—that way, they look better on the shelf. You might want to try that!

♦ V: *In your essay on Jayne Mansfield, you write about your life after you bleached your hair—*

One book states emphatically that the consequences of masturbation are: blindness, death, and softening of the brain!

♦ LP: People treat you completely different when you're blond. I would never have believed it in a million years if I hadn't experienced it myself. Guys just can't handle women with peroxide blonde hair. It's really weird—they completely regress—they *lose* it. I think there's some genetic defect that kicks in only when men see a bleached-blond woman go by. They probably can't explain it themselves.

I live in a neighborhood with a lot of prostitution. You don't have to look a certain way—all that's necessary is for you to be female to have some guy offer you money if you're standing on the wrong side of the street. This got a lot worse when I was blond. It didn't surprise me, but what did surprise me were the guys in the financial district who you might assume would have more manners. If anything, this shows how effective Hollywood's campaign was to promote platinum blond sex bombs, starting with Jean Harlow. Platinum blond equals sex in this society in a way I just never imagined. It shows how thoroughly we've absorbed this image.

♦ V: *Tell us the difference between your marriage and the kinds of marriages described in your books—*

♦ LP: I married somebody who I absolutely love and like. That's what a wedding is useful for: saying publicly that we're making this commitment. Plus, it gave me a reason to have a tremendously great party! I wanted to have a wedding that was very much about me and my husband, and luckily it turned out that way. A lot of weddings in the guidebooks are not about the bride and groom, but some social idea of what weddings are supposed to be: the big poofy white dress, all the attendants, and if something goes wrong your future will be just awful. My wedding date stands out as the day I was able to tell my mom about my tattoo for the first time. It was one of those situations where she couldn't be upset with me because she was so happy! [laughs] I had a blast.

The only place I gave in to wedding etiquette—*wediquette*—is that I tried to think about what Miss Manners would say about me asking a friend to bring a bikini so she could go-go dance at my wedding. I gave in and I didn't ask, but my friend go-go danced anyway in her dress. It was great!

♦ V: *Have you considered doing something on the Internet?*

♦ LP: This woman in Australia has a feminist zine called *Ms .45*, and anything to do with feminism really tweaks people. She was getting all this flack from these guys on-line in the *alt.zine* newsgroup: "Women don't do zines. How do you do zines? Do you have little computers that fit on your stoves?" I just felt, "I

Cover of *Modern Teen*: "Gidget Tells: How to Trap a Man!"

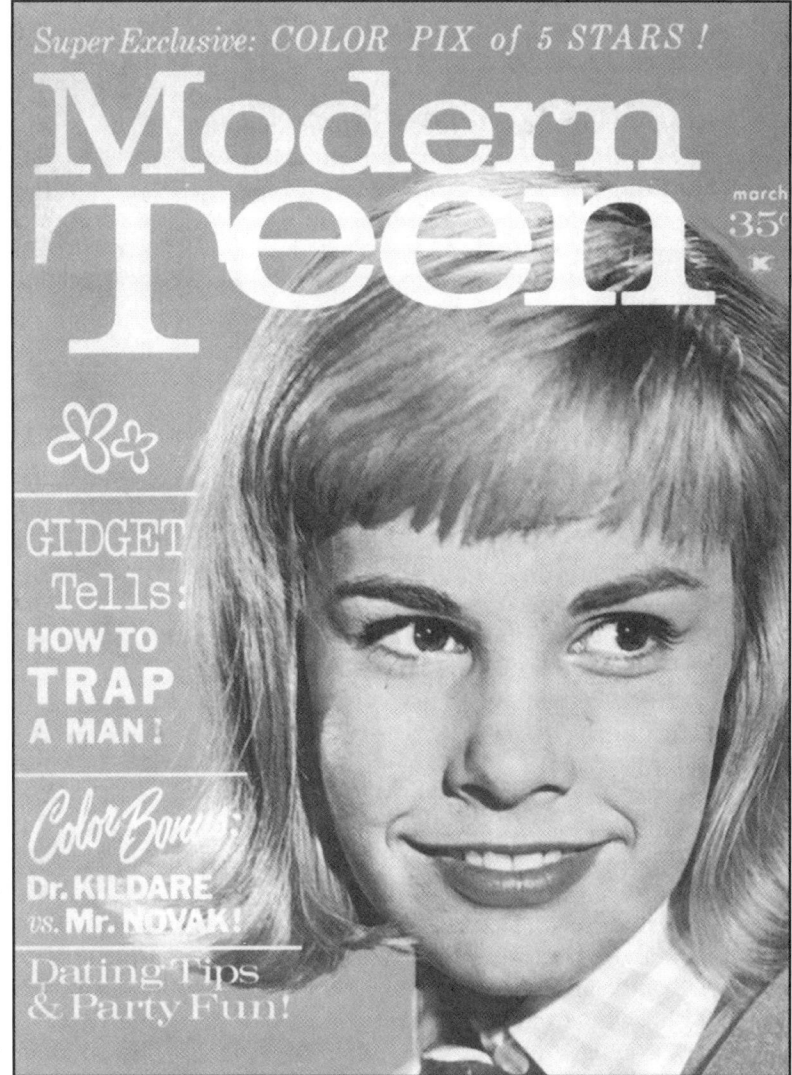

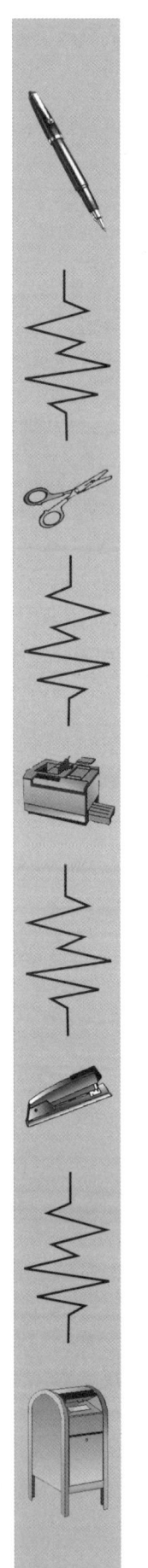

don't want to be involved with a situation where somebody can hide behind a false identity and spout off at me, just because they enjoy spouting off." I don't like the idea of electronic zines—I like *physical objects,* I like paper. I like laying out my zine; I like the fact that you can take it with you on the bus or to the gym or to the bathtub. I sit all day in front of the computer, and the last thing I want to do when I come home at night is sit in front of the computer some *more.* I don't like internet zines.

As far as chatting on-line, that's as bad as talk-radio—I don't want to hear what *idiots* have to say. Mediocre people seem to be what's mainly out there.

That said, I am going to do some kind of web page. It will definitely not be an electronic version of *Mystery Date.* I want to do a site incorporating some of the essays that have appeared in *M.D.*, along with some new features (maybe a "book find of the month"). We'll see what happens. If nothing else, it will expose the zine to a new audience, who may or may not be able to appreciate it.

♦ **V:** *The only thing I really like about the computer-telephone connection is e-mail and information-searching. But the information you can access seems so superficial, and is mostly from mainstream sources—*

♦ **LP:** E-mail is great and that's what I use. As far as chatting on-line, that's as bad as talk-radio—I don't want to hear what *idiots* have to say. Mediocre people seem to be what's mainly out there.

You can do so much more with paper. Just in terms of layout, you're not constrained by the size of the screen. *Mystery Date* is currently 5½″ x 8″, but I could easily make the next issue newspaper tabloid size—or a mini-size, for that matter. But for what I'm doing now, I'm not done with the digest size yet. And the color will always be pink and black.

♦ **V:** *How do you distribute* **Mystery Date?**
♦ **LP:** I'm the world's laziest distributor. Basically, the circulation base is people who have ordered directly from me (mail order), except for Tower, which takes 150 copies. Atomic Books in Baltimore, Maryland also orders it—they have a great mail order catalog and besides, John Waters shops there!

♦ **V:** *Didn't you just see John Waters lecture? How did he look?*
♦ **LP:** He was *so* good! He wore what looked like a dark burgundy or navy smoking jacket with black jeans. He came out and was hilarious. He did questions and answers from the audience, and the best question was from a woman who didn't know that *Serial Mom* was completely fictional and wanted to know which trial it was and if he used the transcripts!

Someone asked what new movies he liked and he said, "*Show Girls,*" which made me really want to see it. He said, "Don't listen to people who say it will never be camp, because it's camp right now." He signed books afterwards; I had him sign the new edition of *Shock Value.* He was so sweet: "Hi! How are you tonight?" I said, "I'm nervous, because I'm going to give you a copy of my zine." He said, "This looks very interesting—I'll read it tomorrow." I'm sure he tosses all the stuff he gets into a big circular file, but what a charming thing to say! Nevertheless, my mouth went completely dry—it was the whole deer-caught-in-the-headlights syndrome.

Personally, I think John Waters is one of the best essayists of our time—brilliant. One of the best things I've ever read is an interview he did with Little Richard that was published in Playboy. It's so hilarious! John Waters is a huge '50s and '60s rock-n-roll fan. I wanted so much to tell him how much I loved that piece, but I froze.

♦ **V:** *Just reading* **Playboy** *is a kitsch activity today—*
♦ **LP:** The interview is brilliant, especially at the end, because Little Richard decides that he wants total control over the article, and John Waters is like, "No, I want to tell people what I really think." In the lecture he did say how bad he thinks people with tattoos are going to look—how they're going to regret it later in their life. [laughs] I was struck by how nice he was offstage. He's one of those great people who are so close to being normal—he does "normal" very well—but he's actually completely wild, like Johnny Marr . . .

Guys just can't handle women with peroxide blond hair . . . I think there's some genetic defect that kicks in only when men see a bleached-blond woman go by.

♦ **JOHNNY BARTLETT:** Back to zines: there's a whole world of specialty newsletters that are like zines. My band released an LP titled *The Exciting Sounds of Model Road Racing,* and this guy who puts out the *Vintage Slot Racers Newsletter* contacted me. He sends out a quarterly (it contains no advertising) to a network of over a hundred people. His subscribers are mostly squares, not hipsters—they probably have no idea what a fanzine *is*. He gets home from his day job, types this thing up and xeroxes it at work. He offered me a free ad and I got about 20 orders from it—that's a high ratio of response.

There are a few zines that have turned into full-blown magazines. *Option* is now a slick and glossy publication, but it used to be a music fanzine that was publishing an A-Z glossary of underground bands and

The term "fanzine" is getting bastardized, just as "thrift store" is: people will get something at an antique store and say, "Yeah, I got this at a thrift store!" They're actually trying to *lower* themselves.

musicians; each issue covered a different letter of the alphabet. For the letter "W" our bass player Mike Lucas sent in a press notice for a fake band we were in, and they mentioned us! *Film Threat* is another example; this guy in Michigan was doing a zine and he sold it to Larry Flynt Publications. The term "fanzine" is getting bastardized, just as "thrift store" is: people will get something at an antique store and say, "Yeah, I got this at a thrift store!" They're actually trying to *lower* themselves.

♦ **V: Lynn, you don't make money on Mystery Date?**
♦ LP: No, I lose money. In fact, my only goal is to eventually break even, but it's not going to happen. Someone at work asked me why I did it, and without thinking I said, "To alleviate boredom." (Why does anybody do anything? "Because I don't like television.") I thought of retorting, "Why do you play golf, you big lug?" I'm lucky I have a job that pays pretty well, because it's not cheap to do a zine. Other people who do zines perhaps live in parts of the country where they have low overhead, but San Francisco is expensive.

Right now zines are like a flavor of the month topic. But just as people have discovered that you can take $500 and put out a thousand 7" singles, so people have discovered that zines are a very low cost way of disseminating information—and it's fun!

Zine-reading is a good way to avoid commercial culture. As all the media outlets conglomerate (soon everything will be owned by just two big corporations), I think people are more and more figuring out the *necessity* to "do it themselves." Zines are a very "punk" literary form, for lack of a better term—they have that real do-it-yourself spirit.

♦ **V: Zines have a contempt for copyright and censorship—you can rip off a newspaper headline and paste it down, or take an advertisement and modify it without writing for permission—**
♦ LP: Exactly. I just want to write about the topics I want to talk about, and oddly enough there seem to be a lot of people interested. I don't want to explore topics in an academic sense right now, and *Vanity Fair* sure isn't interested in publishing any of my material. Also, a lot of zine editors feel safer expressing themselves on paper, so it takes the place of human interaction.

♦ **V: But publishing a zine allows you to break out of your little social circle, and meet interesting, creative people you might not otherwise be able to meet—**
♦ LP: Totally—you get new blood, new thoughts, new ideas, and new inspiration. When I visited Paul Wilson in Arizona, he showed me a built-in linen cupboard in the hallway, opened up three drawers and they all were filled with fake plastic food! I was screaming; it was so funny. There was cake and cake slices, mashed potatoes . . . For some reason that made me very happy—just knowing that there's a person out there with three drawers full of fake food. If he sees an old car on the street he likes, he'll run home and put on a dress and return to shoot these guerrilla video scenes before the owner comes back to move the car. It's all to alleviate boredom; to have fun. I love it—I love the fact that I know people who do things like this. What is this life for if not to have fun? **V**

Mealtime, a 1960 home economics textbook

REFERENCE

Books, stories and media

Grace Paley: short stories

Pink Slip video

$23 from Alpha Blue Archives, PO Box 16072, Oakland CA 94610

Forever Barbie

M.G. Lord (William Morrow & Company, 1994), a journalist and cultural critic who writes intelligently and humorously about Barbie, who she is and what she means.

Where the Girls Are

Susan J. Douglas (Times Books, 1994). Subtitled "Growing Up Female with the Mass Media" and darned if that isn't exactly what it's about.

Rock She Wrote

Evelyn McDonnell and Ann Powers (Delta, 1995). A collection of music criticism written by women. I couldn't put this one down. Filled with lively, intelligent prose, it made me want to run to my desk and start writing.

Mail Order Source

Edward R. Hamilton, Book Dealer, Falls Village, CT 06031. Yes, that's the whole address. Hamilton puts out a newsprint catalog several times a year featuring pages and pages of remaindered books. Textbooks, nonfiction, fiction, even British books—I always find a bunch of stuff I want.

Film reviews from *Mystery Date #3*

Boy With a Knife. Dudley Pictures Co., late '40s/early '50s.

All right, now we enter the juvenile delinquency portion of our program! Narrated by Richard Widmark, this one features Chuck Connors as Brad Williams, youth counselor. He takes on a group of young troublemakers including Joe Martin, who "has hardly ever seen his mother sober," and Harry Jackson, who "gets too much spending money and not enough attention." But it's switchblade-toting Jerry Phillips who is the featured delinquent. Jerry's dad is an ineffectual milquetoast and his stepmother an evil bitch. Jerry, of course, acts out with his knife. The film shows Brad as he slowly works his way into the confidence of the little hellions, eventually enticing them to the "clubhouse," where Cliffie Stone's "Barracuda" blares on the turntable. The narration is mainly of the second-person "you try this, and then you try that" variety, which can be a wee bit wearing. The climactic scene comes as Jerry goes berserk, slicing up the family couch with his blade. Jerry's dad, in particular, is shocked to see his son with a knife. "That's Jerry's . . . equalizer, Mr Phillips," sez Brad, who suddenly appears in the living room with the rest of Jerry's "club," the Regals. Of course, this is just the thing to alert Dad to Jerry's need for attention, and everybody lives happily ever after, Jerry having given his knife to Brad. Having recently seen Chuck Connor's early homosexual porno loop and *Boys Beware* (see below), I have a hard time not smirking when Brad tells the guys he'll pick them up after school and take them to the ball game where "we can have hot dogs and stuff."

Boys Beware. Sid Davis Productions, produced in cooperation with the Inglewood Police Department and Inglewood Unified School District, early-mid 1960s.

This is an amazing film. One day Jimmy hitchhikes home from the park. He is picked up by Ralph. During the drive, they engage in pleasant conversation, and Ralph gives Jimmy "a friendly pat" as he gets out of the car. Ralph tells Jimmy he'll see him again, as he always drives past the park on his way home from work. Sure enough, the next day Ralph picks Jimmy up again. This time they stop for a coke, and Ralph tells some "off color stories." Jimmy's heard stories like these before, so he doesn't think too much about it. They go fishing the next Saturday. Jimmy has a great time, and when Ralph shows him some pornographic pictures, he's curious even though he knows he shouldn't look. At this point, our narrator chimes in: "Ralph was sick, with a sickness that was not visible like smallpox, but was no less dangerous and contagious, a sickness of the mind . . . Ralph was a homosexual, a person that demands an intimate relationship with members of the same sex." Jimmy keeps seeing Ralph, but Ralph demands "payment." We see them climbing the motel stairs together. Jimmy tells his parents, Ralph is arrested and Jimmy is given probation and released to the custody of his parents—incredible. Think about it—first we are told that homosexuals are predatory and that homosexuality is contagious, and then we find out that Jimmy is given probation after being molested!!! The film goes on, telling the story of Mike Merritt, who gets in a stranger's car and "trades his life for a newspaper headline." Be careful, boys, for "one never knows when the homosexual is about; he may appear normal." After seeing this film, I realize that I've been naive about how deep and vicious American homophobia can be. Mind-blowing.

Lynn Peril in her computer room. Photo: Robert Waldman

Personality Test

- Do you feel that your body adequately expresses your most engaging self?

- Do you use your hands and feet effectively?

- Do you have as many men friends as you would like?

- Is your date book filled to the cover?

- Can you "put yourself over"?

- Are you free from self-consciousness?

- Can you talk half an hour without mentioning yourself?

- Do you laugh charmingly?

- Do you know how to make a man talk?

- Are you a good listener?

- Can you entertain a "new" man for an hour?

- Can you be gay without being hoydenish?

- Can you be witty without being caustic?

- Are you often emotionally or socially upset?

- Do you cry easily?

- Do you know how to refuse a date charmingly?

- Do you know how to be disarming?

—from the *Bonomo Original Hollywood Success Course*

AK Distribution

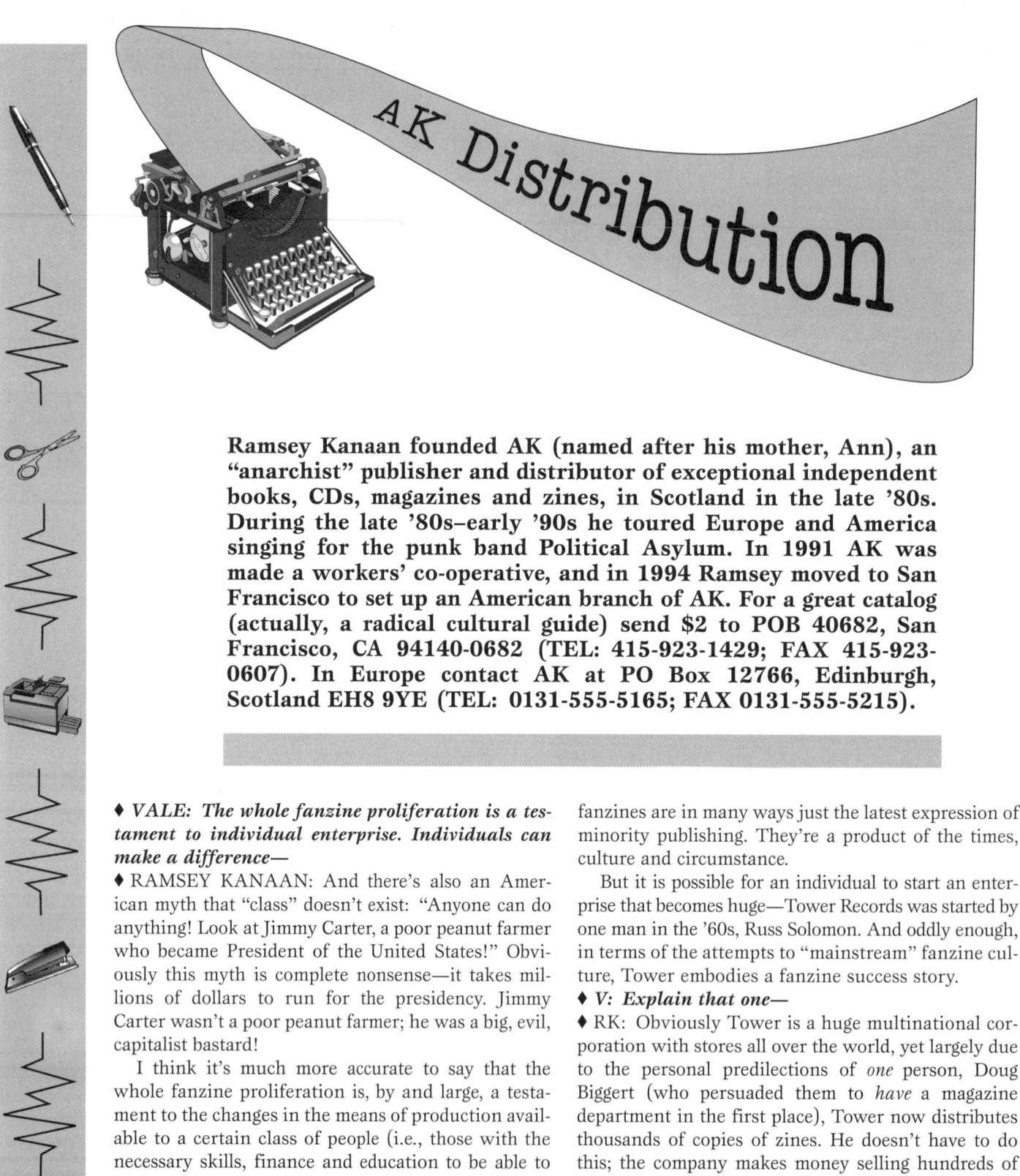

Ramsey Kanaan founded AK (named after his mother, Ann), an "anarchist" publisher and distributor of exceptional independent books, CDs, magazines and zines, in Scotland in the late '80s. During the late '80s–early '90s he toured Europe and America singing for the punk band Political Asylum. In 1991 AK was made a workers' co-operative, and in 1994 Ramsey moved to San Francisco to set up an American branch of AK. For a great catalog (actually, a radical cultural guide) send $2 to POB 40682, San Francisco, CA 94140-0682 (TEL: 415-923-1429; FAX 415-923-0607). In Europe contact AK at PO Box 12766, Edinburgh, Scotland EH8 9YE (TEL: 0131-555-5165; FAX 0131-555-5215).

♦ *VALE: The whole fanzine proliferation is a testament to individual enterprise. Individuals can make a difference—*
♦ RAMSEY KANAAN: And there's also an American myth that "class" doesn't exist: "Anyone can do anything! Look at Jimmy Carter, a poor peanut farmer who became President of the United States!" Obviously this myth is complete nonsense—it takes millions of dollars to run for the presidency. Jimmy Carter wasn't a poor peanut farmer; he was a big, evil, capitalist bastard!

I think it's much more accurate to say that the whole fanzine proliferation is, by and large, a testament to the changes in the means of production available to a certain class of people (i.e., those with the necessary skills, finance and education to be able to afford, operate and/or have access to the fruits of the desktop publishing revolution). There has *always* been a *huge* history of creativity *against the grain*—radical, underground "rabble-rousing" against dominant politics and culture. From the oral tradition of folklore and story-telling to the incendiary pamphleteering of Tom Paine or Thoreau, to the upsurge of underground manifestos, papers and comics in the '60s-'70s, to the dissident *samizdat* tracts distributed throughout Russia before the end of the Cold War, fanzines are in many ways just the latest expression of minority publishing. They're a product of the times, culture and circumstance.

But it is possible for an individual to start an enterprise that becomes huge—Tower Records was started by one man in the '60s, Russ Solomon. And oddly enough, in terms of the attempts to "mainstream" fanzine culture, Tower embodies a fanzine success story.
♦ *V: Explain that one—*
♦ RK: Obviously Tower is a huge multinational corporation with stores all over the world, yet largely due to the personal predilections of *one* person, Doug Biggert (who persuaded them to *have* a magazine department in the first place), Tower now distributes thousands of copies of zines. He doesn't have to do this; the company makes money selling hundreds of thousands of *Playboy, Rolling Stone* and *Spin, et al.* Because of the economics of zines (they're priced cheaply; they have a low profit margin), Tower doesn't actually make money selling 200 copies of a two dollar fanzine. The bureaucracy involved in shipping, receiving, and writing checks—especially if you're a huge corporation—is simply not worth it.
♦ *V: So why should Tower carry zines?*
♦ RK: Two reasons. One, Tower does have this cutting-edge radical *image* (workers are allowed to have

dyed hair, piercings and tattoos), so it's like advertising that they're "hip"—especially to this new generation of kids who are supposedly interested in the avant-garde, cutting-edge, radical underground—the whole "indie" phenomenon. There may be an image justification that is not directly economic.

But I think that Doug believes in, and wants to nurture and encourage, independent publishing—and he's obviously in a perfect position to do it! However, if Doug got hit by a bus (he rides a bicycle to work), the situation could change overnight. It's because of his *personal* drive and interest that Tower carries this huge variety of zines. It's easy for them to sell 200 copies of a fanzine; they just send two copies to each store!

♦ **V: He still has to answer to people above him—**
♦ RK: If you're selling 100,000 copies of *Rolling Stone*, then 200 copies of a two dollar fanzine doesn't really affect your bottom line. For every zine they sell, Tower sells at least 100 copies of a mainstream magazine.

Given that people make a zine for public consumption (as opposed to keeping it as a private journal, or whatever), there's the problem of how it gets out—not necessarily to a wide audience, but to *any* audience. With the desktop publishing revolution, production is actually the easy part—the *distribution* is the main headache. There are no simple solutions to that.

♦ **V: Let's discuss the ethics involved in fanzine distribution. As any "underground" enterprise gets bigger, the issue of "sell-out" becomes a major preoccupation, especially among people who might have an anti-capitalist orientation—**
♦ RK: It's only a small subset of the fanzine world that has anti-capitalist ideals or goals. And an Act of Production in and of itself doesn't imply anything about the actual content, whether in terms of politics or "selling out." Most people *would* sell out, if given the chance! How many zine editors would say "no" if Sony offered them the editorship of a new magazine?

The spectrum of fanzines covers everything. Any topic you can think of, somebody has produced a zine on it (from politics to B-movies to personal travel diaries to model airplane making). Within politics, you have everything from extreme anarchists on one side to extreme Neo-Nazis on the other, all producing independent zines in *mirror-worlds*. Each has their own network of distribution, their own web site on the Internet, their own rock bands—each group has their own *mini-subculture* supporting their cottage industry!

♦ **V: Actually, how do you define a "zine"?**
♦ RK: Something like *Wired* or *Rolling Stone* is obviously a magazine. With the desktop publishing revolution, it's relatively easy to make your publication look as appealing (in terms of sophisticated design and production) as a more mainstream product. In terms of *content,* now the mainstream publications are presenting what was formerly considered more "underground" or avant-garde or obscure—last year's underground punk bands are today's stadium rock acts!

Ramsey surrounded by zines sold by AK Distribution. Photo: Robert Waldman

We're seeing the *mainstreaming of weird, kooky ideas*—from UFO/occult theories (as in television's *X-Files*) to radical politics. And in the last few years everyone from *Time* and *Newsweek* to the *Wall Street Journal* and the *New York Times* has published features on the "zine revolution." The *WSJ* interviewed me for an article that emphasized the mainstreaming of fanzines as supported by the fact that publishers are now producing anthologies of zines as *books*. Since we published the first three issues of *Answer Me* in a book, we're considered a forerunner of this "trend."

The mainstream is stealing, borrowing or assimilating underground ideas—partly because the ideas of many zines are *not* avantgarde! In terms of *content*, a music fanzine photocopied at Kinko's with a circulation of 50 can contain interviews with exactly the same bands as *Rolling Stone* or *Spin;* the only difference is circulation.

♦ **V:** *I saw on the Internet John Labovitz's "E-Zine List," which defined a zine as: "generally produced by one person or a small group, done often for fun or personal reasons, tending to be irreverent, bizarre, and/or esoteric . . . they generally do not contain advertisements, are not targeted towards a mass audience and are generally not produced to make a profit."*

♦ **RK:** I think that's a fairly good definition of the *reality* of fanzines, yet it sounds like a statement of *intent,* which I don't necessarily think is the case at all. While they may not be targeted toward a mass audience, not produced for profit primarily or contain advertisements, this is certainly not to say that any of the editors would object if any of these things were to happen. It's just that they are not in a position to attract advertisers, or sell enough to make a profit, or have wide enough distribution or a format attractive enough to reach a mass audience. It might be more accurate to say that zines by and large are a *hobby,* and as such are not expected to be judged by the standards of a commercial venture.

Actually, fanzines have always had advertising. Often when they start, they advertise things for free, such as a friend's record label or other fanzines. Perhaps the major distinction involves *who* they accept advertising from, and whether it's paid. Music magazines which pride themselves on being "underground," promoting some kind of radical subculture, often will not accept corporate advertising. They won't take an ad from Nike or Absolut vodka, and certainly wouldn't take an ad from Warner Brothers or even Matador Records, because even though they started out independent, Matador workers are now employees of Time-Warner.

Any record label big enough to have a paid employee probably has an advertising budget. Even relatively small labels like Alternative Tentacles, which has about four employees, advertise widely in fanzines.

♦ **V:** *But they don't have to, do they?*

♦ **RK:** Epitaph, a bigger independent label, advertises in mainstream music magazines, but they also advertise in the lowliest (in terms of presentation and circulation) zines—if it's a punk fanzine, I can almost guarantee that Epitaph has paid $50 for the privilege of appearing in it. They sell millions of records because they have videos on MTV and bands which are household names being played on daytime radio, so they don't have to give Johnny or Jeanette Punk $50 to advertise in a fanzine with a circulation of 500. For them, it's probably a conscious political decision to put something back into the underground scene they came out of.

Cover of *Stealworks* by John Yates, published by AK Press

For most advertisers who don't have as much money to spend, however, the fact remains that they *do!* They must figure it's worthwhile. Often they're small record labels or providers of specialty merchandise (for example, a seller of "gothic" jewelry will advertise in a "goth" zine). They think their outlay will be recouped either directly through sales, or by establishing name-recognition for their product—creating a "presence in the marketplace" or whatever.

We're seeing the *mainstreaming of weird, kooky ideas*—from UFO/occult theories (as in television's *X-Files*) to radical politics.

Obviously, capitalism is built on advertising, whether for Cadillacs or detergent. In that sense, fanzines are a microcosm of that economy—I don't necessarily mean that pejoratively. On the most de-politicized level, advertising is about presenting people with information—which is the whole point of fanzines in the first place.

Beyond advertising, a difference between zines and

magazines is circulation—most fanzines print 2,000 or less. But *Maximum Rock'n'Roll, Ben Is Dead* and *Factsheet Five* print nearly 20,000 copies, so are they still fanzines? Circulation is another grey area.

The "labor of love" issue may be a further dividing line: zines are usually produced by unpaid labor. *Maximum Rock'n'Roll* is produced solely by volunteers, and the editor-in-chief, Tim Yohannon, still works a day job. So another definition of a zine involves the economics of production. With most fanzines, the editors don't make a living from the zine. They might get some fringe benefits like free records to review or other zines in trade, but the publication does not pay the rent or put food in their bellies. So if it doesn't pay for itself; if the editor digs into his or her pockets to produce it—that may qualify it as a zine. I'd say 98% of zines simply don't pay for themselves; it's not like sales of issue #1 pay for issue #2. There are lots of hidden costs in publishing, like sending out free review copies to other publications.

Lastly, "professionalism" cannot be a standard because many small zines look very professional, with full color covers and web offset printing. The quality of *Answer Me* is comparable to *Rolling Stone*, which is printed on newsprint. In many ways, given that zine publishing is so broad and the definitions and delineations so blurred, the whole labeling process is arbitrary and irrelevant.

♦ **V: *How do zines make any money at all?***
♦ **RK:** Primarily from advertising or subscriptions—100 subscriptions might pay for one print run, depending on the zine. If enough people pay $10 for a two-issue subscription to a five dollar magazine, that might raise $1,000.

When advertising pays for most of the costs of production, then economically distribution becomes almost irrelevant, because distribution makes little money, given the economics of it all. It might sound like a *Catch-22,* but that's the reality. The distributor takes a cut, the store takes a cut, you have to pay for shipping, so almost the only logical reason to increase your circulation is (in terms of finance): you can charge more for advertising. *Rolling Stone* charges substantially more for a three by five inch ad than *Factsheet Five*; the situation is similar in the fanzine world. For the same ad taking up exactly the same space, you can charge Epitaph exponentially more money if your circulation is 10,000 as opposed to 200. Of course, publications usually list the print run, not what they sell. You can print 10,000 magazines and 90% could be returned by the distributor, but you don't tell your advertisers that!

♦ **V: *How does AK decide what to distribute?***
♦ **RK:** AK is an overtly political project (we are unashamedly anarchists and "left"—if anarchists can even be defined as left!). We straddle the lunatic fringe with glee. We have two criteria. One is if we like it—meaning that it contributes something politically or culturally. We're fairly liberal in our definitions here: when we say "political" we don't just mean something hardcore-anarchist that only talks about smashing the state and killing the President—actually, it's a federal offense to say that! Our definition of "politics" extends into radical culture and the avant-garde, or pop culture and radical art. We sell 200–300 different fanzines, and probably only *five* talk solely about activist politics and how to destroy the state in one easy lesson. So the first reason is whether we like it.

The second reason we distribute a zine is if we think we can sell it. There may be a fanzine we like for whatever reasons (we think it's very witty, or well done, or an interesting "take" on an unusual subject, or whatever), but that doesn't mean we can sell it. We sell music magazines, especially those that offer some cultural or political inspiration, and this includes a couple of hip-hop magazines which are political, sharp, incisive and well-written and designed. Nevertheless, the audience and markets we sell to aren't interested in that particular genre—when we send ten copies to a bookstore, nine are returned.

There are certainly publications that we would like to take but can't. Sometimes it's because they have an exclusive distribution agreement with someone else. More often, it's the fact that a small zine can't afford the economics of distribution. While we do have a substantial mail order business, the vast majority of what we sell goes to stores. We give stores a standard 40% discount off the list price (they pay us 60 cents for a one dollar zine). Hence we ask a 50% discount from the publisher (i.e., we make 10% off the list price as our cut). The publisher has to pay shipping to get the zine to us. Certain publishers simply can't afford to supply us on these terms.

If there were a fanzine on how to make model airplanes, we wouldn't take it. It could be the best zine ever written on this topic, and might make some devastating cultural and political critique besides, but the stores we sell to wouldn't stock a zine on how to

Cover of *Ecstatic Incisions*, published by AK Press, 1992

make a model airplane.

It's not economically viable for us to sell zines at all. The profit margins are too small, and the labor involved is intensive. The average zine sells for two dollars or less, so we might make 20 cents per copy. If we can't sell more than 25 copies of something, it's not worth our while—it's too much of a bureaucratic headache. If you take 25 copies and five bookstores take five each, that means invoicing and packing five separate bundles, shipping them and dealing with returns (if each store returns two copies, you have to issue five credit memos against future sales). So for this two dollar fanzine, even if you sold 20 out of 25 copies, at 20 cents profit each you'd make four dollars! Of the four dollars, two dollars are spent on sending back to the publisher the five copies we didn't sell; there's a bank charge for processing the check we wrote them—basically, the economics don't work! Even if we sell *200* copies of this zine, we're still only making 20 cents each, and it still doesn't work; instead of sending out five bundles, we're sending out 40.

Other products (books and CDs) sold by AK are more profitable—they have a higher retail price, and they subsidize the fanzine sales. On a $10 book, we may make $1.50 to two dollars. These profits pay our meager wages, whereas selling 25 copies of a fanzine doesn't. Nevertheless, we will carry 25 copies of a zine because we think its politics are spot-on, or it's so brilliant that we want to make it available to an uncaring world!

Another source of zine subsidy is the few fanzines that sell 1,000 copies or more, like *Panic Button*—we take their entire print run of 2,000. Certain pop culture zines help subsidize the hardcore political/feminist ones. Admittedly, we have a personal investment in the more political ones like *Fifth Estate,* of which we sell about 40 copies. Again, our decision to distribute zines is *political* rather than economic. And even if we take a zine because it will sell a lot of copies, it's accepted not as a profit-maker, but because it will cut the losses.

Just as most people who consume poetry are poets themselves, most people who consume fanzines are zine editors.

Stores that sell zines are in effect subsidizing them, just like we are; their reasons for stocking them are other than economic. Usually it's because A) they believe in supporting underground publishing, and B) they think that zines are politically and culturally important. Also, they may want to attract a different customer base than the Barnes & Noble store down the street that won't stock zines. But per square foot of floor space, fanzines generate far less income than,

say, CDs or books. A rack that can display 20 two dollar zines can display 100 books retailing for $10–$20 each.

Stores usually won't take digest-size fanzines (5½″ x 8½″) because their racks are not the right size. (They won't take anything *bigger* than 8½″ x 11″ for the same reason.) And usually they won't take something unless it has a glossy full-color cover (or at least a good quality card-stock cover). Ironically, a lot of stores won't carry *Maximum Rock'n'Roll*—even though it's the best selling punk underground magazine—because the cover is newsprint. *Maximum Rock'n'Roll* could double its sales if it had a glossy cover, but the editor refuses to do that.

There are several big independent distributors for zines, like Fine Print and Desert Moon, and because of the way magazine distribution works, they have fairly stringent demands which are out-of-reach of most fanzine publishers. These are typically: 1) full-color glossy cover (if you're printing 200-500 copies, you probably can't afford this); 2) a UPC bar code (if you don't have this, a distributor may charge you 12-20 cents *per zine* to place a bar code on the cover); 3) affidavit returns (the store will only pay for what they sell; at best they'll cut off the masthead and return it. Usually they'll just say, "You sent us 10 magazines, we sold seven and here's payment for seven—you'll have to take our word for this"). At AK, we do whole copy returns if requested; people who publish 500 zines and sell 300 can't afford to have 200 copies thrown away or recycled. But bigger distributors say, "If you can't accept affidavit returns, we won't carry your zine."

Big zine distributors require UPC bar codes because larger stores like Barnes & Noble or Borders demand them—their inventory is computerized.

♦ **V: *What's considered a good sales percentage?***
♦ **RK:** Fifty percent. Eighty or ninety percent is considered phenomenal.

So, on all levels of a fanzine (producing, distributing, and retailing), there aren't really any substantial profits. Fine Print and Desert Moon are making *some* money, but they won't take a zine unless they can sell several hundred, whereas we'll take one if we can sell 25.

Sometimes we sell something if nobody else will, or if we get an exclusive. We're the exclusive importer of *Idler,* a British pop culture magazine celebrating the joys of sloth and not working—it has a radical critique of the work ethic, obviously. It's witty and well done, and we import about 1,000 copies.

The advent of the punk revolution which popularized the concept of D-I-Y [Do-It-Yourself] was accompanied by technology which made increasingly sophisticated publishing available for comparatively low costs and expertise. Scanners are now cheap, and for a relatively low price you can now scan in graphics—cut 'n' paste has become almost obsolete. Twenty years ago, a computer capable of producing a fanzine would have taken up a sizable warehouse space and cost a million dollars, whereas now it costs two grand and can be used by someone with barely more expertise than minimal typing skills.

The whole D-I-Y ethic coupled with the availability of the means of production has obviously resulted in a fanzine *explosion,* both in quantity and quality of zines produced. When Mark Perry produced the first punk fanzine *Sniffin' Glue,* he used a mimeograph machine—Kinko's offers phenomenally more advanced technology today. Paradoxically, on a broad scale, the potential audience for printed material is *shrinking.* Adult illiteracy is rising, and fewer people *want* to read.

In Britain in the 1800s there was a population of under 10 million, most of whom were illiterate and massively poor. There was no such thing as a national distributor, yet Tom Paine's pamphlets sold over 100,000 each! Today, there isn't that long tradition of working class radical political culture, and the alternatives to print media (TV, film and video, Sega games, etc) have never been so dominant and pervasive. Of those few people who do read, probably less than 50% actually shop at bookstores—let alone the kind of small independent store where one might find zines.

So although there has been a huge explosion in zine production, the audience represents a population of mostly college-educated young people. Most people still do not own computers or have access to them, so it's a privileged elite who have the time to produce or read zines.

♦ **V: A lot of the audience for a zine is made up of other fanzine publishers—**
♦ **RK:** Just as most people who consume poetry are poets themselves, most people who consume fanzines are zine editors themselves. It's a very small, inward-looking scene.

In a way, a fanzine isn't *popular* culture. On any level, *music* is a lot more popular than literature. Even small underground music acts can sell 5,000 records, while big "underground" bands sell hundreds of thousands. Those involved in the zine publishing scene may think that *Factsheet Five* selling 15,000 copies is incredible, but it's very much the "big fish in a little pond" syndrome.

♦ **V: Actually, in the book publishing world, a lot of famous authors sell fewer copies than one might think—**
♦ **RK:** Other than bell hooks, Noam Chomsky is the biggest-selling leftist intellectual superstar. He has had a movie made about him, and wherever he speaks several thousand people attend his lecture—as though he were some rock act. People produce CDs on him—everyone's trying to cash in! Chomsky is definitely a big fish in the left, intellectual, radical activist milieu. His best-selling books are the small Odonian Press lecture transcripts which sell for five dollars; they've sold about 65,000 each—whereas Newt Gingrich and Colin Powell have each sold a million of their $23 hardbacks. Of Chomsky's more substantial political

Noam Chomsky CD put out by AK press audio, 1994

work (which includes *Necessary Illusions* and *Manufacturing Consent),* his best-seller is *The Washington Connection.* Published in 1971, it has sold only 30,000 copies (a little over 1,000 copies a year—*nothing).*

However, the avant-garde can have an effect far wider than sales figures might indicate. The Sex Pistols certainly sold far fewer records than Madonna or Michael Jackson or Nirvana or Green Day. Yet obviously the Sex Pistols had a pivotal impact; they revolutionized the way we look at music.

Fanzines that are weird and left-field are never going to be taken seriously by the arbiters of elite intellectual opinion (*New York Times)* or the arbiters of mass culture (MTV*).*

♦ **V: Still, fanzines will continue to be produced—**
♦ **RK:** And the very production of a fanzine means that the editor wants it to be read. Just being involved with the printed word means that most people *won't* be interested. That's the reality, but what excites me is pushing the boundaries of that reality: trying to break through, and make interesting things more available and accessible.

♦ **V: That's what the Beastie Boys' Grand Royal was trying to do—**
♦ **RK:** *Grand Royal* is very much a magazine and not strictly a fanzine. It's aimed at youth culture, and within that is very political (it directly addresses political concerns such as sexism in the music industry, and the censorship of rap). Presumably it has mainstream distribution, plus major advertising support from huge corporations. It's big and chunky, glossy (with a full-color cover), and relatively cheap. It'll be interesting to see how it sells. I think it's great: pushing politics and serious discussions of issues into the mainstream. Whether or not one agrees with the use of corporate backing to do this, it's an attempt to shift the "radical fanzine ethic" into mainstream culture.

Ramsey in drag. Photo: Debs

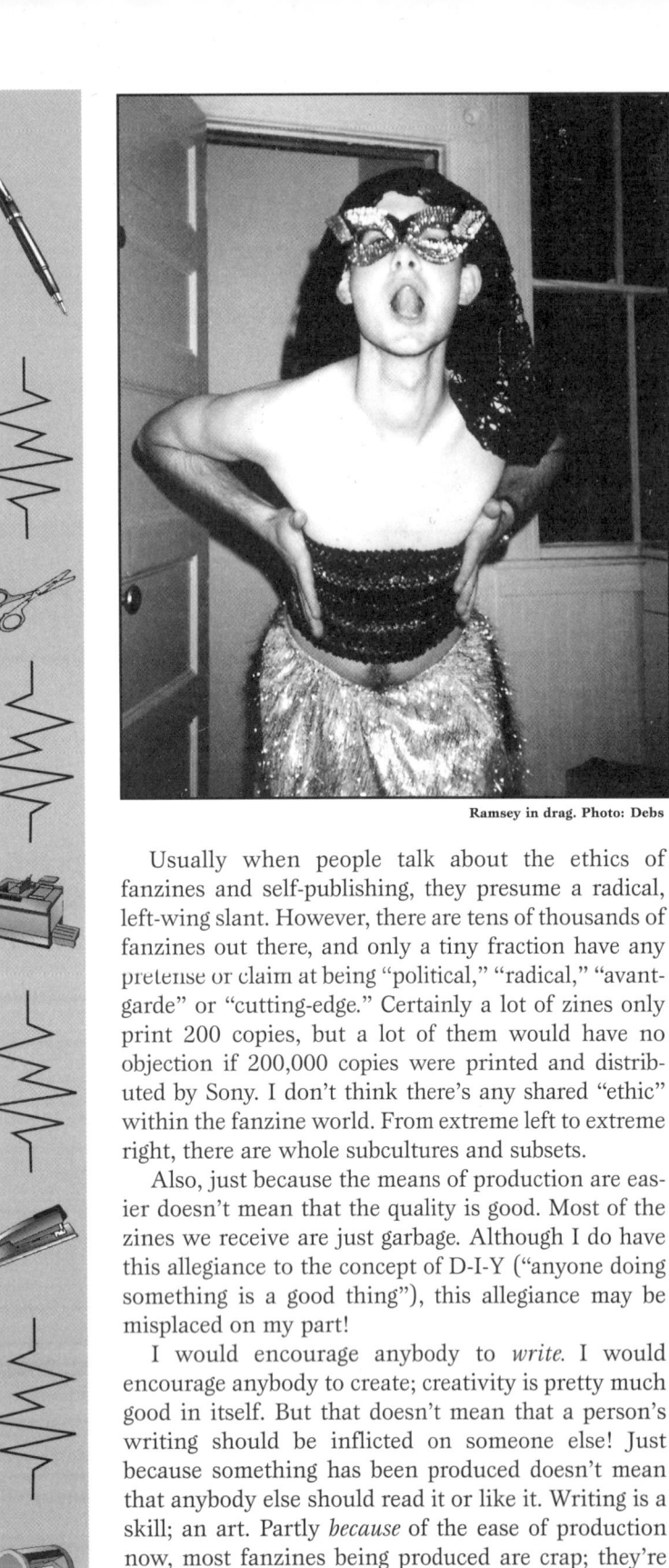

Usually when people talk about the ethics of fanzines and self-publishing, they presume a radical, left-wing slant. However, there are tens of thousands of fanzines out there, and only a tiny fraction have any pretense or claim at being "political," "radical," "avant-garde" or "cutting-edge." Certainly a lot of zines only print 200 copies, but a lot of them would have no objection if 200,000 copies were printed and distributed by Sony. I don't think there's any shared "ethic" within the fanzine world. From extreme left to extreme right, there are whole subcultures and subsets.

Also, just because the means of production are easier doesn't mean that the quality is good. Most of the zines we receive are just garbage. Although I do have this allegiance to the concept of D-I-Y ("anyone doing something is a good thing"), this allegiance may be misplaced on my part!

I would encourage anybody to *write*. I would encourage anybody to create; creativity is pretty much good in itself. But that doesn't mean that a person's writing should be inflicted on someone else! Just because something has been produced doesn't mean that anybody else should read it or like it. Writing is a skill; an art. Partly *because* of the ease of production now, most fanzines being produced are crap; they're badly written and/or badly designed. A good example of bad design was *Vague #16/17*. It took the fanzine "thing" one step further into a trade book format; while totally retaining D-I-Y ethics and having no corporate backing—nevertheless you couldn't fuckin' read it! The type was set against a dark red or blue background, and it may have *looked* "radical" or "cut-ting edge," but the message was missing. It ended up being totally reprinted in order to be legible.

♦ **V: Producing a fanzine has given many people a sense of community they never had before—**

♦ RK: But I would argue that the term "fanzine community" is meaningless. There's no community of ideas. One could say that's a good thing—personally, I don't think fascist fanzines are a good thing, but nevertheless, zines are produced from every conceivable angle, aptitude, inclination and interest. And many thousands of zines are never sold in *any* stores: fan-club and hobbyist newsletters, subscription-only zines, etc.

♦ **V: But people have definitely found new friends through zine publishing; they've attracted a small, though geographically widespread, community based on shared interests. There definitely is a zine community involving radical female publishers whose goal is social change . . . One advantage to self-publishing is: there's nobody censoring you except yourself—**

♦ RK: The whole issue of "censorship" needs to be clarified. If a mom-and-pop store decides not to carry your fanzine for economic reasons, that isn't censorship. If a distributor demands a bar code and affidavit returns, that isn't censorship. If AK doesn't take a fanzine because it's about model airplanes (even though the model airplanes might carry the storm troopers of the revolution!), that's not censorship. One might argue that the issue isn't censorship, but freedom of choice.

To me, censorship is a *power* issue. AK (or a certain store) not carrying a zine doesn't make it not available. We're not suppressing its publication, we're not putting its editor in jail, we're not seizing the zines and engaging in book-burning. Even if we were so inclined, it's not an option!

When something radical is given mainstream media exposure, those who nurtured that particular idea are the first to suffer—they *never* benefit.

In San Francisco, Epicenter [a volunteer-run, not-for-profit store which sells independent records and zines] is constantly being accused of censorship because it chooses not to carry certain items. Sometimes the volunteers who run Epicenter reject zines ("We're volunteering here, so why should we carry something we don't like?"). But that is not censorship. In Bellingham, Washington, the police told a newsstand which sold *Answer Me #4* (the "rape" issue) to remove it from their shelves, as it was promoting violence against women. The owners refused. Now they're being prosecuted by the DA and face up to five years in prison. To me *that* is censorship.

If customs seizes a book—*that* is censorship. When the government says, "We're not letting that into the country," that is censorship. And it's not just a quantitative difference, it's a qualitative difference boiling down to *power* and how you exercise that power.

♦ **V: Government-financed prosecution not only suppresses the existence of the publication, it also jeopardizes the personal life of the publisher, who has to raise thousands in legal fees and could also be thrown in prison. And anyone who's sued gets damaged, because they almost never recover their legal fees—not to mention the stress involved . . . Well, most zines will never get distributed sufficiently to even be prosecuted.**

♦ RK: Again, Tower Records has provided an answer to the problem fanzines face in distribution: getting access to a larger audience. Most of the clientele visiting Tower don't *go* to bookstores. They probably don't live in a town that has a good independent bookstore, and even if one existed, they probably wouldn't visit it. So Tower is achieving the clichéd "getting across to a different audience," which you don't usually reach with your independent or "leftie" bookstore or quality newsstand. They take a lot of fanzines, succeed in selling them, and they pay quite regularly. They expose people to information that is "radical" or "underground"—i.e., not normally seen by mainstream society. Small press, bizarre, non-mainstream publications of whatever hue are being made accessible to a more mainstream audience. This is all true, and more power to Tower for that.

Unfortunately, the chains are a double-edged sword. They are quite actively, deliberately and aggressively putting out of business small, independent stores who have always been, and always will be, the backbone of support for the radical, non-mainstream publication. While chains may give zines wider distribution (the ones that match the correct size, content, cover and bar-code criteria), it is at the cost of the original network which has always supported, nurtured and made possible much of the fanzine culture.

Also, when something radical is given mainstream media exposure, those who nurtured that particular idea or publication or scene are the first to suffer—they *never* benefit. Consistently, any idea that is radical or "out there" gets watered down or modified to comply with what is "commercially acceptable," as defined by the corporate planners. This watered-down version, usually reduced to a few conspicuous elements of style (e.g., a brightly-dyed mohawk and a hand-painted leather jacket) gets marketed. Also, sales actually get taken away from those who kept that idea alive in the first place. In the '70s and early '80s feminist or gay literature could only be found in radical bookstores, but now you can find this at the chains.

Consequently, radical, independent bookstores are losing sales and closing down *en masse* as the chains proliferate everywhere. And of course, once there are only the chains left, there will be nowhere left to buy such literature. Because once the chains have no competition, what incentive is there to stock uneconomical, marginal publications such as zines or feminist/queer literature? There's a great bumpersticker that needs mass distribution: "Friends don't let friends shop at chain stores."

There's a great bumpersticker that needs mass distribution: "Friends don't let friends shop at chain stores."

♦ **V: I hope more small stores (like Naked Eye on Haight Street) spring up and persist in selling zines, even though it's a lot of work. What does the future hold?**

♦ RK: I'd like to see zines keep going for years and just get better and better. I'd like to see production standards and the writing itself keep improving. I'd like to see more thoughtful, more provocative, better researched writing—not just something written "off the top of my head" at midnight in a frenzy and then printed at Kinko's and distributed, *unedited,* for the world to see. *Factsheet Five* is a very worthy publication that lists and reviews many different zines, but it's limited in that it depends on people voluntarily sending in free copies of their fanzine. A lot of worthwhile publications never get mentioned because their editors didn't bother digging in their pockets for postage, large envelope costs, and sending in a complimentary copy.

Of course, I'd like to see independent distribution—both in terms of distributors and stores—develop to a point where we are not constantly at the whim of the corporate media and the chains, in our attempts to get radical ideas out there. We have to develop, build and nurture genuine alternatives—politically, culturally and in terms of organization.

♦ **V: I'd also like to see a zine archive where every zine there ever was is accessible—organized by subject, title, year, editor and contributor. So if I wanted to see all the earliest "Riot Grrrl" zines, I could access them and pay a small charge for copying the ones I really need.**

♦ RK: That would be great. The official libraries of the world aren't set up to preserve information counter to their status quo values, so we need to have libraries to serve *our* needs, our interests, our culture, our lives. And we have to do this for ourselves; the government's never going to do that for us! We have to do this, and fund this, *ourselves.* ∎

outpunk

Matt Wobensmith does OUTPUNK, a queercore record label and zine. To date he has released a dozen 45s and CDs (including Tribe 8, Pansy Division, etc) and four issues of *Outpunk* zine. For information send a self-addressed stamped envelope (or $3 for a sample copy of the zine) to OUTPUNK, PO Box 170501, San Francisco CA 94117.

♦ *VALE: Describe* **Outpunk—**
♦ MATT WOBENSMITH: Outpunk is a queer record label and magazine which I started in 1992. It's not just about being queer, but that's the number one thread that bonds all the projects together.
♦ *V: Tell us about yourself—*
♦ MW: I grew up on a farm near the tiny rural town of Pipersville, Pennsylvania, and moved to San Francisco in 1989. I went to a year of art school and then dropped out. I've been working at a one-hour photo lab ever since—that's what I do forty-plus hours a week—and in my spare time I do my record label and zine. I worked five years at Epicenter record store/punk rock hangout, a collectively-run operation at 16th and Valencia, and I wrote for *Maximum Rock'n'Roll (MRR)* for three years until I quit over a year ago.

Six years after coming here I feel like I'm still adjusting to city life. Certainly a big reason I moved to San Francisco was to be gay—I just *knew* there was a world out there that was better than what I had. I was miserable in Pennsylvania, so this was definitely the right choice. I'm growing all the time—reinventing myself and what I do, and I'm just as thrilled to be in San Francisco now as when I first got here.
♦ *V: Can you tell us your "coming out" story—*
♦ MW: Coming out is a *process*. There are a lot of ways you can "come out": to yourself, your parents, your friends, your job and finally just feeling comfortable being "out." For me, every one of those events took place at a different time in my life. But I *can* say that all the time I've been in San Francisco (since I was eighteen) I've been "out."

I wasn't out before; I came out when I arrived here—I shed my skin. However, people were out at the high school I went to. In fact, people are "out" all over the country, although they may be unhappy or struggling. If I were still back in Pennsylvania, I would not be anywhere near where I am today in terms of my maturity or mental state. I would be out, for sure, but—? People in areas other than San Francisco spend their whole lives never experiencing the freedom we have. Their lives are full of compromise and secrecy—basically, not living up to their full potential.

> **Coming out is a *process*. There are a lot of ways you can "come out": to yourself, your parents, your friends, your job, and finally just feeling comfortable being "out."**

Places like rural Pennsylvania are beautiful, but they're really just a vacuum—there's nothing there. Small towns have small-minded people. If you're smarter and have a desire to see more and know more, you have to get out or you'll suffocate.

At the time I came out, I was also into punk rock. I felt that the two different parts of my life (being queer and being punk) had so much in common. I felt, "Why not be the first to put it all together?" I wasn't really the *first* one to do this, but I had a vision and followed it, and really didn't have anybody as a role model.

Now everybody thinks queer punk was *always* there, but the small-town mentality applies in the city too: in a small town, there's nothing happening unless you *make* it happen. I decided that even if all I had was the four walls of my bedroom, I would make that work for me. I think that queer punk is still a "bedroom" thing—I'm listening to a queer record in my bedroom, and some kid is listening to it in his bedroom. Whether or not they have someone to talk about it with is another story, but there's definitely a growing network.

♦ **V:** *What do your parents do?*
♦ **MW:** My dad's a copyright/patent attorney, and my mother's a housewife—an upper-middle-class family. I'm an identical twin; there's a one-in-a-hundred chance of that happening (when I was growing up I was really into statistics). When you're identical, you're from the same egg as your sibling, so that means you have the same genes.

Unlike some other twins, we didn't get along. I had a lot of trauma growing up—we were trying to be as different as possible. Often twins look similar throughout life, but as we get older my twin and I look more and more different. I have a lot of tattoos and he has none, I have short hair and he has longer hair. My brother is straight and I'm gay (ask him again in five years, maybe he'll give a different answer).

Punk has become, to me, almost the status quo, so what I'm doing is challenging punk.

I was an honor student and my parents had all these hopes for me. In junior high I was really popular, but then I took a sour turn and decided I didn't want to do things like everybody else. I deliberately flunked out of classes. I graduated from high school but cut ties with my parents when I moved here, just to be *myself*. I couldn't be what they wanted me to be: a lawyer, going to school, making money and being straight. Now I think they've accepted me, but I don't talk about what I do. They ask questions like, "Are you making money? Are we going to see you on TV? Are we going to read about you in a magazine?"

Matt in his living room. Photo: Robert Waldman

OUTPUNK
Issue #3 $2.00

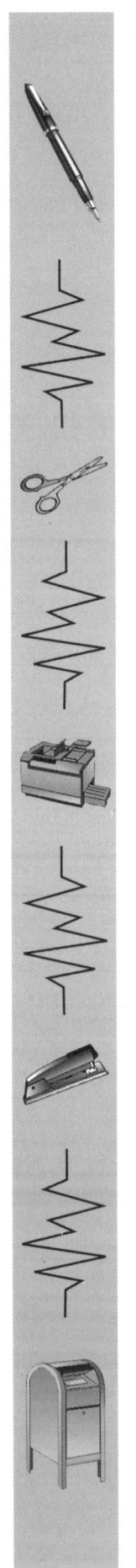

Focus on the Family

Cover of *Outpunk #3*

♦ **V: So in high school you became alienated from your studies—**
♦ **MW:** I just turned off. I came to San Francisco to attend the SF Art Institute—it was my way to escape. Otherwise my parents would not have let me go away as easily as I did. They didn't want me to move 3000 miles away and be who I am. I had an interest in photography and that was what I pursued. Then I landed this killer job at a one-hour lab! [laughs sarcastically]

♦ **V: How did you get into punk rock in a rural area of Pennsylvania?**
♦ **MW:** I learned a lot from college radio and from interacting with certain people in high school. When I was 15 in 1986, I started going to punk shows. This was *way* past the initial waves of the punk rock movement, but for me it was real—I was very into it.

♦ **V: Were there a lot of punks in your high school?**
♦ **MW:** About a dozen.

♦ **V: You were part of a rebellious sub-group—**
♦ **MW:** Sure! However, I don't constantly look at what I do and ask, "Is it punk rock enough?" Punk has become, to me, almost the status quo, so what I'm doing is challenging punk.

♦ **V: Outpunk is a catchy name—**
♦ **MW:** *Outpunk* was a reflection of where I was at when I turned 21. Now I'm 24, and what I'm doing now is more my *own* vision. I always thought, "Being queer is just like being punk—those two belong together." But now I hope to break through this cult of restrictive thinking, this sheep-like mentality that I think punk rock has become, and help get people involved in other interesting areas—that's my goal. It was important to get involved in a "counterculture," but I've always wanted to be different and do things the way *I* wanted to.

♦ **V: But punk provided a support context—**
♦ **MW:** I believed in punk rock and flew that punk rock banner. I came to the city, got involved and totally believed in the cause. I was willing to overlook all these little things that in retrospect were fucked-up. But I was young! Punk was good for me in a lot of ways; the community was supportive, and I needed it.

Now I do *Outpunk,* but that doesn't *define* me—it's a hobby. I haven't gotten to the point where I even consider it as a viable source of income. I think the problem with being forced to live off your hobby is: it would no longer be fun. If I have any goal about money, it's to put out one record that sells well—then I can do fun things on the side. (But if I had to put out a crappy record just because I thought it would sell, that would be fucked—especially if it *didn't* sell. Imagine 10,000 shitty records sitting in your living room!) Actually, selling anything is a compromise to me—I would love to just *give* my records to anybody who wanted them.

I feel like I'm putting out records for myself—creating something for *me* to listen to at home. I enjoy music immensely and I want to be able to share it with my friends or other people. But yes, I would love to have a record that sold really well so I could fuck off and take chances and do things that are really wacky.

> **The small town mentality applies to the city too: there's nothing happening unless you *make* it happen.**

People say there are two roads to success: 1) learn from everything, use your wisdom, take everything into account, and make an educated guess; and 2) ignore the rules! You can't tell what's going to take off and be popular; you never know. If something does well, you can draw conclusions and use them to make a game plan for your next project, but plans don't always work.

♦ **V: When did you start releasing records?**
♦ **MW:** I put out punk singles when I started working at *MRR*. They were really crappily done. Putting out punk rock doesn't require you to do things well. On the next record you hope to correct the part you

116

fucked up on the first one, and you'll make another mistake. Everybody has the same story: you learn by making mistakes. And I've made tons of mistakes putting out records, running a business, and dealing with people.

♦ **V: Describe your support context—**

♦ MW: I used to have my gay friends and my music friends, and they were different groups. I wouldn't tell certain people I dated, "I went to this show last night," and vice versa. I've had friends and confidantes who were queer and punk at the same time, but there wasn't any group context. So I just went ahead and did *Outpunk*. I had help, but basically it was just me. Hopefully other people can learn from me and do it better.

> **My biggest influence has been Bikini Kill . . . we could read the fanzines and substitute the word "queer" for the word "female."**

Even though I put it down a lot now, punk was a big influence on me. Punk showed that you could aspire to be something different, and that there was this thriving subculture that didn't need the mainstream (whatever *that* is). That's where my roots are. There were bands and zines and individuals that were a big inspiration to me.

The thing that really influenced *Outpunk* was not the queer stuff going on—the biggest influence on the so-called "queercore" movement was the feminist movement in music. My biggest influence from punk has been BIKINI KILL (both the music and the fanzines)—Kathleen Hanna has influenced not only Riot Grrrl and all these young women doing things, but queers too, because we could read the fanzines and substitute the word "queer" for the word "female." I would not be so simplistic as to say that queer issues are the same as female issues, but there are a lot of similarities.

Kathleen Hanna was just talking about being a woman in a woman-hating society. She was talking about real issues involving empathy, compassion, as well as intelligence. The first time I got a Bikini Kill fanzine was over four years ago, and it changed my life—I can seriously say that. It took me months to read it, if you can imagine—I knew it was just so amazing. There was this really cool section in issue #2 where Kathleen totally dissected the ten most commonly-used put-downs from guys about the issues she was raising, like: "I know a *guy* who was raped by a woman." And every analysis was totally right on.

As soon as you start doing something like Riot Grrrl, people (particularly the media) put a label on it, and it becomes this other thing, the same way that punk rock has become such a gargoyle. I don't want queercore to be just a label. I don't want it to be a subset of a music scene or a political movement; I think that's limiting and it robs people of their potential.

♦ **V: A Bikini Kill zine is just as truthful and relevant years after it first appeared. It's not like society has gotten that much freer or more enlightened in the past few years. So you started** Outpunk **while working at** Maximum Rock'n'Roll**—**

♦ MW: Working for this big punk rock magazine, *MRR,* I got ads at half price and got to use their computers and copiers and make my flats and lay out my record covers and do a queer punk thing. They were supportive—I have to give them credit. But I paid them back—I worked for free!

♦ **V: How did you pay for the first records you released?**

♦ MW: Before I started *Outpunk,* me and two other friends each came up with $300 or $400 and paid for the first pressing of a single. Then I lucked into an M&D (Manufacturing and Distribution) deal with a local distributor. Looking at my track record, they thought, "Why not pay for his releases? We'll take our cut and he'll take his." I no longer had to put up all the capital. So I went from working with several hundred dollars to several thousand. I can now finance a new release and hopefully sell enough to get my money back. My biggest reward is when people understand what I'm trying to do; regarding this, my favorite

Cover of Outpunk #4

cliché is: "If I have touched just one person, then it's all worthwhile." A lot of people *aren't* enlightened—I have to constantly remember that. This is a battle that's going to be fought forever.

I put out different types of records; I don't just put out one "sound." What excites me is creating *new aesthetics*. Some people have accused me of putting out records that aren't "punk" enough, but to me we don't need that definition anymore. I'm doing things that I think will appeal to people who are into punk, but mainly I'm putting out records that I would personally buy: "This is incredible—why would you deprive yourself of this?" Every record I've put out has sounded different. I may put out a hardcore record or a record that sounds like *No Wave New York* circa 1981; I may put out a rap record or a queer ska record—I put out *anything* if I like it and it's queer—those are my two conditions.

> **I put out different types of records; I don't just put out one "sound." What excites me is creating *new aesthetics*.**

♦ **V:** *You're pushing aesthetic limits—*
♦ **MW:** Exactly. It's *multi-subcultural!* That is a good word to describe the whole queercore thing. Because to us it's not just about an indie rock thing or a punk thing, it's about anything remotely to do with what we do. There are queer hip hop groups out there—*so what* if they don't have guitars; to me they're part of the same struggle. I look at the whole queercore movement as a way to bridge gaps between people, which other movements have failed to do.

Cover of CD released on the Outpunk label.

Fifth Column/God is my Co-pilot split single.

♦ **V:** *What's your definition of a queer band?*
♦ **MW:** My definition of an "out" queer band is: there has to be at least one "out" queer person in the band (and hey—four or five years ago you'd be *happy* to find that), and it has to be someone who somehow shapes the message of the band. Also, they gotta be singing about it; I can't stand ambiguity or compromise—dumbing it down and not telling the truth. I thought this would be really easy: "We're going to have queer bands who are not ambiguous—this is *for* us and *by* us."

Then I put out a record by GOD IS MY CO-PILOT from New York City, and the nucleus of that band is a male and a female, both bisexual and married! That was my best-selling release so far, and I liked it, but a lot of people freaked out, saying: "They're not queer! They're a straight couple; they're just leeching off our space and they've gotten a lot of mileage out of doing this." But there *are* different shades of queer identity; people aren't stamped out by cookie-cutters. God Is My Co-Pilot caused a lot of discussion: [Q:] "Are they queer?" [A:] "Yes, they're queer, but it doesn't mean they're necessarily part of what you're about, or experience what you're into."

Every record I release epitomizes something unique, regardless of genre. I like to get people to listen to something they normally wouldn't listen to. This is also a learning experience; I love learning about new bands and creative people.

♦ **V:** *You referred to what is most valuable about punk, and why it won't die: if you have something to say, yet barely know how to play an instrument, you can release a record in a context that's as anti-elitist as can be, and have a forum to get a record out where people will buy it. There's an international distribution structure that's available, and it's very important to have that.*

♦ MW: The history of subcultures is like a flower: something grows, something else grows out of that, and so on. You have certain roots, and some things work and some things don't. Music provides a means to get a message across. I feel queer punk *borrows* from this or that movement but we don't have to confine ourselves to one thing. We don't have to cheat ourselves or homogenize ourselves into what other people are doing.

♦ V: *So you were disgruntled with punk and decided to publish* Outpunk. *Can you describe your first publications—*

♦ MW: It started as a little thing to give to friends. The first issues were more identity-oriented, like: "I'm queer and I also like music. I'm also young, and have this concern and that concern." Some of those are classic ideas that will be articulated with every new generation. I listed bands that had a queer member—which was and still is a big deal to me. Although now people send me tapes saying "My drummer's queer," and I don't give a fuck—I say, "Make a record that's important to me!" There's a lot more to it than just having a queer member in a band—there has to be a *statement* being made. But back then I was dealing more with isolation and invisibility.

Now I have a certain amount of visibility and power. Recently I woke up and realized, "Wow, I have a lot of friends who are into the same things as me," and that's really wonderful. But at the same time I don't want that to be a sedative: making me think I can slow down or stop, as though the battle has been won. Quite the contrary—I spend just as much time alone now as I ever did. I have friends, and they're there, but at the same time I still have a vision that has to be fulfilled; there's a long way to go.

When I started doing records, a lot of people seemed to like them because they were new and different, and a lot of lip service was paid because they were queer. There's more of a backlash now: "Oh, it's queer—*so what!*" I don't see a lot of people who are really into queer punk and who understand it, but every now and then I go out of town or meet somebody new and realize, "Wow—this is a big deal to *somebody*." Sooner or later those seeds will grow into bigger things.

I'm afraid of backlash, and how things become obscured by history. That's what motivates a lot of us who do things that are political or socially radical. The eighties totally squashed cultural growth; the Republicans caused a huge, large-scale reversal of social rights. The gay movement makes big steps and then people get complacent: "Wow, we got all we wanted." Before you know it, things are back to Square One and are just as horrible. Then the new generation has to come in and fight. I like what the band Sta-Prest said, "Enjoy the spotlight today—tomorrow we'll be monsters again."

Pre-Outpunk 7" release.

I look at the whole queercore movement as a way to bridge gaps between people, which other movements have failed to do.

I fear that every person who's got power will say, "Wonderful! Great!" and kill the emerging queercore movement with kindness and limp-wristed understanding. Then you just give up and don't realize that you really haven't pushed very far—basically, you've been placated and duped into thinking you've accomplished something. I realize now that *you can't ever stop.* If I gave up what I'm doing, I'm afraid it would just go back to where it was and nobody would take up my work. That scares me and keeps me going.

♦ V: *It's amazing what just one person can do by refusing to give up—especially if no money's being made—*

♦ MW: That's true. Also, the other part of what keeps me going is knowing that I'm a thorn in someone's

There's a DYKE in the Pit

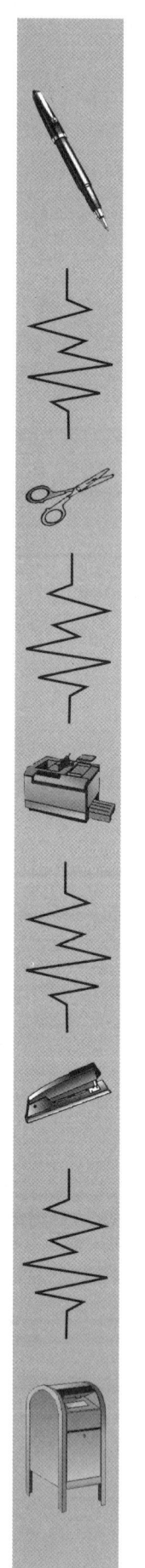

featuring Bikini Kill, Tribe 8, Lucy Stoners, 7 Year Bitch

Outpunk 7" compilation

side. If I were to give up what I'm doing, I think about all the people who would be really happy—and I say, "Fuck you! You can't get rid of me just yet!"

♦ **V:** *You have a life outside* **Outpunk**—*for example, what kind of movies do you like?*

♦ **MW:** I rent a lot of porno movies! [laughs] I like to watch people's reactions when I say that. Gay people are more used to this, but that shocks my straight friends. I like John Waters' movies. I think my favorite movie was *Heathers,* probably because it was a fairly accurate period piece of my high school years. Music is important to me. I write a lot, including articles that I never publish. I spend hours or weeks just thinking, and not being able to sleep. I have worked in a One Hour Photo Lab for the past five years, and that's a whole other story in itself—you live vicariously through a lot of people. It's wonderful.

♦ **V:** *Tell us about that—*

♦ **MW:** When someone brings in their photos, you can find out all their priorities—everyone takes photos of things that are important to them. A person brings in photos and you think, "There's a photo of their house. There's the interior of their house. There's a photo of their bed—they must like their bed. There's a photo of their computer—that's important to them." If there's a nice computer in the background, they obviously don't care about that, because in the foreground is a picture of their cat . . . there's a butthole . . . there's a vase of flowers . . . there's a nice car. You get to see how people's lives are—I didn't know that people could go to Palm Beach every single weekend, but some people *do.*

My job has made me not want to go out and do a lot of things because I've seen it already! Just like people assaulted with images everywhere they go—on advertising or TV—working in a photo lab is really damaging. I used to enjoy photography and looking at photos; now I look at thousands a day and I can't appreciate them. I get off work and don't look at things closely because I've been overloaded. Also, I'm often too judgmental because I've tricked myself into thinking that I know about people—whereas people are a lot deeper than their photos.

For example, friends ask, "Did you go to the Folsom Street Fair?" and I say, "I didn't go this year. But—oh yeah, there was someone sucking dick at the corner of 8th and Folsom. There was a guy taking a piss on another guy at the corner of 9th Street." I was there in ten different people's eyes—however, it was someone else's vision, not my own. But looking at the world through other people's eyes is a poor substitute for going out and seeing things myself—and more importantly, *doing* things myself.

Photos aren't just made for you to look at, they're made to jog your memory of complex experiences you've had. A lot of what I look at are other people's memories. But I can get a different kind of thrill out of certain things that they might not see. I've seen a lot of incredible photos. I realize how sacred people's photos are, and how important privacy is.

My photo lab is in the Castro, and I was shocked when I first started working there: it was the first time I realized that gay people could *have a life.* If you're an outsider, the only way you can know what's going on is to go to bars, and since I've been sober since I was 19, I didn't do that; instead I got involved by working a job. And I couldn't believe it—gay people were everywhere; every person I waited on, more or

Below and pages 121 and 123: graphics by Queer Action Figures, 151 1st Ave. #82, NYC 10003. Reprinted from *Outpunk* #3.

not all lesbians own cats

(but some of us do own guns)

less, was gay. At first it was like, "Wow, it's amazing to be in a gay neighborhood—everything is perfect, I'll never have to worry about anything else my entire life." Then the reality of the situation started to seep in: people are the same anywhere; you get your assholes and your nice people. I like to fight closed-mindedness anywhere I find it, so I felt like I had to challenge the status-quo gay community's values and do things that push people's buttons—

♦ **V: That's punk—**

♦ MW: It's punk without calling itself punk. Any time you have to label something it's a compromise. *Words* are a compromise. You can call it what you want—I'm still going to do it. People say, "That was really punk!" as though rebellion and punk were the same thing. I didn't do it to be "punk," I did it because it was fun.

♦ *V: Even though it's great that there's a relatively safe community in the Castro neighborhood, where same-sex couples can hold hands and live as couples without being driven out of town, and have nice bourgeois homes and face very little job discrimination, still there's a part of me that reacts against any kind of bourgeoisness—*

♦ MW: Absolutely. The older gays are constantly trying to tell you that their values are *your* values—as a "gay community," or whatever. And I used to assert, "We're not part of this gay bourgeois culture!" Now I

> **Previously, I never thought of taking pride in being a butt-fucker! Pansy Division puts topics like this into a context where they're not just tolerated, but *celebrated!***

don't have to constantly scream about it.

Punk can be really pious—about politics above all else; above human feelings and emotions and humanity. I don't want queercore to become like that; a lot of political movements are just *inhuman.* To me, what I do has a sense of humor; I don't take myself too seriously.

The biggest reason that straights even like queer punk or queercore is the fact that it's outrageous. They think that's all it's about. And that's a problem, of course: we're not allowed to assimilate as humans; we're not allowed to be the same way they are, in a lot of ways. We get judged with double standards. But they like the fact that TRIBE 8 can be this militant lesbian group that is shocking to their reality. For this reason, bands who are fuckin' racists or fucked-up people want to play with queer punk bands—they think it's two sides of the same coin. They don't accept the fact that you're just a human being and you're not doing things to shock them or to entertain them. But at the same time we shouldn't be expected to be meek or quiet about things.

PANSY DIVISION is a local gay rock band who are kinda punky. A lot of people think they're too "lite rock" to be punk—but hey, they sing songs about gay sex. They sing about more than just gay sex, but a lot of their songs *are* pretty sex-obsessed.

It's certainly a new thing for people to even sing about sex in a personal way, and in a celebratory way—that is outrageous on its own. Also the fact that it's gay sex—that's supposed to be "dirty." When the singer sings a song called "Ring of Joy" (about your sphincter), *I'm* embarrassed—I'm not going to talk about *that.* But the fact that they set that to music, sing it, and are not ashamed of it, is hilarious.

Previously, I never thought of taking pride in being a butt-fucker! Pansy Division puts topics like this into a context where they're not just tolerated, but *celebrated.* Like taking pride in having a curved dick—whatever! That's wonderful. There's a lot of criticism that comes down on Pansy Division: that provoking outrage through being sexually explicit is a real easy route to take. But hey, you've got to hand it to them—nobody does that. And even if you don't like their music or sexually-explicit lyrics, you've gotta admit they're funny! And it's really not hurting anybody; it's a very positive thing about something that's not considered positive in our society.

What's important here is the sense of self-esteem. Maybe what I've internalized is: "I *should* feel ashamed." Pansy Division get a lot of flack not only from straight people, but from gay people who think they're just a horrible representation of gay people . . . crass and rude and disgusting.

♦ **V: The problem of internalized shame—**

♦ MW: Pansy Division's lead singer, Jon Ginoli, doesn't seem to realize or care about the way people react to him. And that can work in his favor. For example, Green Day, a local East Bay punk band who now sell literally millions of records, decided they wanted Pansy Division to open for them on a tour of arenas—

Cover of Sta-Prest's "Vespa Sex" Outpunk 45.

15,000 people in the audiences. I went with them to a couple shows and was helping them set up a booth to sell their t-shirts, which had a big dick printed on them—and I was afraid! However, Pansy Division was with me, and their attitude was, "These are our shirts!" And with that kind of attitude, the shirts went up for sale, amazingly enough.

I saw Pansy Division play to these crowds—mostly no older than about 14, and totally hostile. I asked Jon about this, and he said, "Well, the people in front really liked us—they were waving and giving us the high five and smiling!" I said, "But Jon, people in the back were chanting 'Fag! Fag! Fag!' and throwing stuff at you!" He doesn't see it that way, he's much more of an optimist. I think that kind of attitude keeps Pansy Division going—

♦ **V: *That works in their favor; it's like leading a charmed life—***

♦ MW: We limit ourselves by our fears; we're guilty of holding back and excluding ourselves from the realm of possibilities just because of our own self-hate. I learned a lot from Pansy Division, and I think other people could learn from them, too.

♦ **V: *We all want wider audiences, but of the "right" people. And again, you may reach that one person alienated in a small town who writes you a very appreciative letter—***

♦ MW: Exactly. That's all we need sometimes. It may be an ego gratification, but it's a wonderful thing.

Right now I'm putting together the next issue of my zine. When you put something out, you put *yourself* out there. You're kind of fragile; you're hoping somebody will validate you in some way. Then, when you get positive feedback, it's almost orgasmic: "Thank god!"

Sometimes I have doubts: "Is this relevant?" Like, you think you're writing something really great, and then you try to get some feedback, hopefully to reignite you to continue what you're doing. And if you don't get any, you start to doubt: "Maybe this isn't such a good idea." Sometimes I think, "Maybe I should get a job at a major label and do something more subversive on that level. Or maybe I should start a corporate-sponsored queer label." There are a lot of *what-ifs*. I just get my cheap thrills doing what I do now, and hopefully it can become successful.

♦ **V: *By "success" do you mean being able to live off your enterprise?***

♦ MW: No—I can't even *comprehend* that! Now, all I can think about is: "If this release doesn't sell, I'm not going to be putting out another record." Right now I can't imagine living without a day job, but it's an interesting thought. I'm a real pessimist sometimes; it's easy to get tunnel vision and be full of despair and not see past your immediate problems: "I owe this person money"; "I've got to pay off that debt"; "I've got to fill all these orders."

Actually, I have gotten some publicity. *Billboard* did a front-page article titled: "Queercore Punk Rock: Ready to Face the Market." I couldn't have conceived of a funnier caption! So any time somebody asks me how *Outpunk* is doing, I say, "It's getting ready to face the market!" There's been a lot of attention paid to queers in music recently, and some people think I'm getting rich, but they don't realize that it's still too ahead of its time. I almost feel like it's too cool to really be popular—too brainy, too smart, too *out there*.

♦ **V: *Are there any other queer punk labels?***

♦ MW: Yes, but I am the only one who has a queercore label. I like "queercore" because it doesn't have the word "punk" in it—it's sort of *multi-subcultural*, as we said. I'm the first rock label that is explicitly queer; I'm not going to put out a straight record. There are other labels owned by queers; there are other labels releasing queer stuff; there are other queer labels putting out queer records, but nobody has made an issue out of it. That's where I'm different.

> **We limit ourselves by our fears; we're guilty of holding ourselves back and excluding ourselves from the realm of possibilities by our own self-hate.**

♦ **V: *Why don't you promote your records in your zine more?***

♦ MW: In doing a zine you're setting your own rules. Your ethics are your own; you're not working under some official publishing ethic. I produce both zines and a record label. I interview people, I've been interviewed; I take out ads, I solicit advertising—I constantly feel like I'm on both sides of the media process. The reason I don't promote my records in my zine more is: I feel there's a conflict of interest in creating the news and covering it, too!

♦ **V: I still don't see "queer" record sections in stores—**

♦ **MW:** We're still in the formative stages. There's the invisibility issue which I'm still fighting: the fact that people don't know we exist. We're getting out there, getting into record stores, getting into the framework of popular culture. The fact is that music can carry your message in a way nothing else can. My magazine gets into places where no other queer magazine gets because it's a music magazine, and I still haven't realized the full potential of that.

♦ **V: Plus, you reach a young audience—**

♦ **MW:** —which is hard to reach. The ideas ride piggyback on the music vehicle. Basically, my idea about the record label is: I can be queer and like these ideas and *all* kinds of music. If you haven't been able to identify with being gay and you're in the closet, you can read *Outpunk* and see that being gay is about being intelligent and having a sense of humor—having fun. Possibly you can identify with that—certainly more than the image you were given before. At the same time, there are plenty of people who are not going to get it. That's why more people should get involved: so that more ideas are out there, and there are more people to identify with. Because I'm one of the only people in the public eye, I get a lot of flak for not being everybody's idea of what they want to see in a gay music label. And I try to realize that *I'm* becoming status quo in a lot of ways.

A lot of media and music magazines are very elitist; not willing to explain something to someone who's a newcomer. Whereas I *want* newcomers. I like people getting into what I'm doing on a gut or entry level. My goal is to appeal to everybody from the entry-level kid whose reaction is: "This is awesome; I want to be involved," to the jaded veteran. It's hard. I'm constantly balancing things, and rejecting topics that require a lot of explaining and contextualizing for kids to understand. I'll think, "They've heard this before; it's too elementary and shouldn't be written about." So I try to find a middle ground, modifying my language and finding a way to present subjects to a wide variety of people age-wise and experience-wise, because everyone's coming from a different point of view.

I remember being turned off by gay magazines, thinking, "This person didn't really want to communicate with me; these words and concepts aren't

---

No one teaches you how to be gay—you learn these things yourself. The gay community just expects young people to assimilate into it somehow.

---

explained. I feel alienated." If I couldn't comprehend something, I felt excluded.

No one teaches you how to be gay—you learn these things yourself. The gay community just expects young people to assimilate into it somehow. I felt that if I put out a magazine that didn't address the fact that young people are reading it (and I'm young), and didn't approach topics from that point of view—that's cheating people.

In every issue I try to tackle concepts and present them in a way that I hope is accessible to kids. In Issue #3 I did a piece on SM. Usually when you see SM sex talked about, it's always in a "shocking" way. To a lot of queer kids, sex itself is really alienating, because you haven't even figured out a lot of things—you're still in this *process.* And people are saying, "Well, I like to be flogged." Or, "I'm wearing my new harness and we're going down to Bondage-A-Go-Go." And the kid is like, "I don't get it. You're just weird." Or, "This is *out there;* it isn't *me,* and why do we have to talk about it?" So I thought, "Let's try to talk about SM in a way that's fun, but not alienating or judgmental." People who were confused about SM sex thought it was really interesting and informative.

In one issue I interviewed a friend of mine who's a male prostitute. He's really eloquent and is not the least bit ashamed. He says, "I look at this as my job and I treat it as a business; this is how I do it; this is how you can do it." It's like a *how-to,* and I think it's very subversive. I got letters saying, "I never read an

Graphic by Queer Action Figures

TRIBE 8

Tribe 8 7″ released by *Outpunk*. Photo: Chloe Sherman

interview like this in my life before . . . I've never known that a prostitute considers himself part of a community . . . I never knew that anybody would be not ashamed to talk about it." Mainstream media never does anything *in-depth;* they just encapsulate everything. And this person painted a real human face on what it is to be a prostitute.

♦ **V: Tell us more about women in the queer punk music scene—**
♦ **MW:** Tribe 8 put out one single on another label, and then I started putting out their records. I put out three records by them before they put out an LP on Alternative Tentacles. They're really good friends of mine and I feel in complete solidarity with them. They're educating people just by *existing.* They're enlightening and entertaining people—I've learned so much just by working with them and watching them—I feel very privileged to know them. And I would buy their records if I didn't know them.

♦ **V: They've been together a long time—**
♦ **MW:** A lot longer than other people who are making much more money than they are. To me, they're super-important as a band, and they have everything to do with what I'm doing and what queercore is about.

Mainstream media never do anything *in-depth*; they just encapsulate everything.

There's a funny Tribe 8 story involving Luke Skywalker (*aka* Luther Campbell, his real name) of Two Live Crew, who were this totally outrageous rap group—really sexist. They got involved in huge controversies in Florida involving obscenity laws and the issue of censorship. Luke Skywalker has a pay-per-view cable TV show called *Luke's Peep Show,* and his producer thought it would be an awesome idea to have Tribe 8 on the show, because even though they're an unlikely pairing, both have been censored.

So all five members of Tribe 8 (plus their manager and publicist) got flown to Miami. Each person had her own hotel suite, and everything was paid for—limousine rides everywhere. They kept trying to call Luke Skywalker to ask, "Luke, what do you want to talk about? What's the gist of this show? Why are we here?" And he kept blowing them off.

Finally they showed up for the show and got on this yacht off the Florida coast. They're sitting with Luke Skywalker, and there's naked and half-naked women running around and sitting on his lap—and he's scared to death of Tribe 8! He started off saying something like, "So . . . you all are *lesbians.* Are you like *straight* lesbians or are you like *gay* lesbians?" And they're thinking, "What the hell is a straight lesbian?" So they started turning the tables on him: "You like to have women naked all around you—you must have a pretty big dick. Why don't you take it out and show it to us?" He was like, "No, no, you show me your tits; show me your tits." "No, no, no, *you* take it off!" He got totally freaked. They filmed for five minutes and that was it—nothing else.

Tribe 8 is outspokenly pro-woman and here's this guy who is considered very anti-woman. The whole press for the show was, "Two unlikely foes united in the cause!" But that's misleading—it's *kind of* funny, but let's face it, this guy's really sexist and these are two sides of a *different* coin. The funniest thing, of course, is that Tribe 8 went and they *won,* on their own terms. As women they're so supportive of one another that they have the strength and the confidence to go out and do something like this.

One writer said that queercore is about women. Queercore came out of the whole Riot Grrrl thing; it was directly inspired by the whole Riot Grrrl feminist movement. And queercore is a place where there are more women in bands than men, which is a dynamic you don't see anywhere else. Women are so much more respected, and are part of the dialogue and what's going on. Someone said, "Queercore is driven by dykes." I think that's totally true.

A lot of journalists who ask, "What's going on in the queercore scene?" don't want to hear about the women. And it isn't just straight music magazines who only want to talk about guys as rock gods, it's also the gay magazines: they're always excluding women. Gay magazines are by definition gay male and don't like women. That ranges from the plain, "We don't want to hear about women; that's not our topic and they're not for our readers," to an old school gay mentality with out-and-out hatred of women. A lot of older gay men are misogynistic and have this outdated separatist view of what the gay community's supposedly about.

I don't think there's anything wrong with lesbians also wanting to be separatist, but at the same time the whole queercore thing has been, for the first time, *both* men and women queers co-exist in the same place.

Queercore is a place where there are more women in bands than men, which is a dynamic you don't see anywhere else.

Homophobia and sexism are two sides of the same coin. If somebody is either one or the other, chances are they're *both.* Anybody who is totally sexist probably hates queers too, so in general feminists and queers fight the same struggle.

♦ **V: Can you peer ten years ahead into the future—**

♦ **MW:** I'm really afraid that ten years from now, queercore will be described in some stupid rock encyclopedia like this: "Queercore was a movement with Pansy Division, and *this* guy band and *that* guy band." Because that's the way music is written about—in revisionist terms. Queer history is the same way. And I don't want to see Tribe 8 as a footnote—to me, they were *the* band. More and more I don't see them getting written about and talked about, and this gets me really mad, because Tribe 8 are really the leading lights of homocore—they were out there before so many other bands, and they don't compromise. They are *the* vital band of this whole scene or idea. So it hurts me to see them not making the money and getting the press that other people get. People need to hear them. When I see them play, I feel like I'm watching history being made.

♦ **V: You're not just critical of the status quo, you're also critical of the status quo in the gay community—**

♦ **MW:** But there is a way to say something inflammatory in a way that isn't considered like a threat, or isn't perceived as too contrary—you're just "saying your opinion." That's an important skill to learn: to express yourself and be outrageous without pissing people off for the wrong reasons. A lot of people use shock value humor which I'm really iffy about: "If it shocks, it's okay." Or "As long as I got this crazy reaction, it doesn't matter how I got it."

There's a lot of that going on in punk, and there always has been. Actually, a lot of really horrible stuff *is* going on in punk, and it's not just about shocking people—it's like an acceptable way to act like a fucking asshole—to be a *bigot,* really. You've got your shock-value, say-anything-to-provoke-a-response crowd. They claim to be cutting-edge. They say they're pushing the boundaries that we, the so-called "p.c." (meaning liberal, left-wing, realistic people who have respect for other human beings) cherish. They want to push our boundaries; they say, "You're humorless; you just don't get the joke. Can't you laugh at yourself?" Forget the fact that everybody else is *already* laughing at me; why *should* I laugh at myself?

Don't kid yourself that they're really "cool" people trying to make "artistic" statements—I don't buy that at all. I think they really *are* bigots, racists, Neo-Nazis and the whole trip. I think they're trying to make prejudice

Lynn Breedlove of Tribe 8, from *Outpunk #1*

Outpunk pin-up #1:

This is a bodacious shot of the lovely and talented Lynn Breedlove of Tribe 8.

Nice tattoos, huh?

> In a scene that's predominantly white, that doesn't want to talk about what race and ethnicity have to do with identity--let alone for us as punks-- that ignores its own "whiteness" for a "colorblind" approach that makes us (and their privilege) invisible, that denies us the specificity of our experiences, well, then what?

> When we're expected to "erase" our racial identities or ignore our non-white, sometimes non-Western cultural backgrounds/experiences or when we're scolded for not being "true" to our "native" cultures, for not being "ethnic enough."

> **Hey you.**

> When some white male punk writes that "racial slurs don't hurt anyone" and that we need a better sense of humor about "those things." (I guess it's "old school" to call someone a chink?)

> **Punks of**

> When a hardcore kid from Connecticut posts on a punk rock e-mailing list about how much he hates "fags and niggers."

> When we're told that punk is a community "beyond ethnicity" because "we're all marginalized here *the same*" even though you're the one who gets called "china doll" or "spic" when you're walking through their neighborhoods, and you remember growing up in the barrio or in an immigrant family or as the only person of color at your school.

> **Color.**

> Contribute to a collective zine by and about people of color involved in the punk scene. Let's talk about our experiences in the "real world" and in the scene, as people of color and as punks. We're also getting together to talk about this stuff and to commiserate, as a chance to talk to each other about these issues where we're usually pretty alone and isolated. For info, write to me, Mimi, at PO Box 4655, Berkeley, CA 94704-0655. Send your contributions to me, too! Or call me: (510) 849-4927.

> Hey, you. White boy/girl. This isn't the time and place for you to 1) rage about how unfair it is that we're doing this without you, and all us mean ol' colored folks are being "reverse racists" because we're getting together and you're not invited, and how we're "just like Nazis" 2) to reasonably argue with us about how punk is an "equal opportunity" space and we should realize that punks face the same marginalization that others –people of color, for instance– do, ha ha, or 3) throw yourself at our collective feet and apologize effusively for personally oppressing us for all those years and that you really want to be our friend so you can better work through your racism, etc. This is for us to talk about *our* issues concerning race and ethnicity and identity, not about yours.

Flyer by Mimi

acceptable and "cool."

♦ **V:** *And who are they serving? Neo-Nazi types love 'em!*

♦ **MW:** I used to work at *Maximum Rock'n'Roll.* Tim Yohannon, the publisher, is not a bad guy; I'm friends with him. But the man is stuck in another time. He has this weird rock'n'roll purist trip, and I honestly feel that this whole musical purism is fuckin' racism, sexism and homophobia all intertwined. There's this weird ethic involving a fear of difference. Tim thinks that rock'n'roll "shakes people up," and that *MRR* is going to shake people up. So they have eight columnists, and five of them are reactionary straight white men who talk about how feminism sucks, and how we're going to start calling people by their racial name—"I'm going to call you *negro,* because I'm trying to be like Lenny Bruce. Words don't mean anything, and I'm protesting linguistic totalitarianism. I'm going to push your buttons and your boundaries, because we're all humans and we're all marginalized the same because we're punks. We're all fighting for The Cause, and I'm just a dissenting opinion."

This guy, Reverend Norb, writes for *MRR* and he calls people "fag" all the time: *fag* this and *fag* that. It's offensive, but he claims he's "taking the word back" as a playground insult. I got really mad for awhile, but I let it go. But kids who think *MRR* isn't racist or sexist or fucked-up read this and conclude, "Well, I hate Nazis, but saying *fag* is okay." Now I see fanzines where kids think it's okay to use the word "faggot."

A couple years ago *MRR* published a Japanese theme issue all about Japanese bands. One columnist, Rev. Norb, wrote about how hot Asian women are— "Oriental girls' eyes look more like vulvii." It's unbelievable! And this is all wrapped up in this package: "Let's talk about Japan. Let's talk about these cool Japanese bands and this cool Japanese fanzine and let's present you with this mixed message." This is a complex issue: *Exoticism.* This is where I draw the line, and I quit *MRR* in protest. In retrospect, I had let a lot of shit go by because I didn't want to see it, and it took this horrible thing to get me to see what was really going on.

♦ **V:** *You brought up the topic of Exoticism—*

♦ **MW:** Which is a big topic. That has to do with objectification, condescension, being patronizing and making a novelty out of other people or cultures. Here, a common attitude is: "Everything that comes out of [Japan] is good." There's the whole Asian Exotic thing—witness the boom in Asian porn video consumption. A lot of it is really hard to call. Do you truly appreciate another culture, or do you single out aspects of it to exploit? However, most people aren't so blatant. They can talk their way around something; they can pass it off as an "intellectual discussion."

♦ **V:** *We were talking about shock chic—*

Anybody who is totally sexist probably hates queers too, so in general feminists and queers fight the same struggle.

♦ **MW:** Another thing about shock value humor: its proponents claim they're not about offending you. But they *love* to see you get offended—that gives them immense satisfaction. So I want to be able to react, "That's the dumbest thing I ever heard. It was so stupid that you didn't even get my attention . . ." Because all they want to do is to provoke you. People deliberately send me stuff to goad me on and get me to comment on it, and I just throw it away.

I wrote an article about fake queer bands because there are all these bands now *pretending* to be gay! But if you're looking for a queer record and there aren't that many, and somebody's passing themselves off as a queer band . . . it's like—there's no media; we don't have media to tell us what is or what isn't a gay band. So I decided to write an article about all these fake queer bands. Every time I saw one of these records I

This is an important skill to learn: to express yourself and be outrageous without pissing people off for the wrong reasons.

was furious: "Fuckin' assholes—this is horrible. I feel cheated, offended and ripped off"—I felt all these different emotions. Then I saw the light: "This is ridiculously stupid—*duh.* What kind of a small mind would produce *this?*" The bottom line is: if nobody cares and nobody gets offended by your record, you're going to be stuck with a few hundred boxes of them! So I laugh at people who spend all this time putting out a dumb joke that doesn't go anywhere.

♦ **V: It's better to take the "higher road" and ignore these vermin, or point out sheer incompetencies and lack of imagination, wit, depth—**

♦ MW: Sure. That to me is the only way you can get through to these people. These editors just want to be noticed: *Notice Me!* Otherwise they'd be *nobodies with nothing.*

♦ **V: They feed on visceral emotional reactions—**

♦ MW: All those people do. Again, *MRR* has eight columnists and more than half of them are like that: reactionary. They're "anti-p.c.," "cutting-edge humor," "push the envelope," and each person supposedly has his own thing. It's easy for the editor, a white guy, to sit back and say, "Well, these are *different* opinions. I'm presenting the *spectrum* of opinions." Whereas in reality, it's the same old fuckin' shit. Make no mistake about it, these people who like shock value humor are bigots. Another "cutting-edge" magazine published a pro-rape issue, and when challenged they claimed, "We're not championing these beliefs; we're just trying to get a *reaction* from you"—

♦ **V: They claim, "I'm just trying to get you to think about a topic that's suppressed or taboo—"**

♦ MW: But what if somebody says, "I read the rape issue of this magazine, and you know what—I agree with him: I *like* rape." What's the editor going to do about this guy interpreting his publication in the "wrong" way? The editor's not going to attack *anyone* for saying that—secretly he'll be pleased, just as he secretly cherishes racist ideas—because that's the support he truly craves.

♦ **V: Can you talk more about the development of the queercore scene?**

♦ MW: There are queercore events happening in other cities, like Homocore Chicago or Homocore Detroit. However, San Francisco is like no other city; there's a huge music scene, a huge gay scene, and there are a lot of things going on here that could be considered queercore. The way I look at queercore is: it's just *people* putting on a show or forming a band or doing a fanzine or simply saying something you agree with—it's a loose network. So far it hasn't been rigidly defined (in terms of fashion or music or ideology), but in the future that will be hard to maintain.

I did an interview for a gay magazine titled *Out,* and afterwards they asked me, "Could you send us some photos of queer punks slamming in a pit at a big show?" [laughs] I said, "No, it's not quite like that. It's more: people like me sitting at home listening to a record." And that doesn't sell magazines. So they dredged out some stock photos of buffed guys with tattoos kissing—that was really funny.

In San Francisco, there's a local group, Q-TIP (Queers Together In Punkness) putting on shows at Epicenter. Again, the problem with anything under the label of "punk" is that you only reach punk-oriented people. Q-TIP has been putting on performances where they have a punk band and a performance artist and an art show on the side. That's kinda cool, because you get people to attend who are sort of like-minded, but who may not know who Born Against or Rancid are. They may not be "down" with the lingo, but they can feel included ideologically because they really are a part of it.

Certain buzz-words can really be alienating, because a lot of times when you use this lingo, people who automatically should be a part of something just turn off. A lot of people don't even have a concept of what a community really is, or could be. To them, a

7" by Behead the Prophet No Lord Shall Live. released by Outpunk

queercore show is just another bar show or rock show. They don't realize the potential of it; that to certain people, it's *life-affirming.*

Make no mistake about it, these people who like shock value humor are bigots.

I'll say it to this day: every time I hear a great new band or discover something good, it's like, I feel like more in step or closer to being human. It's wonderful, and it means everything to me. People who get really jaded don't feel this. The way I look at it is: it's still really early. I try to think globally and see the potential. But I worry that queercore will be defined by its most superficial aspects: a mohawk and slamming in the pit! It's horrible to think that all your work is going to be reduced to something like that. So I'm trying to emphasize working in a community-building direction.

Cover of Pansy Division's *Wish I'd Taken Pictures*

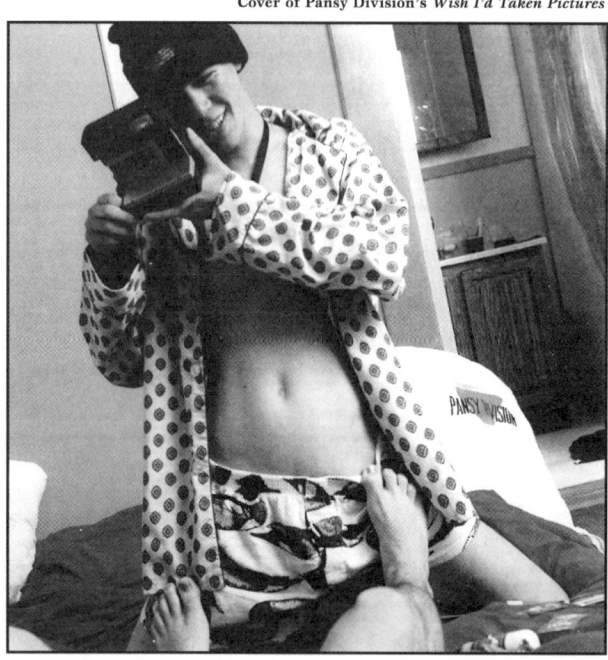

I remember that when I got into punk in the '80s, rap was considered almost the same thing to my friends. It was cool to be into rap like Public Enemy and also into punk. As I got older, I started taking the *MRR* view: "Major labels are bad; that's mainstream music. This is *our* music; it's more organic, more underground." In other words: good/bad; us/them. *MRR* hates rap; rap is not allowed in their pages—let them tell you why; I have my own ideas. Anyhow, I like rap, but I like rock better—I listen to it more. But at least theoretically or ideologically I'm really inspired by rap.

There are the seeds of a queer hip hop scene. It's totally in its formative stages, like where queer punk was five or six years ago. People take queer rock for granted now, but it didn't exist five years ago. To me, queer hip hop is like queercore—it's *queer young people doing it for themselves,* and with music.

♦ **V: Which queer bands should be supported?**
♦ MW: All the bands on my label [!], including Tribe 8, Pansy Division, Sta-Prest (who never play out), Team Dresch, Sister George, Third Sex—there are many more. I have to be really careful. A lot of bands like the fact that people think they're queer.

♦ **V: Why?**
♦ MW: They say, "We like having gay people as our fans, and we're flattered that anybody thinks we're gay, and we'd much rather be perceived as gay or gay-positive than anything else." And that's cool. But on the other hand, it's sort of shock value, hipness, objectification, and it's demeaning sometimes—it's like saying, "I can act this way or pretend to be gay as well." It's misinterpreting queerness as a *choice,* or perceiving it as a *style*—and getting it all wrong. Every little alternative band these days is trying to toy with sexual ambiguity.

♦ **V: Everybody's appeared in a dress by now: Nirvana, Pearl Jam—**
♦ MW: As if wearing a dress equates with homosexuality.

♦ **V: Can you comment on this major media and major label imagery of men in dresses?**
♦ MW: It's hard to say. People say it's a recent thing, but the Rolling Stones appeared in drag on an LP cover in the sixties, and what about *Victor/Victoria,* or *La Cage Aux Folles?* These are major media "transgressions"; I saw *Victor/Victoria* when I was a kid and didn't even grasp it. The thing is, if you get these radical ideas into the mainstream media, it's a victory for sure—you got it there. How it gets perceived is a whole different story.

Also, wearing dresses and pretending to be queer is fucked-up because there's an element of control or manipulation at work. It's like, "We're going to pretend to be gay, and this is what we think being gay is about." It's about being shocking or outrageous or having this style—whatever it is they read into being gay (*their* interpretations, by the way, not mine). They control how it's perceived and how it'll be reported or

Every little alternative band these days is trying to toy with sexual ambiguity.

discussed. The whole big shtick about the singer of Suede is that he *might* be bisexual—like, "I *might* be gay. I might consider sleeping with a guy once." That becomes the extent of what gets covered or talked about in the press. So in the eyes of a magazine, that issue has already been dealt with—it's over.

♦ **V: It's sort of a fake way of dealing with an issue—**

♦ MW: Yes, that's exactly it. It has the same effect as lip service: it weakens it—deadens it in the water. Also, a lot of queer fans of music are willing to sell themselves out because nobody's come to meet them that far before. "Gay people will jump through hoops to be accepted"—I love saying that! I told a reporter, "You know what? Faggots will buy anything!" I said all this totally inflammatory stuff, but it was really true. Gay people aren't used to being accepted, so the community gets behind Nirvana or *anybody* who says something nice about us once. Then we don't cover something cool going on that's queer.

Maybe it's this self-esteem issue: "We're not worthy." It's as if straight people being interested in gay people somehow *legitimizes* us, and that's all we need. We never made it into their media, but if they're willing to meet us only part of the way, that's good enough. So part of the motivation for my operation was (and continues to be): "That's *not* good enough—that's no substitute. *We're doing it ourselves.*"

Outpunk "introduction"

We're here, we're queer and we love punk rock! So what does that mean to the punk scene at large? Do we even care what they think of us? What are their roles in the scenes that we create? I've developed the following list of do's and don'ts that are highly subjective. This is what, if anything, I am saying to straight people who are interested in queer punk.

DON'T:
- Assume that we are complaining just to get attention.
- Pretend to be queer in an attempt to be supportive.
- Flirt with us unless you want us to fuck you.
- Assume that we would want to have sex with you in the first place.
- Tell us that we should be like so-and-so to be "good," "cool" or acceptable.
- Treat us as a novelty.
- Don't bother me.

DO:
- Realize that ideas that you might not understand may make perfect sense to us.
- Understand that queer punk is in its formative stages and may or may not have the expertise, security, or history that the rest of punk has, and that we are creating our own.
- Be supportive without turning it into your self-righteous cause to elevate you among your peers.
- Be aware that for us, punk is something we have chosen to hold on to as our culture, despite pressure to conform to mainstream gay society at large.
- Understand that sometimes we have to do things that aren't "punk" just to function, and that we don't have the easy social scene that straight punks have.

Further questions? Tough shit.

Queer Punk Revolution? What do you think? Do you have a vision for the future? I do. If there's going to be a queer revolution in punk, or a female one, or non-white ones, we really need to think about what we want ultimately, and work towards it. I'm not saying it's that simple, because there are at least two things in our way. 1) the attitudes within punk that treat us like second-class people, and 2) the attitudes within ourselves that prevent us from trying, or that make us want to give up completely. This is no time for self-hate. There is no time for pity parties. It is time for action. You will be as happy as you let yourself be. Don't let anyone tell you differently.

Yes, I know it's not the most eloquent piece of writing, but it's a start. We all need to help each other, support each other, and stop creating division among ourselves. We need to accept the fact that we all may have different ideas of what this is about, but that we are all striving for the same things: love, acceptance, fun and enlightenment. That means withholding judgment if you can't find something constructive to say. It means not making the easy put-down for the sake of being "funny." It's so easy to laugh, it's so easy to hate. It takes courage to be gentle and kind. Thanks Morrissey! Sometimes I think being happy is the most subversive thing you can possibly do.

A message in all this? Check it out. I can't help you. Only you can do that. I don't need to hear how rough it is—I know. I can't write for you or claim to represent you. If I am saying anything at all with this, it is that if I can do it, you most certainly can, too. So fucking do it.

You think you don't belong? You think it's you vs. the world? You say everything excludes you? Well, have you even tried? Do you even know? Are there barriers in front of you or are they in your fucking head? And ultimately, who is responsible for your comfort, anyway? Just wondering.

—from *Outpunk* #3

Fat Girl

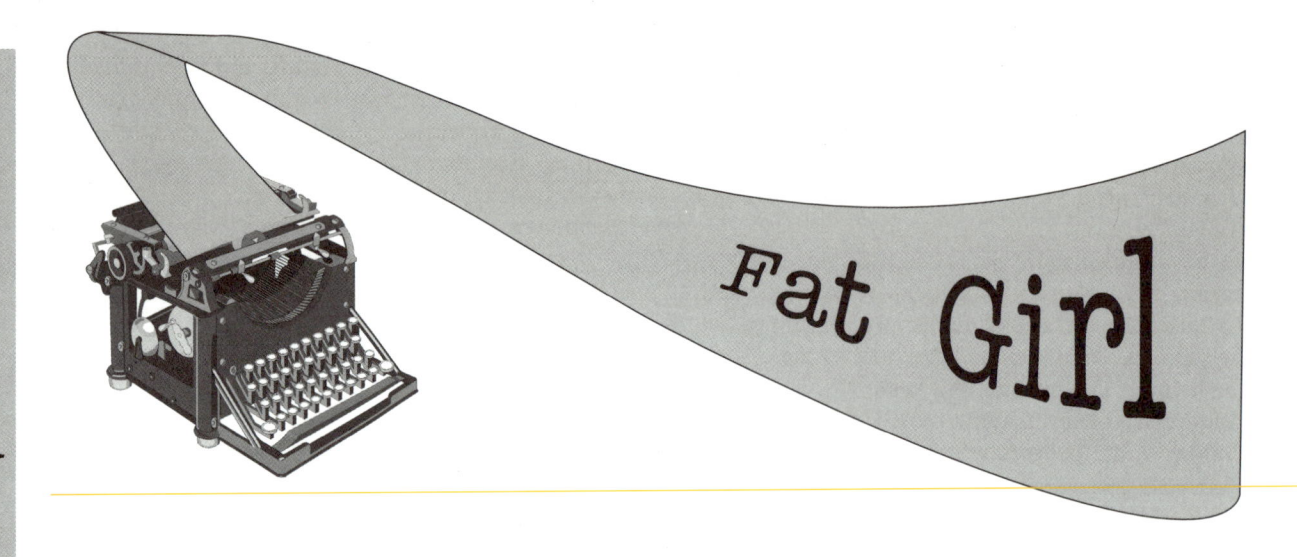

Fat Girl, a magazine "for fat dykes and the women who want them," is published by the Fat Girl Collective (sample issue $5; $20 for four issues from 2215-R Market St #197, San Francisco CA 94114; 415-522-8733). Besides publishing a paper zine, they have a web site: *http://www.fatgirl.com/.* Founding member Max Airborne also runs a private subscriber-only e-mail discussion list for fat dykes: *airborne@sirius.com.* Ten members of the collective (April Miller, Barbara McDonald, Bertha Markowicz, Devra, Laura J., Lisa Brotz, Judy Graboyes, Margo Mercedes Rivera, Max Airborne and Sondra Solo) were interviewed by V. Vale at April's home in the East Bay.

♦ **VALE: *How can you keep a collective enterprise going over the long haul?***
♦ BARBARA: It's hard, because we live in a very competitive, individualistic society. In the very act of getting people together to try to change things, you're involved in a creative process, and being involved in a creative process with multiple people is *always* a challenge! [laughs]
♦ BERTHA: We want to do something creative *while* we're being passive consumers! Or: "Buy our magazine and *then* go out and do something radical!"
♦ APRIL: *She* does the advertising for our magazine.
♦ **V: *I've read that even though the number of publications is increasing, the available pool of readers is shrinking almost daily—***
♦ BERTHA: That's amazing. I read all the time—cereal boxes, whatever's nearby!
♦ MAX: These days, with television and radio everywhere, it's too easy *not* to read.
♦ BERTHA: *Bodily Fluids* was so interesting that I couldn't put it down. It's my bathroom reading—
♦ MAX: "I'm shitting, so I may as well read about it!"
♦ BARBARA: I'm wondering if people are reading less because what's available to them just isn't interesting. The thing about the "Zine Revolution" that's exciting is—now there *are* really interesting publications out there to read, you just have to make the effort to find them. When you find one, it's like finding a *treasure* because a lot of what's being published is boring—it's all about making money. It's not expanding your mind or communicating; it's not interactive. It seems that zines are a response to this vacuum.
♦ DEVRA: Unfortunately, it's still hard to find good zines that you can *really* be into—
♦ BERTHA: Usually you go, "Not my tribe, not my tribe . . . ah, here's one!" When I go to a mainstream magazine stand, I can look through scores of women's magazines and they're all about quick "lite" meals you can make in three minutes!
♦ APRIL: *She* does our "Kitchen Slut" column, which includes guilt-free recipes—
♦ MAX: I can look through hundreds and hundreds of magazines and be lucky to find *one* that's worthwhile.
♦ **V: *Your magazine is unusual in that it's produced in the spirit of a collective enterprise, rather than by a hierarchy or a lone individual. Whose idea was this?* [everyone looks at Max, and laughs]**
♦ MAX: I insisted. Actually, there were three or four of us, and we thought, "We need more people, and it

should be a collective!" At first the others were like, "Oh, come on!" But I kept saying, "Yes, yes!" Since then I discovered that I really have a hard time being in a collective, because I'm kind of a workaholic, and I get resentful when other people *aren't!* I have since left the collective, as have a couple others of us here.

♦ *V: But you're here.*

♦ MAX: Yeah, I'm still part of the family—

♦ BERTHA: It's a collective family—oh yes, we have a secret handshake. To join you have to get your head shaved, turn over all your income and undergo our reeducation program! [laughs]

♦ *V: So tell me about the aims of* **Fat Girl**—

♦ BARBARA: Actually, we wanted to do a publication that was *political, funny,* and *perverse,* and it seemed that the way to do that was to have different people be a part of that process. We made a list of all the fat dykes we'd seen around town that we wanted to meet, and began to approach them. To walk up to another fat woman and say, "Hi! We're doing a zine for fat dykes—would you like to be part of it?" and to see their emotional response when someone is talking to them *openly* about being fat (whether or not they felt comfortable with that)—well, this was an intense process!

♦ BERTHA: We're continuing to work in a collective environment. As hard as it is, it gives you a diversity of voices, there's a lot of different input, and besides—it *feels* good!

♦ MAX: The idea that created the collective was: we wanted to do a zine for fat dykes. And the fact that it's a collective is why it's still around. If it were just me and my little friends—or *big* friends, as it were—the commitment to keeping a zine for fat dykes going wouldn't necessarily be there.

We change and grow (personally, I want to do some new things; I don't necessarily want to spend all my energy working on something just for fat dykes, because I think about other things, too). But it's important that *Fat Girl* stay in existence, because it has brought together fat dykes from all different walks of life, to talk about issues in ways that haven't been done before. It's become almost an institution for some people—

♦ BERTHA: And the visibility is important—fat women are rarely visible in media. This is one of the few places where fat dykes are *out*—in the open.

♦ BARBARA: It took us six months to produce the first magazine, and we spent a lot of that time talking. One of our first endeavors was to put together an "issue statement," so that we had a clear idea of what we wanted to present. We discovered how diverse our interests were, what our heartfelt hopes were, and because we spent a lot of time doing this we were able to incorporate a lot of diversity into our publication: sexuality, smut, and sincere writing about being a fat dyke growing up in this culture and being alienated . . . talking about hard things as well as fun things. We spent a lot of time laying the groundwork, making sure we were inclusive about all of this.

Clockwise from bottom left: Max, Bertha, Sondra, Selena, Barbara, Devra. Photo: Robert Waldman

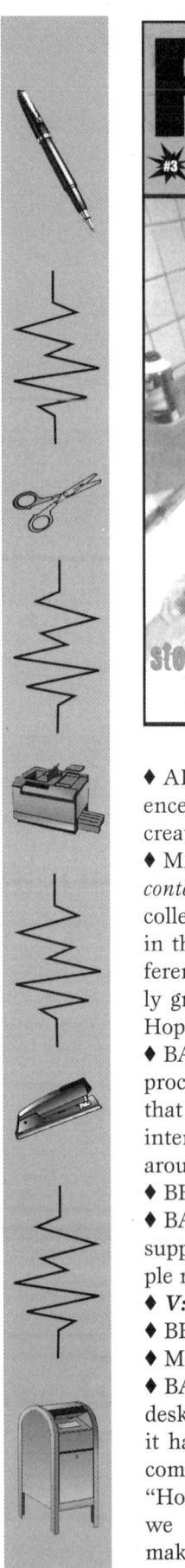

Cover of *Fat Girl #3*, 1995 photo of Crystal Mason by Laura Johnston

♦ APRIL: It's the combination of all of our experiences (different from each other, and the same) that creates the richness of the zine.
♦ MARGO: This is one of the reasons (besides the *content*) that I was drawn to *Fat Girl*. I've worked in collectives for the past seven years, and I really believe in the collective process. You really do get to see different voices represented, and when it works, it's really great! (When it doesn't work, it can be horrible.) Hopefully, this is a *functional* collective.
♦ BARBARA: It has to happen by honoring this process; it's a two-way thing. Personal issues came out that have never been expressed before—it was so intense. Even something basic like "What's fat?" aroused controversy—
♦ BERTHA: "You're not fat enough to be in *Fat Girl!*"
♦ BARBARA: It attracted people who really needed a support group, and support in general—like *most* people need.
♦ **V:** *Your magazine is very slick—*
♦ BERTHA: We're perfectionists!
♦ MAX: It's a labor of love—anal love!
♦ BARBARA: We sat down and learned how to do desktop publishing, deal with printers—how to make it happen. We went to people we knew in the dyke community who had done publications and asked, "How did you do it? What was your process? What do we need to know? What mistakes should we not make?" From Fish of *Brat Attack* we got a distribution list. Networking gave us the skills we needed. People were patient with us: "This is what you need to say to the printer. This is what you need to look for. This is what you do." The fact that we're able to publish is amazing, considering we didn't know how to do any of this before. Several of us took a *QuarkXpress* class to learn how to do layout.
♦ **V:** *How did you pay for the first issue?*
♦ MAX: With my credit card! [laughs] And I have been paid back for every single issue.
♦ BERTHA: We also have some advertising, which we view as a resource for our readers. We were approached by smut advertisers with ads which weren't pertinent to fat dykes, and it felt good to tell them, "We don't want your money!" Other gay and lesbian publications tend to go for corporate advertising, and this affects their content, because they start pandering to the Budweiser ad on the back cover. But we only wanted advertisers that supported us, that *are* us, that liked us, that loved us. Our magazine is too precious to waste!
♦ BARBARA: Being political about the zine means that we also publish a lot of smut that is "borderline"—that potentially plays with pornography laws. But we have been very conscious about all this being within a political context.
♦ **V:** *How do you decide what to print?*
♦ BARBARA: We decided that if we thought something was *hot,* then despite the pornography laws we would go ahead and publish it anyway. There are a lot of zines out there that are political, there are zines that talk about people's personal issues, and there are zines that are smutty—but very few *combine* all of this. Whereas in *Fat Girl* you can turn a page and see a big fat cunt there, and turn a page and find someone talking about a political action they've done.
♦ DEVRA: I think the fact that our sexuality is just there—honestly—is "political." We present just *honest portrayals.* After doing *Fat Girl* for awhile, I would forget how confrontational it is to people.
♦ MAX: We've had our mail tampered with. One day I sent out UPS shipments to 10 different stores and none of them got their zines—that driver had a lot of *Fat Girls!* So we stopped putting "Fat Girl" on the return address and instead wrote "Mary Smith." [laughs]
♦ BARBARA: People are very curious. They see "Fat Girl" and they go, "What?!"
♦ LISA: It's such a taboo, just to say the word "fat"—
♦ DEVRA: That's true. Just on a local level, the personal ads in the *Bay Times* [gay/lesbian weekly] used to say "big" or "plump" or "not skinny." But now they say "Fat, Fat, Fat" all over the place. When *Fat Girl* appeared, a lot of fat activists got a breath of fresh air.
♦ MAX: *Fat Girl* appeared at the same time as *FAT!SO?* We met Marilyn Wann [editor/publisher] at a cafe when she walked up to us and asked, "Are *you* the people who do *Fat Girl?*" It turned out that we lived in the same neighborhood, two blocks from each other. Really strange!
♦ BERTHA: *FAT!SO?* is a small publication for fat

people across the board—not just for *us*.

♦ BARBARA: Fat activism has been going on since the '70s, but there has been a renewal of interest because there's so much stepped-up anti-fat activity going on, everywhere you turn. For example, the White House has been participating in "The War On Fat" with Jenny Craig. Recently I read that participation in diet centers has sharply declined—the diet industry is losing a lot of money because people are starting to *Wake Up and Drop Out* . . . re-examining the Diet Myth, and resisting all the advertising and labeling about everything being "low fat" and "no fat"—

♦ BERTHA: All these "low fat" foods are loaded with chemicals that are all bad for your body—

♦ MAX: —like *Nutrasweet*.

There was a survey in *Esquire* where all these kids said they would much rather be *hit* by a *truck* than be 50 pounds overweight!

♦ BERTHA: While they're telling you to make your body look "better" (according to *their* views), they're putting shit in their products that's going to *kill* you . . . faster!

♦ *V: You mentioned the Diet Myth—*

♦ APRIL: The myth being that if you diet, you'll get thin. I read that 92.8% of people who diet gain all the weight back within two years, plus *more* weight. So if you engage in the cycle that you diet/gain it back, then diet/gain it back, you'll get progressively heavier. Now it's named as a syndrome: weight-loss yo-yo-ing.

However, the whole Diet Myth has more parts to it than that. It's not just: "If you diet, you'll lose weight" (which is by and large untrue). It's also: "If you are thin, life will be perfect!"

♦ BERTHA: "You will be beautiful!"

♦ BARBARA: "Everybody will like you, and nothing will go wrong."

♦ BERTHA: "You'll have a better sex life!"

♦ APRIL: "You'll be wealthier!"

♦ MAX: "Healthy, wealthy, wise—and thin!"

♦ BARBARA: And every single piece of that is untrue.

♦ LISA: I work with very young kids (8-11) who are choking on this American Dream. They tell me, "If I don't eat that candy bar and just eat apples for the rest of my life, I'll stay thin enough." And they're as big around as my little finger! As long as I can remember, the words "thin" and "beautiful" (as well as "fat" and "ugly") have always been connected.

♦ DEVRA: As a woman, no matter what age or size you are, it's generally expected that you're dieting—very strange. There are office pools around diets—

♦ BERTHA: My friend's company has a holiday incentive: if you don't gain weight over Christmas vacation, you get a bonus! [laughs]

♦ SONDRA: And that's really common. There's a myth that you'll be wealthier if you're thin, but that isn't really a myth. There is so much discrimination against fat people; there are so many more costs associated with being fat—like clothing, traveling—

♦ BERTHA: And there's job discrimination.

♦ BARBARA: Fat is definitely a *class;* it pushes you into a different class. (There's a good book on this: *Lesbians Come Out of the Class Closet.*) If women are busy thinking about dieting, this crowds out discussions about the real misogynist, racist events going on around them. A lot is going on in Congress this year, and there's very little coverage in the press—but there sure is a lot of discussion about *obesity* in this country.

♦ MAX: A woman at work told me that she couldn't quit smoking, because when she tried to quit, she gained weight. I asked, "You would rather get lung cancer than weigh more?" She said, "Oh yes!" She went on and on trying to justify her position. I said, "Look. I realize that fat hatred is very prevalent in our culture," and she protested, "Oh no—it's not fat *hatred!* Look at my *frame!*" She just never got it.

♦ DEVRA: There was a survey in *Esquire* where all these kids said they would much rather be *hit by a truck* than be 50 pounds overweight!

♦ SONDRA: And wasn't there another survey where people said they would rather die of cancer than be fat?

♦ LAURA: There's another one where people said they would rather abort fetuses if they knew ahead of time they'd be fat!

♦ BERTHA: And people think we're just whining—

♦ MAX: What a world!

♦ DEVRA: It's amazing what levels people will descend to, to justify fat hatred. People think that if you are fat, you are lazy—no matter what. It's excruciating how deep this goes.

♦ BARBARA: This discussion typifies the dialogue that's been aired in *Fat Girl,* where everything we publish is by and for fat dykes. But many people *outside* the fat dyke community have found something in *Fat Girl* that they have not found anywhere else in this world, and have approached us about how *Fat Girl* has changed how they look at the world, how they write, how they feel about themselves and what they do. The pervasiveness of self-hatred in our relationship with our bodies is so endemic, that when people see us work through this for ourselves, something shifts within *them.* By focusing on what we feel, what we're experiencing and where our anger is, we allow *other* people to re-examine personal issues about their own bodies in a similar light.

♦ BERTHA: The feedback in letters feels really good. All these women have written to us about looking at themselves in a different way: "Now I've done this, and I've done that, and thank you so much for being there!"

from *Fat Girl #3*

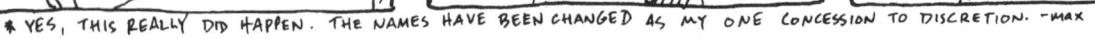

♦ MAX: "Thank you for finally representing me."
♦ BERTHA: "Thank you for showing my body; I opened up *Fat Girl* and there was *my body* in a magazine."
♦ BARBARA: It's been revolutionary: publishing images of fat dykes having orgasms, eating, feeding each other, being happy—just *being*. Breaking these taboos and feeling pretty good about it.

Most of our venues of communication are about selling us something. That's why zines are so exciting: they're really about communication and ideas, not about selling other people's products. Zines are about creating culture and creating community . . .

♦ APRIL: We publish 2,000 issues at a time, and they go out all over the world. We get a lot of letters that say, "I live in Podunk, Utah, and I walked into a store and saw *Fat Girl,* picked it up, and it was the most incredible experience of my life. If I had seen you 35 years ago . . ."

It's inspiring to know that we can *do* something. With all the trauma we get every day, being fat in San Francisco, it's nevertheless much easier here than in the rest of the country. To be able to do something where we have support, and send it out to people who are really solitary . . . well, our whole culture is about hating yourself, and it feels amazing to be able to counter that mentality.
♦ MAX: Like the Voice of America: "It's all okay, everyone—just Be Yourself!"
♦ DEVRA: *Fat Girl* has to do with being "out" in terms of being queer, and also with being involved in SM—which, to be sure, doesn't appeal to everyone. We're not doing one of those cheesy, fake, glossy magazines that doesn't represent anyone; some of those glossy lesbian magazines *pain* me. For someone who feels really isolated, fat and queer in the middle of nowhere, with nobody around who understands, I can imagine that *Fat Girl* provides a much-needed solace.
♦ MARGO: When I look at *Fat Girl*, I see an entire spectrum there. I see pleasure, I see pain, I see fucking, I see wonderful poetry and stories and photographs. I look at it and think, "Anything is possible!"
♦ MAX: On the other side of the coin, some people look at *Fat Girl* and all they see is the fact that it has SM in it, and they won't look any further. We just got a letter from a bookstore owned by a fat dyke in Albuquerque: "Thank you for sending a sample of your magazine. However, given that only a certain percentage of our readers are lesbian, only a certain percentage are fat, and only 2% are into SM, there's no market here for your magazine—
♦ BERTHA: She got it down to 0.15%!
♦ MAX: She doesn't realize that a lot more people than fat SM dykes read *Fat Girl*. Probably 80% of our readers are *not* SM dykes. They're all over the country, doing whatever.
♦ BARBARA: A Different Light bookstore in San Francisco said *Fat Girl* was the highest-selling zine they'd ever carried. They put us up front with the queer glossies.
♦ BERTHA: I wrote back to that woman in Albuquerque: "We're offering you *Fat Girl* on consignment. I would think you might *test* it before you make this assumption that it won't sell in your store." It's amazing; people are so prejudiced—*duh!* [everyone laughs]
♦ BARBARA: And there wasn't a lot of SM in that issue—
♦ DEVRA: Just a photo of you pissing in a cemetery on the back cover!
♦ BARBARA: But is that SM?
♦ APRIL: To get back to the point of humor, we could be really serious and heavy if that's all that we wanted to talk about, but we have to get *through* life, too! And we use humor to do that.
♦ BERTHA: That's why I first did the "Kitchen Slut" column. I wanted it to be fun, silly, sexy, and about food! To be *political* and *funny.* I did it humorously and tongue-in-cheek about sexy, good, *fattening* foods! No guilt allowed in my column!
♦ DEVRA: The first time I read "Kitchen Slut" I was

Cover of *Fat Girl #4,* 1995 photo of Judy Graboyes by V. Markin and J. Segal

laughing out loud—especially at the little captions under your photos.

Everybody working on *Fat Girl* has had to read and re-read people talking about the most intense issues of their lives. It's so heavy that—
♦ BERTHA: —it needed a little bit of heavy cream to lighten it up!
♦ BARBARA: Publishing a zine involves a lot of responsibility. It takes a lot of responsibility to ask someone to pose for you in a revealing way and write about the most personal things that have happened to them regarding their bodies. We're very thoughtful as to where we place each piece when we mix up the articles. One of our mottos is "Go for a ride with *Fat Girl*" and it really is a *ride:* from beginning to end you experience a whole spectrum of emotions.

One of the reasons why it's hard to be in *Fat Girl* and why I recently left the collective is: it's been so difficult to understand what my feelings have been about everything we've published. Everything has happened so quickly that if we were *just* publishing "hard" or depressing content, I feel I might have gone off the deep end! I really needed to stop and step back for awhile. We have created and opened up a lot of dialogue about people's feelings and deep personal concerns, and if we didn't include joy and humor . . . that's the kind of energy people need to go *beyond* the difficult experiences that happen to them.
♦ **V: You're trying to present truth, unwatered-down—**
♦ MAX: That's the idea!
♦ BERTHA: And some of it is fun! We're very silly people.
♦ DEVRA: Some of our better inspirations have come during burnout periods.
♦ MAX: It's kind of ironic that the *truth* is what's so appealing to people, and then for example we went to OutWrite last year (a national gay and lesbian writers' conference) and Barbara from *Fat Girl* was on a panel with members of other publications. The discussion was about gay magazines having sold out to advertising because "that's what the readers really want." We were sitting there going, "Are you sure?!" [laughs]
♦ BARBARA: They even said that their readers weren't intelligent, and that they had to pander to the lowest common denominator! Also, that they have no responsibility to their readers, that people basically aren't too smart, and you don't want them thinking too hard. "They *like* that advertising; they like that glossy feel. That's what they're buying us for. And besides, we're going to be here a year from now . . ."
♦ MAX: —insinuating that *Fat Girl* would not be.
♦ BARBARA: That's what a lot of publishing is about: selling advertising. People don't realize that's what TV is all about. That's what most of our venues of communication are about: *selling us something.* That's why zines are so exciting: they're really about communication and ideas, not about selling other people's products. Zines are about creating culture and creating community (or alienating other people, or writing about the most alienating things you can think of because that's what gets you off, but—hey, you're doing it for yourself!).
♦ DEVRA: This is what feels so life-saving—not just zines, but other D-I-Y (Do-It-Yourself) projects.
♦ APRIL: I feel that the amount of struggling you do to collectively produce a project, and collectively decide what you're going to do, really keeps you honest and strengthens the work. Because all of this is background for what we end up saying and doing, not just in the magazine, but in our *lives*. Magazines that are more corporately-structured don't have a check-and-balance to keep them honest. Our early roundtables were really personal and honest and in-depth because we all had to *work* with each other. Because of this kind of intimacy, we were able to say things *in-depth* in a way that I don't think you can if you don't have that kind of community built up.
♦ BARBARA: In our roundtables (which are transcribed discussions), when talking about fat dyke issues, it's hard to separate all the personal and political issues which we all experience: class, racism, issues around disabilities—the whole spectrum of how we experience life with its different levels of cultural alienation. We were trying to provide a place (and another level of accessibility) where people who perhaps weren't writers or artists could find a voice and discuss important issues.
♦ DEVRA: For *Fat Girl #2* some people sent in their *own* roundtables. It would be so great if more people we don't know would do that.

A woman recently went to a doctor who kept telling her, "You need to lose weight—that's your problem." But her real problem was: she had cancer. She died.

♦ **V: Earlier you mentioned other publications, like FAT!SO?—**
♦ MAX: There's "*Radiance: the magazine for large women*"—
♦ DEVRA: Which just did a big feature on the new generation of fat activists, and didn't include *Fat Girl* or *FAT!SO?*, which have both made a big difference to a lot of people.
♦ APRIL: There's another zine from a young woman, Nomy Lamm, called *I'm So Fucking Beautiful*. A glossy photo book recently appeared, *Women En Large,* plus some other fat women's anthologies.
♦ BERTHA: A woman from England, Lee Kennedy,

From left: Laura, Twyla, April. Photo: Laura J.

sent us a couple of cartoon zines.
♦ MAX: Check out the "resource" sections in *Fat Girl,* which list other publications, books—everything we know, basically, is in there.
♦ BARBARA: Also, Max has put together a web site for *Fat Girl.* We've gotten a lot of press attention from other web publications; one from the U.K. included us in their "Top 50 Most Interesting Sites." *Time* magazine mentioned us in an article on on-line publications; the *Nation* used us as an information resource, too.
♦ MAX: For being such a fringe thing, we sure are popular! Weird!
♦ DEVRA: And our e-zine is very different from the paper zine, for a number of reasons. Resources and announcements are updated before the paper zine appears, of course.
♦ MAX: There is additional information, like I compiled a list of all the songs I could come up with that had any kind of mention of fatness in them. I included as many lyrics as possible and put them on the Web, with links to the web-site of musicians who have done anything related to fat. I'm into resources.
♦ APRIL: In terms of resources, there is the *Fat Lip Readers Theater,* a local fat women's readers' theater group, and *4 Big Girls,* a performance collective of fat black women in Seattle—
♦ MAX: They're fuckin' awesome.
♦ DEVRA: It's definitely not just us; there's a lot out there.
♦ BARBARA: For the recent San Francisco International Gay & Lesbian Film Festival, we were asked to curate a program on fat dyke issues under the heading of Radical Women's Body Politics. Recently I got a call from a woman who curates Florida's International Gay and Lesbian Film Festival—she attended our program and was so affected by it that she took one of the short films and had it run with their top premiere film, which was *The Incredibly True Adventures of Two Girls in Love* (which I have spoken about as so fat-phobic). She was so affected by that—she had her eyes opened—that she said, "I can't in good conscience run this feature film without including something that presents this issue," so she ran this short before the feature. There's definitely been a cultural synergy of ideas; a shift in how people are looking at things, and what they feel comfortable in taking on . . .
♦ DEVRA: We push constantly for other people to get involved at production levels, like for film festivals, Dyke TV . . .
♦ APRIL: By the way, I dance and work with a

choreographer who likes to use fat women dancing—which really flips people out. I search for and collect old videos which feature fat women, and there are a lot of 'em. *The Pajama Game* is one of my favorite films because it has this incredible scene of a middle-aged fat woman dancing a song-and-dance number, which they would never do now. Someday I'll print a resource list of these films in *Fat Girl*.

People are even feeding their infants fat-free formula . . . And there are diet programs for pets now!

♦ BARBARA: Recently, *A Circle of Friends* got a lot of attention. It was supposed to be about the most popular, most eligible boy in school falling in love with this fat woman and dealing with it. The actress they chose wasn't fat at all, and her contract was that she gain weight for the role and have a trainer afterwards to lose the weight. That's a very Hollywood example of how this issue is approached—

♦ MAX: And they couldn't even use a fat actress, for crying out loud.

♦ LAURA: Ricki Lake was fat in *Hairspray*, but now that she has her own talk show she's become thin and weight-obsessed—it's sad. She was beautiful.

♦ DEVRA: In every interview, she says it's the hardest and most "fulfilling" (so to speak!) thing she's ever done. I know; it's sad. JOHN WATERS has been a big inspiration to a lot of us; a bastion of sanity in a weird way. Perhaps it shows.

♦ APRIL: I was excited about two Australian films, *Strictly Ballroom* and *Muriel's Wedding* which both used fat characters of all ages. They lead real lives; they sing and dance. The great thing about *Muriel's Wedding* is: she has this whole life shift; the world becomes wonderful; she finds herself, and it's not about her losing weight. She goes off to the city, dumps her family, finds a guy, dumps the guy, finds a girlfriend who's like a good friend—and it's not about her being thin at the end. I didn't care that she was a normally thin actress who gained weight for the role; the moral of the story was wonderful. Maybe Australians are different from Americans; maybe they're not so weight-obsessed—

♦ MAX: Wait a minute! An American woman married an Australian man whom she met on the Internet. She wanted to move to Australia, and they would not let her in the country because she was 24 pounds overweight! That was in *Newsweek*.

♦ DEVRA: And here in the U.S. a man was released from jail under the stipulation that he lose weight while on parole. He didn't, so they put him back in jail!

♦ SONDRA: If you're overweight, you can't get decent healthcare; they tell you to lose 15 more pounds.

♦ APRIL: Yet they've done studies which show that it's a far more dangerous health problem to be *underweight*. But they never say anything about that.

♦ DEVRA: Also, there's this common fear fat women have about going to doctors. Every time you do, there's this goddamn scale you're supposed to step on—no matter *what* you're going in for! We're trying to publish more resource information from fat-positive health practitioners.

♦ BARBARA: Women are dying in this country because they're being misdiagnosed; they're being told, "You're a fat person; your health problem is that you have to lose weight." Doctors don't take your health issues seriously.

♦ SONDRA: There was a recent case involving a 14-year-old girl whose symptoms were: she was missing her period, and she felt really sick in the mornings. Her mother took her to a gynecologist who said, "You're missing your period because you're overweight." So this 14-year-old girl ended up having a baby she didn't want to have—obviously, she was *pregnant!*

♦ BERTHA: A woman recently went to a doctor who kept telling her, "You need to lose weight—that's your problem." But her real problem was: she had cancer. She died.

♦ LAURA: She personally told me about going to the doctor and saying, "Look, something's wrong," and being told, "No, you just need to lose weight." By the time she was properly diagnosed, it was too late.

♦ APRIL: I've gone to medical appointments where you want them to investigate something specific, and all they talk about is some diet you ought to go on.

♦ SONDRA: They love to tell you that you're "morbidly obese"—

♦ DEVRA: —just the description makes you want to vomit—

♦ MAX: That's the idea! [laughs]

♦ *V: If you present fat-positive medical information in the pages of a professional-looking publication, it's likely to be taken more seriously—*

♦ BARBARA: Our objective was to be very readable, so that people could pick up *Fat Girl* and easily get information and advice.

♦ DEVRA: We were part of a course curriculum at UC Santa Cruz—required reading!

♦ SONDRA: They have an anti-discrimination law there, regarding fat.

♦ *V: Do you have an office?*

♦ BARBARA: No. Production is done in people's homes; the last two issues were done in my bedroom on my Mac.

♦ MAX: When you're a collective, working out of one person's house is difficult. If other people want to do something, they have to come to your home to do it.

♦ BARBARA: It was hard to give up my bedroom to be Production Central for a month. It's like, "I'm going to work now, so you get to use my computer." There was somebody there all the time, except when I was sleeping. But even when I was sleeping, the computer was FTP-ing files! Now I can't stand the sound of the computer—

♦ BERTHA: A slight case of burnout! Flashbacks, nightmares . . .

♦ **V: *So the initial money went to pay for printing, shipping and—***

♦ DEVRA: Syquest tapes.

♦ BERTHA: And if anybody wants to solicit advertising for us, we pay 10%!

♦ BARBARA: Besides us, all the people who read *Fat Girl* make it happen—they send us snapshots, photo booth pictures, their personal experiences, rants . . . if it wasn't for the excitement that readers share with us, *Fat Girl* would not exist. It's about community. That's where the magic is: in that *exchange.*

♦ **V: *What are some other projects you want to do?***

♦ MAX: I want to do a comic zine. For *Fat Girl* I started drawing comics—that was the first time I'd ever tried that. I want to draw about more diverse topics that aren't necessarily appropriate for *Fat Girl.*

♦ BARBARA: I want to do another zine taking the vision that's in *Fat Girl* and extending it to all the other people in the community who are alienated and aren't having their lives represented in the media.

♦ APRIL: I just want to see *Fat Girl* keep going and reach more people.

♦ DEVRA: People have definite taste discrepancies, and come from different places, but there has been a level of respect that has to do with commitment and family. Considering the fact that most people have day jobs, it's pretty amazing that there was a tight group for a year and a half.

♦ **V: *What are your day jobs? Barbara, you work in publishing—***

♦ MAX: And during the evening she's the Secretary of Defense—

♦ BERTHA: —for the New Anarchist Revolution!

♦ BARBARA: Most of us have been anarchist activists for a really long time. To do publishing, I learned what I needed to learn to make *Fat Girl* happen.

♦ LAURA: I'm a barber and I'm not ashamed of that. I use clippers; I'm not a "hairdresser."

♦ APRIL: I was an assistant at a law firm, but the law firm closed—*yes!* It was a very corporate environment with fat hatred, woman hatred; everything that wasn't "straight white male with money" was not okay. And *Fat Girl* was my secret vice: "I do this day job, and at night I bust out and become who I really am!" This feeling is probably true for a lot of people who do zines: this is where their *real life* happens. Anyway, right now I'm unemployed and have my own business making corsets—that's fun.

♦ BERTHA: In the course of *Fat Girl* I also became unemployed. I sell ads for *Fat Girl* and *Cuir Underground*, and I am a *Reiki* healer and teach *Reiki* classes. I also make boxer shorts for big butches and whoever else wants them. In my spare time I do drawings.

♦ MAX: I constantly complain about not having role

Sassy

You may think *Sassy* is just another gross het teen mag, but if you read the August issue, you'll think again. Mentioned on the cover, page 78 and 79 contain a spread entitled "Thirteen reasons not to diet." The reasons:

- 1. Your weight was genetically programmed.
- 2. Dieting slows your metabolism.
- 3. It makes you boring.
- 4. It leads to eating disorders.
- 5. You're always hungry.
- 6. And what is the point?
- 7. You're depriving yourself of essential nutrition.
- 8. You put off living.
- 9. You'll gain it back.
- 10. It's worse for your health to yo-yo.
- 11. You feed the evil diet industry.
- 12. The connection between weight and health problems is iffy.
- 13. It makes you feel bad.
  –from *Fat Girl #2*

Sassy Sells Out

Remember how in *FG #2*, we sing the praises of a glossy teen-mag that makes good with their "10 reasons not to diet list" and a binder that said "If they call you a fat pig, say thanks"? Well, you can forget all that. They sold ownership, and it shows. Their April issue features such heart-warming material as "The truth about fat" (uh, right, and take one guess as to what that is), and a precious photo of a repulsed girl cowering near her salad at the sight of another girl (literally donning pig ears and a snout!) devouring a hamburger & fries. Junior *Cosmo*. **–Devra from *Fat Girl #3***

models. So we have to try to be our own.
♦ BARBARA: Fun, perverse, political—
♦ **V: *And creative.***
♦ MAX: Absolutely.
♦ APRIL: I always felt I was trying to change the world by living my life and being different in the world, but being able to do it through a zine has had a much greater impact. It's like we took the zine and threw it in the water and the ripples were so much bigger than I could ever have achieved by myself.
♦ MAX: We were in *Time* magazine: one sentence with a major typo. They called us "apolitical" instead of "a political" group.
♦ DEVRA: Who would expect an apolitical fat dyke publication? Not me!
♦ **V: *But that's so characteristic of major media. You've had one personal encounter, and they print one sentence which has a gross error. Think about all the other stories you read, which involve dozens of sentences—***
♦ BARBARA: I've been trying to tell people that for years!

Cartoon by Max Airborne from *Fat Girl #2*

♦ **V: This is a terrible question, but—it must be hard for you to find clothes—**
♦ MAX: Uh-huh.
♦ BARBARA: What's so terrible about that question?
♦ APRIL: That is so realistic.
♦ BERTHA: That's the actuality that everybody here has had to live with.
♦ LAURA: In the first issue, there was a survey about "What do you dislike about being fat?" The most common response was: "It's hard to find clothes."
♦ LISA: I remember growing up as a basic femme (which meant clothes were important) and having two shirts and two or three pairs of pants and a couple of pairs of underwear, to wear for an entire year, and thinking to myself, "I'm fat; I'm never going to be able to have clothes and dress the way I want to. I'm fat, ugly, stupid, and lazy." Every time a fat girl walks into a store at age 12 or 13 and can't buy anything, or the mom takes her to the "Large Size" department where all she finds is polyester, it solidifies the notion that "I can't do anything about this—I'm stuck."
♦ DEVRA: Or you gain weight, and can't necessarily afford to buy the clothes that *are* out there. It's grim.
♦ BARBARA: This is why resource networking has been an important part of *Fat Girl*. A lot of people have commented about the zine: "Y'know, you just make being fat so glamorous! Where do you get your bras?" Questions like this are so vital, yet seem silly at the same time. We spend a lot of time just figuring out how to get by. And there's more than just clothes: not fitting into seats, transportation, restrooms, restaurants, flying in an airplane, getting into a wheelchair or ambulance, or through turnstiles—there's so much out there. We really need to share resources with each other, because no one is putting them out there for us.
♦ DEVRA: Only the American Disabilities Act has changed anything to accommodate us. There is still this belief that you should change the size and shape of your body rather than redesign a fuckin' chair!
♦ LISA: Max did a comic in *Fat Girl* that said, "Tired of a world where you don't fit? Try using a *chainsaw!*" It's going to take a lot of people saying, "I'm no longer accepting this crap!" to produce results.
♦ BARBARA: There's an old anarchist song about "Your job and your work are two different things." I may have lost some opportunities in my life, but I've created so many more opportunities through pursuing things in the most honest way for myself.
♦ **V: Max, what's your job?**
♦ MAX: I work for a company doing development for the Web. I keep learning all these new web tools and programming techniques and then I apply them to *Fat Girl*'s web site! Everyone is very thin there—I'm an anomaly. But they knew about my *Fat Girl* web pages—in fact, that's how I got the job.
♦ LISA: I'm a fourth grade teacher and my kids chase me across the schoolyard going, "Hail the fat girl! Hail the fat girl!" I brought *Fat Girl* to school; the kids know all about me.
♦ DEVRA: Age is an issue with us. We put "Not Sold to Minors" on our zine because the reality is: if there's any suspicion of kiddy porn involved, they can raid you and keep all your stuff for months and you'll never get all of it back.
♦ **V: You said that kids as young as eight are already obsessed with being thin—**
♦ LISA: That's why I'm very "out" with kids about fat politics. Sometimes I bring sugar snacks to school that these kids refuse to eat, like little girls who are gymnasts. They eat rabbit food and skip meals and they're sickly. I told them, "You guys, I'm 20 years older than you and I'm fat, and I can outrun you and out-chase you. Does that tell you something?"

I'm not sure why, but it felt really liberating to have a photo published of me pissing! It was printed above quotations from supermodels talking about how they feel about their bodies.

Every minute of the day they get input warning against being "fat and ugly"—*twenty-four/seven*. If you're a girl, it's not okay to be even chunky. Teachers prohibit words that are racist, but they will let kids call each other "fat," "ugly," "faggot," "dyke," and "queer."

Now companies are advertising in *schools:* you see Nike posters of thin gymnasts everywhere. It's all about money.
♦ BARBARA: The government and Jenny Craig have been working on this "Shape Up, America!" project together, and a lot of people who write to us about their experiences of being fat remember their families putting them on diets when they were four and five years old!
♦ DEVRA: People are even feeding their infants fat-free formula!
♦ BARBARA: And there are diet programs for *pets* now; articles are appearing on the obesity of American animals.
♦ **V: Devra, how are you employed?**
♦ DEVRA: I work for a computer science think tank where I'm kind of a high-tech grunt worker formatting documents and doing Web pages; I'm pretty good with *Unix*. I work out at Chinese-Indonesian kung-fu; it's called *Silat*. I used to do a lot of organization and demo work in the SM community, doing play parties, workshops, and having multiple partners *every week!* I used to be much more of a schmoozer and networker; now I'm a hermit like everyone else—I go home from work and hide with my computer.
♦ MAX: Wow, what a depressing picture!

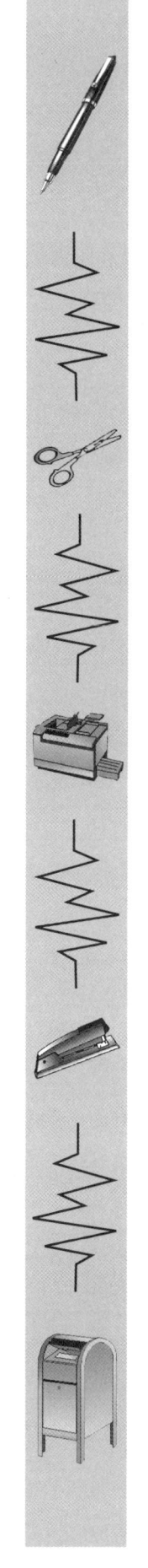

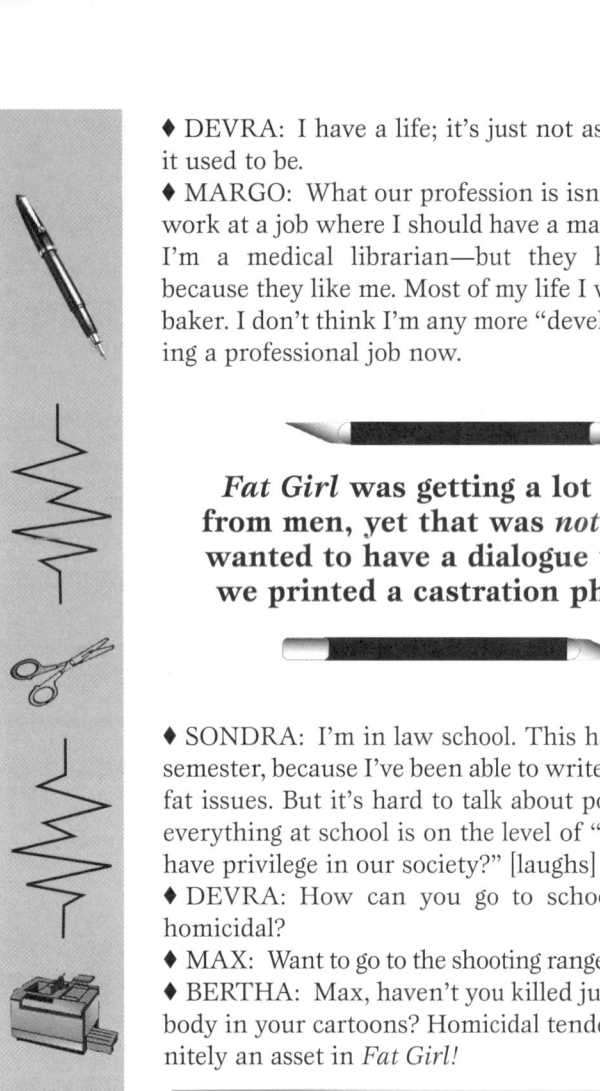

♦ DEVRA: I have a life; it's just not as interesting as it used to be.

♦ MARGO: What our profession is isn't everything. I work at a job where I should have a master's degree—I'm a medical librarian—but they hired me just because they like me. Most of my life I was a cook and baker. I don't think I'm any more "developed" for having a professional job now.

> *Fat Girl* was getting a lot of mail from men, yet that was *not* who we wanted to have a dialogue with. So we printed a castration photo . . .

♦ SONDRA: I'm in law school. This has been a good semester, because I've been able to write about SM and fat issues. But it's hard to talk about politics, because everything at school is on the level of "Do white men have privilege in our society?" [laughs]

♦ DEVRA: How can you go to school and not be homicidal?

♦ MAX: Want to go to the shooting range this weekend?

♦ BERTHA: Max, haven't you killed just about everybody in your cartoons? Homicidal tendencies are definitely an asset in *Fat Girl!*

♦ BARBARA: They're not present, but both Selena Wells and Twyla Stark have been with the collective from the beginning. Twyla worked in bookstores most of her adult life, and Selena worked restoring Oriental rugs; now she's training to do computer animation.

♦ *V: So how did you get the money together for each successive issue? [everyone looks at Max]*

♦ MAX: I go to the bank. [laughs]

♦ BERTHA: We have a new person with a credit card who's going to float us a loan for the next printing—

♦ MAX: $3,500 for printing and tapes, and a few hundred for postage. We pay in cash—interesting experience. "Okay, I've got $3,500 in cash and I'm going to the printer now. Anybody looking at me? Anyone following me?"

♦ BARBARA: The last time we did that was pretty intense; it took about 45 minutes at the bank to get that much cash with a credit card. This was at 16th and Mission, it was really busy, and people were watching what was going on. I got really nervous when we walked out. The bank teller asked, "Do you want this in anything?" and Max said, "No," and stuck the whole wad in her pocket.

♦ MAX: Where else was I going to put it?

♦ BERTHA: In your bra!

♦ MAX: I didn't have a bra—*oh,* in my underwear. Yeah, I'll just give the printer a wad of juicy $100 bills!

♦ BERTHA: We've gotten some contributions from people who want to see *Fat Girl* continue, and have had a few pretty amazing benefits. We got support

Lisa and Margo. Photo: Robert Waldman

from the club MuffDive, Red Dora's Bearded Lady Cafe and Old Wives Tales.

♦ **V: *Do men write you letters?***
♦ DEVRA: Barb gets a lot of fan mail from men who send photos of themselves in lingerie, and write detailed three-page fantasy letters—
♦ BARBARA: *Three* pages—I got this 20-page history from some guy who was trying to have this intellectual/erotic exchange with me. And that's not what we're about.

♦ **V: *You include SM content, which is considered adventurous. What are your thoughts on this?***
♦ BERTHA: We had a whole dialogue in the last issue because someone wrote a letter about this. Basically we said that we're perverts, we enjoy SM, it's important to us, and we're going to print it. If you don't like it, send us stuff you do like and we'll print that, too!

It's important that we print what we believe in. We print what turns us on, what we think is wonderful.
♦ BARBARA: When we started out, the people involved had all been active in the pervert scene. Being truthful and talking about things and really being *yourself* and doing things for yourself, and also doing educational work, is important. This legacy carried over to *Fat Girl*. In the SM community, fat women's sexuality is more visible than in the dyke community as a whole.

♦ **V: *When Good Vibrations first started, I thought it was a courageous enterprise. Just look at how it's grown—***
♦ BERTHA: Remember the back room, the vibrating chair and the little museum?
♦ DEVRA: They still have the museum, the back room, and now they have mail orders, plus a second store in Berkeley.
♦ BARBARA: But at the same time, there are re-virginization groups all over the country now—
♦ MAX: —re-installing their hymens— [laughs]
♦ BARBARA: A lot of them are at universities, and are for men and women who lost their virginity, but want it for marriage. Some women are going in to have surgery for hymen reconstruction. At these clubs, they can meet other virgins—
♦ JUDY: —and virgin wanna-bees!
♦ BERTHA: But that's not what *we're* doing—we advocate de-virginization.
♦ APRIL: Do people go in for that surgery like every month? [laughs]
♦ MAX: Every week... every *day!* "Here I am—back again! I just can't seem to keep it intact!"
♦ DEVRA: You'd think they would just learn about anal sex.
♦ MAX: I wonder if you can be re-virginized *there?*
♦ **V: *... Actually, I think a lot of people can't really deal with fisting. Have you gotten—***
♦ MAX: Yes, a lot of reaction. In the first issue, the centerfold showed someone being fisted, and I think some people might have thought that the fist in question was a large dick or dildo. And people accused us of having men in our zine! I think it was people who didn't know what fisting was.
♦ BERTHA: In the next issue we had to explain to people that there were no dildoes involved—
♦ DEVRA: It was a horse dick!
♦ BARBARA: People just have a lot to get over, regarding sexuality and bodies.
♦ APRIL: One of our "Gear Queen" articles was on toileting, and the problems related to size which people encounter dealing with bathrooms. It attracted a lot of attention on the Internet—
♦ DEVRA: There's a site called "Mirsky's Worst of the Web." He chooses his "worst" for comedy reasons. You click on it and go right to a page. We posted a "Gear Queen" column on butt-wiping tips, and he linked it directly and out of context, which can have an offensive effect.
♦ BARBARA: I'm not sure why, but it felt really liberating to have a photo published of me pissing! It was printed above quotations from supermodels talking about how they feel about their bodies. We all piss, but it's still taboo to show this; the same with fat—people talk about fat, but it's all derogatory. We're trying to help people see through taboos in new and different ways, and feel more comfortable with them.
♦ JUDY: Two different friends told me, after they saw photos of me and Bertha published in *Fat Girl:* "You're a lunatic. You're crazy." It hurts my feelings that my friends, whom I've known for 20 years, think I'm crazy just because they saw photos of me in a sexual way in a magazine.
♦ MAX: Do they think you don't have sex?

We were asked to be on talk shows, but we never quite fit into the topics— we never quite fit into the *chairs!*

♦ JUDY: They think that's so *out there*—you're not supposed to show that.
♦ DEVRA: It's as if you were posing for *Playboy*. People either love it, or they can't get over it.
♦ **V: *What else is on your web site?***
♦ MAX: We provide web space for a straight couple who have devoted their lives to collecting resource information about fat activism. They provide a free database for any topic related to fat—they're great folks—and I designed a few web pages for them. A woman from *Rump Parliament,* another fat activist publication, told them, "Ohmigod—aren't you afraid of being associated with those *lesbians?* Hmm—I guess you'll take help where you can get it, huh?"
♦ **V: *Oh, she's hetero?***

⧫ APRIL: Oppressively so!
⧫ DEVRA: We don't try to win people over who aren't already into us. It's also important to put ideas out there that you as an individual aren't necessarily into, without worrying, "What if people don't like us?"
⧫ APRIL: We're out there to change the world—

Now I have occasional weird feelings of inadequacy because I don't weigh 500 pounds.

⧫ MAX: It's *good* if some people don't like us. Then you know you're doing something right!
⧫ BARBARA: There's more we want to change than just fat issues. But fat is intertwined with so much that needs to be changed.
⧫ LISA: We don't want to go the way of *On Our Backs*. It used to be much more fringe. In the beginning I appeared in chains in an SM spread, but I doubt if they would ever do something like that again. For awhile a lot of people were into *On Our Backs*, but it became very complacent and pathetic. It pandered to a very white middle-class dyke sexuality—
⧫ APRIL: It pandered to straight men!
⧫ BERTHA: It stopped being a dyke publication—
⧫ LISA: And became very BACW (Bay Area Career Woman).
⧫ BARBARA: For awhile *Fat Girl* was getting a lot of mail from men, yet that was *not* who we wanted to have a dialogue with. So we printed a castration photo, and a lot of men were very offended—but anything we print, we're not putting out there for men—

⧫ DEVRA: It made me so happy to see that in print, even though it was offensive. It was one of those *feel-good* moments!
⧫ BERTHA: "If you're a man and you pick up our magazine, you get to read what we have to say"—
⧫ APRIL: "But you can't expect us to have a dialogue with you." I *am* happy that so many gay men read us. Somebody dragged my best friend Clarence into a store and showed him *Fat Girl,* saying, "You've got to read this—this is great. This *IS* punk!" My overwhelming impression of gay men is that they are so size-phobic, diet-conscious and—
⧫ MAX: —workin' out all the time!
⧫ LAURA: I can attest to that, because I'm a barber in the Castro district and I talk to men all day long.
⧫ DEVRA: But if some young punk fat boy publication came out, I'd be into it.
⧫ APRIL: I like how we're bonding across sexuality lines: being out in the world, being fat, and living our lives.
⧫ DEVRA: There are a lot of weird lines out there. At our events, people who I would never think to put in a room together show up.
⧫ **V: *You've been reclaiming fat imagery, stories and history from all of the arts—***
⧫ APRIL: Fat activism as a movement has been going for at least 20 years. We received a poem about Mama Cass, reclaiming her as an icon. The Venus of Willendorf and other goddess images about fat women are now well-known. Max used a photo of circus fat women; in a way they were our fore-mothers.
⧫ BARBARA: A lot of women who've been involved in the fat activist movement for a long time have submitted work—their current writings are being featured. We've made an effort to sustain a cross-generational connection.

Emaciation Stinks!

"Emaciation Stinks!" posters of Obsession waif Kate Moss were plastered all over San Francisco this September. SSIC, the Stop Starvation Imagery Campaign, aims to fingerpoint the distortion of women's images in the media and combat obsession with bodies as objects for products. The posters target Calvin Klein's ad campaign in an attempt to reach teenage girls who are most susceptible to the influence of the diet industry. As founder Kathy Bruin emphasizes, for teenagers it is "do or die." SSIC is raising awareness for women of all ages and encourages boycotting of bad companies. Bruin advocates for women to "exercise their integrity and their personal individuality." Their next poster campaign will be "Bodies aren't fashion accessories," and SSIC has future plans to speak in schools and at fairs. The public is hungry to participate in this dialogue—response to their action has been intense, with hundreds of positive calls as well as national press attention. Interested in raising awareness in your community? Write or call About Face (formerly SSIC) at PO Box 77665, San Francisco, CA 94107 (415) 436-0212.

–**Barbarism from *Fat Girl* #4**

♦ BERTHA: We did a roundtable on this issue, too.
♦ DEVRA: There's also the Queerzine Tradition; a lot of them weren't around for very long and they are sorely missed. For the past 10 years, those publications made a huge difference to us, even though there wasn't a whole lot of fat presence in them. There's definitely been a crossover.
♦ BARBARA: A lot of zines use clip-art imagery. For us, there hasn't been a lot of fat imagery to reclaim. Usually the images are very white and not very diverse, so I feel there's a real need for that kind of art.
♦ APRIL: There used to be more images of fat people around, because they were more accepted. However, the people selecting images for clip art CDs aren't picking those images, so . . .
♦ MAX: That's a project: a fat clip art CD-ROM!
♦ SONDRA: I'm working on a history of legal precedents involving fat issues, and it's tough. Judges are by and large assholes to begin with, and they have stated some horrendously cruel opinions—
♦ BERTHA: —anti-women, racist, prejudiced, fat-phobic, anti-semitic . . .
♦ SONDRA: Although . . . I found a case dating from 1967 where a woman wasn't hired as a substitute teacher because she was too fat. The judge (I don't know where he came from) turned out to be fantastic; he said something like, "Are you kidding? She can do the job. Are you saying that fat people aren't agile? I know a lot of football coaches who would disagree." Today, it would be hard to find a judge like this.
♦ **V: *Are there any Asian women involved in the collective?***
♦ MAX: We had an Asian woman involved, but she moved to New York. Twyla is Chicana—

It's a very strange experience: being very "fringe" most of your life, and suddenly having people read the zine, and coming up and telling you how much they love you.

♦ MARGO: I'm Latina. However, I just joined . . .
♦ APRIL: Being racially and ethnically diverse is important to us, and so is having people who are interested in the same things we're interested in *and* who want to work on the zine. We wouldn't turn anybody away! We did a roundtable on racism, and the choice I made was *not* to be involved in that—because I didn't want to be the person who had to carry all the anti-racist work in the collective. Race, class, culture, weight and size are all really interconnected, and are all topics we will continue to discuss in the zine. They're a part of everybody's life. We have by no means said every-

from *Fat Girl #4*, comic by Max Airborne

thing there is to be said on these topics!
♦ BARBARA: In the first *Fat Girl*, there's an interview with Elizabeth (the Asian woman we mentioned) and she talks a lot about the cultural differences of fat.
♦ DEVRA: There's a submission by a Filipina for the next issue that also discusses that from the perspective of an Asian-American butch. It's interesting; she's well-traveled. She talks about weird cultural assumptions—
♦ MAX: And being fat and Asian, and what's expected of her size as an Asian woman.
♦ **V: *It's fun to be on a roundtable, like now, but most publishing involves so much solitary work—***
♦ BERTHA: I've been taking over distribution (which Max did) and sitting at the computer, and then I get on the telephone, and then pack up orders, and then go to the Post Office—it's amazing how much time it takes to get things done.
♦ BARBARA: Also, we spend a lot of time dealing with people's feelings about publishing their photos and their writing—putting themselves *out there*. It's very emotionally tiring (as well as being rewarding). There are so many community expectations put upon us; I feel like we always have to be "on," ready to promote *Fat Girl*. But that's not who I am first.
♦ **V: *Probably everyone in this room has had to deal with being ostracized, and has dealt with a lot of solitude, and now you're in this great Society of the Future—***
♦ MAX: It's weird! [laughs]
♦ DEVRA: It definitely grew into a family-like feeling. It was the first time I'd been with a *group* of people

who were dealing with fat activism, and it's a support system I never had before. I had fat people in my life, and we'd have issues, but never so interpersonally and so regularly. It's been really great, and interestingly enough, many of us have gained weight in the past year! [everyone laughs] Now I have occasional weird feelings of inadequacy because I don't weigh 500 pounds! My view of reality has definitely twisted around—identity politics get messed with in an interesting way when you deal with this day after day.

♦ BARBARA: We still deal with fat-phobia every day, even within ourselves. Some days I wake up and wonder, "How do I just be *me,* and not a part of this whole collective and not responsible for how everyone else feels about their bodies?"

♦ APRIL: Over the course of doing the zine, I learned that most of us were outsiders and outcasts most of our lives—nerdy or geeky or art-geeks, but always on the fringe. All of a sudden, doing the zine, we're famous and popular and almost "in." It's a very strange experience: being very "fringe" most of your life, and suddenly having people read the zine, and coming up and telling you how much they love you. So this part of the world has changed . . . but the rest of the world still hates me!

♦ DEVRA: We got e-mail from a fat woman who attended one of our fund-raising events with other fat friends. It was pretty much sold-out, and she was in a line waiting to get in, and saw two thin dykes go to the head of the line and chirp, "Oh, there's room for *us,*" and get in! Talk about unclear on the concept!

♦ BERTHA: We would have been totally devastated if we'd known about this.

Most of the people who see our web page are not our community—they're jack-off guys looking for thrills, which is what web-surfing is about for a lot of people.

♦ *V: We've all internalized this society's concepts and expectations which are hostile to our well-being, and it's so hard to eradicate every trace—this syndrome has been titled "The Enemy Within."*

♦ MAX: I think it's interesting to see how much people project on you when they don't know you. They see you in this magazine, you're talking about something important to them, and they develop this relationship to you—and you don't even know about it because you've never met them! For example, I was exchanging e-mail with a fat activist I've never met, and I mentioned that Barb and I were lovers, etc. And she said, "Oh, you can't break up—you're the *dream couple!*" It's like: we can't be real people?! We have to become your *icons?*

♦ DEVRA: That goes with the territory of being public. No one has contacted us to be on a talk show yet, and I am disappointed.

♦ BARBARA: We were asked to be on talk shows, but we never quite fit into the topics—

♦ DEVRA: We never quite fit into the *chairs!* [laughs] I mean like Geraldo and Oprah and Ricki Lake and even Charles Perez. And it's not like I'd actually *want* to do it, but why haven't they contacted us?

♦ BERTHA: Maybe we should send all the talk shows a copy of *Fat Girl.*

♦ *V: But how would you handle this? Because they're just set up to devastate you.*

♦ MAX: I would bring a gun!

♦ BARBARA: I just want to be able to say "No!" My fantasy has been for John Waters to contact us and ask us to be in one of his films—that's my all-time fantasy!

♦ *V: That reminds me—these days, I guess there are no more fashion crimes anymore—*

♦ APRIL: Fat is often seen as a fashion crime, and we're trying to break that myth.

♦ LAURA: That's actually a talk show topic: "You can't wear that!" Fat women aren't supposed to wear revealing clothes.

♦ DEVRA: Laura, will you do a special fashion spread involving horizontal stripes and mini-skirts? [everyone cheers]

♦ MAX: We can all wear white, and wear horizontal stripes!

♦ APRIL: Plus multiple plaid skirts, and floral prints on top.

♦ BERTHA: I used to be a sales rep and wore really bright clothes. I wore an orange jumpsuit once, and this woman came up to me and said, "I really admire you—a woman of *your size* who's willing to wear such a bright color and let everybody see you!" I thought, "This is my orange jumpsuit and I love it—is there a problem here? Am I missing something?"

♦ DEVRA: I was interviewing Jewelle Gomez for *Fat Girl #4,* and she told a story about meeting a woman in an elevator who didn't want to wear any kind of perfume that would draw attention to her body in any way. It freaked me out—I completely forgot about when I was younger and thought, "I don't want anybody to smell anything about me, because fat women smell like—

♦ BERTHA: "Fat women have more body odor—"

♦ DEVRA: Or, "Fat women smell more like—"

♦ MAX: You mean *cunt?* [laughs]

♦ *V: In your publication, you're free to include whatever you want. But have you ever censored yourself for being too "out there"? Because your goal is not to merely produce shock value—*

♦ DEVRA: I censor myself from putting too much cattiness in my writing.

♦ APRIL: I think I'm still censoring myself when I write. A lot of my "process" has been working through feelings of "I can't say that," "You're not allowed to say that," "You're not allowed to *do* that." After I've worked through that and am finally able to put something in print—it seems *that's* what touches people the most.

♦ BERTHA: April did a piece for "Death on Heels," which is a production about the "femme" experience. She talked about being a fat dyke in the community, and had the audience in tears.

If you believe something, set an example and put it out there for everyone to see and respond to and dialogue about.

♦ DEVRA: Every time I see it in the zine, I still cry. Censorship is an issue with our webzine, because most of the people who see our web page are not our community—they're jack-off guys looking for thrills, which is what web-surfing is about for a lot of people.

♦ BARBARA: If someone seeks out the zine in a print form, there's a certain level of participation you have to go through just to find it—

♦ V: *You have to seek out a specialty store; it's not at your local 7-11—*

♦ BARBARA: And the Internet is so diffuse; it lacks that community exchange.

♦ MAX: Each time someone gets a document from our web site, there's a record of it. It tells you what document they got, where they came from, what server they're on, and what they clicked on to get to your page. I can find any place we're mentioned on the net by looking at our log files, and I can trace when people use key word searches to get to *Fat Girl*. We can know that someone searched using "fat bitch" or "naked ladies" to get to *Fat Girl*. And knowing this completely solidified our decision to totally leave off smut—forget it! That's not going to reach the people we want.

♦ DEVRA: All of us feel that what we put in the zine is already incredibly personal. There's so much easy access on the Net.

♦ V: *It takes an exceptional person to mail order—which they should have to do to get your zine.*

♦ MAX: Yep.

♦ BARBARA: Most of the people who drop in on the web are voyeurs, and we're not going to pander to that—let's give 'em *politics* and see what they do with it!

♦ DEVRA: Most of the people who read the paper zine are voyeurs, too, but we do have an unusually high amount of participation from our readers. The letters we get amount to major dialogue—we really have *discussions* going on. It's a shame people have to wait four months for a response. Actually, Max has started a subscription-only e-mail list called *fatdykes,* which has made possible more immediate discussion, compared with letter-writing.

♦ BARBARA: People have written that they've taken *Fat Girl* to their discussion groups and said, "This is something I want to talk about, which I wasn't able to bring up before," or they've read sections to their lovers, or sent portions to their mom. *Fat Girl* is a real pass-around publication; at least 5 people will read each copy.

♦ V: *It's a magical act to change language, take command of your own imagery, and present a new vision of the world in a context of respect, the way you want your vision to be presented—*

♦ BERTHA: It's kind of a cliche to say this, but I think reading *Fat Girl* really does empower women. And that's one of the things I want to see in the world: women empowered, women feeling good about themselves in *all* areas of life. So that we *can* take over the world!

♦ MAX: If you believe something, set an example and put it out there for everyone to see and respond to and dialogue about: "*Okay,* I want to live a life that has no more bullshit. Let's try getting other people to do that, too! Let's publish it! Break the chains!"

♦ BARBARA: That's what's so thrilling about the whole zine movement: so many people are trying to incite other people to *look at the world with a different eye, and be in the world in a different way.* ∇

Dancing girls artwork by Fish from *Fat Girl #4*

REFERENCE

I'm So Fucking Beautiful
$3 sample copy available from Nomy Lamm, 120 State NE #1510, Olympia WA 98501.

FAT!SO?
4 issue subscription $12 from Marilyn Wann, PO Box 423464, San Francisco CA 94142.

The Adventures of Baby Dyke
$4 from Terry Sapp, 4311 Crestheights Rd, Baltimore MD 21215.

Brat Attack
5 back issues, $5 each from Fish & Crew, PO Box 40754, San Francisco CA 94140-0754.

OutWrite
For info: 3525 17th St #6, San Francisco CA 94110.
TEL: (415) 431-7363;
FAX: (415) 431-7362

Ask Gear Queen

Dear Gear Queen,

My girlfriend is a big-assed girl with a huge low-hanging voluptuous belly. Our problem? Skid marks in her skivvies—a PAINFUL subject for both of us. It's not something I've heard other big fat women talk about, but when you reach a certain size it becomes increasingly difficult to wipe and present a spanking clean asshole to the world. It affects her self-esteem and sex life. I know there must be creative fat dykes out there who deal with this same problem on a daily basis and have found solutions for both home and travel toilet situations. HELP!?!?!

Yours in worship,
Searching for a clean hole

Dear Searching,

Just about the time I moved from queen-sized to supersized I attended a workshop/discussion for supersized women at a local NAAFA conference. It was the first time I ever heard toileting and wiping problems discussed, and it really freaked me out. It also made me really glad to discover that I was not the only one to have these difficulties.

Thank you for giving me the perfect opportunity to cover the topic, and please bear with me as I give some background to the uninitiated.

The basic problem is a species design flaw. Arms don't grow longer as needed. As the depth of your body grows the distance from armpit over belly to asshole increases, and there comes a point where your hand just can't reach your asshole anymore. But fear not! Depending on the configuration of your body and the arrangement of the toilet area in question, there are all sorts of things you can do.

Use a bigger stall.

Sometimes if you spread your legs just two or six inches wider your goal will be in reach. Try taking down the tampon disposal box that's sticking into your thigh, using the handicapped stall, or sitting sideways on toilets that are jammed into a corner with lots of space on one side and half an inch on the other.

Try a different angle.

See if holding your stomach out of the way helps. If you've got a smaller butt, maybe wiping from the back is the solution? Or try standing with one foot resting on the toilet seat (like the instructions for putting in tampons), or crouching, or some combination.

Use something to extend your reach.

It can be anything that is long enough, appropriately soft and absorbent, and washable or disposable. I remember women at the NAAFA gathering suggesting the kind of kitchen pot scrubbers with a foam head and hollow handle designed for liquid soap. I imagine you could also use:

- wooden or plastic cooking spoons with toilet paper wrapped around the bowl.
- foam-rubber paintbrushes.
- the kind of kitchen scrubby thing that has a ball of foam wedges or string at the end.
- long strips ripped from an old sheet that you pull between your ass cheeks while holding it taut in both the front and back (like a back scrubber for your butt).

Just be careful not to use things that could injure your anus (scouring pads, brushes, etc) and remember that if you are picking an item to use away from home you need something lightweight that you can store in your purse or bag (unless you don't mind explaining why you always take that piece of vacuum cleaner with you to the bathroom); throw away or rinse out (probably in the toilet: flush, rinse your gear, and flush again); store in a zip lock bag until you get home or somewhere it can be thoroughly washed and dried.

Use a bidet.

Now I have to admit that my only experience with bidets was at my mother's house in Turkey, where the bidet's water spout was carefully positioned to shoot a stream of water at my right ass cheek—not at all useful. However, I believe they are supposed to be used to shoot a stream of clean water over your ass and pussy until they are squeaky clean (if somewhat damp). As a lower-cost alternative to remodeling your bathroom, one was developed by Bill Sabrey, and is sold through Amplestuff, PO Box 116, Bearsville NY 12409. It's a 2-gallon jug with an attached pump handle and tube that attaches (with wire and a suction cup) under the seat of your toilet. A travel-sized version is also available.

Incidentally, this problem is related to another one that may be familiar to some of you: incorrectly fitted dildo harnesses. Most leather workers will understand it if you show them that the hip band they've provided is too short to go around your hips. And they are usually happy to make you a larger one. (If they aren't, go to another leather worker!) However, if the length of the anchor straps—you know, the part that goes between your legs like a g-string or jock strap—isn't also sufficiently lengthened they will pull the hip band low on your body and make the whole arrangement rather…precarious.

Ah, the joys of being deep as well as wide.

Anyway, I hope I've helped you find a workable solution. Wishing you and your girl a lifetime of clean undies,
Gear Queen

Looking for anything in particular? Got some gear tips to share?
Write to the Gear Queen c/o Fat Girl, 2215-R Market #197, San Francisco CA 94114.

—from *Fat Girl* #2

im so fucking beautiful

#1
35¢

Cover of *I'm So Fucking Beautiful #1*, Nomy Lamm

Quotations from Supermodels

Christy Turlington: 1) "You can usually tell when I'm happy by the fact that I've gained weight."
2) "I think, if my butt's not too big for them to be photographing it, then it shouldn't be too big for me."

Christie Brinkley: 1) "I wish my butt did not go side-ways, but I guess I have to face that."
2) "Richard doesn't really like me to kill bugs, but sometimes I can't help it."

Linda Evangelista: "I can do anything you want me to do so long as I don't have to speak."

Beverley Johnson: "Everyone should have enough money to get plastic surgery."

Kate Moss: "It was kind of boring for me to have to eat. I would know I had to, and I would."

Paulina Porizkova: "When I model I'm pretty blank. You can't think too much or it doesn't work."

Cheryl Tiegs: "It's very important to have the right clothing to exercise in. If you throw on an old T-shirt or sweats, it's not inspiring for your workout."

Cindy Crawford: "They were doing a full back shot of me in a swimsuit and I thought, Oh my God, I have to be so brave. See, every woman hates herself from behind."

—selected by Sooty from *Fat Girl #4*

These, and more Deep Thoughts, can be found on Sooty's web site at:

http://www.sils.umich.edu/~sooty/thoughts.html

What do you want from your non-fat allies?

- Open mind. Acceptance. Appreciation.
- Acceptance of who I am, not what I look like. [sic]
- I want you to not talk about yourself being too fat. Don't tell me how fat you feel, all 130 pounds of ya. Don't subject me to complaints about your body and your fat intake, etc.
- I want you not to use fat-phobic language.
- Educate yourself . . . This means we do not try to convert each other—EVER.
- Don't assume I'm trying to lose weight.
- Don't assume that a fat person has a) no self-esteem; b) no will-power or c) no self-control.
- What do I want? Respect! When do I want it? YESTERDAY, TODAY and TOMORROW!!!
- Stop trying to put me on a diet.
- Don't hand me any suggestions on how to cut my fat intake.
- SPEAK OUT on my behalf . . . Do some of the work of objecting to fat-hating places, media, incidents, etc . . . Help in educating the clueless.
- "There is more to life than prettiness. I'll choose stamina!"
- Don't buy into the assumption that being fat is always, for everyone, less healthy than being thin.
- Get the clue that DIETS DON'T WORK!
- To be seen as a sexual human being.
- To be seen as a human being, period.
- To not have every bite of food placed in my mouth scrutinized.
- For them not to be afraid to touch me—fat isn't catching.
- I want to talk about my size and my life—and not be immediately reassured that I'm "not that fat" or to get "nutrition tips."
- I want to be able to be ANGRY (and not fat = jolly all the #@&*$% time!)

—excerpted from a reader's survey, *Fat Girl #4*

RIOTS NOT DIETS

Bunnyhop

Bunnyhop is a pop culture zine produced by editor Noël Tolentino in partnership with co-publisher and software consultant Seth Robson. They met four years ago at U.C. Santa Cruz; their first joint publication was *Waffle*. For a sample issue of *Bunnyhop* send $6 to PO Box 423930, San Francisco CA 94142-3930.

♦ *VALE: What's your background?*
♦ NOËL TOLENTINO: I was born in the Philippines, but my family moved to San Francisco when I was a year-and-a-half old. Then I ended up in Fremont [suburb] until I went to UC Santa Cruz.

A lot of my aunts and uncles live in the Bay Area. I'm the youngest of six kids, and both my parents are C.P.A.s. My parents were able to assimilate into American culture, yet hold on to what they grew up with. It's not that they don't like people of other races; it's just that they stick with "family" in a lot of ways. It's interesting to grow up in America under these circumstances; you're seeing *their* view of the world, but it's not exactly the world you're growing up in.

My parents bought encyclopedias to encourage learning, and I was in honors programs since grade school. My sisters and brother are more academic and conservative than me; I'm the black sheep of the family.
♦ *V: In what way?*
♦ NT: Seeing the "mistakes" that my siblings made, I went an entirely different route. I became interested in a different kind of music and culture and eventually got into skateboarding—my parents never endorsed that. They wouldn't spend a penny on anything skateboard-related, so I took a paper route to get that first "Duane Peters" skateboard.

Skateboard culture is in many ways a rebellion culture, and in the seventh grade that's a big enough deal. Also, being an artist set me apart; everybody else in my family is more business-oriented.
♦ *V: Why did you choose U.C. Santa Cruz?*
♦ NT: They have narrative evaluations as opposed to grades, and interesting professors like Angela Davis.
♦ *V: You were quite young when you started drawing—*
♦ NT: Yes; I drew Snoopy and other cartoon characters, even though I don't consider myself to be an illustrator. In high school I became interested in the basic "weird" art like Salvador Dali and Gustav Klimt. Photography was my focus when I entered college, but then I became involved in making large 3D art installations you could walk through—very tactile. I guess my big "break" came when I went to UC Santa Cruz, where they had just installed a computer lab. It had twenty Macintosh Quadras with 20˝ monitors and all the software installed, ready to go—unlike other schools, where all the equipment is different and the software is pirated. I started teaching myself . . .
♦ *V: How long were you there?*
♦ NT: Four years; I started in the fall of 1990 and graduated with a B.A. in Fine Arts. At Santa Cruz I learned that you're either going to be a "stoner" (lost in drug-taking) or force yourself to *do* something. I didn't particularly care for alcohol or beer, so . . . Then I moved to San Francisco; there's a pretty strong UCSC contingent here.
♦ *V: When were you introduced to the world of zines?*

150

♦ NT: In high school I had this circle of friends who were all skate punks, and a friend of mine, D. Scott Davidson, produced a zine called *Gus*. It was based on skateboarding, freestyle bike riding and punk/literary culture. That was inspirational; I had never seen anything like that and was in awe of the mail he was getting. He produced other zines, too—a few of which I contributed to.

Initially my focus was on the visual arts. However, during my first year at college, I had a writing teacher who saw all this potential in me, and he encouraged me to do creative writing. I met Seth, and when we had our first real conversation, it turned out we had similar interests in music and publishing—we both had a fondness for 4AD Records and 23 Envelope (the graphic end of 4AD; they're now called V23). We decided to do a zine called *Waffle*.

It's amazing how fast technology has improved. Back then, what we had access to was primitive; our first two issues were cut-and-paste, although we used PageMaker to create columns and some custom type. We had an e-mail address and got *no* mail; nobody had e-mail addresses then. The first issues were more xerox collage-oriented. I was responsible for the editorial end and we both did graphics, although lately Seth has been writing.

♦ **V:** *Can you talk more about that first skatepunk zine that inspired you—*

♦ NT: Until the first issue of *Gus* came out I had absolutely no idea that it was in the works. We had a history teacher who let my friend xerox it on the school copier. This teacher was different; he had more of a connection with countercultural values and didn't really use textbooks. When I first saw my friend's zine, I felt envious—jealous even, that *I* didn't think of doing that—I had no clue whatsoever he was working on it.

Earlier, when I was in the sixth grade, I remember wanting to get into fashion design after looking through a lot of magazines. And I wanted to do something with my artistic abilities involving publishing. When I saw my friend's zine, which was based on irreverent material, absurd stories and *factoids* that appealed to my sense of humor, it hit me that this was a medium that could reach out to other people without me having to actually *be* out there. My friend had a P.O. box that opened up another world: getting mail from strangers who were commenting on what he was doing, and sharing their own experiences. This was a whole other means of communication with people beyond the boundaries of your life in a small town. My sense of the power of the written word just didn't *click* until this happened.

I didn't actually publish my first zine until I went to UC Santa Cruz. It didn't hurt that one of the first girls I had a crush on, Miss Kelina, was producing a wonderful personal zine called *The Unmentionable*. Then, after being exposed to *Ben Is Dead*, there was no turning back!

♦ **V:** *You were engaged in a critique of society, or a rejection of certain values, and sharing an interest in lesser-known bands—*

♦ NT: Precisely, and sharing our acquaintance of this world which isn't necessarily fed to us through convenient means, like TV. The process of the school system is infinitely boring, stale and formulaic and the faculty is mostly older white men who are "cruising" on past achievements, not injecting new life into the curriculum. At U.C. Santa Cruz my education was basically a self-made synthesis of graphic design and fine arts, which is what 4AD and 23 Envelope do very well—they work together to create a distinctive visual identity, taking the medium of album packaging to another level. They've influenced many designers.

♦ **V:** *Did you encounter prejudice growing up?*

♦ NT: In school I wasn't too aware of my "Asianness"; it just never seemed like an issue. Now and then I could sense a modicum of racism in what people were saying, but it was never overt or directed personally toward me. I started becoming more aware of racial issues in high school by listening to PUBLIC ENEMY—this wonderfully abrasive sound-collaged noise and political propaganda being shoved down your throat. That first album is still one of the best.

♦ **V:** *How did you fund the* **Bunnyhop** *with the Matt Groening "Binky" cover?*

Noël Tolentino and Seth Robson

♦ NT: Seth saved up money, and I applied for a credit card specifically for the magazine. It's been "maxed" ever since *Bunnyhop* started. The high interest rate encourages me to work harder to get the next issue out! There's a total lack of profit.

When I was first exposed to Matt Groening's work in '87, he was still relatively underground. I was looking at a t-shirt with "Binky" on it, and I had no idea who that was. Then I saw his book, and I completely identified with the work: "I know exactly what you mean, Matt". I was a Simpsons fan from the get-go. So when I did the "Binky" cover [Binky knocking out the Trix rabbit, an ad icon featured on a General Mills cereal box], it was an homage to him.

Countercultural ideas and values come from the outcasts, nerds and rebels. And then, of course, these get co-opted into mainstream culture.

The idea was originally to do a "Geeks and Jocks" issue. My friend Johanna had all these high school photos, and when I saw them I thought, "We should do it like a yearbook!" To me, Binky is representative of the awkward geek who finally prevails over mainstream culture (essentially jock culture or jock rock). As "alternative" culture has become bigger lately, it just seemed like the perfect cover.

When we think about alternative culture, where are the sources? Countercultural ideas and values come from the outcasts, nerds and rebels. And then, of course, these get co-opted into mainstream culture. There's this bizarre connection between the counter-culture and the mainstream that people try not to recognize; there's a definite overlap.

When I did the "Binky" cover, I realized I was using characters that were trademarked or copyright-protected, but I also felt I was creating a scenario that would not otherwise have existed: placing these characters from two different worlds together. This completely recontextualized their characters, and a lot of people understood it. Originally I had wanted to have Jessica Rabbit (from the *Roger Rabbit* film) and the Energizer Bunny in the scene—would that have made a difference? Would all the other companies have sued me?

I had heard from various sources that Matt Groening was a big fan and collector of small press zines, so I got his P.O. box address from Renée French who does *Grit Bath*, a really brilliant comic from Fantagraphics. Being naive, I sent him a copy with a gushing fan letter asking to interview him, and saying that I had been meaning to send it to him but didn't want it to get "in the wrong hands." (Allegedly, when the *Simpsons* first appeared and all these unauthorized "Black Bart" t-shirts appeared, Matt had said that he was "flattered," if filled with "mixed feelings.") Here I was believing that Matt Groening was actually going to open my letter, not realizing that he must receive a ton of mail about his work every day from a whole generation of slackers and counter-cultural do-gooders. I would like to believe that he never saw the letter I received from his lawyers. Now, everyone I know looks at his work in a different light, while still watching it—it's still so funny.

Part of the problem may have been that *Bunnyhop* looks so professional; the cover is embossed and it looks like its print run is in the tens of thousands. Actually, we printed 5,000. I was in L.A. working on the production of *Ben Is Dead* when the letter from the lawyers arrived, and when Seth called and told me, I was completely upset. I recalled the year when it seemed like every episode of the *Simpsons* was a parody of films like *Cape Fear* or *Clockwork Orange*. Each show was packed with cultural asides (scenes, characters, costumes and phrases), so you could watch it over and over and catch different references. So I felt I was just doing something in the spirit of his work, without the *Simpsons* being on the cover. We wanted something rabbit-related; after all, our name is *Bunnyhop*.

♦ *V: How did you first react?*
♦ NT: I thought, "We gotta fight this!" Seth, being a little bit more level-headed, said, "We really don't have the resources to defend ourselves." We were already in the red; we weren't making any money. Sometimes when people sue over copyright, they demand 100% of the profits. I thought, "Sure—since we don't make *any* profits, you can have zero dollars! Go ahead and buy yourself something nice!"

Raggedy Ann and Andy. Cover of Waffle #4

Of course, I felt betrayed. I was having difficulty sleeping—it was so horrible. I wondered, "Are they going to bust into my house?" From a publishing standpoint, the most heinous crime in the world is the fact that people who publish don't make *anything*. And the way things are going we're going to make less—

♦ **V: Paper costs went up 50% in the last year; it now costs 50% more to print a book than it did a year ago—**

♦ NT: And the postage goes up. Everything connected to publishing, like making "Linos" [Linotronic output of halftones or text on photo paper] goes up! *We make no money.* Obviously there is no profit motive. The only "reward" is getting a few free CDs or seeing a few free shows. I try to find jobs that don't take up my whole life, and then reinvest the income back into the magazine, working on the next issue until my money runs out and I have to go out in the "real" world and find another job.

♦ **V: Matt Groening's lawyers demanded you destroy the "Binky" issues and send proof of destruction, right?**

♦ NT: Not only that, they demanded that an apology be printed "in a prominent place" in the next issue of *Bunnyhop*, with text that had to be *approved* by them first! We ended up decapitating Binky's head from the covers and mailing 300 of them in a bag to the lawyers. The act of having to destroy them was horrible. I wrote a cold, minimal apology—and anyone with a keen eye could recognize a little sarcasm in it. The whole experience was incredibly disheartening. I put an insert in the mutilated copies explaining what had happened and left them at certain places. Word got around, and among others, Chris from

Sometimes when people sue over copyright, they demand 100% of the profits. I thought, "Sure—since we don't make *any* profits, you can have zero dollars! Go ahead and buy yourself something nice!"

Negativland offered help in the form of legal referrals—this obviously reminded him of a certain time in his life [when the band U2 sued for an unauthorized parody of a song, plus the unauthorized use of the U2 name on the parody cover art].

There have been other instances of *censorship by threat of lawsuit*. The band (and zine) Thora-zine were threatened by lawyers from the pharmaceutical firm that created the tranquilizer, trying to get them to change their name. Apparently they were okay because they hyphenated the word! In the '60s, comic

Playboy parody. Cover of *Bunnyhop* #6

artist Dan O'Neill got into big trouble because he used Mickey Mouse in a comic strip. And whatever happened to *Hey There, Barbie Girl!*? The publisher was decimated. She only put out two issues.

I wonder if the issue here is irreverence. When you're using or recontextualizing trademarked characters, there's a whole gray fuzzy area. What exactly is the problem here?

♦ **V: The main problem is: lawyers need to invent work to maintain their corrupt lifestyles. Your next Bunnyhop #6 parodied Playboy and Bil Keane's "Family Circus"—**

♦ NT: And I was told, "The *Playboy* legal staff in Chicago is reviewing your cover for possible copyright infringement." Actually, I did a cover for *Waffle* of Raggedy Ann—*that* company could sue me as well. At one point I started wondering, "Do I have any original ideas?" [laughs]

I'm always parodying things, mocking things and impersonating people's voices. The second issue of *Waffle* was a parody of the Sonic Youth *Goo* cover [a drawing by Raymond Pettibon] and *Ren and Stimpy*. I actually gave the original artwork to Lee Ranaldo and he went, "Wow!"—he thought it was the best parody he'd ever seen.

Anyway, for the *Playboy* parody cover, the theme of the issue was normalcy—and how much more absurdly normal can you get than the "Family Circus"? There's a "Dysfunctional Family Circus" parody-zine circulating, and nobody seems to know where it's coming from because there are no credits or address listed. Whoever did it used the original drawings and

153

just replaced the text. So I decided to work on a parody of the family. In many ways, "normalcy" masks dysfunction and oddities and quirkiness. Of course, I had to make the wife of the "perfect family" into a *Playboy* bunny, but with a domestic side as indicated by the rolling pin.

I had been making calls trying to interview Hugh Hefner, a true American icon of sorts. I sent him the yearbook issue and a publicist in L.A. responded: "He's really busy, but please try again." I tried again with a more detailed letter, and sent the *Playboy* parody. Then when I heard that *Playboy* were contemplating suing me, I went, "What—not again!"

♦ **V: What happened?**
♦ **NT:** I immediately called up the publicist and explained that *Bunnyhop* is a small press publication that works thematically and changes its typeface with each issue; we don't have a logo. It's always changing; there's nothing fixed about what we're doing. (Again, the look of professionalism makes it look like it's printed in tens of thousands. We've learned that if you present yourself professionally, people are more responsive and apt to notice you.) After I said that *Bunnyhop* is basically done by two young people working out of an apartment, the publicist understood and intervened on our behalf. I'm really glad I told him, because things could easily have gone somewhere else.

The next time I talked to him on the phone he said, "Well, I've got good news and bad news. The good news is: now that the lawyers understand where you're coming from, and that your work is based on satire and parody, and that nothing's fixed and you're trying to do something that's *cutting-edge*" (I liked it that he used that word), "so they're not going to pursue the case. The bad news is that Hugh Hefner's turning seventy on April 9 (with a 32-year-old wife) and he's ultra-busy—so no interview. But maybe in the future you should try again." I thought, "Well, I'm not sure if he fits in the Clown issue, but we can give it a whirl! The Animal issue—*no*." So this had a happy ending. Now I'm just worried about the Smurfs—that's the next cover I want to do. I'm thinking of combining Sanrio and the Smurfs—combine the two sicknesses!

♦ **V: Then both companies' lawyers can sue you—**
♦ **NT:** The important thing is to take a stand on artistic grounds. Regarding the issue of irreverence, does something necessarily have to be a parody to be in fair use? That's really unclear. It's inevitable that ideas are taken in the world and given new life in some way.

And with parody, does that necessarily make the creator happy? Do they like the representation of their idea? If they don't, they can shut you down. And this alone breaks down communication and the flow of ideas entirely. You can ask permission, but they'll never approve anyway. So is my idea not supposed to exist? Or is it not supposed to exist *in print*? I'll be glad to give 'em 100% of the profits if they really want it!

Also, there's the issue of *similarity*. What if this were R2D2, who does not exist in ink. Do the same rules apply? I don't know—maybe George Lucas needs to make a little more money! It's a ridiculous situation; you need law and money as a means of defense. If you don't have either on your side, you're just dead.

Yet it's important to stand your ground. If they shut people like myself down and prevent such things from happening, this makes it impossible to express criticism of *anything*.

Is criticism the key element? Because if it is, then they're destroying our opinions of anything, or any potential for expansion on their ideas or thought. *Détournement* as a means of cultural and artistic expression is not just important—it's *necessary*. I have this quote from Guy Debord which seems appropriate: "Ideas improve. The meaning of words participates in the improvement. Plagiarism is necessary. Progress implies it.

Ren and Stimpy parody. Cover of *Waffle #2*

It embraces an author's phrase, makes use of his expressions, erases a false idea and replaces it with the right idea." I can't think of any way to improve on that idea for now ... **V**

REFERENCE

The Anti-Aesthetic: Essays on Postmodern Culture by Hal Foster
The Baffler (every issue) POB 378293, Chicago, IL 60637 (312) 493-0413
Society of the Spectacle by Guy Debord
Eightball (every issue) by Daniel Clowes
Dialectic of Enlightenment by Max Horkheimer and Theodor W. Adorno
You Are Special by Fred Rogers
This Rimy River: Vaughn Oliver and v23 published by 4AD
Soul on Ice by Eldridge Cleaver
Deathbird Stories by Harlan Ellison
The Modern Poster by Stuart Wrede
Macworld Photoshop 3 Bible (Second Edition) and *The Illustrator 5.0/5.5 Book* by Deke McClelland
The QuarkXPress Book (Fourth Edition for Macintosh) by David Blatmer and Eric Taub.

History of Zines

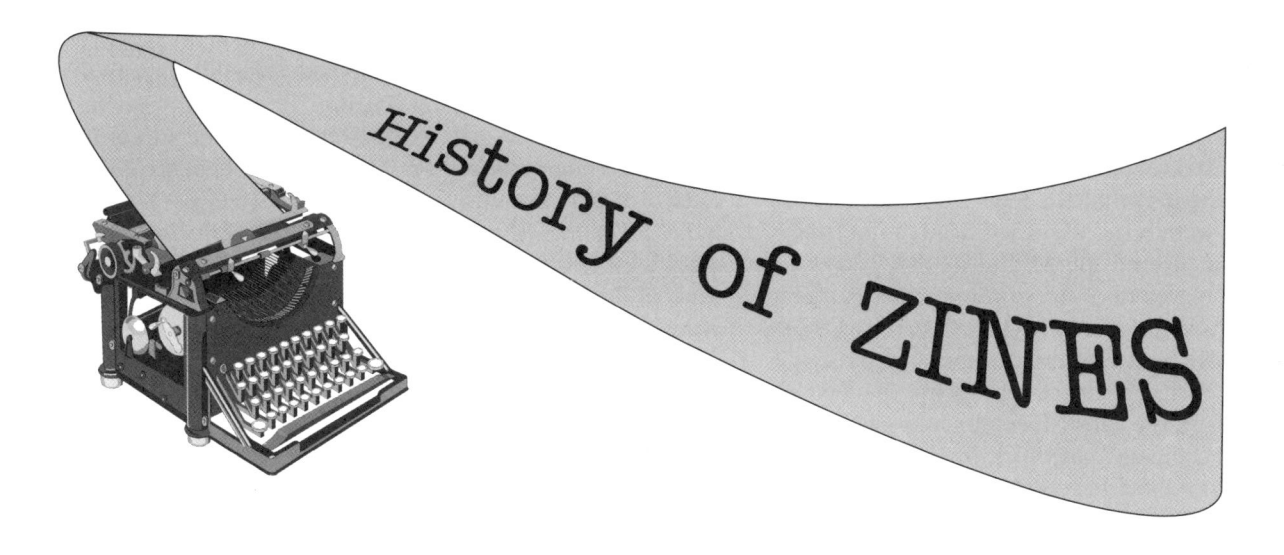

Nico Ordway, a.k.a. NO, was a leading contributor to *Search & Destroy* and a founding contributor to *RE/Search*. Under his real name, Stephen Schwartz, he is a staff writer for the *San Francisco Chronicle*. He has self-published four journals and two books of poetry: *A Sleepwalker's Guide to San Francisco* (1983) and *Heaven's Descent* (1990).

The zine of today—the fullest example we have in history of "self-publication" outside all institutional and industrial control—may be traced to the invention of the printing press.

Broadsides—one-page, letter- and poster-sized sheets with a text reporting news, offering individual satire and other literary works—were a major feature of printed literature from the beginning of the printing press to the end of the 19th century. They were also a form of self-publication that has much in common with the zine, but zines are more than flyers, leaflets or posters. Two post-medieval phenomena in book printing involved large-scale self-publications calling to mind the zine: early Jewish printing and the English-language pamphleteering of the Reformation.

In *The Pursuit of The Millennium*, a magistral account of apocalyptic movements in Europe during the Middle Ages, Norman Cohn describes the impact of the printing press on the development of revolutionary ideas in Europe, which culminated in the Protestant Reformation and the 17th century English Revolution led by Oliver Cromwell.

The anarcho-communistic doctrines of the Ranters, the most extreme English radicals of the Cromwell era, greatly resembled those of their forerunners: the peasant rebels, religious reformers and other dissidents of the medieval period, particularly the Brethren of the Free Spirit. In addition, they anticipated in many ways the radical conceptions of anarchists in the 18th and 19th centuries and this century's Dadaists, Situationists and punks.

But by contrast with the writings of the earlier radicals, we know a great deal about those of the Ranters. As Cohn observes, "Like those of their predecessors, the writings of the English adepts—who were known as Ranters—were ordered to be burnt. But it is much harder to destroy a whole edition of a printed work than a few manuscripts, and stray copies of the Ranter tracts have survived."

The European invention of moveable type by Johann Gutenberg, who printed his Bible in the late 1450s, enabled a series of developments that would completely change intellectual life in Europe. First, mass production of the Bible transformed the attitude toward religious participation of the North European masses. The notion that every Christian believer should have an opportunity to make his own decisions about religion, based on an individual reading of Scripture, laid the basis for the rise of Protestantism. This phenomenon could well be called *self-salvation*.

A second effect was a general increase in literacy, and therefore of self-cultivation. Most importantly, however, for the purposes we are discussing, the spread of printing presses around Europe allowed radical groups and other formerly marginal, unorthodox elements in society—including, notably, Jews—to diffuse their writings among a wider public. The result was the development of self-publication.

It has long been observed that the printing press transformed Jewish intellectual life. Most importantly, exiled Spanish and Portuguese (Sephardic) Jews committed to moveable type many Aramaic and Hebrew texts that are among the finest examples of early printing. Hebrew printing had begun in Spain even before the expulsion of the Jews from that country in 1492; the settlement of exiled Sephardic Jewish typographers around the Mediterranean greatly contributed to the growth of the printing industry. Venice is especially famous for fine Jewish printing, but Sephardic Jewish bookworkers also founded presses at Istanbul and Fez in Morocco, producing the first printed volumes in the Turkish empire and in Africa.

It could be argued that Jewish printing also brought forth the earliest publishers; Christian printers in Venice were commissioned by Jews to print the Bible and other works.

But alongside this early attempt at monopoly, the great majority of Jewish printers in the Mediterranean operated independent print-shops, which allowed Jewish scholars to self-publish religious and mystical volumes.

It has also been noted that the English Revolution produced the first great outburst of self-publication—in which hundreds of isolated Christians, acting on the principles of individual religious choice and responsibility that were at the heart of the Reformation, put their conceptions of faith, church, and reason into print. The Ranter pamphlets were an important example of this genre of printing.

The Ranters as imagined by their contemporaries . . . this woodcut seems to show . . . smoking ranked alongside 'free love' as an expression of antinomianism.

The Ranters were authentic extremist rebels who attracted wide notice beginning in 1650. In London they numbered thousands of people. They were accused of preaching for the expropriation of the rich and collective ownership of property. They were also said to believe that a state of religious grace permitted a man to commit crimes including murder, if he was so motivated, and that women and men should practice free love whether married or not. They were observed cursing in public, smoking and drinking, even in jail, and when challenged to defend their "religion," they "were very rude, and sung, and whistled, and danced."

Cohn writes, "Four Ranters were known to have written books, and despite the best efforts of the authorities copies of most of these books survive." The main examples are the works of Abiezer Coppe (1619-72): *Some Sweet Sips of Some Spiritual Wine*, *A Fiery Flying Roll* and *A Second Fiery Flying Roule*.

Numerous self-published works appeared in England during the Puritan Revolution. Sources on the Ranters include a marvelously-titled survey of the dissident tendencies of the time: Thomas Edwards' *Gangraena: or a Catalogue and Discovery of Many of the Errours, Heresies, Blasphemies and Pernicious Practices of the Sectaries of This Time, Vented and Acted in England in These Last Four Years*, published in 1646.

Similar though smaller explosions of self-publication characterized other religious upheavals of the time, both in the Christian communities and among the Jews. In the latter case, the appearance of the "false messiah" Sabbetai Zvi in the late 17th century set off a new wave of Hebrew book and pamphlet production. But while the bourgeois society that emerged in Europe began in an orgy of self-publication, the later 17th century saw both a temporary decline of the revolutionary impulse and the widespread rise of booksellers, a class of traders who increasingly acted as publishers, commissioning printed works. Although access to both printers and distributors was open to anybody with money, the loss of a sense of religious immediacy—fostered by belief in an imminent apocalypse—dampened the urgency of pamphlet printing.

In succeeding decades self-publication was occasionally employed by poets and other writers. The period leading up to the French Revolution saw booksellers in a major role in intellectual life as distributors for radical social critics. The "clandestine literature" of that time has been brilliantly analyzed by the historian Robert Darnton, whose *The Forbidden Best-Sellers of Pre-Revolutionary France* appeared this year. However, the sexually and politically provocative works that became "underground best-sellers" were typically the merchandise of commercial printers rather than self-publishers: as Darnton shows, there was considerable money to be made in this traffic. But as with contemporary zines, for true pamphleteers and self-publishers money was not the main object.

The great French Revolution saw a revival of self-publication. Pamphlets and self-published journals (for example, the extreme radical Hebert's *Le Pére Duchesne* and Marat's *L'Ami du Peuple*) once again streamed forth from the presses. A harbinger of this development had been seen during the American Revolution, in the form of Thomas Paine's *Common Sense* (January 1776), a pamphlet summary of American grievances against the British crown that became the first non-religious best-seller in American history, reaching a press run in the hundreds of thousands.

But the greatest self-publisher of that time, greater than any American or French figure, was the man who could be called the patron saint of all self-publishers: the poet and engraver William Blake (1757-1827). Blake's books were all self-published, including his greatest works, *The Songs of Innocence* (1789), *The Marriage of Heaven and Hell* (1791) and *The Songs of Experience* (1794). As the French surrealist Philippe Soupault wrote of Blake, "No publisher ever sent him an order."

While political pamphleteering in France declined with the end of the revolution, the phenomenon of literary self-publication grew elsewhere during the 19th century. Self-publication soon became a dominant mode in California, where geographical remoteness from the rest of the country prevented the development of a large publishing industry. Indeed, self-publication remains the main form in which books appear on the West Coast.

An important California exemplar of self-publication was Burnette G. Haskell (1857-1907), a socialist agitator in San Francisco. Beginning in the 1880s, Haskell issued a newspaper, *Truth*, as a platform for a range of political activities. He helped found the Coast Seamen's Union, known as "the lookout of the West Coast labor movement," and launched an unsuccessful utopian colony, Kaweah. But a little-known member of Haskell's circle, the English anarchist William C. Owen (1854-1929), would come to participate in one of the most effective self-publishing enterprises after Blake: the journal *Regeneración* and related books and pamphlets issued in Los Angeles and other North American cities by the Mexican anarchist brothers Ricardo and Antonio Flores Magon. The Flores Magons and Owen, in their persistent self-publishing, may be well and truly credited with the political ferment that, inside Mexico, resulted in the outbreak of the Revolution of 1910.

The period in which Haskell and Owen began self-publishing on the West Coast coincided with the career of Thomas Edison, inventor of the incandescent electric light and the phonograph, and a major contributor to the development of motion pictures. In addition to these achievements, which made possible the greater part of modern pop culture, Edison produced an invention without which the zine might never have emerged as it did: the mimeograph machine.

Edison created a stencil duplicating process adopted by the A.B. Dick Co., which introduced the first mimeograph machine in 1887. Though it was intended mainly for business use, the inexpensive printing technology of the mimeograph led directly to the phenomenon of zines.

But let us not run ahead of history. A "mimeo revolution" in literature did not occur until the 1950s, after the rise of the "little magazine" as a letterpress institution. "Little magazines," a form of self-publication close in spirit to the zine, first emerged as a major literary current in the years before World War I; classic models included *The Blast*, coedited by the writer and artist Wyndham Lewis and the poet Ezra Pound. *The Little Review* was founded in Chicago by Margaret Anderson and Jane Heap, whose names seem to have virtually disappeared, even from feminist historiography.

The Blast was also the title of a periodical edited contemporaneously in San Francisco by the anarchist Alexander Berkman. The anarchists, with their individualist tendencies and emphasis on local initiatives, were the only political movement to seriously stimulate self-publication. Many other anarchist journals were zine-style operations, such as Emma Goldman's *Mother Earth and Man!* issued in San Francisco for many years by Marcus Graham.

The fabled Wobblies, who were decentralized, local and footloose, and had no qualms about declaring their mimeo machines to be (IWW) unionized printing facilities.

Anarchist individualism strongly influenced the art and literary circles in which the "little magazine" flourished after World War I. The Bohemian culture of Greenwich Village produced anarchist and socialist intellectuals such as the artist Man Ray and the journalist John Reed. Their works, along with those of the major poets of the day, appeared in such "littles" as *The Seven Arts*, *291*, *Broom*, *Contact* and a host of others.

Perhaps the greatest of the post-World War I "littles" was *Transition*. Issued in Paris by Eugene Jolas, it published major works by James Joyce, Ernest Hemingway, André Breton and other modernist icons.

The first art movement to base itself almost entirely on self-publication was Dada, with its acolytes producing journals in various European cities. Some of the Dada journals had the added cachet of publishing only one number and then expiring. Important Dada-related self-publication efforts included journals produced in Tbilisi, Georgia by the Zdanevich brothers.

Indeed, the Dada publications may properly be called the first proto-zines in that they were produced purely for the pleasure of their creators and provocation of readers, ignoring or satirizing all canons and standards of journalism. They were, like the zines of today, intended to be ephemeral. But the Surrealist movement that followed Dada was also dedicated to self-publication. The famous Paris colophon "Editions Surréalistes" did not indicate a publisher, bookseller, or other commercial enterprise; it meant only that the Surrealists had produced the writing and paid for the printing. The successive surrealist journals, *La Revolution Surrealiste*, *Le Surrealisme au Service de la Revolution*, and even the luxurious *Minotaure*, were authentic zines. And one of the greatest modernist figures, discovered and praised by the Surrealists, was the fantastical writer Raymond Roussel, author of *Impressions of Africa* and *Locus Solus*—all of whose works were self-published.

The growth of the urban Bohemian classes—the increasing numbers of literary and artistic aspirants in the world's great cities—brought a global expansion of the modernist audience in the 1930s. The same period saw the first "mimeograph revolution," in politics rather than literature. Mimeo was a late acquisition for the Socialists and other leftists before World War I; their loyalty to print workers' unions, as well as their centralized activity and wide audience, decreed that their literature should come from letterpress printshops with the union "bug" proudly displayed, although such was often prohibitively expensive for small radical groups. Mimeo was first used widely among leftists by the ultra-radical syndicalists of the Industrial Workers of the World—the fabled Wobblies, who were decentralized, local, and footloose and had no qualms about declaring their mimeo machines to be (IWW) unionized printing facilities.

Early DADA "zine"

But the sudden flooding of New York, San Francisco and other intellectual centers, with mimeo-produced leaflets, newsletters and journals during the great Depression had its main source in the international activities of the Soviet-controlled Communist Parties. At the same time, the most articulate critic of Soviet reality under Stalin, the exiled Leon Trotsky, expressed himself through a proto-zine: *Byulleten Oppositzii*, or *Bulletin of the Opposition*, a Russian-language journal mainly issued in Paris.

During World War II mimeo played a yet more dramatic role, with production of hundreds of zine-like resistance bulletins aimed against the Axis occupation regimes in France and elsewhere. Leftist mimeo production often reflected, paradoxically, considerable financial resources when compared with those of many literary "little" magazines. Leftists used mimeo because of the practical simplicity of the technology, the ease of transferring machines from place to place, and to evade censorship.

But while their relative affluence and ideological aims distinguished their efforts from truer proto-zines, the leftists' use of mimeo left a mark, particularly in the United States: the popularization of the mimeograph in the West was one of few positive effects of the Communist eruption into world politics. The era saw letterpress ex-"littles" like *Partisan Review* and another proto-zine, *Politics*, produced by Dwight Macdonald, gain notable influence. But letterpress was waning as a dissident medium in America. Mimeo was used in production of a number of important "little magazines" in the "beat" 1950s, such as *Beatitude*, and a whole subculture of "mimeo poets" was visible into the 1960s.

Most importantly, the 1950s saw inauguration of the true zine: the "fanzine" invented by science-fiction enthusiasts. The great advocate for this form of publication was Forrest J. Ackerman.

But the science-fiction fanzines, notwithstanding their typically crude production and limited circulation, were still mainly dedicated to publicizing favorite movies and writers, rather than giving vent to the pure intellectual venturings of the producers. In this regard, the zines of today, which typically focus on concepts, rumors, fads and similar phenomena rather than on commercial promotion, have more in common with the "little" magazines of the mimeo poetry scene.

Mimeo had limitations. It was a messy way to print, although some virtuosi produced well-crafted mimeo editions. Significantly, the most important single self-publishing effort of the '50s and '60s, the French journal *Internationale Situationniste*, eschewed mimeo for the highest standard of letterpress printing, along with expensive metallic paper covers. Like the Surrealists before them, the Situationists were anxious to show mastery of the print medium at the same time as they expressed their contempt for the commodity.

Xerox technology greatly augmented the aesthetic

possibilities available to self-publishers. Before entering into the present epoch of uncontrolled zine-mania, however, we should consider the role of *samizdat*—the most illustrious form of self-publication known in modern times.

Samizdat is a contraction of the Russian words for self-publication. As the Communist system approached breakdown in Europe, self-publication through the typewriter, and, very occasionally, xerox copying, proliferated; the most extensive *samizdat* productions were found in Russia, the former Czechoslovakia and Poland. The threat of *samizdat* was so disturbing for Communist rulers that, for example, dictator Nicolae Ceausescu forbade possession of unmonitored typewriters by Romanian citizens.

These countries also saw creation of some of the weightiest self-published journals in history, including religious organs published by Lithuanian, Ukrainian and Albanian Catholics. Although the power of the Catholic church ostensibly stood behind these efforts, they were typically issued in a manner closer to that of a zine than of established Catholic journals, by individuals lacking regular contact with Church authorities in Rome and, therefore, without church resources and independent of church guidelines. *The Albanian Catholic Bulletin/Buletini Katolik Shqiptar*, for example, which kept alive North Albanian Catholic literary and religious traditions in the face of 45 years of Communist dictatorship, was issued by an exile in San Francisco, Gjon Sinishta, almost entirely on his own.

But mimeo self-publication also burst into the open in China during periods of temporary liberalization; for example, in the Democracy Wall movement of the late 1970s and early 1980s. A landmark account of imprisonment in the wake of that movement was written by Wei Jingsheng, founder of the mimeo journal *Exploration* and advocate of China's "fifth modernization-democracy" (a phrase he coined). Wei's prison memoir, "Q1: A 20th Century Bastille," was first circulated in the West in a smudged English-language version produced on a mimeo by young Chinese anarchists in Hong Kong. As this article was written, Wei was reported facing trial anew in China, for "engaging in activities to overthrow the government."

Similarly, the domination of Chinese literature by "Maoist language" was questioned by a group of young writers known as "misty" or "obscure" in a mimeographed magazine, *Today*. The best of the "misty" writers, Bei Dao, has since become a world-renowned figure.

Since much of this article depends on the Western history of printing, let us note that the history of the zine in Asia, beginning with Chinese block printing, and continuing through the individual "big-character posters" of the so-called "Cultural Revolution" of the 1960s, would require a distinct theoretical analysis.

Today zines constitute a massive counter-industry, spawning such journals as *Factsheet Five* to track them. There are now more poetry and other literary "little" magazines than ever before, most of them, along with such alternative media as FM radio, supported by government through the National Endowments for the Arts and Humanities and the Corporation for Public Broadcasting. It has become something of a cliché to say that experimental and otherwise nonconforming writers and artists must face the probable end of public funding, and therefore reassess the unsubsidized avant-garde movements of the past. But zines carry on the traditions of independent publishing.

> **The threat of *samizdat* was so disturbing for Communist rulers that, for example, dictator Nicolae Ceausescu forbade possession of unmonitored typewriters by Romanian citizens.**

Another "virtual" cliché is the assertion that the modem-equipped home computer offers as many new advantages for the self-publisher as Gutenberg's invention of movable type once did. Certainly, word processing and design programs have provided self-publishers with a long-sought access to better typography and makeup standards.

But what is the future of the zine on, for example, the World Wide Web, and other e-mail? While completing this text, I read, in an article on the WWW in *The New York Times* of November 20, 1995, "Anyone with a modem is potentially a global pamphleteer." However, as shown by Norman Cohn, the beauty of print remains that its distribution is difficult to regulate by the state, corporations, or other hostile powers. Books and print journals still go many places computers and modems cannot; they don't crash, and nobody can pull the plug on them.

Not everybody can afford access to the Web (but not everybody could afford a mimeograph in the 1950s.) Yet unlike the Web, zine production is easily a cash business, requiring no credit checks. Finally, in contrast with Web users, zine producers and other self-publishers do not necessarily seek the largest possible audience. Some aim at the "happy few," readers capable of real comprehension.

What makes a zine? To repeat, a zine is more than a flyer, leaflet, poster, or newsletter. It reflects the unmediated obsessions of the individual producer, in which publicity in the normal sense and other commercial concerns are completely subordinate. Regardless of the particular concerns reflected in their pages, zines are purely libertarian. Zines forever! **V**

quotations

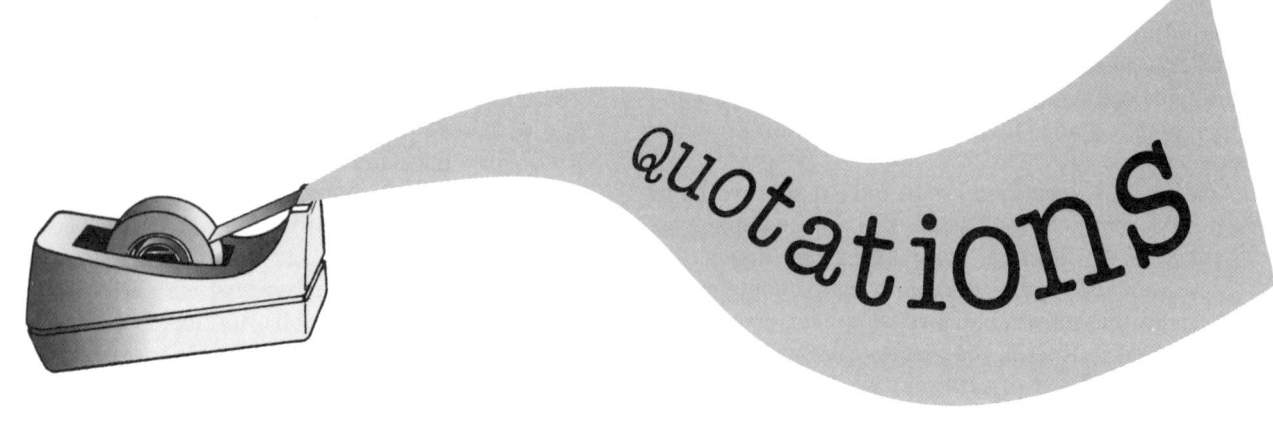

I intend to keep this zine small and personal. It will not be available by subscription, nor will it be on the newsstand. I'll send out a couple hundred copies of this first issue, but be warned, I'll be pruning the mailing list shortly, so if you're interested in staying on it better tell me so. And please, do not review this zine! Just let it be our little secret.
—Mike Gunderloy, founder of *Factsheet Five,* quoted in *Jackpot Years #1*

To design a new civilization, start with designing a new community. To design a new community, start with designing a new family. To design a new family, start with designing a new self. To design a new self, start with yourself. So that's where I start. I look inside myself and ask, "How can I be happy and free and not make other people unhappy and unfree?—*ibid*

Ignorance is the only thing that should be made fun of.
—*Idiot Nation #6* 6678 Washington 3W, University City MO 63130

Whatever it is that we are creating: comix, zines, or maybe you are a doctor or you recycle wine bottles or something, you are keeping yourself alive. You are defending your soul.
—*FREE TO FIGHT!* an interactive self-defense project. c/o Candy-Ass Records, PO Box 42382, Portland OR 97242

Our voice is a weapon.—*ibid*

World peace is actually like this idea that we all strive for by the simple act of lifting or putting down the toilet seat to have some sort of compassion for the next person. Like if you pee on the seat a little bit, you wipe it up 'cause you're thinking, "Oh, I'm not the only one here." —Stella Marrs, *Chickfactor #7,* 245 E. 19th St #12T, NYC 10003

If I don't care about the subject, I can't write about it. All I want is to work for and support myself doing something I like.—*ibid*

Consistency is highly overvalued. Don't be afraid to change your mind for fear of being branded an inconsistent hypocrite. If you *think,* your opinions will change.—*Splatterspleen #3,* POB 4061, St Paul MN 55104

Communication is necessary for any revolution.—*ibid*

I'm not really interested in creating positive images of women. I think that's bullshit . . . I'm going to create other ones, and I can't tell you if they're positive or negative because I don't know. I'm creating something that doesn't, to this point, exist. To me that's the challenge. —Kathleen Hanna of Bikini Kill quoted in *off our backs,* Feb 1993

We have to fight the powers that be no matter how fucked up we are ourselves. And I guess that's what this fanzine's about. We are trying to figure out how we can do these things, enact the revolution right here and right now, and still survive.
—*Bikini Kill #2* c/o The Embassy, 3217 19th St NW, Washington D.C. 20010

I encourage girls everywhere to set forth their own revolutionary agendas from their own place in the world, in relation to their own scenes or whatever, rather than to simply think about ours.—*ibid*

The only way a person brought up GIRL can be "truly" cool is to assimilate into male culture via toughness. By claiming "dork" as cool we can confuse and disrupt this whole process . . . Dorks die when bullets hit them and dorks cry real tears. —*ibid*

It is not our responsibility to explain how boys/men are being sexist anymore than it is our responsibility to "prevent ourselves" from getting raped. It is their responsibility Not To Rape Us and it is their responsibility Not To Be Sexist.—*ibid*

It seems that in most conversations about sexism, men wanna immediately take the focus off of how sexism affects women and put it onto how feminism affects *them.* And once again, men are placed in the middle of the action . . . The assumption that because someone is Pro-girl means that they are anti-male is stupid . . . Why is the emphasis always put on how a feminist feels about men, and not on how she feels about herself and other women?—*ibid*

A belief in instant revolution is just what The Powers That Be want. That way we won't realize that We Are The Revolution. It'll look so hard and far off, someday, someday, that we won't even try to enact it right now.
—*ibid*

The music press really fucked Riot Grrrl over. But they didn't stop us. We're still here, and when they've self-destructed, along with all those other slow, dumb old institutions—we will still be here.
—*GirlFrenzy #5,* POB 148,
HOVE BN3 3DO, UK

It's fun to create something out of nothing.—*ibid*

You can marginalize anyone by dismissing their ideas as eccentric. To some degree we are all odd. Rather than turn to political groups for reassurance and consolation, we should celebrate our eccentricity.—*ibid*

Emma Anarchist Center recognizes the need for oppressed groups to meet free of their oppressors and the queers have been doing just that. Every Tuesday night is Queer Space at Emma (supportive straights can show their support by staying home for this event).
—*Verboslammed,* 8/93, POB 1113,
Portland OR 97207

If, for whatever reasons, you find that the content and opinions within DO NOT reflect your own, then by all means make a fanzine that best expresses yourself.
—*Outpunk #3,* POB 170501,
San Francisco CA 94117

If someone gives me a forum to express myself, I will use it. If that means using "mainstream" channels to do it, then it's all for the better. If you really believe in what you're doing, then why not? By being too cool to publicly talk about these things, we only perpetuate the silence that already exists.—*ibid*

We are dying to fit in. We will give up our lives just to belong. Kids get AIDS, not because they don't know what a condom is, but because they are so desperate to be wanted that they sacrifice everything just to have and be held.—*ibid*

What if I hadn't said I was fat? If I hadn't shown you the picture? What would I look like to you then? The problem is, a lot of fat girls would have probably pictured me thin. "Normal."
—*Adventures of Big Girl #2,* 10006
Greenwood Ave, Seattle WA 98133

I'm angry when I watch television commercials and movies, and when I read literature that is anti-fat and anti-woman. Another term is certainly "fat phobia," just like homophobia—it shows the disease is elsewhere. I am not diseased, the *fear* is the disease.—*ibid*

Factories in third world countries are run by teenage girls who work 18 hour days—they are forced to work overtime, are sexually harassed, and constantly threatened—all to bring us Americans delightful GAP, JC Penney and Eddie Bauer apparel. For every $20 shirt, they get 12 cents.—*Girl Luv #1*

Don't Look Don't Touch Don't Look Don't Touch
—*Nerdy Grrrl Revolution #1*

I want every girl to feel the safety that has never been felt, I want every girl to stare wide-eyed in the glory of her own power. I want us girlz to use our strength and know it's ours to keep. I want every girl to have *his* choices. I don't want there to be a reason for our hate. I want every grrrl to love themselves and feed off their own wisdom. I want all us grrrlz to stand together smirking, eyes closed, for we are safe. I know we will stand basking in our own stunning light of girl unity. I know; I can feel it inside of me.
—Kathleen Hanna quoted in *Smart Ass*
Shea-la, 107 Lindley Av,
N. Kingstown RI 02852

Learn to recognize mindfuck.
—Rebecca Bulldozer, POB 342,
Oberlin OH 44074

The standards of "cool" are not being set by you or by anyone who has anything in common with you!—*ibid*

Because mass media is boring, false, and greedy. Because we can't express ourselves by watching TV. Because we are always told to shut up and consume for the good of America. Because we are told that putting chemicals in our bodies is supposed to be fun. Because we think money should have nothing to do with the quality of life. Because humans are cut off from each other in too many ways already. Because real change is infinitely gradual. Because communication builds inspiration. Because getting mail is fun. Because zines are often under-appreciated in comparison to records. Because slick, glossy, computerized, sterile, is not what we value. Because glue sticks and scissors are the tools of the revolution. Because it's more than music, it's a life. These are all reasons why we are involved in punk and hardcore, and more specifically, why we do zines, and why we started a zine-only mailorder distribution machine. We are small, we are human, we are cut-and-paste, we want revolution.—Irene, Rebecca, Josh, Junglegym mail order, POB 342, Oberlin OH 44074.

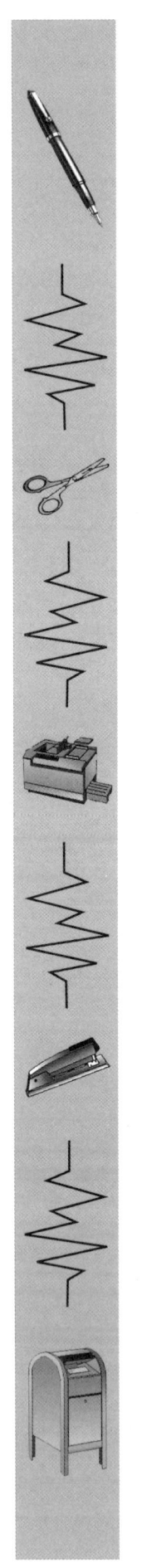

Over 100 million trees per year are used for junk mail. Plus when they are turned into paper pulp, tons of chlorine-bleach pollution is created. Also, marketing companies make money just from selling your name to big corporations . . . Here are some tips on how to deal with junk mail (mostly from Bethesda Co-op Newsletter)
1. Write to the DMA (Direct Marketing Association), Junk Mail Rejection Service, 6 East 43rd St, NYC 10017. Tell them your name, address, all possible misspellings, and tell them to put your name in a block file to stop companies from trading or selling your name.
2. If you subscribe to any big corporate magazines (hopefully you don't), tell them not to trade or sell your name. If you want to figure out who's been giving your name to whom, use different "apartment numbers" for each magazine you subscribe to, to track down the source.
3. If it has a postpaid envelope, mail it all back to them, perhaps with some very heavy objects to increase the rate of postage they will have to pay. Better yet, get a box, put bricks in it, and tape the envelope on the top.—ibid

EXCERPT From *BULLDOZER*:

Every morning and evening there is a great tide of people going to and from their offices. They all look the same, the men in suits and ties, the women in skirts and high heels. These are the masses of the professional class. I learned firsthand what it's like to be among their ranks when I took a corporate office job last summer vacation. I really didn't want a job in an office.

I would much rather have worked in a bookstore or something, but I couldn't find anything else, and I needed the money. It could have been worse, I thought. I could have been drawing diagrams of missiles for military manuals like a friend of mine was doing. I knew my job would be boring and tedious, but I hoped that I could learn something by seeing a different perspective on things, and maybe I could do a bit of monkey wrenching from the inside.

I worked for a consulting firm that dealt with issues of environmental health and occupational hazards. Basically they defend the big chemical companies whose poisoned workers try to sue them. They also provide risk assessment for companies that want to know how much shit they can get away with before they get fined for violating some health, safety, or environmental regulation. The firm's list of clients includes many of the most offensive exploiters of humanity and poisoners of the earth. Exxon, Dow Chemical, AMOCO, Bethlehem Steel, Asbestospray, General Motors, and Nabisco have all paid this firm lots of money to help them avoid regulatory fines and lawsuits, or to get around ones they were already dealing with. They don't want to know how to protect people from their toxins and hazards, because people don't matter. They don't want to lose a lawsuit, be fined by the Occupational Safety and Health Association (OSHA), or get any bad publicity. Here in the corporate world, priorities are upside-down. Money is the single top priority, and people are reduced to mere raw material, to be expended for the sake of profit.

My job was to do the shitwork for the marketing department. I did stuff like filing, copying, faxing, data entry, typing letters, and assembling the pamphlets and stuff that they send to prospective clients. I followed the orders of people whose careers revolved around trying to sell this firm's services. The marketing department was responsible for presenting the company to the public eye. It was a game of appearances, the way advertising always is. The director and her assistant agonized over every detail of the marketing material and whether or not it would give the firm a professional image, right down to the color of the logo. They were constantly stressed out, worrying about getting letters and packets of material out on time, whether the firm would be hired for a case, whether the quality of the printing for the articles they included with the marketing material was good enough, or whether they had enough folders of information left for the president of the firm to take with him on his trip. They spent so much energy turning the worries of the firm into their own worries, when really, their life had nothing to do with this at all. They had become slaves, and ceased to live. Sitting in a cubicle for eight hours a day is not living. I was surrounded by death and by people who had sacrificed themselves to their jobs. If the people in the firm and all the people I saw on the subway and walking around during lunch hour had ever fought against becoming slaves, they had given up and succumbed a long time ago. And how could I blame them? My own power was being diverted towards purposeless and unimportant work which was perpetuating the whole big system, a system in which chemical companies exist, and law suits exist, and firms like the one I worked for spring up wherever they can make a buck. During those two and a half months, it was the hardest struggle for me to keep up my constant fight to keep my brain active, thinking, and learning. I was afraid that if I didn't fight, I would end up like all the others, with nothing but a head full of useless shit.

I felt like I was from a different planet than everyone around me. I couldn't show my real self in the office. I had to wear office clothes and leave my identity at home. So every morning I put on my disguise and boarded the subway, to join the flow of zombies who would spend their day taking orders from people who were taking orders from other people, executing instructions written on endless little yellow sticky pieces of paper or staring into a computer screen at words that mean nothing and have no relation to existence. All this so that they can take home their paychecks which allow them to become consumers. I was surrounded by an army of high-heeled, power-suited slaves who are trapped on the billionth floor of some sterile office building with nothing to look forward to but their next coffee break.

Patriarchy thrives in this climate. Just look at the uniforms for an example. While office clothes for men are designed to make them look dignified, office clothes for women subject them to pain and objectification. High heels may make your legs look sexy, but I thought the function of shoes was to protect your feet and facilitate walking. Heels do the opposite. The firm where I worked was run by a husband and wife team. But it was George, not Susan, whose name was on the letterhead. The men of the firm were prestigious and respected. The women were trying to live up to the superwoman image, with kids and high-powered careers, yet they were still expected to make the coffee and look pretty. It's the same in offices everywhere. There are the men and then there are the girls, and the men say, "Oh, yeah, we're not supposed to call you girls anymore, are we?" All over the city, all over the country, all over the world, the men are patronizing and the women water the plants.

In the office there is this intangible, creepy feeling of evil. When I was there, I felt infinitely small and weak. The power of this corporate behemoth is so extensive, and I felt like there was nothing I could do against it. I wanted to destroy the monster, but the only thing I could do was hate it with all my energy, and fight against having to help this corporate system spread its death and pestilence. This is a difficult thing to do. It might be easy to think you're fighting when you're at a show and everyone around you is fighting the same thing. It might be easy when you're in your room listening to records and screaming the lyrics at the top of your lungs to the neighbors, or when there's a can of spray paint in your hand and no security guards in sight. But it is so much harder to fight when you feel alone, and you're up against the biggest, most powerful force you could ever imagine, way bigger and more powerful than any fascist school administration ever was.

The thing is, I'm really scared. The thought of being sucked into a career like that is really frightening. Yet ultimately, just by needing to eat and consume, everyone is part of the system, and everyone is controlled by it. "What are you going to do, become a hermit?" is the familiar response received when you tell anyone that you want no part in it. It's like that Burn song, "Drown": "I can't break free, and I cannot be me. I don't know what to do because there is no escape from your grasp . . . I'm trapped by my actions . . . I'm drowning." Your only defense against drowning is hate. Hate will mentally separate you from it, even if physically you are a slave. But some days, the scariest days, I didn't even have the energy to hate it anymore. It became easier just to cope, to save my energy for the weekends and evenings.

I held on and did my time, but by the end of the summer I had no solutions. Pilfering office supplies seemed so insignificant. Despite my resistance, I found that I really didn't have the courage to do anything but endure, and comfort myself that at least the money they were paying me would mostly be diverted away from financing more corporate McCulture, and towards worthier things like records and zines. This system which I've been trying to describe has been reduced to so many clichés. It's a "corporate monster" and a "machine." It takes our money and spits back poison. It takes our energy and spits back boredom. If you let it, it will take you and spit back a zombie. I think we are consumers, but really we are consumed.

I am just a tiny person, but this "machine" was created by tiny people, and it needs all of us to participate in order for it to function. My ultimate goal is to refuse to participate. Maybe I can't change it, but I can refuse to let it feed off of me. Listening to records and reading zines and seeing that other people feel the same way as me gives me the inspiration to think and learn and create my own life instead of having it created for me.—Rebecca Bulldozer, POB 342, Oberlin OH 44074

Facts do not cease to exist because they are ignored.
—Billie Strain, *Cross My Heart*

Acting-out memory is a form of unconscious memory in which the forgotten incident is spontaneously acted out through some physical action. It involves either a verbal or bodily act in response to something that reminds one of the original episode . . . Physically acting out part of an abuse memory is a manifestation of this kind of memory. It can also occur under the influence of drugs or alcohol.
—*Discharge #5½*

I only became political once I discovered the language to be so.—*ibid*

Riot Grrrl is not about hating boys. It's about loving girls and loving myself. It should not be about the cool hip punk rock scene. It's not a fashion statement. It's not a haircut. It's not lesbian/bisexual/straight. All it is is a group of females who are *reclaiming their free-*

dom, spitting on the status quo, and tired of being told that a man's opinion is all that matters. Destroy the beauty myth. Live free now. Fuck shit up.
—Jane, "What is riot grrrl, anyway???" (Riot Grrrl, POB 1205, Olympia WA 98507)

hoyden: (hoy-den) n. a noisy, unrestrained girl; a tomboy. hoydenish adj. [origin unknown]—*ibid*

Political Graffiti: It's one of the best forms of art. We used to go around our neighborhood and spraypaint "HOMOSEX RULES" on the side of vans. If you write "QUEER" on a redneck's 4x4 truck, it's pretty much the most effective word you can use to offend him. It really affects his manhood.
—Kurt Cobain quoted in *Ablaze! #10*

I speak through my clothes. —Umberto Eco

Since youth dissent has been sold back to us over and over, the assertion that we may challenge society through our clothes clearly becomes laughable. There is no sartorial style that has not already been mass-marketed . . . We do not need explicit signs in order to recognize one another as revolutionaries, and the spheres in which we operate, often involving intimate contact with the enemy, require that we are sneaky and cunning.
—*Girlspeak,* manifesto of Girl Power International (*Ablaze #10*)

Life in this society being, at best, an utter bore, and no aspect of society being at all relevant to women, there remains to all civic-minded, responsible, thrill-seeking females, only to overthrow the government, eliminate the money system, institute complete automation and destroy the male sex.—Valerie Solanas

Anger makes things happen, then the uncertainty we've been trained in melts into confidence. Self-destruction turns into self-love, and our self-love is our power because we are alive and we're going somewhere, whether we realize it or not.
—Riot Grrrl manifesto in *Ablaze #10*

We're growing, we're underground, and we're denying their power by not talking to them [mainstream media].—*ibid*

Married women have shorter life expectancy than unmarried women; conversely, married men tend to live longer than unmarried men.
—*MADWOMAN #3*

Anarchism: it's not a form of statism. Anarchists don't want to impose their value-system on anyone else. It's not terrorism. The agent of the government—the cop who wears a gun to scare you into obeying him—is the terrorist. Governments threaten to punish any man or woman who defies state power, and therefore the state really amounts to an institution of terror.

Anarchism never relies on fear to accomplish anything because a person who is afraid is not free.

Here's what Anarchists believe: 1) Government is an unnecessary evil. Human beings, when accustomed to taking responsibility for their own behavior, can cooperate on a basis of mutual trust and helpfulness. 2) No true reform is possible that leaves government intact. Appeals to a government for a redress of grievances, even when acted upon, only increase the supposed legitimacy of the government's acts, and add therefore to its amassed power. 3) Government will be abolished when its subjects cease to grant it legitimacy. Government cannot exist without the tacit consent of the populace. This consent is maintained by keeping people in ignorance of their real power. Voting is not an expression of power, but an admission of powerlessness, since it cannot do otherwise than reaffirm the government's supposed legitimacy. 4) Every person must have the right to make decisions about her or his own life. All moralistic meddling in the private affairs of freely-acting persons is unjustified. Behavior which does not affect uninvolved persons is nobody's business but the participants' . . .

All governments survive on theft and extortion, called taxation. All governments force their decrees on the people, and command obedience under threat of punishment. The principal outrages of history have been committed by governments, while every advancement of thought, every betterment in the human condition, has come about through the practices of voluntary cooperation and individual initiative. The principle of government, which is force, is opposed to the free exercise of our ability to think, act and cooperate.

Whenever government is established, it causes more harm than it forestalls. Under the guise of protecting populaces from crime and violence, governments not only do not eradicate random, individual crime, but they institutionalize such varieties as censorship and war. All governments enlarge upon and extend their powers; under government, the rights of individuals constantly diminish.

Anarchism is in favor of a free society organized along lines of cooperation and mutual aid.
—Fred Woodworth (1975), *The Match,* POB 3488, Tucson AZ 85722

Excerpts from *RIGHT NOW. RIOT GRRRL:* The Expansion of Punk Rock:

You know, it's said ("it's said"!? hear me using their language of "objectivity"!) that there is no theoretical basis for feminism—that there is no social need for it. Fuck that. Feminism is punk rock to the schoolworld and the squareworld. Feminism rips up the foundations of our psychology, our history, our political system, our families, our friendships, our sexual lives. It's true, feminism is going for it and people who want things to continue as they are (legalized rape) will tell us we are wrong.

Well, we're not listening to those people anymore. Riot Grrrl. It's like a suggestion, it's like an order. The grrrl probably isn't one who's already been socialized too far down—she's been waiting for the opportunity, like all through history, and sometimes something comes along that makes space, that permits, like a group of women that somehow forms and somehow says, "Yeah, let's do these things we want to do. Fuck philosophy. Fuck punk rock history. GRRRLS ARE THE EXPANSION OF PUNK ROCK AND WE NEED NO JUSTIFICATION. The reasons are on the surface of the world. The reasons we have all-girl meetings are obvious . . .

This is what we do: we use music—playing things as a way of showing ourselves that we can do whatever we want to do. We use them as a way of denying history, of ignoring the messages in our upbringing telling us we can't do certain stuff. WE CAN DO ANY STUFF. Yeah—it's so obvious and it's so straightforward, it's hard to see why there's been all that mystique, why power's been held onto so tightly and knowledge withheld so meanly when it's this easy to claim it—we just use the magic word, and the word is POSSIBILITY. . .

DO STUFF. DO IT. DO - IT - YOURSELF. The backlash is here already. "Ironic" sexism prevails in the music press, they think they've outwitted us because they're still selling papers to 50,000+ kids every week. But only empty things happen fast. We're growing, we're underground, and we're denying their power by not talking to them. They need us, y'see. They need people who are doing things, so they can continue to make money by being seen to always exist at the center of things. But Riot Grrrl isn't centralized, it's not organized, we've no leaders, no spokeswomen, we're not geared up to exploit the press now because you always pay for that kind of stuff in the end . . . They mighta stopped us before but now we are too many for them . . .

Getting guitars; some girls have bits of equipment, and some of us have some money, and some of us can get things cheap—we'll figure out ways. And if all that fails, we got loud voices and we can always find things to hit, things that make good sounds. We can make tapes of our music and swap them, send them, lines of encouragement spinning round from town to town, blocking out boring boyrock, getting more and more ways of saying our thing that's been ignored for centuries.

Hiring venues, doing the sound, making our own shows, inviting who we want—it's our scene where we're not pushed around . . . We're armed with a knowledge of the past. Our voices are not to be diminished. Too many of us, too linked, too wise to it all . . . So much to say, so simply . . . We've got a lot of work to do—not to become media stars, but to fulfill our intentions. We've got a lot of things to define and sharpen.

(contact addresses [may be outdated]: Riot Grrrl, POB 782, Olympia WA 98507; Riot Grrrl Leeds, Box 14, 52 Call Lane, Leeds LS1 6DT, U.K.; Riot Grrrl London c/o Box XX, Ceased to Exist, 83 Clerkenwell Rd, London EC1.)

A vision of the necessity and practicality of removing oppression in every sphere becomes apparent. Once reunited with the gleeful spirit that has whispered obscenities into the ears of everyone you hate, you'll find there's a choice: to return to your previous position on the escalator of sickness, conformity, denial of responsibility for the universal battery farm you are helping to perpetuate . . . or to move from the middle ground of mindless euphoria to a position from which you fuck everything up—setting fire to the escalators, smashing down walls—creating escape routes for those with the imagination to run.—*Girlspeak,* the manifesto of Girl Power International

As women, we've been brainwashed into the sick belief that our surface appearance is the most essential facet of our beings and that we must express ourselves primarily through our shape, clothes, skin, hair, eyes, etc for an audience of judgmental males. Girl Power casts out the internalized stagnant eyeballs to free us into a state of uninhibited self-love in which we fulfill our dreams. Also, and importantly: as women, we are denied any legitimate means of protest about our position, and the adoption of a conspicuous uniform would surely invite assassination.—*ibid*

While men tend to gain societal prestige as they age, the opposite is true for women who are given little real power at any age, and are frequently viewed as one-dimensional sexual ornaments, thus losing our primary usefulness as we age.—*ibid*

Our fight is adrenalin-fueled and essentially fun, following no pre-set program. This manifesto is a carrier of gifts/weaponry, only effective if ideas are stolen or disputed, altered or refuted and spread throughout the *network of brave people linked by a revulsion for authority*. We are prepared to (ab)use philosophy, to put forward statements we know are untrue, in order to stir up stagnant ponds of thought into newly rushing fountains of debate . . . For our purposes authorship is a redundant concept . . . As we stole ideas from numberless sources, there's no copyright on this manifesto—steal any or all of it for your own subversive purposes."—*Girlspeak*

The key to our vision is the deconstruction of gender divisions; not the destruction of any type of person.
—*ibid*

Easy Methods of Generating Girl Time: By denying the necessity of time spent taking drugs, having sex, explaining ourselves to boys, working (for anyone but ourselves), getting "educated" in patriarchal death camp schools, and the murderous rations of housework time and that oh-so important Preparing To Be Watched By The World (make-up) time, we are freed to pursue pleasure and revolution (the two are essentially the same thing).—*ibid*

So I must wrest this language and its forms away from or out of "the majority," to un-man it, to un-American it, even to un-white it, to inconvenience the majority language, to unconventionalize it, even to shame it in an odd sort of way, to question privilege, my own too of course.—Lynn Tillman

Top 10 Riot Grrrl Favorite Books or Authors:
Beloved: Toni Morrison
Backlash: Susan Faludi
House of Spirits: Isabel Allende
Confessions of a Pretty Lady: Sarah Bernhard
House on Mango Street: Sandra Cisneros
Six of One: Rita Mae Brown
Their Eyes Were Watching God: Zora Neal Hurston
Oathbound, Oathbreakers: Mercedes Lackey
Strands of Starlight: Gail Bardens
Women of Brewster Place: Gloria Naylor
Outrageous Acts: Gloria Steinem
Braided Lives: Marge Piercy
Dykes to Watch Out For: Alison Bechdil
Cruelty/Killing Floor: Ai
Shock Treatment: Karen Finley
—Riot Grrrl, POB 11002, Washington DC 20008

Be a dork, tell your friends you love them.
Resist the temptation to view those around you as objects and use them.
Recognize empathy and vulnerability as positive forms of strength.
Resist the internalization of capitalism, the reducing of people and oneself to commodities, meant to be consumed.
Don't allow the world to make you into a bitter abusive asshole.
Cry in public.
Don't judge other people. Learn to love yourself.
Acknowledge emotional violence as real.
Figure out how the idea of competition fits into your intimate relationships.
Recognize you are not the center of the universe.
Recognize your connections to other people and species. Close your mind to the propaganda of the status quo by examining its effects on you, cell by artificial cell.—*Bikini Kill #2*

Marginalized groups must take it upon themselves to educate each other and figure out how to survive in this planet run by pigs . . .—*ibid*

RIOT GRRL IS . . .
BECAUSE us girls crave records and books and fanzines that speak to US, that WE feel included in and can understand in our own ways.
BECAUSE we wanna make it easier for girls to see/hear each other's work so that we can share strategies and criticize-applaud each other.
BECAUSE we must take over the means of production in order to create our own meanings.
BECAUSE viewing our work as being connected to our girlfriends-politics-real lives is essential if we are gonna figure out how what we are doing impacts, reflects, perpetuates, or DISRUPTS the status quo.
BECAUSE we recognize fantasies of instant Macho Gun Revolution as impractical lies meant to keep us simply dreaming instead of becoming our dreams AND THUS seek to create revolution in our lives every single day by envisioning and creating alternatives to the bullshit christian capitalist way of doing things.
BECAUSE we want and need to encourage and be encouraged, in the face of all our own insecurities, in the face of beergutboyrock that tells us we can't play our instruments, in the face of "authorities" who say our bands/zines/etc are the worst in the U.S. and who attribute any validation/success of our work to girl bandwagon hype.
BECAUSE we don't wanna assimilate to someone else's (Boy) standards of what is or isn't "good" music or punk rock or "good writing" AND THUS need to create *forums* where we can recreate, destroy and define our own visions.
BECAUSE we are unwilling to falter under claims that we are reactionary "reverse sexists" and not the truepunkrocksoulcrusaders that WE KNOW we really are.
BECAUSE we know that life is much more than physical survival and are patently aware that the punk rock

"you can do anything" idea is crucial to the coming angry grrrl rock revolution which seeks to save the psychic and cultural lives of girls and women everywhere, according to their *own* terms, not ours.
BECAUSE we are interested in creating *non-hierarchical ways* of being AND making music, friends and scenes based on communication + understanding, instead of competition + good/bad categorizations.
BECAUSE doing/reading/seeing/hearing cool things that validate and challenge us can help us gain the strength and sense of community that we need in order to figure out how bullshit like racism, able-bodyism, age-ism, species-ism, classism, thinism, sexism, anti-semitism and heterosexism figures in our own lives.
BECAUSE we see fostering and supporting girl scenes and girl artists of all kinds as integral to this process.
BECAUSE we hate capitalism in all its forms and see our main goal as sharing information and staying alive, instead of making profits or being cool according to traditional standards.
BECAUSE we are angry at a society that tells us Girl = Dumb, Girl = Bad, Girl = Weak.
BECAUSE we are unwilling to let our real and valid anger be diffused and/or turned against us via the internalization of sexism as witnessed in girl/girl jealousies and self-defeating girl-type behaviors.
BECAUSE self-defeating behaviors (like fucking boys without condoms, drinking to excess, ignoring true-soul girlfriends, belittling ourselves and other girls, etc) would not be so easy if we lived in communities where we felt loved and wanted and valued.
BECAUSE I believe with my whole heartmindbody that girls constitute a revolutionary soul force that can, and will, change the world for real.
—from *Bikini Kill #2*

In a male supremacist society, the only obscenity law that will not be used against women is no law at all.
—Ellen Willis quoted in *Powers of Desire*, ed. Ann Snitow *et al*

Go out and read these important essays and works:
Laura Kipnis, "(Male) Desire and (Female) Disgust: Reading *Hustler*" in *Cultural Studies '92*
Barbara Hobson: *Uneasy Virtue: the Politics of Prostitution*
Gail Pheterson: *A Vindication of the Rights of Whores*
Gayle Rubin: "Thinking Sex: Notes for a Radical Theory of the Politics of Sexuality," in *Pleasure and Danger: Exploring Female Sexuality*
—*Smile For Me* c/o Ananda/Roberto La Vita, 149 Sullivan St #4C, NYC 10012

What does the lie of "femininity" feed off in a capitalist society? The same insitutions that we support. Department stores, weight loss clinics, all female gyms, and thousands of boutiques and jewelry stores. Capitalism has permeated our very souls, turned us into commodity sponges, and by creating an unrealizable image, has assured itself that we will never stop buying it!—Heather, *Order A New World #2*, POB 10081, Olympia WA 98502

To fight pollution, fight capitalism!—Peace Factory, POB 7283, Alexandria VA 22307

RIOT GRRRL...
It's about saying "I CAN" when others are saying "you can't."
It's about insisting on being treated as an equal when it's not convenient for THEM to do so.
It's about daring to say the unspeakable: that WE are still not fully liberated, and we won't stand for anything less.
It's about defying the standards of what is "important" by saying that our personal feelings and experiences are in fact vital to acknowledge and share.
It's about close friendships with girls, without the jealousy and pettiness so common.
It's about deciding you've had just about enough of the shit that's been dished out to you since Day One, and suddenly your rage is realer than anything you've ever felt, and you can't bear to *not* do anything.
It's about not letting our differences (race, class, queer/straight/bi, punk/not punk, etc) divide us, and instead uniting on basis of our commonalities as girls.
It's about healing, and it's about helping each other realize that we all have an incredible strength.
It's about using that strength. We all can use that strength.—Sara, *Out of the Vortex #6*, POB 4619, Gaithersburg MD 20885

Cautious, careful people, always casting about to preserve their reputation and social standing, never can bring about a reform.—Susan B. Anthony

ZINE THEORY: I've been doing a lot of thinking about zines lately. Sometimes I will get a zine that is mostly phone sex ads with curses scribbled over them, and not a lot of substance, and I just don't like those as much as a really well thought-out, dense zine. It doesn't have to be thick, but I like to see some substance. But then I get to thinking, "What right have I to criticize someone else's method of self-expression?" If this particular girl feels very angry about the image of women presented by phone sex ads, and her way of dealing with that anger is to scribble "Fuck you" over them and photocopy this and mail it to me, who am I to disparage that? ...
Everything that a person feels a personal need to put into a zine is valid. I've been thinking a lot lately about zines, especially but not exclusively girl zines, as political tools. The 1970s battle cry, "The personal is political," means to me that our experiences are not isolat-

ed. Everything that happens to us is connected. Every day in the paper I read about a woman getting killed by her boyfriend husband father stepfather and I can't believe it's coincidental. We are hated by this society and need to connect with each other. "Eat meat, hate blacks, beat your fucking wife, it's all the same thing." My harassment, your rape, her murder—these aren't separate instances, but we can only acknowledge this once we start to share our experiences. What outlets do we have for this purpose? Mainstream press, television, movies, the established "alternative" press? Of course not. Only by controlling the medium do we control the message. We are the medium; we are the message. For this reason zines are extraordinarily unique and powerful political tools.

In addition, zines are many people's first contact with the idea of the do-it-yourself ethic. I know this was true for me. It's quite staggering, the first time you truly digest the revolutionary concept that you don't have to depend on other people to do the things you want to get done, you can have full power over that. For me, this zine was my first time being the final critic of my work before it was seen by the public. Always in my life I had handed in my writing to teachers, parents, older writer friends, to give me their opinions about what I'd done, then depended on editors of literary magazines and so on to get my work read by others. Suddenly all this seemed unnecessary. The confidence people gain from this tremendous self-sufficiency can carry over into all aspects of their lives. This is particularly important to kids, girls, minorities—anyone who is discouraged from taking charge in their lives.

So when I critique zines that I receive, I'm not questioning the validity or importance of what the zine-doer has to say. I'm only remarking to myself what about the presentation works or doesn't work for me, so that I can make each issue of Out of the Vortex a piece of work I am satisfied with. Probably some people get our zine and don't like it—that's fine. Just so long as they can still appreciate the spirit behind our zine, and hundreds like it. We all need to break down our walls. And unless something better comes along, I will remain fully committed to the theory and practice of doing zines.—Sara, ibid

---

If you do not tell the truth about yourself you cannot tell it about other people.—Virginia Woolf

---

TEN THINGS MEN CAN DO TO FIGHT SEXISM:

1) Understand that your own attitudes and actions perpetuate sexism and violence, and work towards changing them. Some examples of sexist/abusive behavior: a) pressuring a woman to have sex . . . b) taunting or whistling at women, following women around, embarrassing women in public (sexual harassment). c) controlling women by using threatening gestures, by outshouting women, by interrupting women, intimidation of any kind. d) verbally assaulting women by name-calling, mocking, ridiculing, criticizing, trivializing, and swearing (using the specific gendered terms to harass women); psychological abuse.
2) Confront sexist, racist, homophobia, and all other bigoted remarks or jokes. Say, "Rape isn't funny," or "You could be joking about my sister." Boycott bands, shows, and comedians that verbally assault women.
3) Recognize and speak out against homophobia and gay-bashing. Discrimination and violence against lesbians, gays, and bisexuals is wrong in and of itself. It is also directly linked to sexism (e.g., men who speak out against sexism are often subject to homophobic abuse—one reason why so few men do).
4) Raise money for battered women's shelters and rape crisis centers. If you belong to a fraternity, team, or another student organization, hold a fund-raiser (or collect needed supplies for the centers). Get involved.
5) Don't fund sexism. Don't purchase any magazine, rent any video, or buy any piece of music that degrades women, or portrays them in a sexually degrading or violent manner. Protest sexism in the media.
6) If you know a woman who is being abused, gently ask her if you can help. If you have a friend or relative who is abusing his partner or other women, talk to him . . . Don't remain silent.
7) Read about yourself. Read articles, essays, books about the socially constructed role of masculinity. Examine gender inequality, and read about the root causes of sexual violence. Educate yourself and others about the connections between larger social forces andthe conflicts between individual women and men.
8) Take courses on gender-related topics in school. Take a women's studies class. Contact the women's studies department or the African-American studies department for suggestions.
9) Organize or join a group of men in school, at your workplace, or among friends to work against sexism and violence.
10) Support feminists, who are at the forefront in working to end all forms of violence against children, women, and men. Commit yourself to ending oppression in all its forms.—Keen #2, $1 from Martha, POB 2817, Gaithersburg MD 20886

The dictionary defines "feminist" as a person who believes in equal rights for both men and women. I am a feminist. So is my dad. And he says so proudly. Don't buy the crap that feminism is dead. Declare that you are one, too, because the more of us who refuse to accept the prescribed stigmas, the less the media and society can use them as tools of oppression.
—Kristin Thomson, *Riot Grrrl #6*

THE SMALLER THE FREER: Support small zines because: 1) the larger the zine the more sponsorship it needs and the less freedom it has. 2) the capitalist system destroys the flow of creative ideas. A.K.A. POWER = VOICE. 3) to express is to educate and liberate. The more voices there are the more people will understand.—*Riot Grrrl New York #2*

RIOT GRRRL IS . . .
BECAUSE we girls want to create mediums that speak to us. We are tired of boy band after boy band, boy zine after boy zine, boy punk after boy punk after boy.
BECAUSE I can't smile when my girlfriends are dying inside. We are dying inside and we never even touch each other; we are supposed to hate each other.
BECAUSE we need to talk to each other. Communication/inclusion is key. We will never know if we don't break the code of silence.
BECAUSE we are being divided by our labels and philosophies, and we need to accept and support each other as girls; acknowledging our different approaches to life and accepting all of them as valid.
BECAUSE I need laughter and I need girl love. We need to build lines of communication so we can be more open and accessible to each other.
BECAUSE we need to acknowledge that our blood is being spilt; that right now a girl is being raped or battered and it might be me or you or your mom or the girl you sat next to on the bus last Tuesday, and she might be dead by the time you finish reading this. I am not making this up.
BECAUSE we will never meet the hierarchical BOY standards of talented, or cool, or smart. They are created to keep us out, and if we ever meet them they will change, or we will become tokens.
BECAUSE in every form of media I see us/myself slapped, decapitated, laughed at, objectified, raped, trivialized, pushed, ignored, stereotyped, kicked, scorned, molested, silenced, invalidated, knifed, shot, choked, and killed.
BECAUSE I am tired of these things happening to me; I'm not a fuck toy, I'm not a punching bag, I'm not a joke.
BECAUSE I am still fucked up, I am still dealing with internalized racism, sexism, classism, homophobia, etc, and I don't want to do it alone.
BECAUSE I see the connectedness of all forms of oppression and I believe we need to fight them with this awareness.
BECAUSE a safe space needs to be created for girls where we can open our eyes and reach out to each other without being threatened by this sexist society and our day-to-day bullshit.
BECAUSE every time we pick up a pen, or an instrument, or get anything done, we are creating the revolution. We ARE the revolution.—Erika Reinstein, *Fantastic*, 850 N. Edison St, Arlington VA 22205

To make the liberated voice, one must confront the issue of audience—we must know to whom we speak. When I began writing my first book, *Ain't I a Woman: black women and feminism,* the initial completed manuscript was excessively long and very repetitious. Reading it critically, I saw that I was trying not only to address each potential audience—black men, white women, white men, etc—but that my words were written to explain, to placate, to appease. They contained the fear of speaking that often characterizes the way those in a lower position within a hierarchy address those in a higher position of authority. Those passages where I was speaking most directly to black women contained the voice I felt to be most truly mine—it was *then* that my voice was daring, courageous. When I thought about audience—the way in which the language we choose to use declares who it is we place at the center of our discourse—I confronted my fear of placing myself and other black women at the speaking center. Writing this book was for me a radical gesture. It not only brought me face-to-face with this question of *power,* it forced me to resolve this question, to act, to find my voice, to become that subject who could place herself and those like her at the center of feminist discourse. I was transformed in consciousness and being.—bell hooks

I want to say it so perfect. I want to convince you that everything is going to be fine and that we will all survive this fucked-up world we had no part in creating. I want to take us out of it and not be mere products anymore. In our new world there are no priests no daddys no rapists no alleys you're too scared to walk down alone whenever the fuck you feel like it . . .
—Mary, *Discharge #3*

From *Bulldozer #1*, POBox 342, Oberlin, OH 44074

directory of ZINES

PLEASE OBSERVE SOME MINIMAL POLITENESS WHEN SENDING FOR A ZINE:
1) if you just want a catalog, send $1 & enclose a self-addressed stamped envelope or send 2-4 International Reply Coupons (IRCs, available from Post Office)
2) always send cash (not a check) plus 2-4 stamps (or IRCs) when ordering a zine
3) always write a hand-written letter (no computer letters, please)
4) always write a "positive feedback" letter after you've received a zine
5) be sure to print your name/address legibly on your letter

Daily, zines become unavailable and new zines are produced. This directory is best viewed as a "snapshot" of history rather than an eternal resource (warning: some addresses are defunct). Also, this is but a small fraction of all the zines in existence (*if your zine was not listed, please send us a copy and you will be listed in the next directory*). For currently available zine publications, we highly recommend a subscription to *Factsheet Five*, POB 170099, San Francisco CA 94117-0099 (send $20). Also, check their Advertiser Index for zine distributors' ads. Their back issues are worth ordering as well.

SOME ZINE SOURCES [distribute mostly "slicker" zines; some retail only]:
QVIMBY'S-Steve Svymbersky, 1328 N. Damen Av, Chicago IL 60622 (312) 342-0910. $3 catalog/zine highly recommended: "How to Produce a Zine"
AK DISTRIBUTION, $2 catalog/guide to good books, from POB 40682, San Francisco CA 94140
WOW COOL, 48 Shattuck Sq, Box 149, Berkeley CA 94704 $3 catalog
ATOMIC BOOKS, 229 W. Read St, Baltimore MD 21201 (410) 728-5490
WFMU catalog, POB 1568, Montclair NJ 07042 $3 cat
DESERT MOON, 1226A Calle de Comercio, Santa Fe NM 87505 (505) 474-6311 (zine distributor)
FINE PRINT, 500 Pampa Dr, Austin TX 78752-3028. (800) 874-7082. (zine distributor)
SEE HEAR-Ted, 59 E. 7th St, NYC 10003. (212) 982-6968 $3 catalog
COMIC RELIEF (zines), 1597 Haight, SF CA 94117
BOUND TOGETHER, 1369 Haight St, San Francisco CA 94117 Anarchist bookstore, zine retailer
FLATLAND-Jim Martin, POB 2420, Fort Bragg CA 95437-2420 (707) 964-8326 $3 book catalog, & zine $5
READING FRENZY, 1420 SE 37th, Portland, Oregon 99214
MIND OVER MATTER, 1710 Central Av, Albuq NM 87106
SUBTERRANEAN RECORDS, POB 2530, Berkeley CA 94702
TOWER RECORDS, 2605 Del Monte St, West Sacto, CA 95691 (send your zine for possible distribution to)
NAKED EYE-Steve, 533 Haight, San Francisco CA 94117
POWER TOOT c/o Brian, 55 E 10th St #608, NYC 10003
LEFT BANK, 1404 18th Av, Seattle WA 98122.
RIOT GRRRL PRESS-Sarah Kennedy, 2501 N. Lincoln Ave #261, Chicago IL 60614. $1; send donations!
SEPTOPHILIA, POB 148097, Chicago IL 60614 catalog $2
GERLL ZINE DISTRO-Kelly & Sarah, 656 W. Aldine #3, Chicago IL 60657
RIOT GRRRL LEEDS, Box 14, 52 Call Lane, Leeds LS1 6DT, U.K.
RIOT GRRRL LONDON c/o Box XX, Ceased to Exist, 83 Clerkenwell Rd, London EC1, U.K.
RIOT GRRRL NY, 260 E. 6th St #17, NYC 10003
BASEMENT CHILDREN-Basil, Shayna, Michelle, 1210 Gregory Pl, Downers Grove IL 60515 catalog $1
SUBWAY SISSY ZINE DISTRO-Witknee, 17337 Tramonto #306, Pacific Palisades CA 90272
RIOT GRRL, 345 E. Broadway #331, Vancouver BC V5T 1W5 CANADA
KID REVOLUTION, 4119 Wentworth Av S., Mpls MN 55409
PANDER Distro-Ericka, 4127 Locust #304, KC MO 64110
THE LONG HAUL, 3124 Shattuck, Berkeley CA

THANKS TO THE FOLLOWING KIND SOULS WHO SENT CHRIS TRELA IN NYC THEIR PUBLICATIONS:
20 POUND EMBRYO-4210 W. Emperado St, Tampa FL 33629
3 FEET MINIMUM-934 32nd Av, Seattle WA 98122
8-TRACK MIND-Russ Forster-POB 90, East Lansing MI 48021-0090
ALLEY CAT-820 Frederick St Box E, Oshkosh WI 54901
ALWAYS On My Mind-1550 E. 24th St, Brooklyn NY 11210
AMERICAN CRACKPOT-POB 4794, Louisville KY 40204
AMERICAN WINDOW CLEANER-27 Oak Creek Rd, El Sobrante CA 94803
ANGELZ & REBELZ-11702 Euclid, Cleveland OH 44106
APPLE PIE HUBBUB-263 Bridle Run Ct, Alpine CA 91901
BALLS-POB 202895-New Haven CT 06520-2895
BANAL PROBE-POB 4333, Austin TX 78765
BANANA CONVENTION-536 Essex Pl, Euless TX 76039
BANANA REVOLUTION-66 Osgood St, Andover MA 01110
BATTERIES NOT INCLUDED-130 West Limestone, Yellow Springs OH 45387
BEER FRAME ("A field guide to deriving maximum pleasure from minimum resources")-160 St John's Pl, Brooklyn NY 11217
BEET + PINK PAGES-372 5th Ave, Brooklyn NY 11215
BESMIRCHED-POB 2961, Vista CA 92085-2961
BEYOND BAROQUE-681 Venice Blvd, Venice CA 90291
BEYOND HINDUISM-POB 29044, Portland OR 97210
BLAP-1931 California St #3, Mountain View CA 94041
BLINK-POB 823, Miami FL 33243-0823
BOJI-POB 1876, Hoboken NJ 07030
BOREDOM SUCKS-POB 381 Bard College, Annandale-on-Hudson NY 12504
BRAND X-1717 Iola Drive, Valdosta GA 31602
BUBBA'S LIVE BAIT-POB 824, Knoxville TN 37901
BURN COLLECTOR-307 Blueridge Rd, Carrboro NC 27510
CANNOT BECOME OBSOLETE-POB 1232, Lorton VA 22199
CASHIERS DU CINEMZART (film)-265 E. Oakridge, Ferndale MI 48220
CAUGHT IN FLUX-POB 7088, NYC 10116-7088
CHEMICAL REACTION-POB 65304, St Paul MN 55165
CHODE-POB 9306, Cincinnati OH 45209-0306
CLOWNHUNTER-946 NW Circle Boulevard, Corvallis OR 97330
CLUNKER-373-B Sooy Place Rd, Vincetown NJ 08088
COMPENDIUM-Urban Anthropology, POB 542327, Houston TX 77254
COSMIC PEAS-POB 1063, Englewood Cliffs NJ 07632-0063
CRIMEWAVE USA-POB 675283, Marietta GA 30067-0013
DAGGER, THE-POB 22444, San Francisco CA 94122
DANGER-Dan Kelly comic, from Qvimby's, 1328 N. Damen Av, Chicago IL 60622
DEAD ART LTD-341 N. Milwaukee 5th Flr, Milwaukee WI 53202
DEAL WITH IT-22 Sunset Av, Long Branch NJ 07740-7872
DEMON ANGELA-34 Gramercy Pl #4C, NYC 10003
DISHWASHER-POB 8213, Portland OR 97207-8213 $2
DON'T SAY UH-OH-3328 Poplar St, Port Huron MI 48060
DOWN THE HATCH-Robert Sietsema, 92 Perry St #9, NYC 10014 (about restaurants & food)
DRIVE BY BROADSIDE-POB 470186, Ft Worth TX 76147
DROPKICK THE FISH-639 Whispering Palms, Las Vegas NV 89123-2312
ECHOES REPORT-POB 2321, Mashpee MA 02649
ENDING THE BEGIN-POB 4816, Seattle WA 98104-0816
ENTHEOGEN LAW REPORTER-POB 73481, Davis CA 95617
EVERY GIRL'S DREAM-Carrie Elizabeth, POB 522106, Salt Lake City UT 84152-2106
EXILE OSAKA-3-4 Tanigawa-cho, #202 Tondabayashi, Osaka 584, JAPAN
EXPERIENCE FROST-6135 Utica St, Arvada CO 80003
EXPLODED SCROTUM-515 NW 6th St #23, Corvallis OR 97330
EXTRAPHILE-POB 5585, Arlington VA 22205
FANTASY PIE-479 Sherman St #3, Canton MA 02021
FARM PULP-217 NW 70th St, Seattle WA 98117-4845 recommended
FASCIST-POB 6381, Mpls MN 55406, $1
FED-UP SECRETARY-POB 0573, Chicago IL 60690-0573
FIFTH WALL/LITERARY WHORE-4552 Alabama St, San Diego CA 92116
FLATTER-POB 391655, Cambridge MA 02139-0879 recommended
FOGELNEST FILES-475 Park Ave So. #3300, NYC 10016-6901
FREE BEER-6008 S. 298th Pl, Auburn WA 98001
FRONTAL LOBOTOMY-263 Bridle Run Court, Alpine CA 91901
FROSTBITE FALLS FAR FLUNG FLYER-POB 39, Macedonia OH 44056-0039
GALLERIA-POB 146, Bethel CT 06801
GENERAL ELEPHANT/SKA+-531 Main St #6, Irwin PA 15642
GUN FAG Manifesto-Hollister Kopp, POB 982, Culver City CA 90232 $4
HAVE YOU Seen The Dog Lately-495 Elwood Av #5, Oakland CA 94610
HEINOUS-Steve Mandich, POB 10412, Portland OR 97210 $1 recommended
HEROES FROM HACKLAND, 1225 Evans, Arkadelphia AK 71923
HITCH-Rod Lott, 5504 N. Tulsa Av, Okla. City OK 73112
HUNGRY MAGGOT-2912 N. Main #1, Flagstaff AZ 86004
I WAS NEVER A FAT KID-12702 Lucas St, Cerritos CA 94122
I'M JUST A TORSO-POB 1146, Chico CA 95927
IMAGE GEEK-1100 E. Union St, Seattle WA 98122
INSIDE TRACK-POB 7956, Newark DE 19714-7956
INTERESTING!-Richard Sagall, POB 1069, Bangor ME 04402-1069
INTERZONE-76 Jackson St #8, Hoboken NJ 07030
ISLAND-POB 624, Great Barrington MA O1250
IT'S ONLY A MOVIE-Mike Flores, POB14683, Chicago IL 60614-0683 aboout incredibly strange films
J. CRUELTY Catalog-POB 494, Northfield MN 55057
JAILBAIT-POB 1972, Union City CA 94587-6972
JEM-2380 Lombard St, San Francisco CA 94123
JOEY AUTO MATIC-4405 Bellaire Dr S #220, Fort Worth TX 76109
JOSIE ZINE-POB 5681, Redondo Beach CA 90409
JOURNAL of Unconventional History-Aline Hornaday, POB 459, Cardiff-by-the-Sea CA 92007-9900 $8
JOY PAGE-POB 1520, Evanston IL 60204-1520
JUMBO SHRIMP-POB 667, Prior Lake MN 55372
JUST ANOTHER MENACE TO SOCIETY-4405 Bellaire Dr S #220, Fort Worth TX 76109
KILLING TIMES-Joe Hanson, 11651 Norbourne Dr #316, Forest Park OH 45240-2162
LADIES Fetish & Taboo Society-POB 542327, Houston TX 77254-2327
LAMEGUY-2639 Central Av, Memphis TN 38104
LANGWEILIG-129 Front St, N. Huntingdon PA 15642
LIES-6001-0 Lomas NE #154, Albuquerque NM 87110
LIONESS-13701 Winterberry Ridge, Midlothian VA 23112
LIVING FREE-Box 29 Hiler Branch, Buffalo NY 14223
LOAFERS-POB 2642, St Paul MN 55102-O642
LOAFING THE DONKEY-123 Stonewall #1, Memphis TN 38104-2455
LUCKY/JOY-3302 Descano Dr, Los Angeles CA 90026
MAKING LOSER HAPPY-22 Barton Ln, Cos Cob CT 06807
MANIFIXATION-Box 4531 222 Church St, Middletown CT 06459
MAWEWI-POB 874, Mahwah NJ 07430-0874
MENISCUS-12793 Misty Creek Ln, Fairfax VA 22033
MESHUGGAH-200 E. 10th St #603, NYC 10003
METROZINE-7216 Colgate Av, St Louis MO 63130
MIDDLE GROUND-301 McLaughlin, Santa Cruz CA 95064
MIGRANE-POB 2337, Berkeley CA 94702
MILKY-614 East Union #102, Seattle WA 98122
MONOZINE-POB 598, Reistertown MD 21136
MOONLIGHT CHRONICLES-POB 109, Joseph OR 97846
MOTHER OF INVECTIVE-2506 N. 50th, Seattle WA 98103
MURDER CAN BE FUN-John Marr, POB 640111, San Francisco CA 94109 $4 true crime; deviant culture
PATHETIC LIFE-Doug Holland, 537 Jones St #2386, San Francisco CA 94102 $4 the godfather of per-zines
NECROEROTIC-POB 92303, Warren MI 48092
NOISELESS-Ana Marie Cox, 366 4th St #2, Brooklyn NY 11215 recommended
ON THE POOPDECK-301 E. Longden Dr, San Gabriel CA 91775
OOP-114 Linden, East Lansing MI 48823
OTHER PEOPLE'S MAIL-POB 8695, Austin TX 78713 recommended
OUT OF BOUNDS-Tom W, 957 N. Longfellow St, Arlington VA 22205-1637
OUT YOUR BACKDOOR (travel)-4686 Meridian Rd, Williamston MI 48895
OUT WEST (travel)-408 Broad St #11, Nevada City NV 95959
PHONY TIMES-1709 S. Braddock Av, Pittsburgh PA 15218
PINCH POINT-POB 128, North Lima OH 44452
PINK PAGES-Joe Maynard, 411 Kent Ave, Brooklyn NY 11211, $2
PLANET-1000 E. Apache Blvd #826, Tempe AZ 85281
PLANET POP-POB 485, Pasadena CA 91102-0485
POLAR INERTIA-636 E. Pleasant Hill Road, Carbondale IL 62901
POO POO-POB 8131, Burlington VT 05402
POP NAUSEA-POB 45956, Los Angeles CA 90045
POP SMEAR-105 Thompson St, NYC 10012-3723
PREHENSILE TALES-5556 Bloch, San Diego CA 92122 (like *Beer Frame*)
PRETENTIOUS SHIT-John Cheney, POB 20351, Indianapolis IN 46222-0351
RUBBERBAND-149 South Bull #1, Columbia SC 29205
RUMOR-7340 Huntington, St Louis MO 63121
SACRED CITY-4450 Winslow Pl. N. #3, Seattle WA 98103
SAHIDOMU-2380 Lombard St, SF CA 94123
SATANIC AFTERSCHOOL-POB 06101, Wacker Dr. P.O., Chicago IL 60606-0101
SCAREDY-CAT-STALKER-5535 NE Glisan #5, Portland OR 97213

170

SCENERY-POB 14223, Gainesville FL 32604
S.E.T. Free-POB 10491, Oakland CA 94610-0491 *anti-TV*
SHARK Fear/Awareness-1420 NW Gilman Blvd, Issaquah WA 98027-7001
SHATTERED MIND Jerianne, 106 Murphy Dr #3, Martin TN 38237
SHEMP-593 Waikala St, Kahului HI 96732-1736
SILVER KOOL-629 W. Mountain Av, Fort Collins CO 80521
SINK Full of Dishes-POB 160122, St Louis MO 63116
SKIN TRADE-POB 2583, Hollywood CA 90078
SLOP HUT-POB 85510, Seattle WA 98145-1510
SLUR-3024 Duckworth Dr, Sanatoga PA 19464
SNIPER'S NEST-Trevor Rigler, POB 2351, Galveston TX 77553-2351 $2
SNORKLE-480 2nd Ave #20B, NYC 10016
SPACE AUTOGRAPH NEWS-862 Thomas Av, San Diego CA 92109-3940
SPHERE-341 N. Milwaukee, 5th flr, Milwaukee WI 53202
STUNTOLOGY/TUNEOLOGY-308 S. Buckner, Bloomington IN 47403
SUBLIMINAL VIRGINITY-POB 23483, Pittsburgh PA 15222
TEMP SLAVE-Keffo, POB 5184, Bethlehem PA 18015 #1-6 $10 *recommended, anti-work, black humor*
TEN THOUSAND THINGS-POB 1806, Poughkeepsie NY 12601
TERMINAL BRAIN ROT-7312 Reynard Ln, Charlotte NC 28215
THANK GOD I'M INSANE-3768 Sonoma Av, Santa Rosa CA 95405
THIS IS SO EXCITING!-POB 977, Bryn Mawr PA 19010
TIKI NEWS-Otto von Stroheim, 1349 Preston Way, Venice CA 90291 $2 *tiki culture*, tiki preservation
TIME BOMB-POB 4964, Louisville KY 40204-0964 *anarchist pranks*
TIME TO DIE-611 Capitol Way So. #504, Olympia WA 98501
TOP HAT-POB 24001, Edina MN 55424-1111
TOPOZINE (maps)-Fred Argoff, 1204 Ave U #1290, Brooklyn NY 11209-4107
TRANCE-1450 Clarkson, Denver CO 80218
TV GRIND-Dean Williams, POB 14043, Chicago IL 60614-0043 $3
TWENTY Pound Embryo-4610 W. Gray St #202, Tampa FL 33609
TWISTED NIPPLES-POB 237, Corvallis OR 97339
ULTRAVIOLET Q-TIPS-PSC 54 Box 494, APO AE 09601
UNCOMMON SENSE-POB 466, Middle Village NY 11379
USUAL SUSPECTS, THE-4405 Bellaire Dr S #220, Fort Worth TX 76109
VEINS-2177 Stewart Dr, Hatfield PA 19440
VELOCITY NYC-97 Lexington Av #5A, NYC 10016
VELOUR-POB 2337, Berkeley CA 94702
VERBIVORE-Jeremy Braddock, 532 Laguardia Pl #573, NYC 10012
VIOLATION FEZ-5 Warfield Pl, Northampton MA 01060
VOID OF TOLERANCE-POB 4712, Victoria TX, 77903-4712
VOLCANO-POB 24722, Philadelphia PA 19111
WEST Virginia Surf Report-POB 43662, Atlanta GA 30336-0662
WORLDLETTER-2726 E. Court St, Iowa City IA 52245
WRITER'S RESOURCE GUIDE-POB 58098, Philadelphia PA 19102
YOU COME TOO-1844-1/2 Lincoln St, Eugene OR 97401

OTHER ZINES

4 THE MONEY-Robert Sutter III, In Your Face Publishing, POB 15306, Santa Rosa CA 95402, $1.50
ABLAZE! 17 Wetherby Grove, Leeds LS4 2JH, U.K. *Recommended.*
ABUSE-Rachel Abuse, POB 1242, Allston MA 02134 $5 (#5: body fluids)
ACTION GIRL Newsletter-Sarah Dyer, 543 Van Duzer, Staten Island NY 10304
AGAINST SLEEP AND NIGHTMARE-POB 3305, Oakland CA 94609 $3
AIM-50 Adams St, Newton MA 2160
AIN'T NOTHIN LIKE FUCKIN MOONSHINE, 2667 37th Av, SF CA 94116 $3
ALIEN-Witknee, 17337 Tramonto #306, Pacific Palisades CA 90272 $1
ALIEN GIRL (t-shirt cat)-1215 E Spring Box 36, Seattle WA 98122 $1
ALL THAT, POB 1520 Cooper Sq Sta, NYC 10276 $3 music
ALTERNATIVE PRESS Review-Jason McGuinn & Bob White, POB 1446, Columbia MO 65205-1446 $5
ALTERNAZONE-Patricia K, 14 Loyalist Ct, Markham ON L3P 6A9 Canada
AMAZINE (dyke zine)-POB 720191, San Jose CA 95172 $2
AMERICAN JOB-POB 2284, Portland OR 97208
AMERICAN JOURNAL OF SLOT CAR SCIENCES-1107A Guerrero St, SF CA 94110, $1.32
AMERICAN SALAD BAR-c/o Columbia Univ P.O., POB 250207, NYC 10025-1533
ANARCHIST BOOKLIST-Bob Erler, Libertarian Book Club 339 Lafayette St, Rm 202, NYC NY 10012, $3
ANARCHY-Jason McGuinn & Bob White, CAL PRESS, POB 1446, Columbia MO 65205, $3
AND EVERYTHING NICE-POB 4538, Chico CA 95927
ANGRY Young Women-5525A Coldwater Rd #167, Fort Wayne IN 46825
ANODYNE-Julie-POB 12047, Portland OR 97212
APOLOGY-POB 20065 Greely Sq Sta, NYC 10001-0001 $4
ART ALTERNATIVES-O.B.E., 5 Marine View Pl #207, Hoboken NJ 07030 $5
ARTFUCK-Dan Strachota, 347 Divisadero, SF CA 94117 or Agustin Fuentes, 708 Oak #3, SF CA 94117 $3
ARTISTIC LICENTIOUSNESS-Roberta Gregory, POB 27438, Seattle WA 98125 $3
ASIAN TRASH CINEMA-Tom Wiesser, POB 16-1917, Miami FL 33116, $6
ASIAN Trash Cinema-POB 5367, Kingwood TX 77325 $6
ASSHOLE-Rhino, 190 E. 2nd St #22, NYC 10009 (queer)
ASYLUM FOR SHUT-INS-Msg. Kole, POB 46581, Bedford OH 44146, $2.50 (All Reviews)
ATROCITY-Adrian Furniss, 60 Clarke Rd, Abington, Northampton U.K. NN1 4PW
AUDITIES-POB 1555, Stafford TX 77497 $3
AWAKEN 600-1/2 Grove St N. upper, St Petersburg FL 33701 $1 + 2 stamps
BABY DYKE COMICS-4311 Crestheights Rd, Baltimore MD 21215
BABY SUE-Fievet, POB 8989, Atlanta GA 30306-8989 $3
BAD ATTITUDE-121 Railton Rd, London SE24 0LR, UK $5 (women)
BAD NEWZ-POB 28, 2336 market, SF CA 94114
BAD SEED-Bo Wakeman (gay), 145 Attorney St #6C, NYC 10002 $3
BAD TRIP (60s punk rock)-Bruce Ciero & Paige Howell, 4325 John Wesley Dr, Dallas GA 30132 (770) 445-3086
BAFFLER-Tom Frank, POB 378293, Chicago IL 60637 $5 *recommended*
BALL-BUSTER-Amanda Lynch, POB 3277, Columbus OH 43210
BAMBOO GIRL-Sabrina, POB 2828, NY NY 10185-2828 $2
BANANAFISH c/o Revolver, POB 421215, SF CA 94124
BANNED IN DC-Cynthia Connolly, POB 9743, Washington DC 20016 $12
BAY VEGAN, 564 Mission #134, SF CA 94105
BEN IS DEAD-Darby, POB 3166, Hollywood CA 90028
BI GIRL WORLD-99 Newtonville Av, Newtonville MA 02158 $2
BIFROST (bisexual)-58A Broughton St, Edinburgh EH1 3SA, U.K. $5
BIKINI KILL(grrrl)-c/o K.R.S., 120 NE STATE #418, Olympia WA 98505 *a must*
BITCH QUEEN-POB 1447, Boston MA 02117
BLACKBELT TECHNOFIX-POB 763, Hampshire College, Amherst MA 01002
BLACKEST HEART-Shawn Smith, 3817 San Pablo Dam Rd #614, El Sobrante CA 94803 $6
BLACKSHEETS, POB 31155, San Francisco CA 94131 $5
BLAST, THE-POB 7075, MPLS MN 55407, $2
BLEED-POB 3277, Columbus OH 43210
BLEMISH-8024 Dalton St, Metairie LA 70003
BLOW MY COLON-A. Vegue, POB 1312, Claremont CA 91711-1312
BLOWIN CHUNX-75 Stanton Rd, Brookline MA 02146
BLUE BLOOD-Cyberjunk BLT & Amelia G, 3 Calabar Ct, Gaitersburg MD 20877, $6.95
BLUE PERSUASION-Aaron Lee, 603 E Main #2, Lexington KY 40508 $4 blue movies, etc
BLUE ROSES-Geneva Gano, POB 40674, Portland OR 97240
BLUNDERBUSS-Stephanie Kulick, 857 Fell St, SF CA 94117
BOAS (Bruce Campbell fanzine)-POB 416, Tarrytown NY 10591 $3
BOILED ANGEL-Michael Hunt Publications, Box 226, Bensenville IL 60106, $6.66
BOONPARN-8303 Sycamore Pl, New Orleans LA 70118
BOY DOES HIGHSCHOOL EVER SUCK-540 Los Altos Ct, Santa Rosa CA 95403
BOYCOTT QUARTERLY, POB 30727, Seattle WA 98103-0727 $5
BRAT ATTACK, POB 40754, San Francisco CA 94141-0754
BREAKFAST WITHOUT MEAT-Lizzy Kate Gray, POB 15927, Santa Fe NM 87506 strange music. defunct.
BROW BEAT, POB 11124, Oakland CA 94611-1124 $3
BUGS AND DRUGS, POB 960, Bristol BS99 5QE, England $3
BULLDOZER-Rebecca, POB 342, Oberlin OH 44074 *recommended*
BULLDYKE-Lori, Chatham College Box 206, Pittsburgh PA 15232 2 stamps
BUMPIDEE TIMES-POB 2572, Olympia WA 98507 $1
BUNDLE OF STICKS-54 S. 9th St #132, Mpls MN 54402
BUNNY RABBIT-Amy Fusselman, 51 MacDougal St Box 319, NYC 10012.
BUST (Celina & Betty)-POB 319 Ansonia Station, New York NY 10023
BUSY BEA'S BUSH-Chatham College, BOX 452, Pittsburgh PA 15232
BUTTERCUP-Megan, 803 Ridgeleigh Rd, Baltimore MD 21212 $1
BUZZARD, POB 576, Hudson MA 01749 $3 comic
BYPASS (reviews zines)-POB 148, Hove BN3 3DQ, UK $4
CAKE, 3028 Ewing Ave. S. #201, Mpls MN 55416 $3
CAMPFIRE-Jeffery Kennedy, 250 Page St #1, SF CA 94102, $2, QUEER CULTURE
CAN CONTROL (graffiti)-Box 406, N.Hollywood, CA 91603-0406 $4
CANNONBALL-B. Fissure (hobozine), POB 2054, Phila PA 19103 $2
CAN OF WORMS, POB 1733, Colma CA 94014-0733 $6
CAROL J. ADAMS: THE SEXUAL POLITICS OF MEAT (recommended book)
CASCADIA SALMON-Amber Gayle, 2225 1st Av #207A, Seattle, WA 98121 $5
CATBOX ROOM-Lisa Maslowe, POB 170143, SF CA 94117 $2 comic
CAUGHT IN FLUX-Mike Appelstein, POB 7088 NY NY 10116, $2.
CHAINSAW, POB 11210, Wash DC 20008
CHERRY BOMB-Mandy, 804 SE 25th, Portland OR 97214
CHERUB-11162 Saffold Way, Reston VA 22090
CHICKFACTOR-Gail&Pam, 245 E. 19th St #12T, NYC 10003
CHUCK MAGAZINE-Mike Woolridge, POB 10122, Berkeley CA 94709 $2
CHUM (anti-hip)-POB 148390, Chicago IL 60614-8390 $3
COFFEE NO GIRL-POB 7591, Olympia WA 98507 *good*
COLOUR OF SHADOW-c/o Pariah, POB 55542, Hayward CA 94540 $2
COMATOSE-Aren Rogal, 1092 Lyndhurst Dr, Pittsburgh PA 15206 $1 (13yrs old)
COME AGAIN-353 E 53rd St, NY NY 10022, $5, SM cat
COMETBUS-Aaron, Wow Cool, 48 Shattuck Sq, Box 149, Berkeley CA 94704, $2.50 *classic*
CONTINGENCY CRIER-Doris Hamar, POB 16875, Phoenix AZ 85011-6875, $1
CONTRACT WITH TROUBLETOWN-Lloyd Dangle, POB 460686, SF CA 94146 $5 comic
CONTRASCIENCE. From Basement Children Distro.
CRANK-Jeff Koyen, POB 757, Stuyv Stn, NYC 10009 $3
CREME BRULEE-Abigail Johns, 1705 Summit Av E. #112, Seattle WA 98122
CRUMPY-209 Ridgeway, Little Rock AR 72205
CUIR-3288 21st St #19, San Francisco CA 94110
CUPSIZE-Sasha & Emelye, POB 4326, Stony Brook NY 11790-4326
CURRICULUM VITAE-RD1 Box 226A, Polk PA 16342-9204
CUSP-Sara, POB 4619, Gaithersburg MD 20885 $1
DAFFODIL, POB 124, Willington CT 6279
DAILY COW-David Wyder, 121 Gregory Av #B-7, Passaic NJ 07055
DAME DARCY-Darcy Stanger, POB 591075, SF CA 94159
DANZINE-Teresa, 625 SW 10th #233B, Portland OR 97205
DARK ANGEL-A.R.C. Inc, 500 Pampa Dr, Austin TX 78752-3028 $6
DEAD ON ARRIVAL, POB 191175, San Diego CA 92159
DEAR MOTORIST-The Institute of Social Disengineering, 21 Cave St, Oxford OX4, £1 + envelope, ANTI-CAR
DELERIUM-Sophie Diamantis, 779 Riverside Dr #A-11, NYC 10032 $5
DIESEL-DMP, POB 20547 Salt Lake City UT 84152 (music)
DIMINUTIVE RAGE-Saira, 1951 W. Burnside #1654, Portland OR 97209
DIRT, POB 4438, Richmond VA 23220 $1
DISCHARGE (grrrl)-2501 N. Lincoln #261, Chicago IL 60614
DISEASED PARIAH NEWS, POB 30564, Oakland CA 94604 $3 AIDS humor zine
DISSENSUS-10 Av. Garbalan Bt.J.6., Marseille 13012 France (ed: Alain Maciotta; anarchist)
DISSONANCE-POB 165, Cambridge VT 05444
DIVERSITY (adult/women)-POB 47558, Coquitlam BC Canada V3K 6T3
DLK ZINE-Marc Urselli-Schärer, Via Gorki SN, 74023 Grottaglie, Italy $2
DON'T READ THIS-John, 45 Reno Av, Hamilton ONT L8T 2S5, Canada $1
DON'T SAY UH-OH-Maria Goodman, 3328 Poplar, Port Huron MI 48060 $1
DORIS-Cindy Gretchen O., POB 4279, Berkeley CA 94704 $1
DOUBLE BILL, POB 55 Sta E, Toronto M6H 4E1 Canada
DOUBLE NEGATIVE-Jeff W, 686 Tremont St #1, Boston MA 02118 $1
DREAM SCENE (dreams)-38 Rossi Av #1, San Francisco CA 94118-4218 $3
DREW-JC, POB 791 Berkeley CA 94701, $2, about Drew Barrymore
DROP OUT, 1901 P St #27, Sacramento CA 95814, $1
DUMPSTERLAND-Dave Dumpsterland, POB 267873, Chicago IL 60626, stamp + SASE
DUNGEONEER-Chuck Cosimano, Chicagoland Discussion Group, 3023 N CLark #806, Chicago IL 60657, $5, SM
DUPLEX PLANET-David Greenberger, POB 1230, Saratoga Springs NY 12866 zines, book & cd available!
EAT & GET OUT! (waiters)-POB 267953, Chicago IL 60626-7953 $2
EDNA'S EDIBLES-Sarah Manvel, Sarah Lawrence College, 1 Mead Way, Bronxville NY 10708-5999
EJECTO-POD-Jan Johnson & Brian Curran, 29 Darling St #2 Boston MA 02120, $4
E.L.F., POB 7521, Spokane WA 99207 (L.Peltier support)
ELF LUBE-POB 40320, Berkeley CA 94704
EMERGENCY BROADCAST SYSTEM-329 Lamartine St Ctr, Jamaica Plain MA 02130
EMIT-J Haslam, POB 2499, Vancouver BC CANADA V6B 3W7
EMPIRE, THE-Becky, 416 8th Ave SE, Olympia WA 98502
ENCYCLOPEDIA JUNK HOUSE-Dooley, POB 424036, SF CA 94142, $1
ENGINE, 866 Post #7, San Francisco CA 94109
EUPHORIA-c/o Jordana Robinson, 420 Atherton Hall, Univ Park PA 16802
EVIL TWIN-Amber Gayle & Stacy, POB 12124, Seattle WA 98102 or Postbus 11286, 1001 GG Amsterdam, Netherlands *recommended*
EXEDRA-Kim, POB 422937, San Francisco CA 94142-2937
EXERCISE WITH ALCOHOL-Bruce Clifton, 5606 NE 34th St, Portland OR 97211 $3
EXPOSING MIRAGE. From Basement Children Distro.
EXTRAPHILE-Len Bracken, POB 5585, Arlington VA 22205, $3 diverse, situationist, interesting
FANTASTIC FANZINE (grrrl)-Erika Reinstein, c/o Riot Grrrl Press, POB 1375, Arlington VA 22210
FAT!SO?-Marilyn Wann, POB 42364, San Francisco CA 94142 *recommended*
FEDERATION OF FEMINIST WOMEN'S HEALTH CENTERS-1680 Vine St #1105, Hollywood CA 90028
FEMINIST BASEBALL-Jeff Smith, POB 9609, Seattle WA 98109, $3, MUSIC; one issue had Randy Holden intv
FEMME FLICK-99 Hancock St #4, Cambridge MA 02139 $2 (films/women)
FEMYNIST STICKERS-Donnelly/Colt, Box 188, Hampton CT 06247 $1.50 for 20 stickers (not a zine!)
FERN-Kim, POB 576, Normal IL 61761
FHS-Phil Deslippe, POB 3923 Manchester, CT 06045, $1
FIAT LUX-Lonewolf. Order from Basement Children Distro.
FIFTH ESTATE, 4632 2nd Av, Detroit MI 48201 (anarchist)
FILM THREAT-Chris Gore, LFP, 9171 Wilshire #300, Hollywood CA 90210 $5
FILTH, POB 104, 2336 Market, SF CA 94114 (4 stamps)
FINK-Lana, 1004 S. Granada, Willcox AZ 85643 $2
IN-DE-SIECLE PRODUCTIONS-Lonewolf, POB 40520, Portland OR 97240, ZINE CATALOG
FIREBALL-Terrance, POB 481, Lancaster OH 43130 films
FIRECRACKER-Lara, 297 Alabama Rd, Balitmore MD 21204
FIRECRAQUER/MALEFICE-426 W. Surf #211, Chicago IL 60657
FIRST PERSON-Tracey West, POB 416, Sparkill NY 10976 $2
FISHWRAP, 2130 Broadway #915, NYC 10023 $2 (media criticism)
FIST, 85 St Agnes Pl, Kennington, London SE11 4BB UK $9

FIZZ 1509 Queen Anne Av N. #276, Seattle WA 98109 $3
FLATBED-Doug Jones, 2712 Emerson Av S. #3, Mpls MN 55408 $2 FILM
FLATLAND,Jim Martin, POB 2420, Ft Bragg CA 95437 $4 well-researched conspiracy magazine; bk catalog too
FLOURPOWER. From Basement Children Distro.
FOCUS. POB 17678 Clearwater FL 34622, Free, MUSIC
FOODBOX-307 Blueridge Rd, Carrboro NC 27510
FOOD NOT BOMBS, 3145 Geary #12, SF CA 94109
FOR THE CLERISY-Brant Kresovich, Riga Business School, Riga Technical University, Skolas 11, LV-1010, Riga, LATVIA. Trade only
FREAK SHOW, POB 36002, Regina, Sask, CANADA S4S 7H6 $2 or $1.50 + stamp
FREE THOUGHT, POB 432, Glen Echo MD 20812-0432. Free!
FRONTERA-Yvette Doss, 1509 Golden Gate #304, SF CA 94115 $4
FUCKTOOTH-Jen Angel, POB 43604, Cleveland OH 44143
FUGITIVE POPE-Raleigh Muns, 1178 Margaret Ln, Olivette MO 63132-2319 $1 library
FULL FRONTAL NUDITY-Kyle Rimkus, 20614 S.Driftwood, Frankfort IL 60423 $2
FUNCTION-Dawn, 20946 Bryant St #31, Canoga Park CA 91304
FUNDAMENTALISM IS NONSENSE-POB 37052, Phoenix AZ 85069. $3 *great*
FUNK N' GROOVE-3800 Cottonwood Dr, Blackhawk CA 94506 $3 ('70s)
FUNNY THAT WAY-Brava, 2180 Bryant, SF CA 94110 (queer teen)
FURTHER TOO-40 Darwin Ct, Barlow St, London SE17 1HR, U.K.
G IS FOR GIRL-715 Willey St #2, Morgantown WVA 26505
G.B. JONES book, GOC, 76 Greene St, NYC 10012 $9
GAY RAJ (lesbian)-1516 E.Pike #303, Seattle WA 98122 $3
GAYBEE-POB 343, Portland ME 04112-0343
GEARHEAD-Mike LaVella, POB 421219, SF CA 94142
GEE-ZUZ-297-810 W. Broadway, Vancouver BC V5Z 4C9 Canada. $2
GENETIC DISORDER-#13, POB 151362, San Diego CA 92175 $2 + 6 stamps (Pranks)
GERBIL, POB 10692, Rochester NY 14610 $3 queer
GERM OF YOUTH-1321 88th St SE, Oly WA
GERMS ZINES, 3410 First St, Riverside CA 92501
GET OFF MY WAGON-Sandy Stork & Steve Smith, POB 16041, Oakland CA 94610, $4
GET WHAT YOU WANT-Mary Anderson, 418 Duboce, SF CA 94117 (dyke comix)
GIANT ROBOT (Asian American culture)-Eric Nakamura, POB 2053 LA, CA 90064, $5,
GIFT IDEA-Seanna, POB 73308 Washington DC 20009, 35¢
GINGER'S HUT-Judy, 79 W St #4F, Worcester MA 01609, $2, stamps or trade, DYKE CULTURE
GINGER'S RAG-Ginger Vitus, 117 E Louisa #348, Seattle WA 98102
GIRL FIEND, POB 960, Hampshire College, Amherst MA 01002
GIRL GERMS-MollyAllison, POB 1473, Olympia, WA 98507
GIRL LUV-Olivia, 3233 Juliet St, Pgh PA 15213 $2
GIRL, INTERRUPTED-Witknee, 1024 Chautauqua, Pacific Palisades CA 90272 $2
GIRLFRENZY-Erica, POB 148 HOVE BN3 3DQ U.K., $4, UK
GIRLHERO-Megan Kelso, 4505 University Wy NE Box 536, Seattle WA 98105, $3
GIRLIE MAG-POB 7118, Ann Arbor MI 48107 $3
GLAMOUR GIRL-Merry Death, 6784 Stump Rd, Pipersville PA 18947 $1
GLOBAL MAIL (mail art)-POB 597996, Chicago IL 60659 $3
GLOBEHEAD (geography)-POB 10376, State College PA 16805 $2
GLUT-Jim Testa, 418 Gregory Ave, Weehawken NJ 07087, $2, MUSIC
GO METRIC, 30-28 34th St #4G, Astoria NY 11103
GO ON, FUCKER!-Donna Han, 2850 21st St, SF CA 94110 $3 comic
GODDESS JUICE-Andee, 656 W. Aldine #3, Chicago IL 60657
GODS & DOGS-Jim Blanchard, Beef Eye, Box 20321, Seattle WA 98102, $3.50, GRAPHICS
GOGGLEBOX-Jennifer, POB 250402, Columbia Station NYC NY 10025 $2
GOURMANDIZER-POB 582714, Mpls MN 55458-2714
GOZAR MY Love: a journal of car livin', POB 15071, Berkeley CA 94701-6071 $4
GRADE D BUT EDIBLE-Marko Krabaschaque, Rt 1 Box 304, Whitwell TN 37397
GREAT GOD PAN, 763 Capp, SF CA 94110 $1 Heino, etc
GRIND-Jason, Box 2830, Mesa AZ, 85214, $2, MUSIC
GROPE-Kirsten, POB 543, Arcata CA 95521 $1
GUERITA-POB 2115 MHC, S Hadley MA 01075
GUMPTION-Sheri Trudeau, POB 7564, Ann Arbor MI 48107, $1
GUNK, 16 Lord Stirling Rd, Basking Ridge NJ 07920
GUTSY-Megan, 3019 Norsewood Dr, Rowland Heights CA 91748, $1 + 2 stamps or trade
GYNEPHOBIA-Sarah Stanfield, 812 Duke St N, Rockville MD 20850
GYPSY LIZARD TOES, Box 475, Hampshire College, Amherst MA 01002
H2SO4-Jill Stauffer, POB 423354, San Francisco CA 94142
HABITUAL FREAK, 10896 Montego Dr, San Diego CA 92124
HAIRY LEGGED MAN-HATING FEMINIST GAZETTE-POB 2821, Iowa City IA 52244, $1.50
HANGING TREE-Jeff Levine, 1574 Hayes, SF CA 94117 $1
HARBINGER-39120 Argonaut Way #127, Fremont CA 94536 (class war)
HATE & HOPE-Rachel c/o Chris, 11 Harrison Pl, Newcastle, U.K.
HEADPRESS (shock)-POB 160, Stockport, Cheshire SK1 4ET, UK $7
HEARTATTACK Ebullition, POB 848, Goleta CA 93116 (805) 964-6111 $1 punk rock zine & record label
HEAVY ROTATION #6 + free tour diary-Bob Suren, POB 3204, Brandon FL 33509-3204 $1.50
HELIOPHOBE-Forrest, 6636 Fisher Rd, Dallas TX 75214
HELL AND DISNEYLAND-RO, 6320 N Magnolia St #35, Chicago IL 60660
HELL KITTY-31 Creek Ln, Mt Royal NJ 08061
HELLO KLITTY, Rebecca, 287 Sussex St, SF CA 94131 $1
HELP-Lance, 137 Tamarack #12, Henderson NV 89015
HER POSSE-PaulX, POB 15137, Boston MA 2215 queer
HEY THERE, BARBIE GIRL-POB 819, Stuyvesant Stn, NYC 10009 $2
HEY YOU KIDS!-Stephanie, 999C Edgewater Blvd #299, Foster City CA 94404
HIDING PLACE-Marie Koetje, 1659 Lamberton Lk Dr, Grand Rapids MI 49505, RIOT GRRRL
HIP MAMA (kid-raising), POB 9097, Oakland CA 94613 $4
HISTORY OF NIGHTMARES-Stacy Wakefield, 2225 1st Av #207A, Seattle WA 98121 $20 handmade book
HOBOS FROM HELL, POB 2497, Santa Cruz CA 95063 $8
HOLLYWOOD BOOK AND POSTER, 6349 Hollywood Blvd, Hollywood CA 90028 (213) 465-8764. video source
HOLY TITCLAMPS-Larry Bob, POB 590488, San Francisco CA 94159 queer source guides
HOMOCORE-Tom Jennings, World Power Systems, POB 77731, SF CA 94107, $2
HOMOTURE-POB 191781, San Francisco CA 94119-1781
HOS & PIRATES (ex-*Homotiller*)-from Claudia, POB 460695, San Francisco CA 94146-0695
HOT BUTTERED GEEK-Mike, 885 St Charles Dr, Thousand Oaks CA 91360
HOT LAVA MONSTER-61 Park Plaza #21, Daly City CA 94015
HOUSE O' PAIN, POB 120861, Nashville TN 37212 $2
HUGGY BEAR-c/o Catcall, 142B St Paul's Rd, Islington, London N12U, U.K.
HUMANS IN THE MUSHROOM FIELD, POB 66, 4068 Queensland, Australia
HUNGER STRIKE-121 Bookshop, 121 Railton Rd, London SE24 UK $2 (eating disorders)
HUNGRY FREAKS-POB 20835, Oakland CA 94620 $4
I AGAINST ME-Scott MacDonald, 10 Dahl St, Warren PA 16365
I KICKED A BOY-Leah Baldo, 6857 Compton Hgts Cir, Clifton VA 22024
I SCARE MYSELF, POB 426857, SF CA 94142 $2 grrrl
I STILL BELIEVE-Greye Pineda, POB 1595 Cooper Sta, NYC 10276
I'M NOT SHY I JUST HATE PEOPLE-Toad, Revolutionary Knitting Circle c/o Eden Stein, Suite 114, 1144 Sonoma Av, Santa Rosa CA 95405
I'VE WRITTEN A LETTER-John Sanchez, POB 0573, Chicago IL 60690 $2
ICON-Denise Ratliff, 4104 24th St #181, SF CA 94114, Free, DYKE CULTURE
IDIOT NATION-Steve, 6678 Washington 3W, University City, MO 63130
INDUSTRIAL NATION #10, 614 W.Belmont, Chicago IL 60657-4529 $3
INQUISITOR (media studies)-Daniel Drennan, POB 132, NYC 10024 $5
INSIGHT-John Livingstone, POB 51592, Kalamazoo MI 49005-1592 $4
INTERFACE, POB 1209, Chicago IL 60690 $3 "industrial"
INTERNATIONAL VIRUS, POB 313, Farmington MI 48332-0313 $3
INTERPOL-Matt Janovic, 3540 N. Tillotson #347, Muncie IN 47304 $2
INTERROBANG?!-Sharon, 3288 21st St #33, SF CA 94110
IRON FEATHER JRNL-Stevyn Prothero, POB 1905, Boulder CO 80306 $2
JABONI YOUTH-Alec Bemis, 9 Rockhagen Rd, Thornwood NY 10594, $1
JAPANCORE, POB 8511, Warwick RIU 02888
JIGSAW c/o K.R.S., 120 NE State #418, Olympia WA 98501
JJO, POB 624, Alameda CA 94501 $2
JUNK MAGNET-Nicholas Freeman, POB 11501, Berkeley CA 94712
JUST LIKE A GIRL, 120 NE State #181, Olympia WA 98501
JUXTAPOZ, 1303 Underwood, SF CA 94124 $4 slick alternative art 4-color magazine
KEEN-Martha, POB 2817, Gaithersburg MD 20886 $1
KEN KNABB CATALOG, POB 1044, Berkeley CA 94701
KETCHUP-Mad Am and God S, 3603 Sexton St, Alexandria VA 22309
KHORONZONE KIDS, POB 579 Station P, Toronto ONT Canada M5S 2T1 $4
KILL THE ROBOT-Jason. From Basement Children Distro.
KILLING TIMES, 11651 Norbourne Dr #316, Forest Park OH 45240-2162 $2
KINGFISH, POB 13641, Berkeley CA 94701
KISS MY PINEAPPLE-Beth Allen, 1538 Fulton #B, SF CA 94117 $1 (ukelele)
KITCHEN TABLE WOCPress, POB 908, Latham NY 12110 free catalog
KITTEN KORE, POB 66561, Los Angeles CA 90066
KNEE DEEP IN SHIT-Brian Davis, 588 South St, Windsor Ont, N9C 2W9 CANADA $1 (graphics)
KOMBAT, POB 20931, Indianapolis IN 46220 anarchist
KOMOTION, POB 410502, San Francisco CA 94141-0502
KRASH, 1202 E Pike #751, Seattle WA 98122 $2 music
LADIES HOMEWRECKING JRNL-Bianca, 2415 Fortham St, San Pablo CA 94806 $1
LAST PROM, 137 S. San Fernando Blvd #243, Burbank CA 91502
LEDGERMAIN-Edward Dean, POB 15637, Santa Fe NM 87508 $2
LEZZIE SMUT, POB 364 1027 Davie St, Vancouver BC Canada V6E 4L2 $6
LIAR-Danielle, 2452 N California, Chicago IL 60647
LIBEL-Jenna De Lorey, 4040 Olive Av, Sarasota FL 34231 $1 *one of the best*
LITTLE FREE PRESS-Ernest Mann, #113, 714 3rd St SE, Little Falls, MN 56305
LONDON Psychogeographical Association Newsletter, Box 15, 138 Kingsland High St, London E8 2NS UK $10
LOST I.D., 700 E. 9th St #20, NYC 10009. (212) 979-2477
LOVE AND RAGE, RAF, POB 3606, Oakland CA 94609-0606 (class war)
LUMPEN (Lumpen Times), 2558 W. Armitage Av, Chicago IL 60647 $3
LUMPY HEAD-Ann/Rachel, 424 Q St NW #3, Wash DC 20001
LUSY'S ANGRY-Rebecca, 287 Sussex, San Francisco CA 94131 $1
MAD PLANET-Sarah Dyer, 543 Van Duzer St, Staten Is NY 10304, $1
MAD WOMAN-Helena Perkins, 1514 Hilly Hil Dr, Champaign IL 61821, $2-FEMINIST
MADWORLD SURVIVAL GUIDE-Box 791377, New Orleans LA 70179 $1.50, RIOT GRRRL
MADWOMAN-Helena Perkins, 1514 Holly Hill, Champaign IL 61320 $2
MAILBOMB. POB 1312, Claremont CA 91711-1312 $2
MAMASITA-Bianca, 2415 Fordham St, San Pablo CA 94806 $1
MARIKA-Tesc Mod 3126, Olympia WA 98505
MAXIMUM ROCKNROLL-POB 460760, San Francisco CA 94146-0760 $2
MAYBE-Shosh Cohen, 2001 Haste #3, Berkeley CA 94704 $2
MCJOB-Julie Peasley, from AK Distribution
ME FIRST-2 Bloor St W Ste 100, Box 477, Toronto ON M4W 3E2, CANADA, $2
MEASLY ATTEMPT-POB 11333, Pleasanton CA 94588
MERCURY RISING-Howard Williams, San Francisco (bike messenger zine)
MICKEY ROURKE #5&6, POB 2284, Portland OR 97208
MOE MAGAZINE-Bob P, POB 320753, Tampa FL 33679
MOGWI-James, 240 Pacific Av, Staten Island NY 10312 (718) 967-2416 $1
MOLE-Jeff Bagato, POB 2482, Merrifield VA 22116 $3
MONS OF VENUS+, POB 22354 Memphis TN 38122 $2 (or: 3566 Walker Ave, Box 1203, Memphis TN 38111)
MOO JUICE-Britton Walters, 1573 N. Milwaukee Ave #444, Chicago IL 60622 $2
MOTORBOOTY, POB 7944, Ann Arbor MI 48107 $4 mag.
MOUSIE-Anna, Box 440478, Somerville MA 02144 $2
MOUTH (disability rights), 61 Brighton St, Rochester NY 14607-2656 $2
MS. 45, POB 2063, Fitzroy MDC, VI 3065, Australia $1 or 4 IRCs
MS. AMERICA-Sarah, POB 148421, Chicago IL 60614-8421
MUDFLAP, 666 Illinois, San Francisco CA 94107
MY LAST NERVE-Carol Petrucci & Cheri Haines, POB 3054 Madison, WI 53704, $1.50 or 6 stamps
NARCOLEPSY DREAMS-Jaime Crespo, POB 112, San Anselmo CA 94979
NEAR MISS (squatting)-Brendan, 156 Rivington St #1, NYC 10002 $1
NERDY GRRRL REVOLUTION-Nomy Lamm, 4221 Indian Pipe Loop, tesc P107, Olympia WA 98505 & Val Taylor, 3232 Mottman Rd SW #I-4, Olympia WA 98512
NEW ARCHAIC, POB 45133, Seattle WA 98145
NEWSPEAK (catalog & zine), 5 Steeple St, Providence RI 02903 $3
NO DUH, 2 Aldie St, #1 Allston MA 02134
NO IDEA #11 (CD), POB 14636, Gainesville FL 32604-4636 $5
NO LONGER A FANZINE-Joseph Gervasi, 142 Frankwood Av, Blackwood NJ 08012 $2
NO LONGER SILENT!-Eliza Blackweb, POB 3582 Tucson AZ 85722, $3
NO MEANS NO-1780 Wrightstown Rd, Newtown PA 18940 $1
NO ROOM 4 SQUARES-Max Ginnis, 5537 Old Ranch Rd, Sarasota FL 34241 $2
NOBODADDIES-POB 95094, Pittsburgh PA 15223-0694
NOBODY YOU KNOW-Jason McGraw, POB 42585, Portland OR 97242
NOISE-Bjorn, 1043 Grand #252, St Paul MN 55105-3002
NOISELESS-Ana Marie Cox, POB 14666, Berkeley CA 94712 $2 *a must*
NOT BORED-POB 3421 Wayland Square, Providence RI 02906
NOT EVEN-BOX 950 McIntosh Student Centre/3001 Broadway, NYC 10027
NOT YOUR BITCH-Christine Johnston, POB 2484, Denver CO 80201
NOTEBOOK-18839 Lansing St, Orlando FL 32833
NOTEVENZINE-Daisy Rooks, POB 18119, Washington DC 20036 $1
NOTHING DOING-Brandan Kearney, Box 591075, San Francisco CA 94159
NOTHING YOU'VE EVER HEARD OF-Dave Neeson, 1349 Fond Rd, Lyndhurst OH 04124
NOTTA BABE-1800 Floyd Av, Richmond VA 23220
NUTHING SACRED-Jay Sosnicki, POB 3516, Los Angeles CA 90078 $4
OBSCURE Publications-Jim Romenesko, POB 1334, Milwaukee WI 53201
OCHO Y MEDIA-POB 81332, San Diego CA 92138 $1
OFF OUR BACKS-OOB Collective, 2337 18th St NW, Basement Office, Washington DC 20009, $2.50
OFF THE DEEP END-Tim Cridland, POB 85874, Seattle WA 98145 $4
OHTAZINE, 1602 Lewalani Dr #204, Honolulu HI 96822 $2
ON THE RAG-OTR, PSC 3 Box 1024, APO AE 09021
ONE WAY MAILORDER-po box 6966, Gulfport MS 39506
ONGAKU OTAKU-Mason Jones, POB 170277, SF CA 94117 $4 Japanese music zine, in English
OOMPA! OOMPA!-89 Park Dr #4, Boston MA 02215
OPEN EYE, BM Open Eye, London WC1N 3XX, UK $5
ORDER A NEW WORLD, POB 10081, Oly WA 98502 $1
OUT DAMN SPOT-1016 Crispell, College at New Paltz, New Paltz NY 12561-2491
OUT OF BOUNDS, 957 N. Longfellow St, Arlington VA 22205 $3
OUT OF THE VORTEX-Joan & Sara, POB 4619, Gaithersburg MC 20885, $1
OUTHOUSE-Anna Christensen, POB 1040, La Mesa, CA 91944, $1

PADDLE BALL-Matthew, 22133 Mulholland Dr, Woodland Hills CA 91364

PANIC BUTTON-Ben Weasel, POB 66722, Chicago IL 60666-0727 $1

PANOPHOBIA-Jen & Sarah, POB 148097, Chicago IL 60614 $2

PAPERBACK JUKEBOX-Valerie Cashman: Northwest Music & Arts, 222 SE 16th, Portland OR 97214

PARANOIA (exposes)-POB 3570, Cranston RI 02910 $4

PASTY-Sarah-Katherine, 6201 15th Ave. NW #P-549, Seattle WA 98107 $2

PAWHOLES-Deborah & Karen, POB 81202, Pittsburgh PA 15217 $3 (a "Do-Me Feminist" Reader)

PEACE FACTORY, POB 7283, Alexandria VA 22307 booklet on urban guerrilla postering; catalog. Send $1

PENGUIN GIRL PRESS-Eden Stein, 1144 Sonoma Av #114, Santa Rosa CA 95405

PHALANX-Brian, 7100 E. Evans #329A, Denver CO 80224

PINTO-Sara Lorimer/Tina Herschelman, POB 2244, Oly WA 98507

PIXXIEBITCH-Zoe, RDL Box 37B, Montrose, PA 18801, $1

PLEASURABLE PIERCINGS-Wild Bill, 7 Garfield Ave, Hawthorne NJ 07506 (catalog)

PLOTZ-Barbara, POB 819 Stuyvesant Sta, NYC 10009 $1 ex-publisher of *Hey There, Barbie Girl!*

PMS-Rik, POB 2563, Cambrtidge MA 02238 $1

POCHO-Esteban Zul/Lalo Lopez, POB 40021, Berkeley CA 94704 or POB 63052, East LA, CA 90063 $2

POINT OF INTEREST-Jay, 1134 17th Av #302, Seattle WA 98122 $1

POKE-A-DOT-Marzy Quayzar, POB 42, Oroville WA 98844 $2

POOK, 10451 Mulhall #39, El Monte CA 91731 $2

POOR, THE BAD & THE ANGRY (class war)-POB 3305, Oakland CA 94609

POP TARTS-Revolutionary Knitting Circle c/o Eden Stein, Suite 114, 1144 Sonoma Av, Santa Rosa CA 95405

PORN FREE (tattoo issue)-POB 1365 Stuy Sta, NYC 10009

POUT-Meghan Lake, 251 Rollingwood Dr, N Kingsown RI 02852, 50¢ or trade

POWER CANDY-Ericka Bailie, 4127 Locust St #304, KC MO 64110

PR WATCH-John Stauber, 3318 Gregory St, Madison WI 53711 $2

PRESENTLY OUT OF PRODUCT-Ronni Tartlet, 3917A Castleman, St Louis MO 63110 or An Canteloupe, 1910 E. Marion, Seattle WA 98122

PREVAILING WINDS (watchdog)-POB 23511, Santa Barbara CA 93121 $5

PRINCESS-Diana Morrow, 151 First Ave #129, NY NY 10003 $4 good intv with Kahleen Hanna in #1

PRINCESS, 175 Fifth Ave #2416, NY NY 10010

PRIVACY (watchdog)-POB 28577, Providence RI 02908 $2

PROBABLE CAUSE-David Gold, 825 Surfside Blvd, Surfside FL 33154 $2

PROFANE EXISTENCE (anarcho-punk)-POB 8722, Mpls MN 55408 $2

PROVE IT-Alice Borealis, 2802 Parkview Terr, Baltimore MD 21214-3137 $1

PUCK-2336 Market, San Francisco CA 94114 $6 HUMOR

PULP-Katherine Valentine, POB 1856, Hollywood CA 90078

PUNK PLANET-Julia Cole, POB 1711, Hoboken NJ 07030

PUPIL-Val. Order from Basement Children Zine Distro.

PUPS-POB 510, Southwick MA 01077 $2

PUSSY CAT VISION-Lauren, 7014 Charles Ridge Rd, Balt MD 21204

PUSSY GRAZER-POB 20553 Tompkins Sq Sta, NYC 10009

PUSSYCAT MAGAZINE-Mark D, 39 Cedar Terrace Rd, Chapel Hill NC 27516 $2

PUSSYCAT-Melody, 11600 N 75th Ave #135, Peoria AZ 85345

Q-VALUE-David, 8450 Robinson, O.P. KS 66212

Q-ZINE-2336 Market St #14, San Francisco CA 94114

QUEENIE-Sarah Kate, 434 Woodlawn, St Louis MO 63119

QUEER NATION, POB 34773, Washington DC 20043

QUEERPUNK!, POB 1320 Stuyv Sta, NYC 10009

QUEERZINE EXPLOSION-Larry-Bob, BOX 591275, SF CA 94159-1275

QUIT WHINING-POB 2154, Mt Holyoke College, S Hadley MA 01075

R2D2 IS AN INDIE ROCKER-Jeff Czeka, 515 W Buffalo St, Ithaca NY 14850-4103 $2

RACCOON-Laurie Tull, 144 Browning Ln, Rosemont PA 19010

RACECAR MAGAZINE-Rae Sturtevant/Helen Williamson, POB 410010 SF CA 94141 $3

RAG-Erin, 379 Fox Pass, Hot Springs AR 71901

RAGE-POB 2962, Rapid City SD 57709, 25¢

RAGE-POB 17401, Worcester, MA 01601

RALLY 6-Holly Brown, POB 1457, Bental Centre, Vancouver BC CANADA V6C 2P7

RALPH-Box 505, 1288 Broughton, Vancouver BC CANADA V6G 285 free jazz-oriented sheet

RANTEX-POB 3458, Berkeley CA 94703

RED HANKY PANKY-Rachel House, 23 Whateley Rd, E.Dulwich SE22 9DA U.K.

RED PLANET-POB 3684, Oakland CA 94609-0684

REIGN OF TOADS-Kyle Silfer, POB 66047, Albany NY 12206 $4

RENEGADE GIRLZ-Zoe, RDI Box 378, Montrose PA 18801

REPTILES OF THE MIND-Kat, POB 10087, Knoxville TN 37939-0087 $1

RETICENCE & ANXIETY (dyke)-POB 2552, Austin TX 78768

REVEAL, POB 2611, Bloomington IN 17402-2611 $2

REVOLUTION RISING, POB 3843 LA CA 90078 $1

REX RESEARCH, POB 1258, Berkeley CA 94701-1258

RHYTHM OF THE RAIN, POB 1784, Olympia WA 98507-1784 $1

RIOT GEAR, POB 190176, San Francisco CA 94119-0176

RIOT GRRRL NYC, POB 188 Cooper Sq Station, NYC 10003

RIOT GRRRL, POB 7453, Arlington VA 22207

RIOT GRRRL, POB 11002, Wash DC 20008

RIOT GRRRL, 1800 Floyd Av, Richmond VA 23220

ROCK AGAINST SEXISM-POB 390643, Cambridge MA 02139 $2

ROCK CANDY-Marie, 1659 Lamberton Lk, Grand Rapids MI 49505 $1

ROCK FOR CHOICE, 8105 W 3rd St #1, Los Angeles CA 90048. They sell feminist stickers

ROCKRGRL-Carla DeSantis, 7 W 41st Ave #113, San Mateo CA 94403 $5

ROCTOBER-Jake Austen, 1507 E. 53rd St #617, Chicago IL 60615 (weird music)

ROESSIGER-Tim, 1E5 Desert Sky Rd, Tucson AZ 85737

ROUGE-Roger Evans, BM Rouge, London WC1N 3XX, UK. $6 (gender issues, etc

RUMP compilation, POB 18510, Denver CO 80218 $5

RUNT, POB 261, Merion PA 19066

RUTABAGA, POB 184, 48 Shattuck Square, Berkeley CA 94704

SANDBOX-Vid Jain/Sylvie Myerson, POB 150098, Brooklyn NY 11215 $5

SATANIC AFTERSCHOOL SPECIAL, POB 06101, Chicago IL 60606-0101

SCAREDY-CAT STALKER-Krista Garcia, 5585 NE Glisan #5, Portland OR 97213 $1

SCIENCE GEEK-Steve Spatucci, POB 8641, Trenton NJ 08650

SCRAM-Kim Cooper, POB 461626, Hollywood CA 90046-1626 $4

SCREAMING BETTY #1-3-POB 1007, Amherst MA 01004

SCREAMS FROM INSIDE-Carissa, POB 13044, Minn MN 55414

SECOND GUESS-Bob Conrad, POB 9382, Reno NV 89507 $2.50 (Tom Frank, *Baffler* interview)

SEVENTH STREET-Eden Stein, Penguin Girl Press, #114 1144 Sonoma Ave, Santa Rosa CA 95405

SHAG STAMP-Jane, POB 298, Sheffield S10 1YU, UK $3

SHAVED ANUS-c/o Paul, 26 Belgrave St, Brighton BN2 2NS, England

SHE (Asian film stars)-POB 969, Centralia IL 62801 $4

SHE'S THE BOSS-Andrea, 501 W Meetinghouse Rd, South Kent CT 06785 $1

SHELF LIFE-Sheryl, POB 91260, Santa Barbara CA 93190 $3 *recommended*

SHOCK CINEMA-Steve Puchalski, POB 518 Stuyv Sta, NYC 10009 $3

SHOCKING IMAGES-Mark Jason Murray, POB 7853, Citrus Hts, CA 95621 (film) $4

SIC-TEEN-Rev Norb, POB 11173, Green Bay WI 54305

SIMBA-Ms Vique Martin, 20 Brangwyn Way, Brighton, Sussex, BN1 8XA U.K.

SIMPLE LIVING NEWS-POB 1884, Jonesboro GA 30337

SINK FULL OF DISHES-POB 160122, St Louis MO 63116 $2

SIPAPU-Noel Peattie, 23311 Country Rd 88, Winters CA 95694 $4

SISTERSTRIKE-2940 SE Woodward, PDX OR 97202, $2 (women's self-defense)

SKINFLINT NEWS-POB 818, Palm Harbor FL 34683-5639

SLIGHT EXPRESSION-Leah Urbano, 679 Portola #210, SF CA 94127 $2

SLUDGE POND-Maria Knopp, 3419 Plaza Dr, State College PA 16801 $2

SLUG, 2120 S. 700 EA, Salt Lake City UT 84106

SLUMBER, POB 139, Cazadero CA 95421

SMACKS #5, Hey Grrrlz!, Box 364, 1027 Davie St, Vancouver BC Canada V6E 4L2 $2

SMACKS,SMART ASS-Shea'la, 107 Lindly Av, North Kingstown, RI 02852 $1

SMART LIKE EVE-Ann Carroll, 152 N. 33 St #C, Omaha NE 68131

SMELL MY FINGERS!-Lucky Pierre, POB 191152, Sacto CA 95819 $1

SMILE FOR ME-Ananda La Vita c/o Roberto La Vita, 149 Sullivan St #4C, NYC 10012 (212) 777-0449

SNAKE OIL-Bro. Randall, 6102 Mockingbird #374, Dallas TX 75214 $2

SNARLA-Miranda July, 301 Heller Dr #281, Santa Cruz CA 95062

SNIPEHUNT, POB 3975, Portland OR 97208 $10-4 issues

SNIPER'S NEST, POB 2351, Galveston TX 77553-2351

SOMETHING WEIRD, POB 33664, Seattle WA 98133 (206) 361-3759 $5 good video catalog

SOUR MASH, 361 60th St, Oakland CA 94168

SOURPUSS-Sara, 330 Ophelia St, Pittsburgh PA 15213

SPAWN OF SATAN-Joshua Doom, 640 E. 11th St #5E, NYC 10009 $3

SPEC-Matthew Jaffe, POB 40248, SF CA 94140 $3

SPECTRE #4, POB 474, Lexington KY 40585-0474 (Leilah Wendell) $5

SPEECHLESS-Megan, 2940 Childers, Santa Cruz CA 95062

SPEED KILLS-Scott Rutherford, POB 14561, Chicago IL 60614 $5

SPINSTERWITCH-Jenni Aquilina, 3354 Palm Aire Ct, Rochester Hills MI 48309 $2

SPIRALS UPWARD-Basil, 1210 Gregory Pl, Downers Grove IL 60515

SPLATTERSPLEEN-Amanda Maude Huron, POB 4061, St Paul MN 55104, $1

SPUN-Rudeboy, POB 40021, Eugene OR 97404

SPUNK, POB 1641, Tucson AZ 85702

SQUARE PEGS-Carrie, Equinox, 903 Pacific Av #207A, Santa Cruz CA 95060 queer

STALKER Miss B&K, POB 268173, Chicago IL 60626.

STICKY GREEN'S ZINE-Sticky Green, POB 27663 LA CA 90027, $2.50

STINKBOMB-Suzie, POB 3166, London E6 3TH, U.K.

STRAIN-2103 Coleman St, Olympia WA 98502

STRANGE FRUIT-POB 421872, San Francisco CA 94142-

STRANGE LOOKING EXILE-Robert Kirby, POB 300061, Mpls MN 55403

STRUCTURE (feminist)-Judy, 79 West St #415, Worcester MA 01609, $2,

STUMBLE-Renée Bessette, 59 Brentwood Ln, Fairport NY 14450, $2, music

STY ZINE #18-19, 300 N. Bryan, Bloomington IN 47408-4144 $3 for both

SUBWAY SISSY-Witknee, 17337 Tramonto #306, Pacific Palisades CA 90272 $1 distribution catalog

SUCK DON'T BLOW, POB 170214, SF CA 94117 $2 x-taboo

SUPERDOPE-Jay Hinman, 520 Frederick #33, SF CA 94117 $2 (music)

SURF CITY BLACK BANNER, POB 7691, Santa Cruz CA 95061 (class war)

SWEETHEART-Princess Robin, 6505 Esplanade #1, Playa Del Rey CA 90293

SWIVEL ACTION-Jason Pruitt, POB 40674, Portland OR 97240-0674

TABLETOP-Sue Tabletop, POB 10114, Baltimore MD 21285

TAKE BACK YOUR LIFE-Profane Existence Collective, POB 8722, Mipls MN 55408 (Free; WOMEN'S HEALTH CARE)

TALES OF BLARG, POB 4047, Berkeley CA 94704

TANTRUM, POB 190176, SF CA 94119-0176 $4

TEEN FAG-Gordon Gordon, POB 20204, Seattle WA 98122

TEENAGE BOMBSHELL-Katy Weselcouch, 6234 Wynmore Dr, Cicero NY 13039

TEENAGE WHORE BOOK, 1780 Wrightstown Rd, Newtown PA 18940

THAT GIRL-Kelli Wms, POB 170612, SF CA 94117

THE EMPIRE, 416 8TH Ave SE, Olympia WA 98501

THEE DATA BASE-The Data Collectiv, POB 1238, Glasgow G12 8AB, UK

THEORYSLUT-POB 426965, SF CA 94142, $3.50, THEORY

THORN-Kelly Martin, 2300 Market St, POB 23, SF CA 94114, $3.50, ACTIVISM

THREE THOUSAND EYES ARE WATCHING ME-Vicky Jedlicka, 102 E. 19th St #206, Mpls MN 55403

TIGHTWAD Gazette, RR1 Box 3570, Leeds ME 04263-9710

TOMBOY-Jo, 3375B Merrill Rd, Aptos CA 95003

TOMMY, 58 Schrader, SF CA 94117 $1

TOO FAR-Adrienne (Spitboy), POB 40185, Berkeley CA 94704-4185 $2

TOP?-Judy Ricardi, 79 West St #4F, Worcester MA 01609, $1 + stamps or trade

TOUCH YOURSELF-Kenmore Station-Box 15109, Boston MA 02215

TRANSIENT SONGS-Amber Gayle, 2225 1st Av #207A, Seattle WA 98121 $11

TRANSSISTERS, 4004 Troost Av, Kansas City MO 64110 $8

TROUBLEMAKER'S HANDBOOK, 7435 Michigan, Detroit MI 48210 $15

TURTLE WAX-Jen, POB 109, Chilton WI (from Gerll Distro)

TWB, $2 from 1780 Wrightstown Rd, Newtown PA 18940

TWENTY BUS-Kelli Williams POB 170612, SF CA 94117, 20¢ + stamp, BUSES

TWENTY-TWO FIRES, 4200 Pasadena Pl NE #2, Seattle, WA 98105-6064 $3 ppd guide to Washington zines

TWISTED TIMES (pranks), POB 271222, Concord CA 94527 $3

UBUIBI, 1333 GROVE, San Francisco CA 94117

UFO MUSEUM, 500 W. Cermak #504, Chicago IL 60616

UGLY MUG-Rachelle, 140 Harvard Av #321, Allston MA 02134 $2

UGLY, 410 E. Denny Way #224, Seattle WA 98122

UNMENTIONABLE, POB 7219, Santa Cruz CA 95061

UNSIGHTLY, 4758 Ward NE, Salem OR 97305 $2

UP YOURS-Sarah Kate, Box 25, 470 E Lockwood, St Louis MO 63119

VEGETARIAN CATS & DOGS (book), (800) 435-9610

VELOCITY-Beth Barnett, 7540 N Pennsylvania St, Indianapolis, IN, $1.35

VERBAL ABUSE-315 Park Av S Room 1611, NYC 10010

VERBOSLAMMED-Rebecca, POB 1113 Portland OR 97207, $1 women's culture

VERY VICKY-Meet Danny Ocean, POB 383286, Cambridge MA 02238, $3 enigmatic comic series

VIDEO WATCHDOG-Tim Lucas, POB 5238, Cincinnati OH 45205-0283 $6

VIVID-1664 FULTON ST, San Francisco, CA, 94117

VK, Mark Aaron, 2245 E. Colorado Blvd #104, Pasadena CA 91107-6921

WARPED REALITY-Andrea Feldman, POB 2515, Providence RI 02906 $3

WEEKLY WORLD CRUZ-Jim Jones, 244 Mission St, Santa Cruz CA $1

WEIRD FLOWER, POB 366, Sta B, Toronto ONT CANADA M5T 2W2 $5

WHAT'S THE BUZZ-Sara, 1118 Mission #E, SC 95060

WHEN SHE WAS GOOD-Jenny, 18309 W Anderson, Sand Springs OK 74063

WHERE DO YOU GO WHEN YOU DIE?-Star Seifertr, 317 17th Av SE, Oly WA 98501 $2 comic

WHOREZINE, 2300 Market #19, San Francisco CA 94114

WHY CAN'T I BE YOU?-Meg Z, 12119 Trailridge Dr, Potomac MD 20854 (teen)

WIG OUT-Girl Trouble, POB 44633, Tacoma WA 98444

WIGLET, 382 Wyandotte Av, Columbus OH 43202

WILDCAT, BM Cat, London WC1N 3XX, UK

WINGNUT-Wes Wallace, POB 603128, Providence RI 02906

WIVES TALES-Britton, POB 81332, San Diego CA 92138 $2

WOMAN'S CIRCLE-3102 Stamp Student Union, College Park MD 20742 $2

WOMEN'S MUSIC PLUS, 5210 Wayne, Chicago IL 60640 (send SASE)

WOMEN'S UNDERGROUND MUSIC DIRECTORY FOR NYC-Leah Huddleston, 56 Sterling Pl #3, Brooklyn NY 11217, $3 + 2 stamps, MUSIC

WOMYN'S Rap Sheet c/o Squat or Rot, POB 20691, NYC 10009

WOOLLYBUGGER-Jeff Fuccillo, POB 1832 Olympia, WA 98507, $2

WOOZY, POB 4434, Melbourne Uni, Parkville 3052 Australia $10 ppd

WORLD Domination Review-Larry Taylor, 5825 Balsam Rd, Madison WI 53711, $1

WORLD OF FANDOM, 2525 W. Knollwood, Tampa FL 33614-4334 $5

Y IS FOR YUCK-Camilla Camilla, POB 420424, SF CA 94142 $2 comic

YAWP (grrrl), POB 752723, Dallas TX 75275-2723 $2

YOUR FLESH-Peter Davis, POB 583264, Mpls MN 55458-3264 $4

YOUS-Andreas, 3019 Abell Av, Baltimore MD 21218 $1

YOUTH REVOLUTION c/o Riot Grrrl Press, POB 73308, Wash DC 20009

Z MAGAZINE, 18 Millfield, Boston MA 02115 $4 (political)

V/SEARCH Catalog RE/SEARCH

From V. Vale, former co-publisher of RE/Search

"A pantheon of alternative culture...The books offer a keyhole view of a carefully crafted world of the bizarre and function as road maps for trips past the boundaries of the mainstream."
–MIRABELLA

"From cinema to industrial music, feminism to fiction, each volume tours like an exotic travel guide..."–RAYGUN

"[RE/Search] mines the fringes of culture for material that breaks down barriers and reverses preconceptions...one of the most vital presses of the '90s"–WASHINGTON POST

"Obviously, the RE/Search editors are fascinated with society's fringe elements, and since most bikers also enjoy life on the edge, it's not surprising that we're gonna share some of the same interests as the fun-loving gang at RE/Search."
–IRON HORSE

"A consistent standard can be applied to RE/Search: you can extract first-rate information about and thoughts of worthy artists and activists that are not available elsewhere."
–BOSTON PHOENIX

"RE/Search noses out role models who show that you can be creative at any level against a society's control processes, myths and mental overlays that prevent people from expressing their individuality."–SAN FRANCISCO WEEKLY

"RE/Search makes a study of the extremes of human behavior –saluting individualism in an age of conformity."
–ADVOCATE

"RE/Search examines some of the most arcane fringes of subculture with a thoroughness usually found only in academia."–REFLEX MAGAZINE

♦ This book you are holding is the first volume of the *V/Search* series, a new publishing venture by V. Vale in San Francisco.
♦ For the past 20 years V. Vale has brought uncompromising, cutting-edge content and innovation to the staid, predictable world of publishing. While working at City Lights Bookstore, and with seed money from Allen Ginsberg and Lawrence Ferlinghetti, in late 1976 Vale began his first publication, the now legendary "zine" *Search & Destroy,* which advocated punk rock as an in-depth cultural revolt whose motto was (and continues to be) "DO IT YOURSELF (DIY)." The punk rock "lifestyle" and culture remain influential two decades later.
♦ In 1980, wishing to expand beyond punk rock culture, V. Vale founded *RE/Search*, was its original editor-in-chief/publisher, and remained co-publisher/co-editor for its duration. *RE/Search* has exerted a major cultural influence disproportionate to numbers sold. *Incredibly Strange Music* has changed the face of musical aesthetics, inspiring the "Cocktail Nation"; *Modern Primitives* inspired a massive tattoo/body piercing movement (still expanding); *Incredibly Strange Films* stimulated widespread interest in little-known/neglected films; *Angry Women* is used as a feminist text on many college campuses; *Industrial Culture Handbook* launched a movement of musicians such as Nine Inch Nails; *Freaks* stirred up interest in the lost arts of the circus sideshow; etc... And now, hopefully, *ZINES!* will inspire even more cultural subversion and creativity!

ZINES! Vol. One: *Incendiary Interviews with Independent Publishers*

In the past two decades a quiet revolution has gained force: over 50,000 "zines" (independent, not-for-profit self-publication) have emerged and spread—mostly through the mail, with little publicity. Flaunting off-beat interests, extreme personal revelations and social activism, zines directly counter the *pseudo-communication* and glossy lies of the mainstream media monopoly. These interviews with a dozen zine creators capture all the excitement associated with uncensored freedom of expression, while offering insight, inspiration and delight. Included are: *Beer Frame, Crap Hound, Fat Girl, Thrift SCORE, Bunny Hop, OUTPUNK, Housewife Turned Assassin, Meat Hook, X-Ray, Mystery Date* and more! 8½x11″, 184 pp, over 200 illustrations, quotations, zine directory, index. ISBN 0-9650469-0-7 **$18.99**

"Another incredibly strange manual of subversion from the visionary who brought you *Pranks!, Modern Primitives* and *Incredibly Strange Music*."–Jello Biafra

"Interviews outstanding, unusual publishers of 'zines' like *Beer Frame* and *Mystery Date*... will inspire the most passive couch potato to turn off the TV and start actively communicating."–Last Gasp Newsletter

LOOK FOR ZINES! Vol. Two
$15 postpaid special on orders received by Oct. 1, 1996 (save 35%)

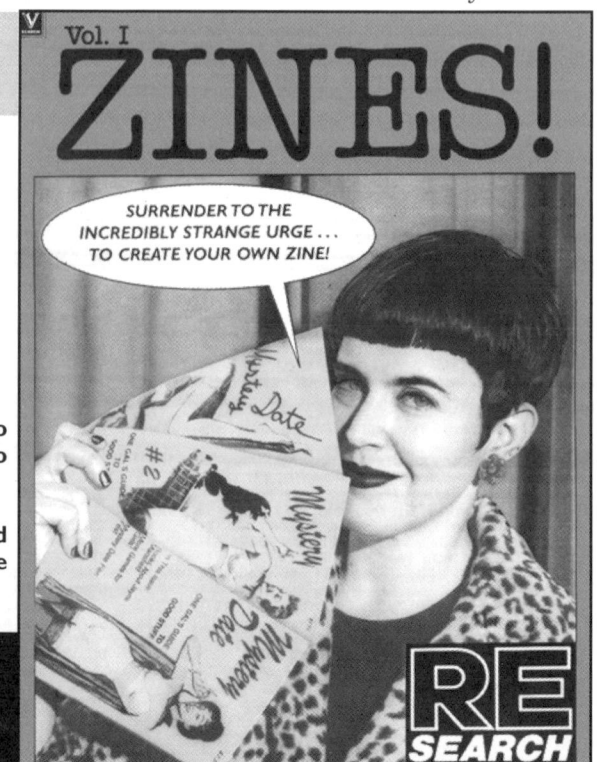

RE/SEARCH BACKLIST

#16: RE/Search Guide to Bodily Fluids by Paul Spinrad

Table of Contents: Mucus, Menstruation, Saliva, Sweat, Vomit, Urine, Flatus, Feces, Earwax & more
This guide sparks a radical rethinking of our relationship with our bodies and Nature, humorously (and seriously) spanning the gamut of everything you ever wanted to know about bodily functions and excreta. Each bodily function is discussed from a variety of viewpoints: scientific, anthropological, historical, mythological, sociological, and artistic. **Topics include:** constipation (such as its relationship to cornflakes and graham crackers!); the history and evolution of toilet paper; farting; urine (including little known facts about urinalysis); earwax; smegma as well as many other engrossing topics! 8½x11″, 148pp. **$15.99**

"A stunning new release... *The RE/Search Guide to Bodily Fluids* is a must buy."–BIKINI
"This is an important work that shouldn't be ignored, packed with fascinating facts on excreta."
–LOADED MAGAZINE

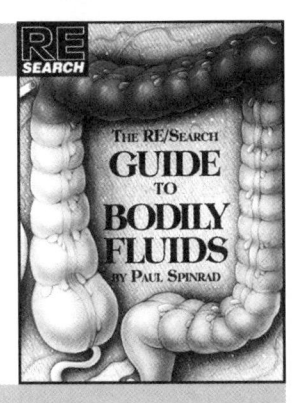

#15: Incredibly Strange Music, Vol. Two

A continuation of the territory investigated in Volume I. Interviews include: Jello Biafra (spoken word activist), Yma Sumac (Inca princess-diva), Bebe Barron (creator of the *Forbidden Planet* soundtrack), Juan Garcia Esquivel, Elisabeth Waldo (*Realm of the Incas*), organist and mystic Korla Pandit, Rusty Warren, Ken Nordine (*Word Jazz*), Robert Moog, plus obsessive collectors such as the Reverend Warren Debenham (10,000 comedy records). **Categories include:** Outer Space, exotica-ploitation, Brazilian psychedelic, singing truckdrivers, yodeling, sitar-rock, abstract female vocals, religious ventriloquism, moog, theremin, harmonica, and much more! 8½x11″, 220pp, over 200 photos & illustrations. **$17.99**

"RE/Search advances the case for individual reappropriation of this sonic diaspora where, in an uncharted space free from MTV pabulum, one can still toss some exotica on an 8-track, crank up the volume, and experience the eclectic sublime."–SF BAY GUARDIAN
"Fans of ambient music, acid jazz, ethno-techno, even industrial rock, will find the leap back to these genres an easy one to make."–ROLLING STONE

#14: Incredibly Strange Music, Vol. One

Incredibly Strange Music surveys the territory of neglected "garage sale" records (mostly from the '50s-'70s), spotlighting genres, artists and one-of-a-kind gems that will delight and surprise. **Genres examined include:** "easy listening," "exotica," and "celebrity" (massive categories in themselves) as well as more recordings by (singing) cops and (polka-playing) priests, undertakers, religious ventriloquists, astronauts, opera-singing parrots, beatnik and hippie records, and gospel by blind teenage girls with bouffant hairdos. Virtually every musical/lyrical boundary in the history of recorded sound has been breached; every sacred cow upturned. 8½x11″, 208 pp, over 200 photos. **$17.99**

"This book will change your life."–MIRABELLA
"Alfred Hitchcock's *Music to Be Murdered By* is just the tip of the iceberg. *Incredibly Strange Music*, a catalog of the wackiest discs ever made, goes where few audiophiles have ever gone."–ENTERTAINMENT WEEKLY
"... incredibly amazing... a must read for those interested in freeing themselves from contemporary artistic self-consciousness."–HIGH PERFORMANCE

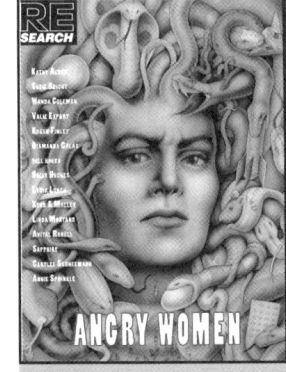

#13: Angry Women

16 cutting-edge performance artists discuss critical questions such as: How can revolutionary feminism encompass wild sex, humor, beauty, spirituality *plus* radical politics? How can a powerful movement for social change be *inclusionary*? A wide range of topics is discussed *passionately*. Armed with contempt for dogma, stereotype & cliche, these creative visionaries probe deeply into our social foundation of taboos, beliefs and totalitarian linguistic contradictions from whence spring (as well as thwart) our theories, imaginings, behavior and dreams. 8½x11″, 240 pp, 135 illustrations.**$18.99**

◆ Karen Finley ◆ Annie Sprinkle ◆ Diamanda Galás ◆ bell hooks ◆ Kathy Acker ◆ Avital Ronnell ◆ Lydia Lunch ◆ Sapphire ◆ Susie Bright ◆ Valie Export ◆ and many more...

"The view here is largely pro-sex, pro-porn, and pro-choice... Art and activism are inseparable from life and being. This is the 13th step, beyond AA's 12: a healing rage."–THE VILLAGE VOICE
"This book is a Bible... it hails the dawn of a new era–the era of an inclusive, fun, sexy feminism... Every interview contains brilliant moments of wisdom."–AMERICAN BOOK REVIEW

#12: Modern Primitives

An eye-opening, startling investigation of the undercover world of body modifications: tattooing, piercing and scarification. **Articles & interviews:** *Fakir Musafar* (Silicon Valley ad executive who has practiced every known body modification); *Genesis & Paula P-Orridge* describing numerous ritual scarifications and symbolic tattoos; *Ed Hardy* (editor of *Tattootime*); *Capt. Don Leslie; Jim Ward; Anton LaVey* (founder of the Church of Satan); *Lyle Tuttle; Raelyn Gallina* (women's piercer) & others talking about body practices that develop identity and philosophic awareness and explore sexual sensation. 22 interviews, 2 essays, quotations, sources/bibliography & index. 8½x11″, 212 pp, 279 photos and illustrations. **$17.99**

"All of the people interviewed are looking for something very simple: a way of fighting back at mass production consumer society that prizes standardization above all else. Through 'primitive' modifications, they are taking possession of the only thing that any of us will ever really own: our bodies."–WHOLE EARTH REVIEW
"The photographs and illustrations are both explicit and astounding... This is the ideal biker coffee table book, a conversation piece that provides fascinating food for thought."–IRON HORSE

RE/SEARCH BACKLIST

#11: Pranks!

A prank is a "trick, a mischievous act, a ludicrous act." Although not regarded as poetic or artistic acts, pranks constitute an art form and genre in themselves. Here pranksters such as Timothy Leary, Abbie Hoffman, Monte Cazazza, Jello Biafra, Earth First!, Joe Coleman, Karen Finley, John Waters and Henry Rollins (and more) challenge the sovereign authority of words, images & behavioral convention. This iconoclastic compendium will dazzle and delight all lovers of humor, satire and irony. 8½x11", 240 pp, 164 photos & illustrations. **$17.99**

"The definitive treatment of the subject, offering extensive interviews with 36 contemporary tricksters ... from the Underground's answer to Studs Terkel."—WASHINGTON POST

"Men never do evil so completely and cheerfully as when they do it from religious conviction."—Pascal

#10: Incredibly Strange Films

Spotlighting unhailed directors—*Herscell Gordon Lewis, Russ Meyer, Larry Cohen, Ray Dennis Steckler, Ted V. Mikels, Doris Wishman* and others—who have been critically consigned to the ghettos of gore and sexploitation films. In-depth interviews focus on philosophy, while anecdotes entertain as well as illuminate theory. 13 interviews, numerous essays, A-Z of film personalities, "Favorite Films" list, quotations, bibliography, filmography, film synopses, & index. 8½x11", 224 pp, 157 photos & illustrations. **$17.99**

"Flicks like these are subversive alternatives to the mind control propagated by the mainstream media."—IRON HORSE

"Whether discussing the ethics of sex and violence on the screen, film censorship, or their personal motivations ... the interviews are intelligent, enthusiastic and articulate."—SMALL PRESS

#8/9: J. G. Ballard

A comprehensive special on this supremely relevant writer, now famous for *Empire of the Sun* and *Day of Creation*. W.S. Burroughs described Ballard's novel *Love & Napalm: Export U.S.A.* (1972) as "profound and disquieting ... This book stirs sexual depths untouched by the hardest-core illustrated porn." 3 interviews, biography by David Pringle, fiction and non-fiction excerpts, essays, quotations, bibliography, sources, & index. 8½x11", 176 pp, 76 photos & illustrations by Ana Barrado, Ken Werner, Ed Ruscha, and others. **$14.99**

"The RE/Search to own if you must have just one ... the most detailed, probing and comprehensive study of Ballard on the market."—BOSTON PHOENIX

"Highly Recommended as both an introduction and a tribute to this remarkable writer."
—WASHINGTON POST

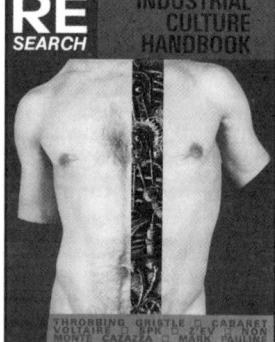

#6/7: Industrial Culture Handbook

Essential library reference guide to the deviant performance artists and musicians of the *Industrial Culture* movement: *Survival Research Laboratories, Throbbing Gristle, Cabaret Voltaire, SPK, Non, Monte Cazazza, Johanna Went, Sordide Sentimental, R&N,* and **Z'ev**. **Some topics discussed:** brain research, forbidden medical texts & films, creative crime & *interesting criminals*, modern warfare & weaponry, neglected gore films & their directors, psychotic lyrics in past pop songs, *art brut*, etc. 10 interviews, essays, quotations, chronologies, bibliographies, discographies, filmographies, sources, & index. 8½x11", 140 pp, 179 photos & illustrations. **$13.99**

"... focuses on post-punk 'industrial' performers whose work comprises a biting critique of contemporary culture ... the book lists alone are worth the price of admission!"—SMALL PRESS

#4/5: W.S. Burroughs, Brion Gysin, Throbbing Gristle

Interviews, scarce fiction, essays: this is a manual of ideas and insights. Strikingly designed, with rare photos, bibliographies, discographies, chronologies & illustrations. 7 interviews, essays, chronologies, bibliographies, discographies, sources. 8½x11", 100 pp, 58 photos & illustrations. **Topics discussed** include self-defense, biological warfare, the possibility of Revolution, utopias, assassination, con men and politicians, lost inventions, turning points in history, the JFK killing, dreams, ideal education, Hassan I Sabbah, nuclear weaponry, cloning, the cut-up theory (and practice) for producing prophetic writing, Moroccan trance music, the Dream Machine, art forgeries, Manson, the media control process, prostitution, the possibilities of video, etc. **$13.99**

"Interviews with pioneering cut-up artists William S. Burroughs, Brion Gysin and Throbbing Gristle ... proposes a ground-breaking, radical cultural agenda for the '80s and '90s."
—Jon Savage, LONDON OBSERVER

RE/SEARCH BACKLIST

RE/SEARCH #1, #2, #3—*the shocking tabloid issues*

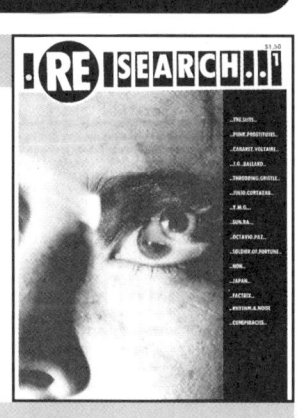

Deep into the heart of the Control Process. Preoccupation: Creativity & Survival, past, present & future. These are the early tabloid issues, 11x17", full of photos and innovative graphics.
◆ **#1:** J.G. Ballard ◆ Cabaret Voltaire ◆ Julio Cortazar ◆ Octavio Paz ◆ Sun Ra ◆ The Slits ◆ Robert K. Brown (editor *Soldier of Fortune*) ◆ Conspiracy Theory Guide ◆ Punk Prostitutes ◆ and more.
◆ **#2:** DNA ◆ James Blood Ulmer ◆ Z'ev ◆ Aboriginal Music ◆ West African Music Guide ◆ Surveillance Technology ◆ Monte Cazazza on poisons ◆ Diane Di Prima ◆ Seda ◆ German Electronic Music Chart ◆ Isabelle Eberhardt ◆ and more.
◆ **#3:** Fela ◆ New Brain Research ◆ The Rattlesnake Man ◆ Sordide Sentimental ◆ New Guinea ◆ Kathy Acker ◆ Sado-Masochism (interview with Pat Califia) ◆ Joe Dante ◆ Johanna Went ◆ SPK ◆ Flipper ◆ Physical Modification of Women (anticipated *Modern Primitives*) ◆ and more.
$8 each, full set for $20 WHILE THEY LAST!!

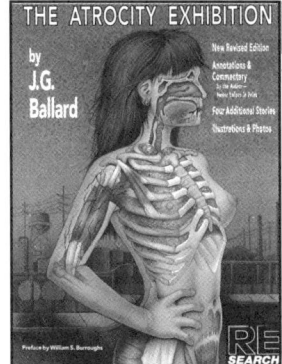

The Atrocity Exhibition *by J.G. Ballard*

A large-format, illustrated edition of this long out-of-print classic, widely regarded as Ballard's finest, most complex work. Withdrawn by E.P. Dutton after having been shredded by Doubleday, this outrageous work was finally printed in a small edition by Grove before lapsing out-of-print fifteen years ago. With four additional fiction pieces, extensive annotations (a book in themselves), disturbing photographs by Ana Barrado and dazzling, anatomically explicit medical illustrations by Pheobe Gloeckner. 8½x11", 136 pp. **$13.99**

SIGNED HARDBOUND: Limited edition of 300 signed by the author on acid-free paper. —almost gone! **$50.00**

"*The Atrocity Exhibition* is remarkably fresh. One does not read these narratives as one does other fiction . . . one enters them as a kind of ritual . . ."
–SAN FRANCISCO CHRONICLE

Freaks: We Who Are Not As Others *by Daniel P. Mannix*

Another long out-of-print classic book based on Mannix's personal acquaintance with sideshow stars such as the Alligator Man and the Monkey Woman. Read all about the notorious love affairs of midgets; the amazing story of the elephant boy; the unusual amours of Jolly Daisy, the fat woman; the famous pinhead who inspired Verdi's *Rigoletto*; the tragedy of Betty Lou Williams and her parasitic twin; the black midget, only 34 inches tall, who was happily married to a 264-pound wife; the human torso who could sew, crochet and type; and bizarre accounts of normal humans turned into freaks–either voluntarily or by evil design! 88 astounding photographs and additional material from the author's personal collection. 8½x11", 124 pp. **$13.99**

"RE/Search has provided us with a moving glimpse at the rarified world of physical deformity; a glimpse that ultimately succeeds in its goal of humanizing the inhuman, revealing the beauty that often lies behind the grotesque and in dramatically illustrating the triumph of the human spirit in the face of overwhelming debility."–SPECTRUM WEEKLY

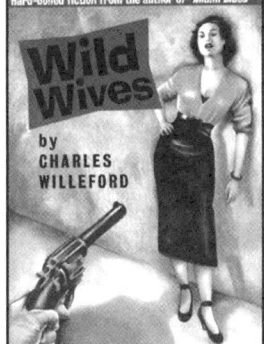

Wild Wives, *a novel by Charles Willeford*

A classic of hard-boiled fiction, Charles Willeford's *Wild Wives* is amoral, sexy, and brutal. Written in a sleazy San Francisco hotel in the early 1950's while on leave from the Army, Willeford creates a tale of deception featuring the crooked detective Jacob C. Blake and his nemesis–a beautiful, insane young woman who is the wife of a socially prominent San Francisco architect. Blake becomes entangled in a web of deceit, intrigue and multiple murders in this exciting period tale. 5x7", 108pp. **$10.99**

"Mr. Willeford never puts a foot wrong, and this is truly an entertainment to relish."–NEW YORKER

High Priest of California *a novel & play by Charles Willeford*

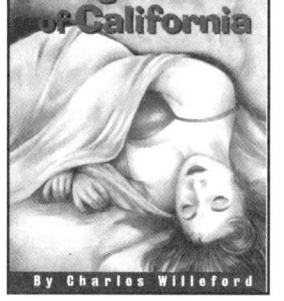

Russell Haxby is a ruthless used car salesman obsessed with manipulating and cavorting with a married woman. In this classic of Hard-boiled fiction, Charles Willeford crafts a wry, sardonic tale of hypocrisy, intrigue and lust. Set in San Francisco in the early fifties–every sentence masks innuendo, every detail hides a clue, and every used car sale is an outrageous con job. 5x7", 148 pp. **$10.99**
"A tempo so relentless, words practically fly off the page."–VILLAGE VOICE

> We must ever contradict ourselves; we must always welcome the opposite of our thought and scrutinize what worth this opposite may have . . . Every day you must make war against yourself."–Nietzsche

177

RE/SEARCH BACKLIST

The Confessions of Wanda von Sacher-Masoch

Finally available in English: the racy and riveting *Confessions of Wanda von Sacher-Masoch*—married for ten years to Leopold von Sacher-Masoch (author of *Venus in Furs* and many other novels) whose whip-and-fur bedroom games spawned the term "masochism." In this feminist classic from 100 years ago, Wanda was forced to play "sadistic" roles in Leopold's fantasies to ensure the survival of herself and her 3 children—games which called into question who was the Master and who the Slave. Besides being a compelling story of a woman's search for her own identity, strength and ultimately, complete independence, this is a true-life adventure story—an odyssey through many lands peopled by amazing characters. Underneath its unforgettable poetic imagery and almost unbearable emotional cataclysms reigns a woman's consistent unblinking investigation of the limits of morality and the deepest meanings of love. Translated by Marian Phillips, Caroline Hébert & V. Vale. 8½x11", 136 pp, photo-illustrated. **$13.99**

"Extravagantly designed in an illustrated, oversized edition that is a pleasure to hold. It is also exquisitely written, engaging and literary and turns our preconceptions upside down."–LA READER

The Torture Garden *by Octave Mirbeau*

This book was once described as the "most sickening work of art of the nineteenth century!" Long out of print, Octave Mirbeau's macabre classic (1899) features a corrupt Frenchman and an insatiably cruel Englishwoman who meet and then frequent a fantastic 19th century Chinese garden where torture is practiced as an art form. The fascinating, horrific narrative slithers deep into the human spirit, uncovering murderous proclivities and demented desires. Lavish, loving detail of description. Introduction, biography & bibliography. 8½x11", 120 pp, 21 photos. **$13.99**

"...sadistic spectacle as apocalyptic celebration of human potential...A work as chilling as it is seductive."–THE DAILY CALIFORNIAN

"Here is a novel that is hot with the fever of ecstatic, prohibited joys, as cruel as a thumbscrew and as luxuriant as an Oriental tapestry. This exotic story of Clara and her insatiable desire for the perverse and the forbidden has been hailed by the critics."—Charles Hanson Towne

"...daydreams in which sexual images are mixed nightmarishly with images of horror."—Ed. Wilson

Bob Flanagan, Super-Masochist

Bob Flanagan, 1952-1996, was born in New York City, grew up with Cystic Fibrosis (a genetically inherited, nearly-always fatal disease) and lived longer than any other person with CF. The physical pain of his childhood suffering was principally alleviated by masturbation, wherein pain and pleasure became linked, resulting in his lifelong practice of extreme masochism. In deeply confessional interviews, Bob details his sexual practices and his relationship with long-term partner and Mistress, Sheree Rose. He tells how frequent near-death encounters modified his concepts of gratification and abstinence, reward and punishment, and intensified his masochistic drive. Through his insider's perspective on the Sado-Masochistic community, we learn about branding, piercing, whipping, bondage and endurance trials. Includes photos by L.A. artist Sheree Rose. 8½x11", 128 pp, 125 photos & illustrations. **$14.99**

"...an eloquent tour through the psychic terrain of SM, discussing the most severe sexual diversions with the humorous detachment of a shy, clean living nerd. I came away from the book wanting to know this man."–DETAILS MAGAZINE

SPECIAL OFFERS

The Definitive S&M Library (Save $16!)

Offer includes *RE/Search #12: Modern Primitives* (see page 175 for description), *Bob Flanagan: Super-Masochist*, *The Confessions of Wanda von Sacher-Masoch*, and *The Torture Garden*.
Special Discount Offer: $52 ppd. Seamail/Canada: $58.

Incredibly Strange Music CDs and books! (Save $17)

Offer includes *Incredibly Strange Music* CDs Vol. One & Two and *Incredibly Strange Music* books Vol. One & Two.
Normally $75 with shipping and handling; NOW: all four items only $58 postpaid! (AIR Europe $79. AIR Australia/Japan $84

"I am not interested in policing the boundaries between nature and culture–quite the opposite, I am edified by the traffic. Indeed, I have always preferred the prospect of pregnancy with the embryo of another species."
–Donna Haraway, *Primitive Species*

RE/SEARCH MUSIC

Incredibly Strange Music, Vol. One (CD or cassette)

On this CD you will hear a rousing version of the "William Tell Overture" whistled by the blind virtuoso Fred Lowery; the '70s hit song "Up, Up and Away" played on an unbelievably out-of-tune sitar (with string arrangement); and a song off the LP *From Couch to Consultation* titled "The Will to Fail" (about the Freudian "failure complex"). Energizing instrumentals include a frenetic track performed on the xylophone ("Minute Merengue" by Harry Breuer) and a rapid-fire guitar version of "Flight of the Bumble Bee" by Buddy Merrill. Dean Elliott's "Lonesome Road" (everything *including* the kitchen sink) counterpoints Dave Harris's "Dinner Music for a Pack of Hungry Cannibals." The mind-boggling denouement is "A Cosmic Telephone Call," a 7-minute excursion into the trance-inducing world of Kali Bahlu, a self-styled guru, complete with atmospheric sitar accompaniment. Cheap enlightenment!
CD $16; cassette $7 special—buy one for your car & one for a friend!

Incredibly Strange Music, Vol. Two (CD only)

This CD includes an array of dynamic, inspirational obscurities such as Lucia Pamela's barnyard frenzy "Walking on the Moon"; instructional tracks on "How to Speak Hip" by Del Close and John Brent; selections from Ken Nordine, the father of *Word Jazz*; a stirring sitar rendition of "The Letter"; an exceptionally eerie version of "Join the Gospel Express" by singing doll Little Marcy; a mile-a-minute vibraphone instrumental by swingin' vibemaster Harry Breuer, "Bumble Bee Bolero"; "Terror" as sung by the exotica vocalist Bas Sheva, who died suddenly and tragically (the arrangement is by Les Baxter); Billy Mure's vivacious virtuoso version of "Chopsticks Guitar"; "The Letter" by the Nirvana Sitar and String Group; "The Mummy" by Rod McKuen *AKA* Bob McFadden & Dor; and more! Comes with extensive booklet of liner notes and full-color reproductions of the original LP covers.
CD **$16**

The Essential Perrey & Kingsley (CD)

Two fantastic, classic LPs (*The In Sound from Way Out* and *Kaleidoscopic Vibrations*) combined on one hard-to-find, currently out-of-print CD available exclusively from RE/Search mail orders. This CD contains *all* the tracks recorded by the Perrey-Kingsley duo, including such masterpieces as "Unidentified Flying Object," "The Little Man from Mars," "Cosmic Ballad," "Swan's Splashdown," "Countdown at 6," the hilarious "Barnyard in Orbit" (featuring animal sounds), "Spooks in Space," "Girl from Venus," "Electronic Can-Can," "Jungle Blues from Jupiter," "Computer in Love," "Visa to the Stars," "The Savers," "Umbrellas of Cherbourg," "Strangers in the Night" (anti-sentimental rendition), "One Note Samba-Spanish Flea," "Lover's Concerto," "Third Man Theme," "Fallout," "Baroque Hoedown," "Winchester Cathedral," "Carousel of the Planets," "Toy Balloons," "Moon River," "Mas Que Nada," and "Flight of the Bumble Bee." All the tracks were painstakingly spliced together by hand in a labor of love which will never be repeated! CD **$16**

Ken Nordine *Colors* (CD)

V/Search is proud to distribute Ken Nordine's *Colors:* a kaleidoscope of riotous sound and imagery. This pioneer of "Word Jazz" delivers "good lines" which are as smooth as water, inviting the listener to embark upon a musical fantasy evoking ethereal images of every poetic hue. Timeless in his spirit, Nordine stands alone as a speaker, writer and conceptualist. An essential addition to the musical library of the hip connoisseur. Far out! CD **$16**

Eden Ahbez *Eden's Island* (CD)

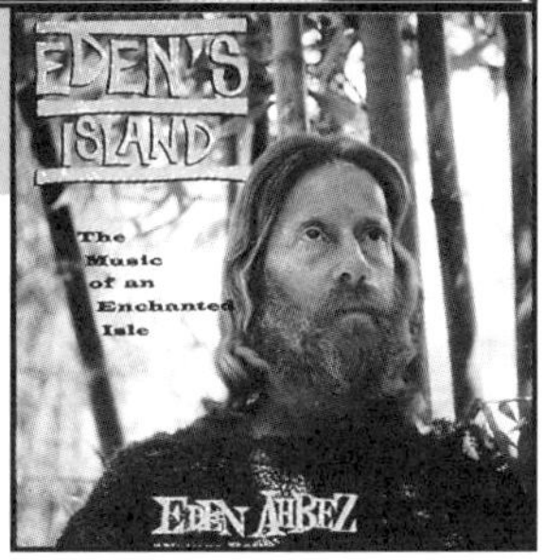

The most recent addition to V/Search's musical offerings. Released in 1960 on Del-Fi records, it "is a bizarre cross between exotica, '50's pop, and Beat-Era lyricism, whose genius was probably unintentional." In *Incredibly Strange Music,Vol. I*, Mickey McGowan calls *Eden's Island* "one of the truly strange masterpieces on record." This CD reissue contains additional tracks not on the original, rare LP. Limited edition. CD **$16**

SPECIAL OFFERS

The Complete V/Search CD Library! (Save $19)

Offer includes *Incredibly Strange Music* CDs Vol. One & Two; *The Essential Perrey & Kingsley*; Ken Nordine's *Colors*; and Eden Ahbez's *Eden's Island*.
IN SHORT—EVERYTHING ON THIS PAGE!! Normally $84 with shipping and handling; **NOW: all CDs only $65 postpaid! ($75 postpaid Air Mail Overseas)**

ALTERNATIVE OFFERS

Search & Destroy

Incendiary interviews, passionate photographs, art brutal. Corrosive minimalist documentation of the only youth rebellion of the seventies: punk rock (1977-78). The philosophy and culture, BEFORE the mass media takeover and inevitable cloning. Crammed with information and inspiration.

- ◆ **#1** Premiere issue. Crime, Nuns, Global Punk Survey.
- ◆ **#2** Devo, Clash, Ramones, Iggy Pop, Weirdos, Patti Smith, Vivienne Westwood, Avengers, Dils.
- ◆ **#3** Devo, Damned, Patti Smith, Avengers, Residents, TG, etc. **!OUT-OF-PRINT!**
- ◆ **#4** Iggy Pop, Dead Boys, Bobby Death, Jordan & the Ants, Mumps, Metal Urbain, Helen Wheels, Sham 69, Patti Smith.
- ◆ **#5** Sex Pistols, Nico, Screamers, Crisis, Suicide, Crime, Talking Heads, etc.
- ◆ **#6** Throbbing Gristle, Clash, Nico, Talking Heads, Pere Ubu, Nuns, UXA, Negative Trend, Mutants, Sleepers, Buzzcocks.
- ◆ **#7** John Waters, Devo, DNA, Cabaret Voltaire, Roky Erickson, Clash, Amos Poe, Mick Farren, Offs, Vermillion & more.
- ◆ **#8** Mutants, Dils, Cramps, Devo, Siouxsie, Chrome, Pere Ubu, Judy Nylon & Patti Palladin, Flesheaters, Offs, Weirdos, etc.
- ◆ **#9** Dead Kennedys, Rockabilly Rebels, X, Winston Tong, David Lynch, Television, Pere Ubu, DOA.
- ◆ **#10** J.G. Ballard, William S. Burroughs, Feederz, Plugz, X, Russ Meyer, Steve Jones, etc. Reprinted by Demand!
- ◆ **#11** The all-photo supplement. Black and White.

$5 each. Incomplete set: 1-2, 4-11: $39

Louder Faster Shorter
Punk Video by Mindaugis Bagdon

San Francisco, March 21, 1978. In the intense, original punk rock scene at the Mabuhay Gardens (the only club in town which would allow it), the AVENGERS, DILS, MUTANTS, SLEEPERS and UXA played a benefit for striking Kentucky coal miners ("Punks Against Oppression!"), raising $3,300. The check was actually mailed and received. One of the only surviving 16mm color documents of this short-lived era, LOUDER FASTER SHORTER captured the spirit and excitement of "punk rock" before revolt became mere style. The filmmaker was Mindaugis Bagdon, a member of *Search & Destroy*, the publication which chronicled and catalyzed the punk rock "youth culture" rebellion of the late '70s. "Exceptionally fine color photography, graphic design and editing" (S.F. International Film Festival review, 1980). 20 minute video in **US NTSC VHS Format** only. $15

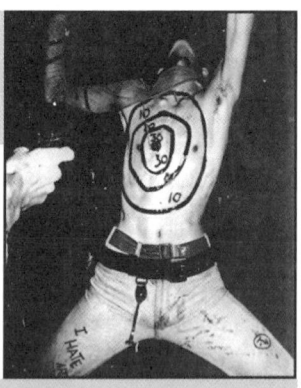

Tattoo Time *edited by Don Ed Hardy*

- ◆ **#1: NEW TRIBALISM** This classic issue features the new tribal tattooing renaissance started by Cliff Raven, Ed Hardy, Leo Zulueta & others. $10
- ◆ **#2: TATTOO MAGIC** This issue examines all facets of Magic & the Occult. Tattooed Charms, Sacred Calligraphy, Dragons, and Christian Tattoos. $10
- ◆ **#3: MUSIC & SEA TATTOOS** Deluxe double book issue with over 300 photos. Mermaids, pirates, fish, punk rock tattoos, etc. $15
- ◆ **#4: LIFE & DEATH** Deluxe double book issue with fantastic photos, examining trademarks, architectural and mechanical tattoos, the Eternal Spirit, a Tattoo Museum, plus the gamut of Death imagery. $15
- ◆ **#5: ART FROM THE HEART** All *NEW* issue that's bigger than ever before (128 pp) with hundreds of color photographs. Featuring in-depth articles on tattooers, contemporary tattooing in Samoa, a survey of the new weirdo monster tattoos, and much more! $20

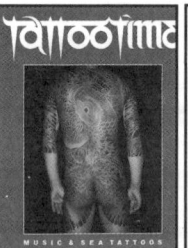

Halloween
by Ken Werner

A classic photo book. Startling shots from the "Mardi Gras of the West," San Francisco's *adult* Halloween festivities in the Castro district. Beautiful 9x12" hardback bound in black boards. 72 pp. Black glossy paper stock. This shocking hardcover photo book is an absolute steal at this price; when stocks are exhausted that will be it! $11

Sidetripping
by Charles Gatewood

Unforgettable, deviant fringe photographs by Charles Gatewood. Deep focus commentary by William S. Burroughs. A classic photo book, long out of print. Available here in a *limited offering*, as-is condition. As intense as Larry Clark's *Tulsa*, and equally as rare. 9x12". Warning: *perfume de molde*. For persons possessing an iron constitution and a steel stomach. **Only $10 while they last!**

MORE SPECIAL DISCOUNTS

Just RE/Search Library: (Save $30!) All RE/Search serials

Offer includes the RE/Search #1, 2 & 3 tabloids, #4/5: Burroughs/Gysin/ Throbbing Gristle, #6/7: Industrial Culture Handbook, #8/9: J.G. Ballard, #10: Incredibly Strange Films, #11: Pranks!, #12: Modern Primitives, #13: Angry Women, #14: Incredibly Strange Music, Vol. 1, #15: Incredibly Strange Music, Vol. 2, Bob Flanagan: Super-Masochist, and #16: RE/Search Guide to Bodily Fluids by Paul Spinrad.
Special Discount Offer Only: $178 ppd. Seamail/Canada: $190.

The Classic RE/Search Library: (Save $19!) All RE/Search classic reprints

Offer includes *Freaks: We Who Are Not As Others*, *The Torture Garden*, *The Atrocity Exhibition*, *The Confessions of Wanda von Sacher-Masoch*, *High Priest of California* and *Wild Wives*.
Special Discount Offer: $68 ppd. Seamail/Canada: $74.

The Complete Library: (Save $71!)

Includes all issues of RE/Search (both offers above), PLUS the first issue of V/Search AND all available issues of Search & Destroy (1-2, 4-11)
Special Discount Offer Only: $290 ppd. Seamail/Canada: $320.

Incredibly Strange Library: (Save $11!)

Includes Incredibly Strange Music Vol. One, ISM Vol. Two, Incredibly Strange Films. Special Discount Offer Only: $49 ppd. Seamail/Canada: $55.

Subscriptions to V/Search

You will receive the next three books published by V/Search, either our numbered interview format serials or WHATEVER! **$40.** Overseas/Canada: **$50.** *Sorry no library or university subscriptions. Libraries and universities please place individual orders from this catalog.*
SUBSCRIPTIONS SENT SURFACE MAIL ONLY! NO AIRMAIL.

ORDERING INFORMATION

MAIL: V/SEARCH Publications
20 ROMOLO #B
SAN FRANCISCO, CA 94133

OR

PHONE: Orders may be placed Monday through Friday: 10 AM to 6 PM PST
PH (415) 362-1465, FAX (415) 362 0742

Cash, Check or Money Order Payable to V/Search Publications OR Charge to Credit Card: VISA or MASTERCARD Only

SHIPPING & HANDLING CHARGES

DOMESTIC CUSTOMERS: first item $4; add $1 per additional item; for priority mail add $1 per order.
INTERNATIONAL CUSTOMERS: SEAMAIL: first item $6; add $2 per each additional item; **AIRMAIL:** first item $15; add $12 per additional item.

PAYMENT IN U.S. DOLLARS ONLY
ATTENTION CANADIAN CUSTOMERS: We *do not* accept personal checks even from a U.S. dollar account! Send Cash or International Money Orders Only! (available from the post office)

TITLE	#	TOTAL
SUBTOTAL		
CA residents add 8½% sales tax		
Shipping and handling (see above)		
TOTAL		

SAVE YOUR INDEX! (SEE BACK OF THIS PAGE) PHOTOCOPY THIS FORM OR JUST WRITE THE INFORMATION ON A SEPARATE SHEET!!!
HAVE YOU ORDERED FROM US BEFORE?
YES   NO circle one

NAME

ADDRESS

CITY, STATE, ZIP

VISA/MASTERCARD #:

EXP DATE:

SIGNATURE:

SEND SASE FOR CATALOG (or 4 IRCs for OVERSEAS)

DO YOU KNOW SOMEONE WHO WOULD LIKE TO RECEIVE OUR CATALOG?

NAME

ADDRESS

CITY, STATE, ZIP

index

1001 Ways to Make Love 47
15 minutes of fame 42
23 Envelope 151
4 Big Girls 137
4AD Records 151
666 Cold Remedy 23
8-Track Mind 14

◆ AB ◆

AK Distribution 106-113
Ackerman, Forrest J. 158
Acorn Books 91
Activism 53
Addams, Charles 41
Advertising 10, 25-26, 28, 31, 35, 41, 43, 47, 49, 65, 90, 108-109, 120
Airborne, Max 130-149
Alien Sex Fiend 62
Almond, Marc 62
Alpha Blue Archives 92-93
Alt.zines 7, 102
Alternative Television Access 43
Alternative Tentacles 108, 124
American Cemetery 33
American Disabilities Act 141
American Dream 133
American Me 57
American Revolution 156
American Woman's Cookbook 98
Amps, 53
Anarchists 157, 159
Anderson, Margaret 157
Answer Me! 109, 112
Art Chantry 44
Atomic Books 102
Attoxico 58
Autonomy 95
Backlash 119
Bad Religion 58, 85
Banderas, Antonio 57
Bartlett, Johnny 11, 13, 103
Bauhaus 62
Bay Times 132
Beatitude 158
Beer Frame 22-33
Ben Is Dead 7, 109, 151-152
Bennett, John M. 81
Berkman, Alexander 157
Beyond the Looking-Glass: America's Beauty Culture 94
Bicentennial 16, 19, 21
Bikini Girl 95-96
Bikini Kill 53-55, 58, 64, 70, 117
Bikini style underwear 21
Billboard 122
Binky 151-153
Black Sparrow Press 76, 82
Blake, William 157
Blast 157
Boggs, J.S.G. 26-27
Bonomo Original Hollywood Success Course 98
Bonomo, Joe 98
Borealis, Alice 80
Bowles, Paul 76
Bowling 22
Boy With a Knife 104
Boys Beware 92, 104
Bra-less tops 21
Bracero programs 52
Brady Bunch 16

Brand loyalty 30
Brannock Device 22-24
Brannock, Charles 23
Brat Attack 132
Bratmobile 70
Breedlove, Lynn 71
Brethren of the Free Spirit 155
Breton, André 157
Brewer's Dictionary of Phrase and Fable 45
Brewton, Johnny 74-87
Bride's Primer, The 93
Bright, Susie 81
Brink, Bruce 78
Broom 157
Brotz, Lisa 130-149
Brown, Tina 25
Bukowski, Charles 74, 76, 78, 81
Bulletin of the Opposition 158
Bunnyhop 7, 150-154

◆ CD ◆

Burroughs, William S. 76
Cage, John 74
Caifanes 58
Calter, Carey 80
Capitalism 24
Carmichael, Starch 78
Carroll, Jim 81
Casper Spook 54
Catcall Retaliation Ideas 66
Ceaucescu, Nicolae 159
Censorship 46, 49, 103, 111-113, 124, 153
Chain stores 113
Chambers, Marilyn 77
Cher 69
Cherkovski, Neeli 74, 81
Chicano Moratorium 52
Childish, Billy 81
Chomsky, Noam 111
Chumbawamba 42-43, 47
Circle of Friends, A 138
Circulation 109
Cisneros, Sandra 57
Clam jerky 23-24
Classism 64
Clowns 42, 45
Coca Cola 27
Cocteau, Jean 68
Cohn, Norman 155-156, 159
Coleman, Wanda 76
Collins, Patricia 80
Collision, R. 43, 47
Coming out 114
Commercial culture 103
Common Sense 156
Connors, Chuck 92
Consumer culture 22-23
Consumerism 26-27, 72
Contact 157
Cooper-Hewitt Museum 82
Coppe, Abiezer 156
Corned mutton 23, 29
Corp. for Public Broadcasting 159
Cox, Ana Marie 17
Craig, Jenny 133, 141
Crap Hound 34-49
Creamy Head 23, 29
Creeley 76
Cromwell, Oliver 155
Crown for Athena 53
Crucifix in a Deathhand 76

Crush On You 95
Dada 155, 157
Dali, Salvador 150
Dao, Bei 159
Dark Shadows 88
Darnton, Robert 156
Dead Boys 95
Dead fads 16
Deathcare business 33
Debord, Guy 154
Decline and Fall of Western Civilization 85
Demographics 25-26
Depression, The 158
Desert Moon 110
Desktop publishing 106-107, 110
Desperado 57
Devils 45
Devra 130-149
Dickies 78
Diet Myth 133
Distribution 107, 109-110, 113
Do-It-Yourself (DIY) 43, 55, 71, 86, 110, 111-112
Dogma Munditas 58
Don't Be a Dope 98
Dover Books 44
Duchamp, Marcel 26

◆ EF ◆

Eating disorders 68-70
Economics of oppression 72
Economics of zines 110
Economy 26, 61
Eden 21
Edison, Thomas 157
Education 61
El Mariachi 57
Empirismo 58
English Revolution 155-156
Epicenter 112, 114, 127
Epitaph 108
Equalism 69
Esquire 98, 133
Esquire's Handbook for Hosts 98
Exciting Sounds of Model Road Racing 103
Excuse 17, 54
Exoticism 126
Exploration 159
F.Y.P. 54
Factsheet Five 7, 82, 109, 111, 113, 159
Family Circus 153
Fantagraphics 152
Fat Girl 130-149
Fat Lip Readers Theater 137
FAT!SO? 132, 136, 147
Feminist Dictionary, A 69
Fifth Estate 110
Film Threat 103
Filth 43, 47
Fine Print 110
Firefox Enterprises catalog 31
Flares 21
Flores Magon, Ricardo and Antonio 157
Folsom Street Fair 120
Fondled, The 54
Forster, Russ 14
Franciscan Starburst 96
Frederick's of Hollywood 98
"Free to Fight" 64, 66

French Revolution 156
French, Renée 152
Friedman, Seth 82
Frigid Fluid company 33
Fugazi 71
Fugs 47
Fuller, Buckminster 74

◆ GHI ◆

Gacy, John Wayne 84
Gay community 120-121, 123-125, 129
Genderism 69
Genet, Jean 91
Gig 15
Ginoli, Jon 121-122
Goad, Jim 8
God Is My Co-Pilot 118
Goldman, Emma 157
Gomez, Jewelle 146
Good Enough to Eat 53
Good Man Is Hard To Find, A 91
Good Vibrations 143
Goodwill 11, 16
Graboyes, Judy 130-149
Graham, Marcus 157
Grand Royal 111
Green Day 121
Grit Bath 152
Groening, Matt 151-153
Guerrilla Girls 69
Gunderloy, Mike 82
Gus 151
Gutenberg, Johann 155, 159
Hagen, Nina 62
Hairspray 138
Hanna, Kathleen 58, 70, 117
Harlow, Jean 69, 101
Haskell, Burnette G. 157
Heap, Jane 157
Heathers 120
Heavens to Betsy 54
Hebrew printing 156
Hefner, Hugh 154
Hemingway, Ernest 157
Hemp 46-47
Hernandez brothers 78-79, 85
Hernandez, Jaime 82
Hey There, Barbie Girl! 153
High Weirdness By Mail 90
Hine, Thomas 27
Hoff, Al 6-21
Holifield, Dave 78
Home economics books 92, 93
Homeless 54
Homocore Chicago 127
Homocore Detroit 127
Homophobia 124, 126
Hooks, bell 111
Hot Pants 21
Housewife Turned Assassin 50-67
Huasipungo 58
Hydrox 24, 27
"I Love You This Much!" statues 15
I'm So Fucking Beautiful 67, 136, 147
Ice beer 27
Idler 110
Image bombardment 120
Immigration 56
Impressions of Africa 158
Inconspicuous consumption 22, 24,

26, 32
Incredibly Strange Music 11
Incredibly True Adventures of Two Girls in Love 137
Independent bookstores 113
Internationale Situationniste 158
Internet 6-7, 18, 102, 107-108
Irony 15, 19, 31
Irony victim 15

◆JK◆

J, Laura 130-149
J. Paul Getty Library 82
Jigsaw 70
Jingsheng, Wei 159
Johnson, Ray 81
Jolas, Eugene 157
Joy Division 62
Joyce, James 157
Kanaan, Ramsey 106-113
Kandykorn Jackhammer 78, 82
Kaufman, Bob 82
Keane 15, 19
Kennedy, Lee 136
King, Mike 47
Kinko's 36, 111, 113
Klimt, Gustav 150
Kohler, Francis 77, 83
Kraut Juice 23, 29
Kupferberg, Tuli 47

◆LM◆

L.A. Weekly 54, 70
La Cage Aux Folles 128
Lake, Ricki 138, 146
Lamm, Nomy 67
Leary, Timothy 81
Lee, Stan 78
Lesbians Come Out of the Class Closet 133
Letter U and the Number 2, The 43
Letterpress printing 158
Lewis, Wyndham 157
Liberace 92
Linquistics 69, 70, 126
Little Review 157
Little Richard 102
Locus Solus 158
Log-rolling 20
Lois 66
Lolita 91
Los Crudos 57
Lucas, George 154
Lucid Nation 53
Lujon Press 76
Lukas, Paul 22-33
M&Ms 25
Macdonald, Dwight 158
Mad Magazine 17, 76
Magnet program 51, 60
Mail 90
Mail art 80
Mainstream media 28, 31-32, 59, 62-63, 103, 107-108, 111, 113, 123, 128-129
Maldita Vecindad 58
Mama Cass 144
Manufacturing Consent 111
Markowicz, Bertha 130-149
Marr, John 20, 88, 103
Marriage of Heaven and Hell 157
Martinez, Ruben 57
Masacre 58, 68
Mason, James 91
Matador Records 108
Maximum Rock'n'Roll 109-110, 114, 117, 125-128
McDonald, Barbara 130-149
McDonalds 37
McMemories 37, 40
Meat Hook 68-73
Melmac 9
Menstruation 92, 94, 96, 99
Mexican community 52
Mexican immigrants 50
Mexican stereotypes 52, 56-57
Mi Familia 57
Micheline, Jack 74
Mickey Mouse 153
Miller, April 130-149
Mimeograph 111, 157-159

Miss Manners 102
Money Man 27
Monroe, Marilyn 69
Moreno, Rita 57
Morrissey 129
Mother Earth and Man! 157
Mother's Book 99
Movable type 159
Ms .45 102
MTV 18, 111
Multi-subculturalism 118, 122
Murder Can Be Fun 7, 88
Muriel's Wedding 138
Murphys, G.C. 17
Museum of Bad Art 15
Mystery Date 88-105
Nabokov, Vladimir 91

◆NO◆

Naked Eye 113
National Endowments for the Arts and Humanities 159
Necessary Illusions 111
Negativland 43, 153
Neuman, Gary 62
New Wave 95
New York Magazine 32
New York Press 32
New York Times 17, 23, 111, 159
New Yorker 25
Newsweek 37
Nine Inch Nails 62
No Comprende 43, 47
No Poetry 81
No Wave New York 118
Noise 54
Noiseless 17
Norb, Reverend 126
Norte, Marisela 57
Nosedive! 47
Nostalgia 24
O'Connor, Flannery 91
O'Neill, Dan 153
O'Neill, Eugene 91
Odonian Press 111
Olmos, Edward James 57
On Our Backs 144
Option 103
Oreo cookies 24, 27
Osmond, Donny and Marie 95
Out 127
Outpunk 114-129
Outsider, The 76
OutWrite 136
Owen, William, C. 157

◆PQ◆

Package design 25, 30
Paine, Thomas 106, 111, 156
Pajama Game, The 138
Pale Fire 91
Panic Button 110
Pansy Division 121-122, 125, 128
Paper 46, 76, 82-83, 153
Paper size 110
Partisan Review 158
PBS 76
Peezlee, Julee 14, 81, 84
People magazine 19, 40
Pepsi 27
Peril, Lynn 9, 11, 13, 20, 88-105
Perry, Mark 111
Perutz, Kathrin 94
Pettibon, Raymond 153
Pickers 12
Pink Slip 92
Platinum blonds 101
Playboy 153-154
Pneumatic Press 78
Pocari Sweat 23
Poetic Justice 58
Politics 158
Pollock, Jackson 76
Polyester 21
Pop culture 19, 94
Pop, Iggy 95
Pound, Ezra 157
Prejudice 56, 61
Presley, Elvis 7

Printing press 155
Product design 29
Production 109
Products 22
Propaganda 35, 37, 43, 93, 98, 101
Prostitution 123
Protestant Reformation 155
Psychic Sparkplug 82
Public Enemy 128, 151
Punk 57, 66, 70, 85-86, 95, 103, 110, 114-129, 144
Punk Rock Spectacular 95
Punk zines 95
Pursuit of The Millennium 155
Pyrotechnic needs 31
Q-TIP 127
Queer band definition 118-119, 126
Queercore 114-129
Queercore influences 117, 124-125
Race 72

◆RS◆

Racism 60, 64, 126
Radiance 136
Ranaldo, Lee 153
Ranters 155-156
RAW 76
Ray, Man 157
RE/Search Guide to Bodily Fluids, The 130
Reed, John 157
Regeneración 157
Ren and Stimpy 153
Repatriation 52
Revolution from Within 72
Revolution Rising 50, 53-55, 58, 62-64, 66, 68, 73
Riding in Cars With Boys 100
Riot Grrrl 17, 50, 53-56, 58-59, 62-64, 66, 69-73, 117, 124
Riot Grrrl bands 18, 71
Riot Grrrl zines 17-18, 70
Rivera, Margo Mercedes 130-149
Robson, Seth 150-154
Rolling Stone 28, 47
Rolling Stones 128
Ronald McDonald 35, 41, 43
Roosevelt, Eleanor 67
Roussel, Raymond 158
Rump Parliament 143
S.F. Art Institute 80, 115
S.U.N.Y. at Buffalo 82
Salvation Army 6, 11
Samizdat 106, 159
Sanford and Son 10, 13
Sassy 17
Scholastic Book Club 91
Science-fiction fanzines 158
Secret Service 26
See Hear 95
See Saw 54
Self-defense 63-64, 66
Self-salvation 155
Sergio 52
Serial Mom 102
Sesame Street 9
Seven Year Bitch 71
Sex education 36, 92, 96, 99-100
Sex Pistols 111
Sexism 111, 124, 126
Shargel, Delia 77
Shaw, Jim 15
Shields, Brooke 43
Shifting ahead 12
Shock value 102, 125-128
Show Girls 102
Simpsons, The 152
Siouxsie and the Banshees 62
Sister George 128
Sisters of Mercy 62
Situationists 155, 158
Skywalker, Luke 124
Slug Fest 43
Sniffin' Glue 95, 111
Snipehunt 47
So You Want to Raise a Boy? 99
Solo, Dan X. 44
Solo, Sondra 130-149
Sonic Youth 53
Soupault, Philippe 157
Spam 29
Spandex 21
Sperry, Chuck 82

Spheeris, Penelope 85
Spiegelman, Art 76
Spitboy 54
Spy magazine 20
St. Vincent de Paul 11
Sta-Prest 119, 128
Steinem, Gloria 72
Still Life 54
Strecker, Candi 11, 13, 20, 93
Strictly Ballroom 138
Subscriptions 109
Suede 128
Suicidal Tendencies 85
Sumac, Yma 86
Surrealists 157-158
Switched at Birth 54
Synthetic Fabrics 20-21
Tampons 94-95

◆TU◆

Tannen, Deborah 70
Taxidermy 30
Team Dresch 128
Tejaratchi, Sean 34-49
Temping 6, 8
That Girl in Your Mirror 96
Third Sex 128
Thompson, Hunter S. 77, 83
Thora-zine 153
Three's a Crowd 91
Thrift karma 14
Thrift SCORE 6-21
Tight Jeans 21
Tijuana No 58
To You, Girls 100
Today 159
Tolentino, Noël 150-154
Tonga Room 97
Total Package, The 27
Tower Records 102, 106-107, 113
Townsdowner 43
Transition 157
Tribe 8 71, 121, 124-125, 128
Trotsky, Leon 158
Truth 157
Tummy Ache 53
Twinkies 97
Two Live Crew 124
U2 43, 153
UC Santa Cruz 138, 150-151
Unmentionable, The 151
Updike, John 20
Vague 112

◆VWXYZ◆

Van Dyke Catalog 30
Van Slyke, Mark 77
Velez, Lupe 56
Vicky, Milwaukee punk 96
Victor/Victoria 128
Vietnam War Moratorium 94
Vonnegut, Kurt 20
Waffle 151, 153
Warhol, Andy 19
Washington Connection 111
Waters, John 43, 102, 120, 138, 146
What Every Young Man Should Know 98
Widmark, Richard 92
Williams, Robert 78, 81
Wilson, Paul 96-97, 103
Wobblies 158
Wobensmith, Matt 114-129
Woman's Guide to the Language of Success, A 70
Women En Large 136
Wood, Natalie 57
Woolworths 17
World of Modelling 94
World Wide Web 137, 159
X-Ray 74-87
Xerox 46
Yohannon, Tim 125
You Just Don't Understand 70
Zdanevich Brothers 157
Zine audience 111
Zine definition 108-109, 159
Zines, history of 155-159
Zoot Suit 57
Zvi, Sabbetai 156

BUNNYHOP

Hey There, Barbie Girl!
Issue N° 2/spring 1994 — $2.00
"Our Barbies, Ourselves"

CENSORED!

Lawyers for the Mattel Corporation and the Matt Groening Corporation sent cease-and-desist letters to the above publications, citing copyright violations. *Hey There, Barbie Girl!* terminated, and the remaining copies of *Bunnyhop* #5 bearing a parody of Groening's "Binky" character were destroyed. Now you know who to boycott . . .